OLD CHINA HANDS
and the Foreign Office

Old China Hands

AND THE FOREIGN OFFICE

NATHAN A. PELCOVITS

Published under the auspices of

AMERICAN INSTITUTE OF PACIFIC RELATIONS

by the KING'S CROWN PRESS, *New York*

1948

To My Wife

Preface

This is a study of the opinions and attitudes on Anglo-Chinese relations held by British merchants engaged in the China trade and of their relevance to the formation of British foreign policy toward China in the half-century between the Treaty of Tientsin and the Treaty of Portsmouth. It is, further, the story of that repeated clash between the Old China Hands and the British Foreign Office about the premises of Anglo-Chinese relations, despite their basic agreement on the aims of foreign policy in the Far East. In sum, it is an analysis of the reasons which could lead *The Times* to exclaim in 1875, apropos of a periodic crisis in those relations, that Britain did not want another India in the valley of the Yangtze.

The ultimate "Chinese question," posed by mercantile pressure on Lord Russell in mid-century and, in more acute form, on Lord Salisbury forty years later, was whether China would become Britain's second India. The issue was always pressed in veiled form. But the upshot of mercantile demands would tend to push the Government into a position from which it could not withdraw without falling heir to the substance, if not the form, of the Manchu legacy. This path the British Government refused to follow: it is the contention of this work that the Foreign Office reached this reluctant decision when the Board of Trade convinced the rest of Whitehall that the China trade would never be worth the expense of war or sovereignty. Old China Hands were never able to shake the fundamentals of this decision. The most their pressure accomplished was the adoption of a policy of wheedling gradual reforms out of China and ensuring that Britain would secure the largest slice of pie during the Battle of Concessions. But with this modest result the taipans were never satisfied.

This hypothesis—that for half a century there existed a fundamental clash between mercantile and official attitudes on British policy toward China—contradicts the theory, repeated from authority to authority, that Britain's China policy was shaped primarily by the pressure of the

English business world in China, particularly by the more powerful local firms, such as Jardine, Matheson & Co., in commerce, shipping, and enterprise, and the Hongkong and Shanghai Banking Corporation in the field of investment. Thus, T. W. Overlach states it as an axiom that "While British foreign policy usually is largely directed by public opinion, the constant absence of any public opinion regarding China, based on a lack of interest in this remote country, had caused the policy of the Foreign Office to be guided by the advice of the individuals and firms most prominently associated with China." [1]

Similarly, J. O. P. Bland, sometime *Times* correspondent in China and later representative of British financial interests in railway loan negotiations and himself an Old China Hand closely associated with the internal politics of the China Association, assumes that British foreign policy "represents in the main the collective opinions and interests of British traders." [2] This, despite his own conviction (which, as an Old China Hand, he could not fail to hold) that in the immediate period following the Treaty of Tientsin the Foreign Office, persuaded that the fabulous Chinese trade could not be forced open by the sword, became committed to a policy of "benevolent non-interference," [3] a policy which ran contrary in every respect to that advocated by organized mercantile opinion.

It is not certain on what the accepted theory is based. Overlach finds it sufficient to quote the China Association letter to Lord Salisbury, published in the Parliamentary Papers,[4] which warned of the encroachment of the Franco-Russian bloc on the Yangtze. But, as will be demonstrated later in this study, the China Association was itself convinced that Lord Salisbury was neglecting their advice. Dr. Philip Joseph, too, in his careful study, *Foreign Diplomacy in China*, consistently implies that because Britain's sole interest in China was commercial, it therefore follows that the pressure of commercial interests determined policy.

On the face of it, no more plausible thesis could be suggested. None would question that Britain's primary interest in China was commercial; Lord Balfour, in his oft-quoted Manchester speech of January 10, 1898, referred to British trading interests as "our sole interests" in China. Nor can it be denied—and this study will demonstrate the point time and again—that in particular matters and on particular issues, official policy was but a translation of organized mercantile demands. The commercial and political concessions which Sir Claude MacDonald

---

1. T. W. Overlach, *Foreign Financial Control in China* (New York, 1919), pp. 45–46.
2. *Recent Events and Present Policies in China* (London, 1912), Chap. X.
3. *Ibid.*
4. China No. 1 (1899), No. 25.

secured from a prostrate China in February, 1898, actually *was* the China Association program of 1892 and 1896. Indeed, by a careful selection of documents it is possible to strengthen the *ex parte* argument, grounded on the familiar imperialist theory, that commercial interests *cum* economic pressure at home determined foreign policy in the China seas.

It is an argument pat, far too pat and simple, for it fails to account for the outstanding and primary fact that throughout the half-century following the Treaty of Tientsin, merchants and officials were consistently and with few exceptions on opposite sides of the fence on most issues raised in Anglo-Chinese relations.

Curiously enough, the theory which stresses mercantile interests and economic "factors" has been advanced by studies based almost exclusively on sources discovered in diplomatic documents. No serious effort, to the knowledge of this writer, has been made to tap other sources, such as business correspondence or mercantile association records. Most of these are, of course, hard to come by. But sufficient are available to warrant reconsideration of the whole subject. Included are the records of British Chambers of Commerce, the Minute Books and correspondence of Jardine, Matheson & Co.,[5] and documentary sources at the British Board of Trade.[6] These present a total picture which differs substantially from the partial view published in Parliamentary Papers. It is upon these sources, along with Foreign Office records, that this study is based.

A study of this nature inevitably becomes an account of what Professor Arthur MacMahon has termed the "political aspects of associational bodies." [7] For private interests concerned with political issues and with attempts to influence policy do not operate singly but in associations. This is as true in foreign as in domestic affairs. Old China Hands—even in such powerful houses as Jardine, Matheson & Co.—operated through their Chambers of Commerce at Hongkong and the treaty ports and directed intense, propagandistic efforts to enlist the support of the home Chambers. At critical periods, also, committees of merchants were formed in London to press the mercantile view on the government. But it was not until the organization of the China Association in 1889, and the formation of its Shanghai and Hongkong Committees several years later, that mercantile interests were provided with a permanent,

---

5. Brought from Hongkong and stored at the University Library, Cambridge University. These cover principally the period from 1840 to 1880.

6. Covering the period from 1860 to 1885.

7. Cited in S. B. Clough, "Clio and Mars," *Political Science Quarterly,* Sept. 1945.

unified, powerful instrument for the propagation of their views. The close relations which existed between the Association and the Foreign Office assured Old China Hands that their views, if not always accepted, would always be heard. During the high period of Far Eastern affairs, from 1894 to 1905, the story of mercantile opinion and attitude is, therefore, essentially the history of the China Association.

This study is concerned with opinion and attitude; and, only obliquely, with influence. The study of pressure in politics is, under the best of circumstances, a hazardous affair. Particularly is this true when we deal with documents which, unless they are themselves historical facts, can but serve as evidence of sequence, not consequence. Influence does not operate in a straight line; and, only a subscriber to the devil theory of history or one who has misread Marx will see a direct pipe-line from the Hongkong and Shanghai Bank through the Cannon Street offices of the China Association to the Foreign Office. At best a contrapuntal relationship between commercial and imperial interests might be established. An association representing the China trade, itself a synthesis of conflicting views, cannot pretend to an exclusive claim on government even in its own bailiwick. Time and again in the study which follows the inescapable conclusion that such an association cannot hope to attain its maximum program is brought out. The China Association was never able to convince the Government that British commercial and financial interests in China, important and powerful though they were, were worth the imperial cost of establishing a Yangtze protectorate or even of a government guarantee for railway concessions.

The study was conducted under a fellowship of the Social Science Research Council, its basic research being completed in London in September, 1939. To the Council and its staff, particularly Miss Laura Barrett, I am grateful for material assistance enabling me to undertake this work and for introductions abroad which smoothed the path of research. I am happy to acknowledge my indebtedness to Mr. E. M. Gull, Secretary of the (British) China Association, for putting at my disposal the invaluable records of that organization; to Dr. G. Atkinson and Mr. Michael Greenberg who helped me find my way through the Jardine papers at the University Library of Cambridge; to Mr. D. G. M. Bernard of Matheson & Co. and to Sir Charles Addis, Mr. G. Leveson and Mr. W. Spalding of the Hongkong and Shanghai Banking Corporation for special favors; to Lord Mancroft and Mr. C. B. Dunwoody of the Associated Chambers of Commerce of the United Kingdom; to Mr. R. C. Booth of the Manchester Chamber of Commerce, Mr. Eli Devons of the Joint Committee of Cotton Trade Organisations, and

Dr. Arthur Redford of the University of Manchester for guidance to research materials in that city; to Professors Sir Charles K. Webster, J. B. Condliffe, and H. L. Beales of the London School of Economics and to Mr. G. E. Hubbard and Mr. F. C. Jones of Chatham House for stimulus and counsel; to Mr. J. O. P. Bland for rare talk about the Far East; to Dr. C. G. Parsloe of the Institute of Historical Research and Mr. R. M. Hinton of the Institute of Bankers for research guidance; and to the staffs of the Board of Trade library, the Public Records Office, the British Museum and the libraries of Cambridge University and Columbia University. In Paris I had the benefit of talks with Dr. Tracy B. Kittredge of the Rockefeller Foundation, Professor Etienne Dennery and M. Roger Lévy of the Centre d'Études de Politique Etrangère, and M. Guy Lacam of the Banque de l'Indo-chine.

It is with deep appreciation that I acknowledge my primary obligation to Professor Nathaniel Peffer who first awakened my interest in Far Eastern problems and whose counsel and encouragement attended me throughout the preparation of this book. To Professors S. B. Clough, J. P. Chamberlain, M. T. Florinsky, P. C. Jessup, Grayson Kirk, R. M. MacIver, Lindsay Rogers, J. T. Shotwell and Schuyler Wallace, and my other friends and teachers at Columbia University, I owe a long-standing debt of gratitude for inspiration, for helpful criticism, and for ten years of cumulative kindnesses which I can never hope to repay. I am also indebted to the American Institute of Pacific Relations for sponsoring publication of this book and to Mr. Henry M. Silver 2d of King's Crown Press for his careful and sympathetic handling of the manuscript.

Contents

Introduction:
Folklore of the Treaty Ports

*"The Chinese character is not about to change, and
the experience of the past may guide us still"*—
R. S. Gundry, President of the China Association,
to Sir Edward Grey, July 16, 1906.

IF—playing a game for scholars—one were to choose at random
among the documents expressing mercantile attitudes at critical periods in Anglo-Chinese relations, the probability is high that the
date of the document selected could not be guessed without looking at
the label. For it is characteristic both of those attitudes and of the issues
they treated that what the forty heads of Manchester firms wrote to
Lord Palmerston in 1839, British merchants in Shanghai could repeat
to Lord Elgin in 1858 and again to Sir Rutherford Alcock in 1868; and
the China Association could take up the identical refrain in 1898 and
1906. When commercial treaty revision was being canvassed at the
dawn of the twentieth century, the Shanghai Committee of the China
Association found it "not inopportune" to refer the attention of the
British Consul-General to "the old expressed opinions by British merchants in China upon the questions at issue," adding: "It is indeed noteworthy to remark how little many of those questions have altered during the last forty years, what little progress has been made toward their
elucidation, and how closely the representations of British merchants
today coincide with those made by their predecessors at the time of
attempted revision of Treaties in 1869." [1]

There is an element of *déja vu* in everything dealing with mercantile
opinion on British policy toward China in the 1890's and 1900's; of
having treated those problems, written those memorials, read those
complaints, listened to the debates in the Cannon Street office of the
China Association forty years ago. Not alone attitudes, but the very

issues remained constant. When the Mackay Treaty was being negotiated at the turn of the century, merchants and Chambers were somewhat wearily demanding the same rights, the same broad interpretation of Articles 12 and 28 of the Tientsin Treaty that their fathers had
demanded in the 1860's: more open ports, steam navigation on inland
waterways, railway development, inland trade and residence, recognition of the total immunity of foreign goods from inland taxes, the firm,
immediate and local redress of grievances; in general, as they put it,
"enforcement" of treaty rights and the maintenance of British prestige
in the face of Chinese industrial backwardness and governmental du-
plicity. The demand for "effective occupation" of the Yangtze advanced
in the summer of 1899 and again during the Boxer crisis was but an
extension of the traditional mercantile view that only by the assertion
of British sovereign might, exercised through puppet viceroys without
reference to Peking, could that administrative security be assured without which trade and enterprise were doomed to stagnation.

Nor was there any basic change in the mercantile view of the proper
role to be played by British authority in opening China to British private
enterprise. It was the function of government to open the whole of
China as one vast Treaty Port, by force and an occasional "little war"
if necessary; to assume the responsibility (and imperial expense) of
security for British persons and property throughout the Middle Kingdom, if need be by extending the King's Peace to the Yangtze; to assure
British commercial predominance in China both against the dead-weight
of Chinese obstruction and against foreign rivals. Despite repeated
frustration, mercantile hopes that the policy of conciliation and benevolent non-interference toward Peking would be repealed were never
completely dissipated; but these hopes were, without exception, followed by resentment at the inevitable compromise into which the
British Government was forced after each crisis.

The clash between Old China Hands and the Foreign Office—sometimes exhibiting the nature of a feud, at others, as during the honeymoon between China Association and Foreign Office in the period immediately following the Sino-Japanese War, lying dormant—was a
constant struggle between the mercantile demand for an all-out attack
on Chinese backwardness at whatever cost, and governmental reluctance
to undertake the responsibility even of quasi-sovereignty in China. It
was, fundamentally, a clash between the merchants' folklore which pic-
tured the infinite potentialities of the China trade and official conviction that this vision had been grossly exaggerated. No matter, therefore, what concessions were granted to commercial interests—and they
were many and not unimportant—they would always be regarded as

too little and too late. For, in essence merchants and officials differed as to the advisability of Indianizing the Manchu Empire. The stakes were high; and it was inevitable that the official policy of piecemeal and gradual extension of the frontiers of economic opportunity in China should be branded in the mercantile press as an abdication of Britain's imperial responsibility.

To the eye of the foreigner—particularly the Frenchman [2]—no such fundamental cleavage between government and business was evident. Was not Britain's interest in China primarily, almost exclusively, commercial? Who could deny that the British sword had twice, even thrice, hacked away at Chinese stubbornness to cut open a path for trade and enterprise? Who could doubt that Britain was daily accumulating a larger and larger share of China's trade and real estate? And, was not the British Minister first in line to obtain concessions from the unfortunate mandarins in Peking?

The foreigner could not understand the reason for mercantile resentment and did not see what was so evident to the inhabitants of the Bund and their retired partners reminiscently drinking a Shanghai Flip in the Thatched House Club in London—that through sheer pusillanimity the Foreign Office was intent on abandoning an Empire which could be had at a bargain price. To them it often appeared that an official conspiracy blocked the path to the acquisition of a bigger and better India. Nor did their view of the proper function of government change with the current mode of political economy taught in the universities. In 1860, as in 1900, it was the task of government to force open the Chinese oyster with a sword and of business to gather the pearls. They spoke the language of the latter-day Joseph Chamberlain at least a generation before Imperialism became fashionable.

But the basic clash between the China Hands and the Foreign Office arose not from differing political and economic views; primarily it stemmed from a difference of opinion as to the probability of discovering a pearl in the Chinese oyster. The mercantile view was a derivative of the folklore which had been built up around the China trade. Pottinger's rosy vision of Manchester mills hardly able to produce enough stocking stuff to meet the demands of some four hundred million Chinese customers well served the propaganda of the Treaty Ports. For if this were even partially true, what sacrifices, what expense, what governmental responsibilities were too great to realize it? China was the Eldorado never fully explored, whose riches in concessions and customers were immeasurable. Never, in his soberest or most despairing moments, would the Old China Hand admit the devastating charge of official critics that the very nature of China's domestic economy, its self-sufficiency, was bound to condense the fabulous dream into a relatively meager reality.

According to mercantile folklore the obstacles to the dream's realization were overwhelmingly political rather than economic. If only *likin*, the symbol of oppressive inland taxation, were abolished; if only the Government would take up a firm stand at the Tsungli Yamen or, better still, deal directly with the Yangtze viceroys as the Government of India with the Maharajahs; if only the fleet on the Asiatic Station were doubled and gunboats patrolled the length of the Yangtze; if only the British Government would secure and then guarantee railway and loan and manufacturing concessions. This was the ever-recurring theme, the *leitmotif* in mercantile attitude. Occasionally this vision would also stir the home Chambers who would then back up the Old China Hands. Indeed, the various projects for tapping the rich western provinces through a Burmese back door was, for half a century, Lancashire's own version of the China dream, and literally hundreds of memorials were sent to the British Government urging construction of a railway from Rangoon to the Yangtze.

The British Government's decision to reverse Palmerstonian policy and adopt one of caution and conciliation stemmed directly from the conviction that the prospects and potentialities of the China market had been so exaggerated as to dictate a reconsideration of the premises which had previously formed Anglo-Chinese policy. It was this conviction which made Cobdenite overtures popular. The Mitchell Report of 1852, revived by Lord Elgin in his dispatches six years later, stressed the pessimistic view that the self-contained nature of Chinese economy would never allow an appreciable extension of her foreign trade. Even the Select Committee of 1847 could see no way out of the depressed state of the China trade except in an improbably expanded consumption of tea in England. Sir Frederick Bruce's instructions to support the tottering imperial authority of Peking against the Taipings, which so aroused the opposition of the merchants, as well as his decision to back the nascent maritime customs, were a direct reflection of the growing view that no further commitments were to be assumed by British authority in China. And, in 1869, the Board of Trade officially declared that the time had come for the country to awaken from the China dream: the insignificant prospects of the China trade did not warrant the risks of forcing upon China those major administrative, fiscal and industrial reforms which a unanimous mercantile opinion demanded.

The importance of the China dream in the formation of policy toward China, neglected by most historians, has not been overlooked by economists. As Professor C. F. Remer noted in 1926: "The general fact about

China's trade as a whole which strikes the student as most noteworthy is its small volume," considering the size of the country.[3] From 1865 to 1885, for example, China's net imports showed an almost negligible growth from sixty to eighty million Haikwan taels, an increase even more negligible than the figures appear to demonstrate when it is noted that the tael dropped in that period from 6/8 to 5/3 sterling.[4] Even when the upswing occurred in the 1890's, China's foreign trade did not exceed 1.5 percent of the world total. The point stressed by Remer, as it had been by Mitchell more than seventy years previously, is that the self-contained nature of China's economy precluded the expansion envisaged by the merchants.

It may be remarked that the limited size of China's foreign trade has usually been veiled by expressions which call attention to the "vast potentialities." The trade of China has always exerted a certain power over the imaginations, of those who have written from the point of view of trade promotion. Such writers commonly accept four hundred million as the population of China and proceed upon this doubtful fact to build the most fanciful calculations of the magnitude of the trade to be expected. . . . Every advance in the penetration of foreign trade into China has brought out exaggerations of this sort . . . [and] . . . this viewpoint has had its influence upon the policies of governments. . . .[5]

The influence of this viewpoint, however, was so much greater on mercantile attitude than on government policy that the very essence of the clash lies in this disparity. The British Government, ever skeptical of the potentialities of the China market as depicted in mercantile "trade promotion," pursued a policy of limited advances and conciliation from the 1860s to the end of the century; and it was only the menace of international rivalry which led to a partial espousal of the mercantile line.

But it proved only partial. Fundamentally, the British Government never departed from this policy of limited liability. Even its vigorous action in the Battle of Concessions was not an adoption of the mercantile program but rather an attempt by "counterpoise" and counter-concession to protect existing British preponderance against international rivalry. The test came in 1899 and again in 1900 when Old China Hands demanded that Britain establish a protectorate over the Yangtze region and assume the leadership in the fiscal and administrative reform of China. This the British Government emphatically refused to undertake. And with its refusal Old China Hands were convinced that they had lost the struggle. Only the vested interests identified with the "chosen instrument" of the Foreign Office—the British and Chinese Corporation—to whom the bulk of the railway concessions were granted, were sufficiently content to accept the official policy of limited commitments. For the overwhelming majority of merchants, entrepreneurs, and business interests it was the final defeat.

Out of the folklore which grew up in the China trade, the latter built up a body of principles and a program of action which they urged upon Chambers of Commerce and upon a reluctant government for fifty years following the Treaty of Tientsin. This program exhibited an amazing consistency through the years and was itself translated into an orthodox code of opinion believed and propagated as doctrine by Old China Hands. Its essentials, which are woven into the story which follows, may be briefly summarized.

First, it was gospel that political rather than economic obstacles prevented realization of the potentialities of the China market. "Illegal" *likin* and other inland dues were strangling trade. Because merchants were not free to reside and trade in the interior, only the outer fringes of the Middle Kingdom had been touched. In effect, it was held that only when the whole of China was converted into one vast Treaty Port would China become what it might be. Again, reading into the Tientsin Treaty their own broad interpretation, merchants insisted that if the Treaty were properly "enforced" their rights would include everything from abolition of internal taxes to a comprehensive privilege of trading and residing throughout the whole of China.

Arguing from the decentralization of the Empire and the impotence of Peking authority in the provinces, Old China Hands, further, called on the government to face reality and deal with the local viceroys. This was not a theory first advanced during the Boxer crisis, as is often supposed, but served traditionally as part of the mercantile program. Its manifestations ranged all the way from insistence on giving consuls power to employ force locally for redress of grievances to the widespread campaign for "effective occupation" of the Yangtze. Politically, it was on this issue that merchants and officials differed most bitterly, the former criticizing through the years the official policy of bolstering Peking and treating China as a civilized state in international relations.

As a fourth tenet Old China Hands built up a sort of cracker-barrel philosophy of the Treaty Ports on the proper way to handle "Orientals" and "Oriental authorities." The latter were never to be trusted and would squirm out of international commitments as soon as pressure was removed: ergo, never remove the pressure. It was only under the tutelage of the white man (ranging all the way up to British) that they might serve in commercial and fiscal administration. It was, moreover, the mandarins and not the people that wanted to exclude foreigners. It was an integral part of the folklore that the Chinese, a trading and business people, would participate in foreign trade on a vast scale under British guidance once mandarin squeezes and obstructions were removed.

Fifth in the list of the articles of faith was the conviction that Chinese backwardness rather than international rivalries was the chief obstacle to overcome in order to secure for Britain the realities of the China market. Even at the height of the battle for concessions in 1898 the China Association did not lose sight of this fact; and in 1906, as in 1868, Old China Hands were demanding that the British Government force upon China those administrative and fiscal reforms without which the door would never be truly open.

Along with this came the ever-renewed cry for a policy of "vigor," of dealing firmly with Chinese obstruction and procrastination. On this point, merchants never equivocated. While skirting around the problem of what should be done in the event British pressure led to the collapse of native authority (the chief headache of the Foreign Office), mercantile opinion would hint that the establishment of a British protectorate —in the style made fashionable in Egypt—would not be a calamity. It goes without saying that agitation for an increase of British naval forces in the Asiatic Station and of the garrison at Hongkong was a traditional concern.

Nor were Old China Hands ever reluctant to request government aid for their private ventures. Long before the Battle of Concessions, the Hongkong and Shanghai Banking Corporation secured official aid in concluding the loans of 1877 and 1884, though there was much searching of souls in the Foreign Office as to the propriety of making Her Majesty's Government a partner to the deal. To the merchants, their private interests were "national interests" and the concept of laissez-faire is conspicuously absent from mercantile briefs. Enterprise in backward areas, it was held, required strong government backing. This was particularly true when the growth of foreign competition in the nineties threatened British economic predominance in China. And the attempt to persuade the government to assume the role of guarantor in railway loans became a major phase of the mercantile program at the turn of the century.

Finally, in the face of strong dissenting opinions from both Shanghai and Manchester, organized mercantile opinion adopted a definite stand favoring a policy of spheres of influence in China. Convinced that the partition of the Manchu Empire was inevitable, the home Chambers of Commerce under the leadership of the China Association regarded a British protectorate of the Yangtze region as the only acceptable solution of the crisis. Far from welcoming the Open Door diplomacy which Lord Salisbury embraced, with a sigh of relief, in 1899, the China Association devoted its effort toward persuading the Foreign Office that only by the "effective occupation" of the British sphere would Britain's preponderance in the China Seas be maintained. And, it is noteworthy that this policy was urged before, during and after the Boxer crisis. Not until 1905 were mercantile circles convinced that their policy would never see official adoption. To them that was the ultimate defeat and the end of an era.

PART 1

End of the Rainbow

I

The Tientsin Treaty

"The paramount difficulty and danger to be avoided in our dealings with China is all unnecessary contact between British traders and the natives"—Louis Mallet of the Board of Trade, 1863.

WITHIN less than five years after the signing of the Treaty of Nanking on August 29, 1842, the Chinese dream which Britain had purchased at the price of the Opium War began to show evidence of lacking substance. The signing of the treaty had been the signal for another rush after the profits anticipated from its benefits. Canton, Amoy, Foochow, Ningpo and Shanghai had been opened as Treaty Ports to British mercantile enterprise. The monopoly of the Cohong had been abolished. Under Article X transit dues were commuted upon the payment at the port of a moderate scale of duties, later set at one-half of the equally moderate tariff scale; and what was later to become the most vexing of problems in Anglo-Chinese commercial relations was thought to have been settled. Hongkong was ceded to Great Britain as a colony and entrepôt for trade.

Despite these benefits, the value of British exports in 1850 exhibited practically no increase over 1843, while in 1854 it was even less.[1] Just as aggravating as the small volume were the twin evils of fluctuation and overtrading which characterized the China trade. Overoptimism was ever a staple of that trade. Robberds & Co., a Norwich firm which exported woolens on consignment to Jardine, Matheson & Co., at Hongkong, was even willing to speculate on future profits in tea in the hope that the market for woolens in China would become steadier.

Although the price continues so unprofitable, still we trust that your care in investing the proceeds, with the aid of our plan for disposing of them here, will bring out a satisfactory result. We also hope that these sales by reducing the late very heavy stock in China . . . will produce the effect anticipated in our letter of 22 March 1845. The late depression of your market has evidently discouraged speculators, and if we can only keep the price at a fair medium rate, there will be no inducement for them to interfere again . . . On all these grounds we hope that we may now look forward to a steady regular trade, without those fluctuations, by which your market has hitherto been so much disturbed.[2]

This on March 31, 1846, but the date matters little for it was a constant refrain. Respectable Yorkshire and Lancashire manufacturers, as well as the taipans in Hongkong and Shanghai, might blame fluctuation and the uncertainty of trade on the speculator, but business with the Far East was always something of an adventure in speculation. Manchester merchants who shipped on consignment to Jardine, Matheson & Co., could never know the state of the market for their shirtings nor whether they would receive in exchange a shipment of Congou tea or a bill drawn on Matheson & Company of London.[3] The search of Robberds & Co. for "steady and satisfactory" transactions in the future, which was the sole reason "we have persevered in our shipments under such an unpromising aspect of things," was to become the common pattern.

Very embarrassing also was the fact that while the demand for British manufacture remained limited and unsteady, profits could be made by the few who invested in opium. The following from George Armstrong of Liverpool to Jardine, Matheson & Co. is a commentary on the whole China trade.

I have the honour to acknowledge receipt of your letters of the 26 March one of which gave cover to account sale of the 10 chests of opium, forwarded to you by Geo. Armstrong & Co. and a remittance for the net proceeds, on draft on Messrs. Matheson & Scott for £1372 which has been duly accepted—the result of this operation is quite satisfactory. I am obliged by your promptitude in closing it so soon. I only wish you could be as successful with the shipments of piece goods on my own and j/a with Messrs. Matheson & Scott, but I fear from the wretched position of your markets that it will take a considerable time to rally.[4]

The "wretched position of your markets" was a repeated complaint. From the period of the depression of 1846–47, Jardine, Matheson & Co. found it more and more difficult to persuade manufacturers to gamble on the China market by continued shipments of goods on consignment. "Manufacturers of respectability" were demanding advances on shipments and were forcing Jardine's to purchase at least fifty percent of goods shipped on their own account.[5] Fluctuation and overtrading on a serious scale were reported from China at least every other year. The following, from Jardine's monthly report for June 1850, is typical:

"Our last monthly advices informed you of the unfavourable turn our market had taken for Imports. This we confirm and advise serious fall in cotton yarn and shirtings, vessels with further goods causing glut that for a long period will not easily be got over, particularly as the present demand by dealers is confined to immediate wants." [6]

The Select Committee on Commercial Relations with China, appointed in 1847 to investigate the causes of the long depression, assigned purely economic reasons for the restricted nature of the China market. The result of extended intercourse had "by no means realized the just expectations which had been naturally founded on a freer access to so magnificent a market." [7] The difficulties, said the Committee, arose neither from want of demand in China nor from foreign competition. The trouble was due to the difficulty of finding a return: the payment for opium absorbed the available supply of silver, and only tea and silk were left to balance the import of foreign manufactures. But how much tea could the United Kingdom and the United States, the two chief consumers, swallow? The first warning, then, was an economic one—that the market was not fabulous but restricted. The second was political:

We feel ourselves warranted . . . in reminding our fellow countrymen residing in foreign countries, that while they are entitled to expect that the whole force and influence of their country should be put forth for their protection, when injured in property and person; yet that the interests of Commerce are best consulted by studying a conciliatory demeanour, and cultivating the good-will of the nations with which they traffic.[8]

The most optimistic verdict the Committee could give was that the trade might be "further extended from time to time." The handwriting was already on the wall, but the merchants interpreted the symbols in their own way.

From Alexander Matheson, head of the house of Matheson & Co. in London, and commercial affiliate of Jardine, Matheson & Co. of Hongkong, the Committee heard the orthodox mercantile chant. Political obstacles were mainly to blame for the restricted trade. Governmental sins of omission and commission accounted for the continued slump. Was not Hongkong being stifled by taxes and land regulations and the "opium farms" which attempted to control trade in the drug? It was, Matheson insisted, none of the Government's concern to prevent opium smuggling by the registry of Chinese vessels. Another complaint was the "laxity and subservient policy pursued by the British representative" toward Chinese officials. Asked if he could suggest "any means by which an opening might be made to the Imperial Court of Pekin" as a means of bringing pressure to bear for the enforcement of treaty rights, Matheson replied: "No, not at present. I think we are losing ground in China, instead of gaining ground; I mean politically." [9] It was to become a familiar mercantile tag. "To what do you attribute that?" he was asked. "In every instance where an Englishman gets into trouble in China, the British authorities instead of protecting their own subjects, almost invariably take the side of the Chinese; they seem to treat their own countrymen in a way that is not at all calculated to impress the Chinese with respect for them." [10]

It was the expression of a consistent attitude. And it sometimes proved convincing to the home Chambers of Commerce. An active correspondence between the newly formed British Chamber of Commerce at Canton and the Manchester Chamber of Commerce convinced the latter that the restricted trade was due to official tolerance of the hostile attitude of native authorities at Canton and to the illegal exaction of inland dues.[11] The Canton Chamber was particularly chagrined because the Board of Trade had refused to recognize its status; it was therefore unable to make representations on its own.[12] The Manchester Chamber addressed several memorials to Lord Palmerston voicing "great anxiety" over the condition of British trade with China. On July 19, 1849, the Chamber repeated the recommendation that a searching inquiry be instituted by the Government "into the causes which have led to the present result and into those by which the state of ill feeling [at Canton and the other treaty ports] is sustained and fomented." [13] Nor was the Chamber in doubt as to the cause. "Our trade with China will never be fully developed until the right to sell and purchase is extended beyond the ports to which we are now restricted." [14] Manchester demanded that "remonstrances of Her Majesty's Government and a firm vigilance on the part of the Representative at Hongkong put a stop to future infractions of the Treaty."

In its 29th Annual Report to the membership (February 11, 1850) the Chamber's Board of Directors reiterated the complaint that "under the cloak of a liberal import tariff" the government of China "endeavours in secret and indirect ways to oppose itself to the introduction of foreign manufactures by encouraging native jealousies and screening native aggressions." [15] There was but one adequate solution: an advance beyond the five treaty ports. "The strictly enforced limitation to five places on the seaboard prevents the growth of better personal feeling between the races, and keeps concealed the causes of our stunted trade with China." [16] Just four months later, on the occasion of the death of the Chinese Emperor, Manchester again voiced "the disappointment universally felt in respect to the results expected from the

Treaty of Nanking," and again urged Lord Palmerston to rectify "the mistake made in limiting the right of ingress to five coastal ports." [17]

This, of course, was a basic repudiation of the conclusions reached by the Select Committee; and it is noteworthy how early mercantile attitude was set. Welcoming the appointment of Dr. John Bowring as Governor of Hongkong and Superintendent of Trade in China, the Manchester Chamber expressed the hope that "he may be invested with such powers as may enable him to extend British interests not only in China but in Japan, Siam, and other countries contiguous to those seas." [18] The memorial forwarded to Lord Clarendon on January 26, 1854, emphasized two cardinal points in mercantile folklore:

(a) "without permission to go into the interior of the country our trade with China must remain stunted and crippled"; and

(b) "the introduction of British manufactures into the interior is delusively prevented by *internal imposts* unknown and unrestricted." [19]

The China trade continued to feed on hope. "Mr. Rylands wishes me to state," wrote their Hull agent to Matheson & Co. of London, "that he very highly appreciates the services of your China friends, and that although there is a heavy loss upon the shipments under review, the Hull Co. were quite prepared for this and trust that the long-continued depression in China, being about to yield to a better state of things, they will be enabled at no distant day to renew their shipments with better hopes of a favourable market." [20] But, as the Jardine-Matheson correspondence reveals, trade with Hull and Manchester never sustained a real boom and the only constant factor was fluctuation. Jardine, Matheson & Co. were forced to purchase more and more Manchester goods on their own account in order to influence consignments.[21]

Was there a hidden China trade? And could it be tapped by opening more treaty ports and suppressing the exaction of inland dues as Manchester and the Old China Hands were contending? It was to be a perennial cry raised by mercantile circles for the next fifty years. The basis of their policy rested on the assumption that the potentialities of the China market were limitless.

Few were the voices to dispute this thesis in the early days. Among them was that of Mr. Mitchell, assistant magistrate at Hongkong, who prepared an exhaustive report in 1852 for Sir George Bonham, then Governor of Hongkong and Superintendent of Trade, aimed at exploding the mercantile dream. It was apparently pigeon-holed at Hongkong and did not come to the attention of the Foreign Office until 1858 when Lord Elgin enclosed it with one of his own dispatches.[22] The Mitchell Report reached the radical conclusion that not political obstacles such

as inland taxes or restriction to five treaty ports on the littoral accounted for the failure of the Chinese masses to consume large quantities
of British manufactured goods, but the self-sufficient nature of the
Chinese economy. China, he argued, would never be a large market for
Manchester goods because its domestic economy was so organized as to
provide durable homespun textiles at a price England could never
effectively challenge. In effect, Mitchell denied the assumption of the
Select Committee that *demand* for British manufactures existed, and
only means of payment was lacking. It would, he argued, always be so.
For the year ending December 31, 1851, British manufactured goods of
a gross value of £1,500,000 had been imported into China, as against
opium imports of six million and £1,500,000 in other goods from India.
The figures, Mitchell emphasized, were important and indicated an
inevitable trend. His analysis warrants extensive quoting.

It seems a strange result [he writes] after ten years of open trade with this
great country, and after the abolition of all monopolies on both sides, that China
with her swarming millions should not consume one half so much of our manufactures as Holland or as our own thinly populated North American or
Australian colonies.

But this seemingly strange result is a perfectly natural one to those who are
sufficiently acquainted with this peculiar people and have marked their thrifty
habits and untiring industry. . . .

When we opened the seaboard provinces of this country to British trade ten
years ago, the most preposterous notions were formed as to the demand that
was to spring up for our manufactures. Our friends in Manchester and even
their counterparts on the spot out here . . . seem to have all gone mad together
upon the idea of an open trade with "three or four hundred millions of human
beings." They straightaway began to bargain and barter, in imagination, with
"a third of the human race," and would not be convinced that it was possible
to throw more into the newly opened markets than they were capable of clearing off. Sir Henry Pottinger told them that he had opened up a new world to
their trade, so vast, "that all the mills in Lancashire could not make stocking
stuff sufficient for one of its provinces," and they pinned implicit faith to a statement to which their own fond wishes stood sponsor. Now as we could not possibly find a better one, I take Sir Henry Pottinger's own hyperbole and try to
exhibit how utterly unfounded from first to last was this splendid fabric of His
Excellency's imagination. . . .

Pursuing his analysis Mitchell discovered the "great fact" that the
export of manufacturing stuffs to China was less by nearly three quarters
of a million sterling at the close of 1850 than at the close of 1844. How
had it happened that such a splendid vision had resulted in such a
"meagre reality"? The answer lay in the nature of the Chinese economy.

British manufactures were in competition with native home industry. "Our cloth must displace native manufacture—and it will never succeed in doing so." The Chinese peasant worked his own loom. The Fukien farmer traded his sugar for northern cotton which he then carded, spun and wove into a heavy, durable material; after harvest time the entire peasant family was engaged in producing homespun. Only the hong clerks, the bookkeepers and shopkeepers wore the neater, but less durable and far more expensive, British long cloth. This was the reason why Britain had failed to break into the China market and why her export to China would always be comparatively small.

All other factors, Mitchell concluded, were inconsequential. "Even if merchants could lay down goods duty free in the very heart of the provinces the boon would not result in any appreciable increase of their consumption. The industry of China can beat our power looms by a great deal more than five percent."

This was indeed a fundamental challenge to mercantile folklore; and although Mitchell's prophecy that at the end of fifty years China would be taking no more than four million sterling in British manufactures was to prove overly pessimistic, the deflationary attitude expressed in his report was to prove basically correct. And it became the premise of official policy. Lord Elgin reported from Shanghai in 1858 that Mitchell was still confirmed in his views. Elgin himself thought it contained "much valuable information" and intimated that it accorded with his own opinion.[23]

Aside from his antipathy to the blood and thunder attitude of the merchants,[24] it was Lord Elgin's basic acceptance of the Mitchell thesis which accounts for his opposition to the mercantile attitude on China. He cautioned "that British manufacturers will have to exert themselves to the utmost if they intend to supplant . . . the fabrics produced in their leisure hours . . . by this industrious, frugal, and sober population. It is a pleasing but pernicious fallacy to imagine, that the influence of an intriguing mandarin is to be presumed whenever a buyer shows preference for native over foreign calico." [25]

With the *Arrow* incident resolved, Lord Elgin stopped off at Shanghai, enroute to Tientsin to sign the treaty. He was welcomed by representatives of Jardine, Matheson & Co., Dent, Beale & Co., Moncrieff Grove & Co., Gibb, Livingston & Co., and lesser British merchants who addressed to him the hope that "the blow thus struck may finally subdue the hostile spirit so long evinced by the Cantonese," and that the "result of Your Excellency's exertions we trust may be more fully to develop the vast resources of China, and to extend among the people the elevating influences of a higher civilization." [26] Elgin managed to be barely polite in his response. Apparently convinced by the Mitchell Report, he read the Old China Hands a lecture which they were to resent for the next two generations.

The expectations held out to British manufacturers at the close of the last war between Great Britain and China, when they were told that a new world was opened to their trade so vast that all the mills of Lancashire could not make stocking stuff sufficient for one of its provinces, have not been realized and I am of the opinion that when Force and Diplomacy shall have done all that they can legitimately effect the work which has to be accomplished in China will be but at its commencement.

When the barriers which prevent free acess to the Interior of the Country shall have been removed the Christian civilization of the West will find itself face to face not with barbarism but with an ancient civilization in many respects effete and imperfect but in others not without claims on our sympathy and respect. In the rivalry which will then ensue Christian civilization will have to win its way among a sceptical and ingenious people by making it manifest that a faith which reaches to heaven furnishes better guarantees for public and private morality than one which does not rise above the earth.

At the same time, the machino-facturing West will be in presence of a population the most universally and laboriously manufacturing of any on the earth. It can achieve victories in the contest in which it will have to engage only by proving that physical knowledge and mechanical skill, applied to the arts of production, are more than a match for the most persevering efforts of unscientific industry.[27]

The basic conflict between merchant and official was also evident in British consular opinion on mercantile demands for liberty to visit the interior and free navigation of the larger rivers as desirable concessions in the new treaty.[28] Rutherford Alcock, who was to become Britain's Minister at Peking ten years later, in 1857 bitterly criticized the mercantile proposal. He charged that many foreign merchants, "under no effective control," were converting "privileges of access and trade into means of fraud and violence."[29] Protected by treaties from the action of native authorities they had "launched into a wholesale system of smuggling and fraudulent devices for the evasion of duties." Access to the interior would increase this evil. The object of British policy should be to restrict the trade, limit points of contact, and support Chinese authority in its efforts at control.

This difference was to become full-blown ten years later. Meanwhile, mercantile circles through the Shanghai Chamber of Commerce called for the following concessions in the new treaty: reduction of the tariff to five percent ad valorem (specific rates having proved to be higher); legal admission of opium; respect for the transit passes which covered foreign goods on which the commuted inland charges had been paid at the port of entry; representation at Peking; and, above all, the right to travel and reside in the interior.[30] If this were attained Shanghai anticipated a vast extension of the China market for British goods. Again they argued that if "obstructions" were removed and treaty rights "enforced" British manufacture could compete with native products. It was to become a familiar chant.

The Treaty of Tientsin was signed on June 26, 1858. On the whole it incorporated the major expectations of the merchants and Lord Elgin reported that the mercantile communities were satisfied.[31] The Tientsin Treaty served as the ultimate basis of Anglo-Chinese diplomatic and commercial relations throughout the period here under review; neither the Chefoo Convention of 1876 nor the Mackay Treaty of 1902 produced any fundamental change. Its provisions may be briefly summarized.[32]

Direct diplomatic relations were established, Britain and France exercising the right to "appoint Ambassadors, Ministers or other diplomatic agents to the Court of Peking," while China consented to establish a board for foreign affairs (Tsungli Yamen). The rights of British subjects were defined with the principle of extraterritoriality more fully recognized. Questions in regard to rights of property or person arising between British subjects were to be subject to the jurisdiction of British authorities. In the case of criminal acts offenders were to be tried and punished by the law and jurisdiction of their own authorities. In mixed cases grievances were to be brought before the British consul who enlisted the "assistance of the Chinese authorities, that they may together examine into the merits of the case" if no amicable solution had been reached. The right of the consul to control his subjects was thus fully established; to assist him a cruiser might be stationed at each of the treaty ports. Britain's right to most-favored-nation treatment was reaffirmed.

Articles IX-XI contained the new concessions. Newchwang, Tangchow, Taiwan in Formosa, Swatow and Kiungchow were opened to trade and Chinkiang was to be opened within a year. The Yangtze was opened to British merchant shipping as far as Hankow, and three river ports were to be established upon the restoration of internal peace. British subjects might *travel* for pleasure or trade to all parts of the interior under Consular passport countersigned by local authorities.

Articles XII and XXVIII, which were to figure prominently in mercantile disputes, deserve separate attention. The former, originally of minor concern dealing with the subject of land purchase, reads: "British subjects, whether at the ports or other places, desiring to build or open houses, warehouses, churches, hospitals or burial-grounds, shall make their agreement for the land or buildings they require, at the rates prevailing among the people, equitably, and without exactions on either side." The innocent phrase "or other places" was seized upon by mercantile circles as a joker and for the next fifty years it was interpreted as providing British merchants with the privilege of residing and establishing warehouses in the interior. In effect, mercantile opinion kept harping on the need for so interpreting this clause as to open all of China as one vast treaty port. It was principally this right which they claimed in urging "enforcement" of the Treaty of Tientsin.

Article XXVIII attempted to deal with the difficult question of inland dues. The Treaty of Nanking had provided for free transit after payment of the tariff and a fixed transit duty. No specified scale had been established and British merchants even then complained of arbitrary and illegal exaction of inland duties. The Tientsin Treaty provided for publication of a fixed scale, but gave the British merchant the option of clearing his goods of all transit duties by the payment of a single charge at the port of entry or at the first barrier passed by goods to be exported. On payment of this commuted tax, a transit certificate (or transit pass) was to exempt goods from "all further inland charges whatever." Of no great significance at the time, the issue of inland dues was to become of primary importance when provincial authorities insisted on levying additional inland taxes on both native and foreign trade to pay the cost of the Civil War. Inland taxation—particularly in the form of the destination tax *likin*—became the favorite scapegoat of Old China Hands in rationalizing periodic depressions in the China trade.

The treaty was welcomed by the business community since, in the main, it embodied the concessions demanded. In fact, its strictly commercial articles followed very closely the recommendations of the Shanghai memorial.[33] But the merchants were wary. From the start it was realized that not the letter of the treaty but the spirit in which it would be interpreted by British authority would determine the extent of the advance made. In its circular report of August 9, 1858, Jardine, Matheson & Co. accurately gauged mercantile sentiment. "These concessions, if faithfully carried into effect, may be regarded as highly favourable and fully as much as under present circumstances could have been reasonably looked for." [34] The benefits of the treaty, Jardine's admitted two years later, were "substantial" but only "while pressure continues to be exerted." [35] This was to become the mercantile keynote. Few, however, were as blunt as John Thacker, an Old China

Hand who was convinced that the treaty would be of little use unless "carried into effect at the point of the bayonet."[36]

Even apart from differences over the meaning of carrying the treaty "into effect," this attitude was bound to produce a cleavage between merchant and official on future policy toward China. For, officially, a reversal of Palmerstonian methods was inaugurated. The Foreign Office agreed with Sir Frederick Bruce, the Minister at Peking, that a new era must follow the treaty. If the China market did not warrant a British India on the Yangtze, neither did it mean that Britain could tolerate another Turkey in the Far East. As Bruce noted: "The weakness of China rather than her strength is likely to create a fresh Eastern question in these seas."[37] This meant treating China as a responsible power and eschewing the road of local pressure for redress of grievances. But if the central authorities were to be held responsible, something must be done about fortifying the weak, Imperial authorities. This meant, among other things, bolstering the Peking government against the Taiping rebels; it meant lending the support of British authority to the nascent maritime customs; it meant stern instructions to British consuls and naval authorities to refer the redress of grievances to Peking and not to enforce it by independent local pressure.

All this was anathema to the taipan mind. The correspondence of Jardine, Matheson & Co. bristles with repeated denunciations of Bruce's failure to observe a neutral attitude toward the Taipings, thus interfering with Jardine's trade.[38] That and official support of the foreign maritime customs were held responsible for the stagnation of trade in 1861–62.

We firmly believe that the long period of stagnation to which the Import trade at Shanghai has been subjected, would have been avoided, if the policy of strict neutrality had been persisted in on our part, and it is therefore devoutly to be wished that the large reinforcements of troops, which, it is reported, have been asked from the Home Government in order to subdue the rebellion, may not be granted, as we are convinced, that both the Import & Export trade in China cannot fail to be seriously prejudiced by a renewal of hostilities owing to the heavy taxes, which the Taepings will levy on all Goods, passing in and out of the provinces which may be in their possession.[39]

The policy advocated by Jardine's was the recognition of de facto authority by the Taipings in certain districts, "and sanction their levying moderate transit duties therein."[40]

But what particularly exercised Jardine's, as it did the other merchants, was the active support lent by Bruce to the foreign maritime customs, which not only bolstered Imperial authority but prevented lucrative smuggling and uncontrolled trade with local authorities. This was the major issue in mercantile-official relations in the two years following the establishment of direct relations with Peking; and it was the first defeat sustained by the Old China Hands. Although Jardine's might pretend to dismiss Bruce's support of the Chinese customs as a "hobby" to which he was willing to sacrifice all British interests,[41] it was early recognized that in the resolution of this question lay the future of Anglo-Chinese relations.

The foreign Inspectorate of customs had its origin in a local arrangement at Shanghai in 1854 when the temporary occupation of that port by the rebels had resulted in the collapse of the customs system.[42] To prevent smuggling and the uneven collection by native officials, it was reorganized under the inspection of three foreigners nominated by the consuls of the Treaty Powers. Objection from local Chambers of Commerce was immediate. Partly this was due to the conviction that efficient collection at Shanghai and not at other treaty ports was unfair; although the Board of Trade found that native collections at Foochow were fair and did not put Shanghai at a disadvantage.[43] The policy then favored by most Chambers of Commerce and reluctantly advocated by the Board of Trade in 1856 was that the system be abolished and the one employed at Canton be made universal; at Canton the British merchant did not come into contact with the native customs but traded with the compradore or native dealer who "arranged" his own terms with the customs.[44] A similar effort to establish a foreign inspectorate at Foochow in 1857 was also discouraged by the Board of Trade at the instance of the merchants.[45]

In 1861, following the new policy of assisting the Imperial authorities to set China's house in order, Bruce lent his active assistance to China in drawing up regulations to guard against customs frauds and in reorganizing a new customs administration under the supervision of foreigners in the employ of China. Mercantile opposition, led by Jardine, Matheson & Co. was immediate and vigorous and enlisted the innocent support of the Chambers at home. To Sam Mendel of Manchester, Jardine's wrote on March 30, 1861, that despite the opening of the Yangtze

we may observe that the country is in a state of desolation, and that the duties now collected at the foreign custom houses are being applied to Imperial and not provincial wants. The effect of this last circumstance is to cause additional Imposts to be levied on the transit of goods in the Interior, and the foreign customs and their obnoxious regulations being supported and we may say almost enforced by the British authorities in China we fear that the benefits which may accrue from the new treaty will be very much smaller than might reasonably have been expected.[46]

The increase in transit dues was but one of the evils assigned to the inspectorate. Business was stagnant and the honest collection of customs dues did not help. To Matheson & Co. Jardine's reported that "at Shanghai local trade is dull as ever, & Tientsin where business looked promising . . . will be swamped by oversupplies." [47] The reason was the same.

The new custom house there whose arrangements are utterly unsuited to trade, is seriously impeding transactions as well as annoying the residents and no abatement of the evil can be looked for. Indeed the entire foreign custom house system has become such an obstruction to business and rapidity of communication in China, and is so unequal and unjust in its operation, that the sooner foreigners cease to uphold it the better and it is much to be desired that influential persons at home connected with the trade would make a move in this connection. [48]

This was the signal for a campaign to abolish the system. Both the Shanghai and Hongkong Chambers addressed the Foreign Office and called on the home Chambers for support. The Glasgow Chamber wrote to Lord Russell their conviction that the foreign inspectorate was collecting "arbitrary dues" and that the British Minister and Consuls "do not afford that assistance to the merchants" which the situation demands. [49] Glasgow had acted upon the recommendation of the Hongkong Chamber and the urging of a Mr. William Paton, a business correspondent of Jardine, Matheson & Co. [50] without too direct a knowledge of the extent to which even the larger China houses were engaging in smuggling. The other home Chambers acted as innocently, depending for their China intelligence on the taipans and the China Chambers they controlled. Controlled is none too strong a word, particularly for the Hongkong Chamber of Commerce which was run almost as a department of Jardine, Matheson & Co.

The Hongkong Chamber in adding its memorial to the flood denouncing Bruce and the foreign inspectorate came closest to revealing the crux of mercantile resentment. Complaining bitterly against Bruce's approval and support of China's efforts to enforce customs regulations, the Chamber argued that British officials were there to aid in the development of trade, not to support Imperial authority.

Another class of remedies depends entirely on the alteration of tone in the Government and its representatives. If Ministers and Consuls can be induced to see that one chief object of their being placed in China is to protect, develope and encourage trade, and not merely to demand blind obedience to every requirement of the native authorities, or of the Foreigners employed by them, a great point would be gained. [51]

An intensive campaign to arouse mercantile opinion at home was inaugurated. Jardine, Matheson & Co. told the manufacturers that Bruce's support of the Imperial authorities and of the foreign inspectorate system was responsible for China's failure to consume British goods which were flooding the market. "Should our present policy be continued it is greatly to be feared the consequences will prove most disastrous to Trade." [52] The Hongkong and Shanghai Chambers complained to Manchester that exemption certificates were not being honored and that transit dues were being levied arbitrarily; disputes over customs, they held, should be decided by British consular authorities and not by the mixed court, which insisted on respect for Chinese customs regulations. [53]

The campaign was only partially successful. Glasgow refused to memorialize the Foreign Office again, being "unwilling to trespass too frequently on the attention of the British Government as it would injure its influence at headquarters by doing so." [54] Manchester Chamber of Commerce, under the urging of John Pender (later an M.P. and promoter of the first telegraph line in China) and Sam Mendel, Jardine's agent in Manchester, at first resolved to memorialize the government and send a deputation to Earl Russell "with a view to remedying the evils complained of . . . which are of a nature to materially interfere with the important trade of this district with China." [55] However, the subcommittee appointed to investigate the grievances alleged in the Hongkong and Shanghai complaints concluded that most of these had been redressed and that Bruce's action was not to be condemned. [56]

In response to mercantile complaints, however, the Foreign Office conducted a quiet inquiry. Lord Elgin, asked for his opinion, not only approved the course taken by Bruce but remarked caustically that "to the best of my recollection it never was suggested to me that I should use the power I possessed to compel the Chinese government to divest itself of its power of enacting regulations for the protection of its revenue and of imposing penalties for the breach of such regulations." [57] The Board of Trade, after full investigation, gave its unequivocal support to Bruce's policy, remarking that satisfaction of mercantile demands would result in undermining Chinese authority, an eventuality which must be prevented at all costs. [58]

This clash between Whitehall and the China Hands, as it would soon be evident, was more than a disagreement over the mode of customs collection or the legality of inland taxation. Now, as later, the dispute was being conducted in veiled terms. For what the merchant desired was governmental support of his own broad interpretation of the Tientsin Treaty—so broad as to disregard Chinese authority and permit him to conduct his operations over the length of China on his own terms. Trade was bad—it was never really good—and the only way to tap the fabulous market was by the removal of all "obstruction." The British Government, intent on preventing the breakdown of Chinese authority, became committed to its support. Inevitably, that meant support against its own subjects. Whitehall was not prepared to assume the responsibility of governing China. Its position was not the result of an aberration suddenly conceived by Lord Clarendon under the hypnotic spell of Mr. Anson Burlinghame, as mercantile propagandists later contended; it was a policy already determined in 1862.

The conflict was soon to come out into the open. Despite the rebellion, Chinese authorities opened the Yangtze to trade under very liberal regulations; the foreigner was even permitted to enter Kiukiang and Hankow. Clashes between British subjects and natives, as well as growing difficulty in collecting customs and internal duties, however, led the authorities in the summer of 1862 to adopt more stringent trade rules. A flotilla of customs cruisers enforced tighter customs regulations; trade on the Yangtze was again restricted to the open ports; and the assumed privilege of establishing hongs and warehouses in the interior was withdrawn. The practice had grown up with the tacit consent of Chinese authorities, although no such right had been granted by treaty.

The outcry was strident. The larger houses, as well as the smaller speculators, were thrown into consternation. The *Shanghae Recorder*,[59] a newspaper founded and financed by Jardine, Matheson & Co., kicked over the traces and openly advocated what it had up to then been hinting: that all tariffs be abolished and treaty restrictions removed, that trade be conducted through personal arrangements with local authorities for landing and shipping goods; all central authority, it recommended, should be ignored. Even the Hongkong *China Mail* [60] was shocked by this attitude. "If merchants expect protection they must adhere to the terms of the treaty under which we can demand such protection; if they insist on doing a lucrative smuggling trade on the plea that no preventive service exists, they must not complain when China, with our advice and assistance, provides a fleet of cruisers that can neither be bribed nor frightened."

Sir Frederick Bruce, enclosing these press excerpts, reminded the Foreign Office that the promoters of the *Shanghae Recorder* had consistently opposed all attempts at enforcing the treaties between China and the foreign powers and had denounced the organization of "an honest customs-administration." His interpretation is illuminating.

No doubt, if the Chinese executive were to continue in its former condition, the proposed policy would be favorable to the interests of the large houses in China, for their command of capital would give them a decided advantage in corrupting the local authorities, and they would conduct their trading operations in armed vessels which would overawe opposition. But this monopoly would not be beneficial to the manufacturing interests of Great Britain and the calculations of its promoters will be defeated if the Chinese are in possession of a naval force.[61]

Nor was this view, in its essentials, confined to the larger houses. While the *North China Herald* and the *China Mail* [62] might object to Jardine's open espousal of taipan gunboats on the Yangtze, mercantile opinion was fully aroused by China's attempt to restrict trade within the limitations defined in the treaty. Already choleric as a result of Bruce's continued support of the maritime customs administration, merchants regarded the Chinese regulations of 1862, which attempted to push foreign trade back to the treaty ports, as an ominous development. For the first time, a more considered statement of mercantile policy was advanced, and it is striking that this first assertion laid down two strategic lines which future generations were to follow: the legal argument and the political argument. The legal approach advanced a broad interpretation of the Tientsin Treaty, so broad as to allow merchants to trade without restriction throughout the Middle Kingdom. The political, invariably complementing the legal approach, argued the necessity for continued application of pressure on China if treaty privileges were not to be lost.

This statement of mercantile policy was laid down in the Shanghai British Chamber of Commerce memorial of September 4, 1862 to Earl Russell, signed by twenty-eight leading firms and merchants. It objected to China's attempt to "dispute the right of foreigners to trade upon the Yangtze river excepting at the Consular ports" and her further decision to establish custom-houses at Kiukiang and Hankow. The latter objection was admittedly specious, but the former was based on the unique mercantile interpretation of treaty rights. Most significant was the mercantile objection to the issuance of a circular by the British Consul at Kiukiang that it was the view of Her Majesty's Minister that no right to rent or establish hongs and warehouses in the interior or reside there permanently could be derived from Article XII. As pointed out above,[63] the merchants had been arguing that the phrase "or other places" in the Article on land purchase had granted this privilege. Having advanced this treaty interpretation, the merchants concluded on a note of policy:

In calling your Lordship's attention to these two points, which in themselves we regard as of the first importance to our future trade with China, we would respectfully urge what past experience amply proves, that in dealing with an Asiatic nation like the Chinese, any surrender of a right is attributed by them to any cause rather than forebearance on our part, and on that account, if no other, such a surrender should never be made; and we are of the opinion that a firm and decided tone in demanding all privileges accorded to the British nation by the late Treaty of Tientsin, will best preserve that peace which all classes, and more especially merchants, are so anxious to maintain.[64]

The argument was ingenious and, within a very few years, was to be translated into a catechism of mercantile folklore. Bruce, to whom a copy of the memorial was sent, and who was already convinced as the result of recent clashes in the interior that "the most serious difficulty we have to contend with is the misconduct of foreigners themselves," [65] could hardly fail to dispute each point. He was convinced that "the right claimed to trade at all places on the Yangtze River, together with the privilege of erecting hongs and warehouses in the interior," had never been conceded under the Treaty of Tientsin. In China's decision to limit trade to the open ports "there is no restriction of a previous concession." Certainly, so long as foreign disorders, "which the Chinese are too timid, and we are unable, to repress," occur, no further concessions could be asked.[66]

As respects the right to open warehouses in the interior, it is one which cannot, in my opinion, be sustained, either on the letter or on the spirit of the Treaty. . . . The word "places" was introduced to prevent any chicanery on the word "ports"; and the clause was intended to refer to any other ports or places not mentioned in the Treaty which the Chinese government might hereafter consent to open to foreigners. But it was not intended to open by a side window the whole of China to British residents, which is the construction put on the words by the Memorialists.[67]

The difference between merchant and official was more than a dispute over treaty interpretation. It was a difference in policy. The "restricted interpretation" was official rationalization for a policy of limited commitments in China. Neither the extent nor the kind of trade warranted the doubtful benefits of forcing the trade upon the inland provinces. Convinced by the Mitchell thesis, which had been confirmed in Colonel Neale's Trade Report of December 20, 1861,[68] that the prospects of the China trade must fall far short of the Pottinger dream, the Government was hardly prepared to revert to that "bold" policy demanded by the merchants; its imperial costs were bound to prove greater than its commercial returns. A forward policy or a failure to back Peking might lead to the disintegration of Imperial authority. Was Great Britain ready to accept the responsibility of governing a China in collapse?

It was, as the Foreign Office saw it, a problem for the Board of Trade. Already disturbed by the strong mercantile objections raised against the foreign inspectorate system, the Foreign Office submitted the Shanghai Memorial of September, 1862 to Louis Mallet and J. E. Tennent, undersecretaries at the Board of Trade, for expert comment. Their minutes on the Shanghai dispatch became policy. While agreeing with Bruce in rejecting mercantile pretensions, Mallet realized the more fundamental implications raised by the memorial.

It is evident that the Chinese Govt have conceded more than they were at all bound to do—and probably more than their real interests justify.

The paramount difficulty and danger to be avoided in our dealings with China, is all unnecessary contact between British traders and the natives. The class of Britons who press into this new and untrodden field of enterprise is mainly composed of unscrupulous & reckless adventurers who seek nothing but enormous profits on particular transactions and care little for the permanent interests of commerce—still less for the principles of truth and justice. These men always cloak their injustices under the guise of patriotism and civilisation —and appeal to the British Govt as "Cives Romani" but I have seldom seen a case in which their total disregard of honesty was so apparent.

I would submit that the F.O. should be told that in the opinion of the Board there is nothing in Articles X or XII to justify the pretensions of these merchants—that the Chinese Govt have faithfully fulfilled their Treaty engagements both in spirit & in letter—and that consequently H.M. Govt has no ground for remonstrance.[69]

Tennent agreed, holding that there was no justification whatever for the Shanghai view, and the Board of Trade letter to the Foreign Office of February 17, 1863, stressed that no right to trade outside the treaty ports could or should be claimed. And not only on legal grounds but on grounds of policy.

They believe so far as it is possible for H.M. Government to regulate the intercourse of British subjects with the Chinese authorities and population in places beyond Consular control, the one great object which should be steadily kept in view, especially during the continuance of the present internal disturbances, is to diminish by every means in their power, the points of contact between them.[70]

Two further points were stressed by the Board, both of which became significant premises in the formation of official policy.

Instead of pressing the Chinese government to relax regulations necessary for their own protection My Lords consider H.M. Government should give them on all occasions their moral support in resisting undue encroachments on their

authority and in checking those forms of commercial enterprise which however profitable to individual traders, are fatal to the permanent interest of trade.

Secondly, while regretting to find itself at variance with "so important
a body as the Chamber of Commerce at Shanghai on a matter which involves one of the fundamental principles which should animate our
commercial relations with China," the Board

cannot forget that, as a general rule, the interest of the mercantile class engaged
in the trade with Asiatick countries is not of so permanent a character as is the
trade with European and Anglo-Saxon communities—and that from this cause
there arises a constant tendency to look rather to immediate than to prospective
and permanent advantage.[71]

Mallet's view as to the temporary and insignificant, not to say speculative, nature of the China trade was not just one man's opinion in
Whitehall. For it served, almost verbatim, as the official reply which
Sir Edward Hammond, Permanent Undersecretary at the Foreign
Office, dispatched to Shanghai.[72] The parallel is evident. Hammond not
only supported Bruce on the customs issue but completely rejected the
Shanghai view as to the legality and desirability of extending trade
inland. No right to reside, trade or establish warehouses in the interior
was recognized by the Government. Nor was it to be sought.

Lord Russell believes that, so far as it is possible for Her Majesty's Government
to regulate the intercourse of British subjects with the Chinese authorities and
population in places beyond consular control, the one great object which should
be steadily kept in view is to diminish by every means in their power the points
of contact between them.

Instead of pressing the Chinese Government to relax its regulations,
the British Government "will give them their moral support in resisting
undue encroachments on their authority and administration, and in
checking those forms of commercial enterprise which, however profitable to individual traders, are fatal to the permanent interests of trade."
Apparently out of deference to the taipans, Hammond did not include
the Board of Trade's slighting contrast of "Asiatick" with European
trade. But on the implication of that comparison it based future policy.
    Thus as early as 1863 official policy was defined and from the very
start it clashed with mercantile premises about the China trade. The
Board of Trade, champion of commercial interests, could see nothing
but a temporary, speculative trade and urged caution and retrenchment. The "one great object" of official policy was to diminish points
of contact between British traders and native customers.
    This became the first staple in British official policy. The other, whose

origin came to be attributed to the inauguration of the "Clarendon policy," [73] was first enunciated by Lord Russell in 1861 and repeated by Lord Stanley in 1867. Committed to the support of Imperial authority and to the recognition of Peking as a responsible, sovereign government in international affairs, the Foreign Office instructed its consuls that henceforth treaty disputes and the redress of grievances arising out of anti-foreign disturbances or differences with native officials were not to be solved by local pressure but referred to Peking for diplomatic settlement.[74] As a corollary, Bruce emphasized that this meant the constant exercise of discretion on the part of British subjects to avoid giving offense to the Chinese and on the part of British consuls to meet local authorities in a spirit of compromise.[75] In his instructions to Consul Forrest at Kiukiang at about the same time, Bruce took occasion to redefine official policy. Cultivate good understanding with native authorities and the people, he admonished the consul.

Where there are difficulties that you are unable to overcome, you must refer the case, after exhausting all amicable means, to Peking; but avoid, as much as possible, menace. Her Majesty's Government has reiterated its instructions that Her Majesty's Consuls are not to appeal to it, except in cases where the lives of H.M. subjects are threatened, or their property endangered by riots. Abuse of authority by the Chinese, or delay in doing what we are entitled to demand, are not sufficient causes to warrant violent measures. The effort must now be made to settle such disputed questions through the intervention of the Imperial authority. . . .[76]

Lord Russell approved.[77]

Occasion for the implementation of these instructions was not long in coming and under circumstances which brought the lesson home to mercantile interests. A certain Captain Sullivan, representative of Jardine, Matheson & Co., became involved in an argument over an alleged breach of contract concerning the sale of a shipment of camphor at a Formosan port and was severely beaten by the local taotai's men. Captain Sullivan appealed directly to Captain Moresby of H.M.S. *Snake* for assistance in securing redress, but the latter refused to act without consulting G. P. Browne, the British Consul at Taiwan. Browne, on instructions from Bruce, not only rejected the appeal, but read both Captain Moresby and the litigants a lecture on proper procedure.

With respect to the mode of dealing with cases in which the Treaty rights of H.M. Subjects are violated, I have to inform you that H.M. Government has issued instructions that in no case whatever is force to be resorted to unless the security of British life or property is threatened. I must warn you against the assumption that because a violation of right has been committed you are justified in obtaining redress for it by force. The desirable object to be attained is that of forcing the local officials to observe the Treaty and protect H.M. Subjects in the exercise of their privileges through the pressure brought to bear on them by the Peking government and thus to escape the false position in which we have hitherto been placed of coercing the local authorities and people and thus doing the work of the Imperial Government.[78]

This procedure became a mainstay of British policy in China. It was repeated on several occasions throughout the next several years.[79] Nor was it reversed with a change in Government, for it was not a function of Liberal principles but a manifestation of Whitehall policy. Thus, Lord Stanley reiterated the Foreign Office view, during the Newchwang disturbances in 1866, that "Her Majesty's Government are very averse to the employment of Her Majesty's forces on shore in China even to meet a sudden emergency," and approved Sir Rutherford Alcock's procedure in calling upon the central Chinese government to assume the responsibility of maintaining order throughout the Middle Kingdom.[80]

Thus the twin principles of reducing contacts with the natives and of holding the central authority responsible for the good order and observance of treaty rights did not originate with the advent of Lord Clarendon to the Foreign Office. They became official policy soon after the signing of the Treaty of Tientsin when the Board of Trade convinced the Foreign Office that Britain should cut her commitments in China. Despite mercantile pressure which reached a climax at the end of the 1860s the Government early became disillusioned about the potentialities of the China market. British interests there would be neither permanent nor would they amount to much. Further concessions forced from China, resulting in a real "opening" of the country as the merchants demanded, would lead to internal anarchy. Anarchy, in turn, meant the collapse of native authority and the inevitable substitution of some form of British sovereignty. But if British interests were destined to be temporary and limited what justification could there be for assuming the cost and responsibility of extending commitments to protect those interests? Commercial interests in China would always remain particular, even speculative, interests; never, imperial.

This became the premise of British official policy until the end of the century; and even then the Foreign Office retreated from it only partially and reluctantly. Without an understanding of this element and the significant part it played in the formation of British policy toward China, the development of that policy in the nineteenth century cannot be grasped.

II

Lord Clarendon
and the Old China Hands

"The opening of the country is their cry, 'progress' is their motto, war is their object. Trade is slack at present. It is necessary to live, and Micawber-like, they hope for something to turn up in the general disruption it would infallibly produce"—Peking Correspondent of *The Times*, quoted in the House of Commons, March 29, 1870.

H ISTORICAL motives are rarely documented and always difficult to assess. But Britain's China policy cannot be explained except on the premise that Whitehall's estimate of the prospects of the China market were markedly bearish. This alone explains the Board of Trade's reaction to the Shanghai Memorial of 1862 and the Foreign Office decision to eschew local pressure and support the tottering Manchu authority. Official attitude was set within two years after the ratification of the Tientsin Treaty. It was not a function of the Liberal triumph of 1868; Clarendon's Declaration of that year but dramatized and brought to a focus all the points already at issue.

Admitting that Britain was in China for trade, what were the prospects? Would China ever prove a major outlet for Manchester goods or a major field for British enterprise? Trade figures were hardly promising; and for Whitehall the inference was as obvious as it had been for Mitchell. Remove all the political obstacles of which the merchants complained—restriction of trade to treaty ports, arbitrary inland taxation, personal insecurity, a too strict customs administration—and the effect on trade would be negligible, for the potentialities of the China trade were limited. This premise the merchants disputed, and it was from this difference in premise that the clash over policy arose. Whether to bolster Peking authority or to step boldly into the provinces and establish the

King's Peace; whether to force railways and big business on a reluctant China even at the risk of war and anarchy; whether to adopt that "bold policy" for which the Old China Hands clamored—all these would be solved in accordance with the view one took of the commercial prospects of the Middle Kingdom.

While the conflict between merchant and official was already defined in the time of Bruce, it was the coincidence of treaty revision and the Burlinghame Mission at the end of the sixties which translated it into a public issue. For the first time Anglo-Chinese policy was debated in unveiled terms as a clash between the Foreign Office and the Old China Hands. Mercantile success in preventing ratification of the Alcock Convention was a victory not without a Pyrrhic quality for it postponed basic treaty revision for another thirty years, while the tempest over the Burlinghame Mission served the Liberal Government with an opportunity to put a moral stamp of approval on a policy already firmly held.

There was no getting around the trade figures. Business in the mid-sixties was still stagnant and far from certain. As early as August, 1865, Jardine's was complaining of unprofitable trade, of over-trading and speculation which they attributed to "the inordinate number of Banks in China, and to the monetary facilities with which they flood every commercial channel." [1] And although they looked forward to "a cautious, quiet, business for some months to come," [2] 1866 was to prove disastrous with a severe depression unprecedented in the China trade. An entire want of confidence prevailed and the most sinister rumors in regard to the stability of firms resident in China were current as the result of disclosure of peculation and failure by McKellar & Co. at Hankow.[3] Jardine, Matheson & Co. spoke of the "undisguised collapse which the vent here for manufactures has experienced." [4] Their business correspondence sounded an almost hysterical note.

The pressure to sell which exists all around renders it plain that many of the sales of shirtings have been purchased by means of borrowed capital, and threaten, when brought to resale, to most unduly prejudice the quittance of the very stocks that the kind of business they represent has contributed to accumulate. Our argument is that but for the baseless, fictitious support extended to prices during the past two or three years by local speculations (the operators being Chinese as well as Foreigners) so heavy a stock of shirtings might not have been accumulated, and we cannot too strongly deprecate the unwarrantable facilities made available to speculators by the competition for the employment of funds existing among the various Banks. . . .[5]

But it was to prove more than the result of speculative excesses. Over-optimism and over-trading had again seized the China market. "In a commercial and monetary sense," Jardine's wrote in their New Year's report for 1867, "no year has opened in China so gloomy as this." [6] A widespread disbelief in the stability of all trading firms, insolvency of many establishments, the precarious position of most banks characterized the China trade throughout 1866 and most of 1867. And although confidence revived somewhat toward the end of the latter year, British consuls found it necessary to issue a warning that "the vicissitudes and losses which have characterized foreign trade in China are traceable to the over-trading of those interested." [7] A consular report on Shanghai trade in 1869, more than two years after the depression was presumably over, pointed out that overloading of the market still led to losses.[8] More significant, the report warned of "ominous symptoms that the maximum of consumption has nearly been reached."

Typical of mercantile reasoning in the face of continued depression and stagnation was the Annual Trade Report on Hankow for 1869, distributed to the taipans by E. Townsend & Co.[9] Hankow had not prospered as an outlet for Manchester goods because these were funneled through Shanghai, whence the cost of transhipment was high. "At present all the advantages of this port are reaped by natives and speculators, who make purchases in Shanghai for resale here, thus creating more middlemen between the manufacturer and consumer." There was hardly any limit to the market for Manchester products in Hankow "if such could be imported at low cost and of good wearing material." Having established the economic axiom that good material will sell at a low price, the Townsend Report proceeded to recount a bit of current mercantile folklore on the cause of trade stagnation. The exaction of inland duties was primarily to blame. But the fault lay not with the illegal action of local tax gatherers but with British government policy. "The bane of the present policy is that it tends solely to centralisation of all power in Pekin, it being apparently not generally known that this country is in fact a confederation of states under one Emperor . . . so that the forwarding of all Customs duties to Pekin has compelled the authorities to raise further revenue by local taxes."

Not only was business uncertain and trade restricted; its distribution was passing into native hands. The foreign merchant, squeezed by native competition, cried to his government for unrestricted access to inland markets. At Kiukiang the British Consul reported in 1868 that the import of Manchester goods was improving but the business was largely in native hands.[10] At Canton, Consul Robertson submitted a pessimistic report in response to the Minister's inquiry on the desirability of inland travel and residence for foreigners. "The fact of the import trade in merchandize at this port being entirely in the hands of Chinese . . . renders increased privileges in the navigation of inland waters a matter of less consequence to the foreign merchant at this than at any of the other open ports." [11]

To the taipans this was the essence of heresy; for even as late as 1898 the opening of the West River from Canton was a basic demand of the Hongkong Chamber of Commerce and the China Association, the restriction on navigation of inland waters being regarded as a primary obstacle to the expansion of foreign trade. Even more heretical was Robertson's view that "the foreign merchant makes a great mercantile mistake in desiring the diffusion of trade over a wide area. . . . Concentration not extension should be the object. . . . I believe myself that the deplorable results which have attended foreign trade in China during the past few years are attributable in great measure to the opening of the Yangtze River."

"Concentration not extension should be the object"!—what better proof to the merchant that British officials were sabotaging British commercial interests in China.

Not all British consuls agreed, of course. In reply to a circular inquiry in the spring of 1869, by Sir Rutherford Alcock, the British Minister, the consuls emphasized that the task of distribution of foreign goods in the interior was being taken over by Chinese traders. But they differed as to diagnosis and cure: as a result of surveys among mercantile firms the Consuls tended to reflect local opinion.[12] At Amoy, the Consul was convinced that "the diversion of foreign trade at this port into Chinese hands is almost entirely owing to the operation of likin duties"; Foochow reported that natives were taking over internal distribution because of their superior knowledge of language and markets and lower overhead; Hankow also insisted that "it is the transit pass system which alone keeps any of the import trade in the hands of the foreigner" until such time as residence and travel in the interior would be conceded.[13]

These views did not differ materially from mercantile opinion. Consul Robertson at Canton, however, regarded the diversion of trade into native hands with equanimity.

There is no doubt that being in Chinese hands will, to use the words of Lord Clarendon . . . "tend to a larger development of trade in British goods" and consequently what the local mercantile establishment may lose will be recouped tenfold to the home manufacturers by the increased demand. . . . There is every prospect that as far as Imports are concerned the business of Foreign firms in them will ere long be simply agency.[14]

To Whitehall the situation was daily becoming clearer. Not only was China far from the pretended Eldorado of mercantile vision, but the trade was passing into native hands. What was more, far from being harmful to Manchester manufacturers it might prove beneficial as Robertson argued. Was the promotion of local mercantile establishments in China then worth the vigorous policy which merchants demanded in the name of imperial interests?

It was against this background that the battle over treaty revision and the reappraisal of British policy toward China, brought into focus by the Burlinghame Mission, were undertaken. Mercantile opposition to the Alcock Convention was not, as is sometimes claimed, a narrow objection to specific provisions such as the rise in opium tariff or the transit dues arrangement. The issue then raised was much more profound, and the argument centered on the direction which British policy toward China was to adopt. Was it to be expansion or consolidation? Was tariff revision to be used as the occasion for pressing those "reforms" on China which would open the country to British enterprise even at the cost of Chinese independence? The solution lay in one's answer to the question: was the Chinese market worth the assumption of further imperial commitments? For the Old China Hands in Shanghai and London, and even for Manchester manufacturers subjected to their propaganda about the fabulous China market, a forward policy—pressure for reforms, for unrestricted trade on Britain's terms, for railway and telegraph and mining concessions—was well worth the risk of China's collapse. Whitehall and its spokesmen were fully convinced that it was not. Gradualism, a Chinese revolution by consent, a policy of *festina lente* as the learned Minister Sir Rutherford Alcock called it, was the wiser course. For Britain, it was argued, was not prepared—for economic as well as imperial reasons—to accept the responsibility of governing China. As Alcock put it, Britain should not risk more than the hesitant forward step from waiting to hoping.

In the late spring of 1867 Sir Rutherford Alcock, Her Majesty's Minister to Peking, made a grand tour of the treaty ports with an eye toward sounding out mercantile opinion precedent to treaty revision, scheduled for the following year. At Kiukiang on the Yangtze the merchants complained of the illegal exaction of transit dues and the failure of the transit pass system; further they requested the right for foreign steamers to navigate the Yangtze and Poyang Lake.[15] At Chefoo the merchants drew a rosy picture of prospective trade with Shantung, Honan and Shansi if the projected railway from Chefoo to Tsinanfu were constructed and permission to operate coal mines in the district were granted. Trade could progress if only it were unregulated and unrestricted.

Every advantage is taken of the letter of the treaty to interpret it in a harsh sense, and we are constantly threatened with confiscation of our goods on frivolous pretexts . . . owing to the unwillingness of the Customs to meet us in a proper spirit. We are constantly obliged to ask the help of the Consul against the exactions and annoyances thus sought to be imposed on us; we feel them more acutely because our own countrymen are the instruments for such illiberal action.[16]

At Chinkiang the merchants paraded the usual complaints about internal taxes, but they touched on what was to become a major issue in emphasizing that treaty enforcement depended on continued local pressure on Chinese authority. "We would also suggest the necessity of granting enlarged powers to H.B.M. Consuls in their intercourse with the native authorities, as mere remonstrance and protest go but a very short way with such a class of men as the body of Chinese officials." [17]

In his reply to the Kiukiang merchants, Alcock for the first time hinted at the more restrictive view the Government took of treaty revision. It was a two-sided affair. Revision, once opened, would provide the Chinese with an opportunity for pressing their own demands. They had been opposed to steam navigation of the Yangtze; but that might be accomplished. He granted that the problem of inland taxes which Chinese provincial officials continued to levy "under a thousand different pretexts and names" had not been resolved by Elgin's formula of commutation. But, he added, "whether Foreign Governments had the right in all cases to prohibit such exercise of territorial sovereignty or not, it was quite certain that none of them had the power to prevent it, because that would require a surveillance there was no means of exercising." [18] Did the mighty British Empire indeed have no "means of surveillance," or was it unready to apply them?

The Foreign Office (Lord Stanley) very much approved Alcock's reply to the merchants. But it set him a difficult task. On the one hand the Foreign Office sanctioned his catering to mercantile opinion: "those opinions must always be valuable even though it may not be politic or even possible to give full effect to them." On the other, Lord Stanley was pleased that Alcock was "prepared to take into account the interests, the feelings and to a certain extent the prejudices of the Chinese Government and people." The "true policy" to be advocated is that which "shall combine the suffrages of both parties in some common system." Lord Stanley then proceeded to express the official Britannic attitude, an attitude which was later to be attributed to Lord Clarendon and the Liberal Government by publicists and Old China Hands:

Her Majesty's Government neither wish nor have they the right to impose sacrifices on China even though they may be convinced that the inconvenience of such sacrifices will be only temporary, whereas the benefit which will result from them will be lasting. We must not expect the Chinese, either the Government or the people, at once to see things in the same light that we see them; we must bear in mind that we have obtained our knowledge by experience extending over many years, and we must lead and not force the Chinese to the adoption of a better system. We must reconcile ourselves to waiting for the gradual development of that system, and content ourselves with reserving for revision at a future period, as in the case before us, any new arrangement which we may come to in 1868.[19]

On the same day that government policy was set by Lord Stanley, the Foreign Office inquired of the Board of Trade as to the advisability of consulting the British Chambers of Commerce on treaty revision. The Foreign Office pointed out that Alcock had already invited suggestions from the mercantile community in China.[20] The Board of Trade agreed that though "most of the merchants in this country interested in the Chinese trade have representatives in China" it would be politic to approach the home Chambers.[21] On September 5, 1867, consequently, an appropriate letter was circulated.

Chamber replies were remarkably indifferent. Some tabled the letter, several replied that they were not concerned, while the remainder expressed satisfaction with the current tariff.[22] The Bradford Chamber of Commerce thought the matter could be left entirely to the China Chambers. The Belfast Chamber of Commerce was not even aware that linen and linen fabrics, in which they were particularly interested, were included in the China tariff schedule.[23]

Far different was the reaction in mercantile circles in China. Determined that the time for adopting a strong stand had arrived and that they could not afford to let the opportunity slip, merchants and Chambers of Commerce fired a barrage of memorials, in response to Alcock's circular letter of May, 1867, probably unprecedented in British commercial history. And the subsequent campaign, which became entangled with the political situation attending the Burlinghame Mission, ultimately succeeded in enlisting the support of all the important home Chambers of Commerce.

The burden of the 1867 memorials was that partial revision and tariff reform was not enough; a fundamental change in Chinese administration and determination on the part of the British Government to force upon the country an industrial and political revolution to the advantage of British commercial interests were required. The axiom underlying all the memorials was that with political obstacles removed the long-anticipated blossoming of foreign trade in China would follow. Between September and November of 1867, the Shanghai, Foochow, Amoy, Tientsin and Hongkong Chambers submitted memorials along this line; their unanimity was impressive.[24]

Shanghai, repeating the argument it had advanced in 1862, stated that the Treaty of Tientsin had all the requisite provisions for an expanded trade, if only the treaty were correctly interpreted and properly enforced. Import trade was slow because of (a) the obstructiveness of native officials, (b) illegal transit dues, and (c) a "general denial" of the privileges which the treaty was intended to secure. The design of the treaty had been to throw open the "producing and consuming districts to foreign capital and energy." Because of the retrogressive views of native officials, upheld by "influential quarters," this design was being frustrated. As a result of restrictive interpretations, merchants had lost the right to reside and establish warehouses in the interior, illegal inland excises were universal, and British representatives failed to secure redress for grievances against the Chinese. Correct interpretation and a change in official attitude was the only revision needed, according to the Shanghai merchants.

Foochow went even further, requesting not only residence in the interior, but that the entire coast of China be opened to foreign trade and shipping. Amoy merchants stressed the need for establishing a "radius of immunity" from *likin* taxes around treaty ports (they suffered more severely from this tax, as a special levy had been imposed in Fukien province); they also suggested that the tariff schedule (already at the low figure of five percent ad valorem) be halved. Tientsin, after covering minor grievances, laid down the heaviest barrage: throw open the entire country "to Christianity and commerce"; build railways and telegraph lines; extend communications and widen opportunities for exchange of goods.

The full implications of the mercantile demands were immediately seized by British officials in China, particularly by the senior consuls. Winchester, in forwarding the Shanghai memorial to Alcock, included his own extensive comments, which the Foreign Office regarded as important enough to submit to the Board of Trade for special observation. Despite his expressed sympathy for mercantile aims, he could not refrain from criticizing the Shanghai memorial for ascribing treaty failure to the non-exertion of pressure by diplomatic and consular officers. The treaty was actually "ahead of Chinese administration" in assuming that the Chinese government was centralized and possessed of authority in the provinces. To meet mercantile desires consuls would have to be provided with authority to threaten native officials with gunboats; but the weak Chinese government could never subsist against such "stringent displays of foreign influence." [25]

This, of course, was the focal point, as Winchester noted. In revision "the problem always is what concession can be demanded of the Chinese government without straining its authority." So long as this was true any encouragement to open additional ports on the seaboard would be useless and futile.[26] Sufficient waste of mercantile capital had already been experienced at the British concessions located at Chinkiang, Kiukiang and Hankow; the extent of China trade did not warrant further establishments nor would the privilege of residence in the interior be of any value "except for shooting and excursions."

Similar was the view expressed by Consul Robertson in his comments on the Hongkong Chamber's memorial, but with added vehemence.[27] Scarcely able to veil his indignation at the *ex parte* attitude of the Hongkong merchants, Robertson denied that the treaty had been unfulfilled "both in spirit and letter." All privileges accorded by treaty had been granted without that "passive resistance" charged by the Chamber. As for the mercantile desire to see a "restoration of the prestige of H.B.M. Consuls" by allowing them to exercise an "occasional display, if not employment, of more than moral force when dealing with Chinese authorities," Robertson regarded the suggestion so inadvisable as to require "no comment." Hongkong had demanded that import duties on textiles be halved; Robertson's pertinent comment was that "competition and running up the markets had had more to do with the depression of trade than anything else—and it would be the same if merchandise and produce entered duty free."

A wide gulf separated mercantile and official views on Anglo-Chinese policy. Alcock, in forwarding the 1867 memorials, favored a compromise policy based on gradual concessions which would not disturb Chinese authority. "Between the desirable and the practicable there is a great gulf at present, which must be bridged over by progressive steps towards the reconstruction and improvement of the internal administration of the Empire, before anything very practical or effective can be done in the direction pointed out" in the memorials.[28] Official and merchant might agree as to the need for reform but they differed as they were to differ for the next generation, as to the advisability of taking steps which might lead to China's collapse. Jardine, Matheson & Co. thought the potentialities of the China trade were so great that the risk was worth taking; inland residence would prove to be "the open sesame to that extension of British trade upon the confines of which we hover." [29]

The problem faced by Britain, as Alcock saw it, was the pace at which China could endure internal reform and survive. The mercantile program boiled down to four essentials: (a) relief from inland and local taxes, including transit dues and *likin* (destination tax); (b) greater facilities for access to the interior, involving rapid introduction of railways and steam navigation on inland waters; (c) the privilege of residing in the interior near the centers of industry and production; (d) establishment of a mixed tribunal with security for execution of awards against Chinese defaulters. But how were these to be attained? Only through drastic internal reform. But internal reform could be effected only gradually and through a policy of patience and forebearance. Without "foreign meddling and attempts at dictation" slow progress might result; but never at the rate demanded by the merchants. Otherwise Britain must be prepared to govern the country. "I believe the true policy of Foreign Powers is to wait." [30]

By the end of the year (1867) the difference between merchant and official was defined and it was already obvious that fundamental issues of policy, not individual measures of treaty revision, were in the balance. Forwarding the last of the mercantile memorials to the Foreign Office, Alcock submitted an estimate of the situation. The general identity of features in all the memorials, Alcock notes, led the press in China to draw the "erroneous deduction" that the views set forth were wise and the proposals "practicable and expedient in the interests of the merchants, whether consistent with treaties and the law of nations or not." But whether the British people were prepared to inaugurate a new policy in China designed to ensure an interpretation of the Treaty "exclusively in accordance with the wishes and interests of merchants irrespective of all other considerations of policy or justice, must be very doubtful." New concessions could be forced upon China only by pressure "with all the danger attending such violent action and sudden innovation on the customs, traditions and habits of a vast Empire." The foreign powers had had their chance for revolution during the Taiping rebellion, but for narrow commercial reasons this was checked. Now the situation would not admit "of hot haste or the introduction of sweeping changes and must of necessity be effected by slower methods." And if collapse is to be avoided China must be allowed to work out her development in her own way.

The assumption of superiority and right of dictation which pervades the whole of these memorials, insofar as they may be adopted by Foreign Powers constitutes one of the greatest impediments to progress under such circumstances. Internal organization and administrative reforms are the most pressing wants in China; but it is precisely in these that every nation of any independence claims for itself the right not only of initiation but direction, and is disposed to resent the meddling of foreign states.[31]

Alcock for the first time points out the full implications of mercantile demands. The changes pressed in the memorials could not be forced upon China "unless Foreign Powers are prepared to take upon themselves the full responsibility of such a policy and govern China themselves, under a protectorate." He envisages the possibility of dismemberment or division of Chinese territory; but this would be to the interest of no power. "Conquest and occupation have been spoken of; but it is difficult to see to what uses, political, military or commercial, any portion of China could be applied by European powers." Merchants on the spot might gain a temporary advantage but this program was not to Britain's interest. "Those who suffer in their material interests and feel from day to day the injury inflicted upon them by the maladministration and often the bad faith of Chinese officials may very naturally feel impatient and little inclined to forbearance, but it behoves Governments to take action on larger grounds, and with greater regard for future and permanent interests."

But the Old China Hands were hardly prepared to accept Alcock's plea for caution. The Hongkong press, jubilant over the unanimity of mercantile opinion and universal support for "treaty enforcement," beat the drums for "another Palmerston." [32] New memorials were pouring in. The Shanghai Chamber, concerned about the lukewarm attitude displayed by the home Chambers to treaty revision, inaugurated a publicity campaign designed to secure their support. Even as Alcock's dispatches counselling gradualism were reaching Whitehall, Chambers of Commerce in London and Lancashire and Scotland were systematically circularized by the Shanghai Chamber.[33] The letter of January 24, 1868 was the first of a series. In disarming fashion, the Shanghai merchants pointed out that the "most essential questions which the Chamber has urged upon the consideration of H.M. Government are the *bona fide* admission into the country of English manufactures, and as connected with this, the right to reside in the interior for purposes of trade." After reviewing the detailed suggestions for revision which the Chamber had adopted—including the apparently innocent one that "transit dues be collected by local officials"—Shanghai came to the core of the issue: that without a fundamental change in British policy treaty revision was meaningless.

For experience of British traders under the treaty had demonstrated rather "the necessity for a watchful and firm policy in its application than the want of any essential modification in its plan." The occasion was ripe for putting commerce in China on a "firm basis," and an aroused and informed public opinion at home should bring its influence to bear. The Chinese, a great trading nation, were not enjoying the full benefits of the treaty because of the obstruction of the mandarins, while foreign merchants equally found that their representatives refused that support which had been anticipated from the opening of a Legation at Peking. But, "removed from any contact with Foreign merchants, and the influence of public opinion, the Foreign Ministers become in a measure advocates of Chinese exclusiveness rather than of the extension of Foreign trade, and the result of such views can only be obviated by the urgent representations of all the Chambers of Commerce in England."

This was the Old China Hand partyline, peddled to British public opinion when occasion demanded. The reaction at home was none too warm. Many of the Chambers pigeon-holed the Shanghai letter. Belfast indicated that it wished no changes in the tariff and saw no reason for revision of any kind.[34] The Chambers still regarded the issue as strictly commercial and best left in the hands of China firms. At the annual meeting of the Associated Chambers of Commerce of Great Britain, however, an entire session was devoted to "Our Trade with China" in the light of revision.[35] The presence of Edward Milsom, briefly introduced as a "merchant of Shanghai," stimulated the discussion. Milsom's presentation constituted a review of the Shanghai memorial of 1867 and the circular letter to the home Chambers. The treaty was basically sound but had not been "enforced"; the increase in trade had been "much less than expected" because of illegal exactions and denial of treaty privileges; the Government should be pressed to secure those measures which would bring about "freedom of British trade and immunity from illegal imposts . . . [and] . . . liberty for British subjects to settle throughout China for purposes of trade and manufacture."

The discussion which ensued indicated how far apart home manufacturers and China merchants were in their appraisal of the issue; and how early the political implications of treaty port demands were recognized. The following is paraphrased:

MILSOM: The great difficulty foreigners had to contend with in dealing with the natives was to get contact with producers and consumers.

LUPTON (representing London): Was the Chinese government strong enough to protect English goods in the interior?

MILSOM: No, that was the point. "It had been tottering for 200 years . . .

and had been kept up so long by British aid." The corruption of officials was such that there was no remedy except foreigners going into the country and looking after their own interests themselves!

LUPTON: Then you propose English protection should be afforded them?

MILSOM: We suggest that foreigners should themselves look after their own goods and when anything goes wrong appeal to the Minister at Peking.

LUPTON: But we have been given to understand that the system is such that there can be no protection except by force.

MILSOM: That is unfortunately so.

LLOYD (President of the Associated Chambers): Then you want the treaty not revised but extended.

MILSOM: We want to be enabled to carry our goods into the country and to dispose of them there.

W. E. FORSTER (of Lancashire): I understand you wish to have the treaty so revised that instead of ports only being opened to British trade the whole country shall be thrown open. Suppose, then, the position of a merchant in a town in the interior far from gunboats, do you propose that English lives and property should go there at their own risk, our government not being bound to help them? that they should go armed? or that we should hold the Chinese government responsible for their safety?

MILSOM: The Chinese government should be held responsible. The natives are friendly and only the mandarins make difficulties.

Members were not convinced and the question was tabled for future study. For a moment, though, the issue had been clarified: adoption of the Shanghai program would commit the British government to a further extension of responsibility for protecting trade in the interior. On the whole, however, the home Chambers were not aroused. Liverpool was typical. After postponing action for six months, the Chamber wrote to the Foreign Office favoring adoption of the Shanghai recommendations, but not pressing the crucial issue of inland trade and residence.[36]

Public opinion had not responded to the Shanghai gambit, and the storm over treaty revision was postponed. Alcock, meanwhile, continued to pour his voluminous dispatches into the archives of the Foreign Office in an attempt to convince the Government that the mercantile view was shortsighted and that only a policy of gradualism and conciliation would serve the true interest of Britain. In a confidential report to Lord Stanley on New Year's Day, 1868, Alcock noted that the situation on revision was more encouraging but that the best they could hope for was that "instead of *aspettiamo* as our sole motto we may now add *esperiamo*." Whatever reforms might be secured they were bound to fall "far short of what merchants have demanded," for these were dependent on "organic changes in political and fiscal administration of government" which could only be effected by the sword.

It seems to be very easy for a few foreign merchants at Hongkong, on the outer confines of a great empire of which they have but little knowledge, to suggest changes and deal lightly with the grave questions to which they give rise. The responsibilities of government do not weigh upon them, and it is perhaps natural that they should fail to see, or seeing give little heed, to the difficulties which make their suggestions impracticable. They do not always see their own interests in a very clear light. And judging by the melancholy failures and bankruptcies within the last two or three years, they are but uncertain guides even in matters of trade and the conditions of commercial prosperity.[37]

It was in the same dispatch that Alcock outlined the theoretical origins of the Burlinghame Mission, its relation to treaty revision and to the policy underlying Anglo-Chinese relations. This was Alcock's argument: While it might serve the interests of France ("which had no trade of importance present or prospective") to throw everything into confusion "on the chance of establishing a protectorate over all or some provinces of China," Britain's interests would best be served by saving the Chinese Empire from disorganization. Maintaining China's territorial integrity and political independence was to Britain's long-term benefit. To accomplish it a policy of forebearance, of gradual reforms, was the only feasible one. "Railway, telegraph, mines, foreigners in public service—all these may shortly be adopted on one condition— that they are left free from dictation and control as to the selection of their agents and the time or conditions of their employment, and *feel* free from galling interference of foreign powers and their diplomatic and consular agents." [38]

It was to preach this gospel that the Burlinghame Mission, which Alcock had been instrumental in promoting, was formed by the "advanced party" at the Tsungli Yamen. Mr. Anson Burlinghame, former United States Minister to China, set out in the company of Chih Kang and Sun Chia-Ku to urge upon the Western powers formal acceptance of the doctrine which Bruce and Alcock had been advocating; it was a policy already implicit in every dispatch from Lord Russell and Lord Stanley. But it was destined to go down in history and to be subjected to bitter denunciation by Old China Hands as the "Clarendon Policy."

Disturbed by mercantile pressure for drastic treaty revision and by the first rumblings of anti-foreign sentiment in the provinces, Prince Kung, leader of the advanced party in the Tsungli Yamen, welcomed the proposal that the returning American Minister Anson Burlinghame might serve as a Chinese apostle "to state China's difficulties and inform the treaty powers of her sincere desire to be friendly and progressive." [39] To Peking, Burlinghame was to play the role of a buffer against foreign pressure for that precipitate reform which the merchants were urging. First news of the Burlinghame Mission received a surprisingly warm reception in all circles. Alcock's view has been noted above. But even among residents at the treaty ports the Mission was at first welcomed as a wedge for introducing some measure of reform in China.

This was to prove an aberration and opinion was to change radically. But in January, 1868, as Burlinghame in Shanghai was preparing for his trip to San Francisco, uncertain of the reception which awaited him, treaty port sentiment was favorable. Even Alcock was happy to quote the local China press as favoring the objectives of the Mission: "extension of intercourse, extension of commercial relations. And the right mode of attaining these objects is admitted to be argument and persuasion, rather than menace of violence." [40] James Barr Robertson, Shanghai correspondent of the London *Daily News* who usually reflected treaty port opinion, took pains to explain the point of view of Burlinghame's principals at the Tsungli Yamen:

The changes they had already introduced were really revolutionary, considering the condition of the empire; and while they were progressing, and willing to progress, they could not lose sight of the important fact that upon them devolved the responsibility of governing the empire and maintaining it in its integrity. . . . It was not necessary, and it would be very unwise, to introduce every possible change that foreigners could conceive within the almost momentary space of ten years; but with a steady policy of gradual progress they would be able to advance with security to the empire, and with satisfaction to foreign governments.[41]

Lord Stanley, too, received the intelligence of Burlinghame's Mission "with great satisfaction," as unmistakable evidence "of the desire of the Imperial Government to maintain the most friendly relations with European states." [42] Stanley's cordial reception of the idea of the Mission, whose purpose was no secret, is itself sufficient evidence that the "Clarendon policy" was not an innovation of the Gladstone Cabinet. It was fully in accord with the instructions which both Russell and Stanley had been sending to British representatives in China throughout the sixties.

But the honeymoon period did not last long. It is difficult to date the beginning of that rabid opposition to the Burlinghame effort which was to characterize mercantile opinion throughout the next few years and whose overtones were still discernible in statements made a generation

later. Basically, of course, mercantile opposition was already implicit in
the hostility shown by the Chambers to any conciliatory measure advocated by Alcock during the long process of treaty revision. For that
hostility was growing and even before Burlinghame was regaling the
citizens of San Francisco with visions of a China ready to exchange goods
and thoughts with the West, treaty port sentiment had become suspicious. The feeling that the shrewd Oriental had put something over on the
foreigner was strengthened by the renewed antagonism to basic treaty
revision displayed by the right wing of the Yamen. Memorials from
Chinese officials in the southern and western provinces breathing a spirit
of hostility to the foreign devils were reported by Consul Robertson that
spring. And Alcock himself was disturbed by the "disorder and mis-
government prevailing throughout the Empire at the present time" and
referred to the "general features of anarchy and helplessness in governing powers as of special interest at this moment when the question of the
revision of treaties is under consideration." [43]

The London *Daily News'* correspondent recovered from his January
aberration and now reflected the opinion of the treaty ports that
Alcock's policy of gradualism and forbearance was of a piece with the
Chinese camouflage being spread by Burlinghame. The *Daily News* advised the Foreign Office to make up its mind before the arrival of Burlinghame whether "to insist on or to abandon the full advantages of the
Treaty as to the right it gives of free access and residence in the interior
of China." [44] So aroused was Alcock that he accused the journal of dis-
playing complete ignorance not only of treaty interpretation but of the
state of affairs in China. If foreigners were scattered throughout the Empire by what means could they be secured against civil disturbances?
"Would the merchants have each foreign government, as often as such
cases arose, proceed at once to acts of retortion, by seizing Chinese property or laying violent hands on the customs?" How long could relations
proceed under such a system?

Besides, Alcock pointed out, merchants did not understand their own
economic interests when they appealed to government for access to inland places. For despite mercantile dreams, China would never serve as
a major outlet for British goods and capital.

When the Treaty of Tientsin was made the cry for more ports and opening of
the Yangtze to Hankow was equally unanimous and loud. Their desire was
granted and with what result let the universal bankruptcy, the nearly total
transfer of the foreign trade into native hands, and unoccupied land at all the
ports . . . attest. I doubt whether there is a single merchant in China now who
does not rue the day that the wish of the whole mercantile body was acceded to,
and more ports from Newchwang to Swatow were opened to Treaty. [45]

The gulf between official and mercantile attitudes was widening. The *Daily News* reported "a strong wish in China" for the removal of Alcock, who had become too mandarin-minded, and his substitution by someone fresh from "the political life of Europe." Alcock said this meant: "We want a Minister who knows what should suit our interests and who does not know and will not ask what the Chinese Government can safely promise and fairly be expected to perform." [46] If the British government followed mercantile advice, he warned, it would lead to the collapse of China.

But Alcock's major talking point against mercantile demands was the argument, repeated in dispatch after dispatch, that it was the restricted nature of the China market and the commercial malpractices of merchants, not political obstacles, which accounted for continued commercial stagnation. It is with a note of restrained glee that he comments on the Trade Memoranda on Shanghai, prepared by the principal merchants at that port and forwarded by Consul Winchester. For these embodied the hard-headed consideration of the economic factors which limited the China trade, factors ignored by the merchants in their political memorials.

I am glad to find in them a frank recognition of many of the true causes of the depression from which the trade has long suffered. The memorials so persistently kept these out of sight, attributing all the difficulties and losses to the action or inaction of Governments and authorities, that it is satisfactory to know there are some merchants at least who can take a larger view of the conditions of success and the requirements in this country.[47]

As one merchant had put it, in an indiscreet moment, "in pushing into the country we do but run after a shadow." But Alcock was convinced that only bitter experience would satisfy the Old China Hands that the demands in their memorials were economically as well as politically unwise. He was angered at the tacit cover-up of business malpractices which prevailed in the treaty ports, writing to Consul Winchester that he would have been pleased to see a formal condemnation of the actions of the bankrupt firm of McKellar & Co., which had engaged in large-scale defrauding of Chinese in Hankow.

The absence of any condemnation from the various Chambers of Commerce of acts in one of their own body which defrauded and ruined so many Chinese dealers, while they discredited the whole Foreign Mercantile community, is in curious contrast with the alacrity both Chambers and collective bodies of these same merchants have shown in the most sweeping and indiscriminate censure of others, and their readiness to charge the Chinese and their own authorities with collusion and bad faith. It is evident that there are two measures in use, one for mercantile, and another for official classes, and that they have nothing in common.[48]

Alcock's public censure of McKellar & Co. further strained already difficult relations with the merchants. The Shanghai Chamber of Commerce took umbrage at what they considered "an unwarranted interference on the part of any Minister with the right of merchants individually and collectively to determine for themselves what should be the mode of conducting business in China without advice or warning from Minister or Government." [49] In his public reply to the Shanghai Chamber, Alcock denied that any such "principle of absolute independence could be admitted."

So far as Imperial interests and British commerce were affected, the actual merchants resident at any time in the country, could enjoy no such unlimited right to do whatever might seem good in their own eyes, wholly irrespective of the injury they might be inflicting upon the trade of their country, and all the permanent and future interests of a national character connected with the present course of development.[50]

So vexed was Alcock by the tenor of this dispute that he deemed it necessary, in order to justify himself to the Foreign Office, to make a detailed survey of all recent instances of mercantile malpractices on the basis of facts furnished by the local press "wholly dependent on the mercantile class for support" and therefore not unfair to them. He found enough "to justify not only what I may have written, but the worst that has ever been said of the commercial morality, the tone of public opinion and the want of sound judgment or forecast in those who constitute the mercantile communities in China and Japan at the present date." [51]

Alcock's dispatch criticizing both the attitude and basic honesty of the mercantile communities had hardly been sealed in the diplomatic pouch at Peking when an event on the other side of the globe furnished Shanghai opinion with the ammunition needed to combat the effects of the Burlinghame Mission. Carried away by the exuberance of his own inspired oratory, Burlinghame told the leading citizens of New York, at a banquet held in his honor on June 23, 1868, that only by a policy of forbearance could China be brought into the comity of nations; that China, "emerging from the mists of time," was only too willing to accept reform and railways and international law; and that she asks only that "those treaties which were made under the pressure of war" be given "a generous and Christian construction." Leaning heavily on imagination, Burlinghame averred "that there is no spot on earth where there has been greater progress made within the past few years than in the Empire of China." But it was Burlinghame's peroration which really raised Shanghai fever:

Yet, notwithstanding this manifest progress, there are people who will tell you that China has made no progress, that her views are retrograde; and they tell you that it is the duty of the Western treaty powers to combine for the purpose of coercing China into reforms which they may desire and which she may not desire—who undertake to say that this people have no rights which you are bound to respect. In their coarse language they say, "Take her by the throat." Using the tyrant's plea, they say they know better what China wants than China herself does. Not only do they desire to introduce now the reforms born of their own interests and their own caprices, but they tell you that the present dynasty must fall, and that the whole structure of Chinese civilisation must be overthrown. I know that these views are abhorred by the governments and the countries from which these people come; but they are far away from their countries, they are active, they are brave, they are unscrupulous, and, if they happen to be officials, it is in their power to complicate affairs and to involve, ultimately, their distant countries in war. Now it is against the malign spirit of this tyrannical element that this Mission was sent forth to the Christian world.[52]

Old China Hands could hardly fail to regard this as anything but a declaration of war. Indignation in Shanghai reached an apoplectic high. James Barr Robertson, in reviewing the effect of the speech two years later, could find nothing more kind to say for Burlinghame than that he had "placed the China question before his auditors in what we conceive to be an utterly distorted light, and as we think wholly misrepresented the attitude of the Chinese Government towards foreigners." [53] The *North China Herald,* which had originally welcomed Burlinghame's mission, declared that his "absurd description of China in a public speech at New York has covered him with ridicule from all who know how widely different is the original from the picture." [54] These were the kindest comments. So worked up was the Shanghai Chamber of Commerce that it sponsored an exposé of Burlinghame by Johannes von Gumpach, who emerged some years later with a ponderous volume of almost nine hundred pages entitled *The Burlinghame Mission: a Political Disclosure, Supported by Official Documents, Mostly Unpublished.*[55] What hurt particularly was that Burlinghame "with nothing but falsehood on his lips and guile on his brow . . . imputes to honest men who mean well by China a tyrannic policy and destructive views of his own invention, in order that he may hold them up to the abhorrence of the West and the governments of the West." [56]

Frederick Wells Williams' comment that the vehemence of mercantile opposition derived from their realization that they were "in the position of men who had long appropriated unfair but uncertain privileges at the expense of weaker parties, for whom at last a public champion had appeared" [57] is an inadequate judgment. There were reasons more immediate and more basic for the merchants' reaction. For not only was the issue of treaty revision still in the balance, but the whole future policy of Britain toward China was being reappraised. The very essence of mercantile propaganda since the spring of 1867 had been directed toward convincing the Government that the Bruce-Alcock line of moderation and gradualism was unwise and contrary to Britain's interests; yet, here in Burlinghame an unexpected and powerful ally had joined the opposition. What was more, he had in New York pointed his finger at the mercantile community as the principal source of China's international troubles. And Burlinghame was proceeding to London.

Alcock, who was daily becoming more lukewarm to the Burlinghame Mission as its successes strengthened the stubbornness of the Yamen in treaty revision negotiations, saw clearly enough that Burlinghame's principal aim was to combat the bellicose attitude and political pretensions of the Shanghai traders. The core of the treaty with the United States, which Burlinghame had signed at Washington on July 28, 1868, lay not in its commercial provisions but in Article VIII.

The United States . . . do hereby freely disclaim and disavow any intention or right to intervene in the domestic administration of China in regard to the construction of railroads, telegraphs, or other material internal improvements. On the other hand, His Majesty the Emperor of China reserves to himself the right to decide the time and manner and circumstances of introducing such improvements within his dominion. . . .[58]

This self-denying provision expressed the essence of Burlinghame's diplomacy. There was, Alcock clearly understood, only one way to interpret its significance: "This public disclaimer of all right to adopt a meddling or coercive policy for the advancement of foreign trade would seem to be especially directed against the mercantile communities in China and perhaps some Foreign States prone to advocate or adopt a policy of compulsion." [59]

Parenthetically, it is interesting to note that while Alcock himself was the chief advocate of the policy of self-denial expressed in the American treaty, he cautioned the Foreign Office that it might be followed by a treaty of alliance between the United States and China in which the former would play the role of protector "and at the same time try if they could not wrest from Great Britain its vast commerce and predominance as a nation in the East." If such were the case, he argued, the very basis of England's China policy might have to be radically altered. He concludes his dispatch with a remarkable forecast of the new issues which were to arise at the end of the century when Britain's virtual monopoly was threatened.

It is, in truth, difficult to determine what are the limits of the possible in these Eastern countries, to any European power willing to incur the risk of failure and ready to pay itself in territory or exclusive rights of exploitation or monopoly of sources of revenue. It is not in accord with the modern policy of Great Britain to seek dominion or prestige and riches by such means, but neither can we very well sit by inactive if any attempt be made to carry out schemes of this character. Other Western powers would certainly see with no favorable eye any effort on the part of the United States to appropriate what is now the property of all.[60]

At the Foreign Office the dispatch was marked "For the Queen."

Long before Burlinghame reached London, treaty port sentiment was already dead set against the Mission and even Alcock was viewing it with suspicion. Not only had the popular acclaim experienced by Burlinghame in America strengthened Prince Kung's opposition to almost every measure of reform proposed during the negotiations for treaty revision;[61] at the same time what was to prove an epidemic of anti-foreign demonstrations and riots, culminating in the Tientsin Massacre of 1870, commenced in Chinkiang and Yangchow in August, 1868. Alcock's attempts to press for vigorous measures of redress while Clarendon's conciliatory policy was being pronounced in London accounts for the British Minister's disillusion with the Burlinghame effort. It was this coincidence which led Alcock to regret the support he had originally lent to the Mission, not that Clarendon *"alla plus loin que ne le desirait son conseiller,"* as Cordier remarks.[62] For Alcock was subsequently to support the Clarendon Declaration, and he was among the minority which recognized that it was but an extension of the traditional diplomacy pursued by Bruce and himself.[63] It was rather the timing than the fact of the Clarendon policy of conciliation which accounts for the hostility of the diplomatic corps in Peking.[64]

The Yangchow affair of August, 1868 thus has a direct relation to the formation of that policy. Moreover, the affair was known to the Foreign Office when the Clarendon Declaration was drafted and accounts, to a large extent, for the emphasis placed in that document on the responsibility of Imperial authority for redress to victims of anti-foreign outrages. On August 22, 1868 the Building of the (British) China Inland Mission at Yangchow was sacked and set on fire, following anti-foreign incitement by local literati. W. H. Medhurst, the British Consul at Shang-hai, proceeded to Yangchow, escorted by H.M.S. *Rinaldo* which took the missionary refugees on board and returned to Shanghai. Medhurst's re-quest for an indemnity was refused as soon as the *Rinaldo* departed.[65] He therefore returned in November, accompanied by two warships, and succeeded in forcing the Nanking Viceroy to pay the indemnity and promise guarantees against future outbreaks. Medhurst himself be-lieved that it was the presence of the gunboats and the threat of violent action which had produced this result.[66]

The reaction of the Foreign Office to the Yangchow affair is instructive for two reasons: it indicates that the Clarendon policy did not originate with Clarendon, and it provides a clue to the correct interpretation of that document. On December 6 Hammond at the Foreign Office minuted Alcock's account of the Yangchow affair as follows:

I do not like this very much. I think Alcock should insist at Pekin on redress and if they hesitate and are unable on their own means to afford it, he should offer British cooperation holding them responsible if they refuse it. But I cannot think it desirable for us to take direct action against the local governor unless in the last extremity. *Such a course is contrary to our policy which is to hold the central government responsible for fulfillment of Treaties.*[67]

To this Lord Stanley added that he was "inclined to agree" but would leave action to his successor. The Liberal Government took office the following day, with Lord Clarendon as Secretary of State for Foreign Affairs. The Hammond draft thus not only stated the gist of the Claren-don policy, which was proclaimed at the end of the month, but declared it to be the continuation of policy which Britain had been following all along. This was also Alcock's view.[68]

Buringhame's conversation with Lord Clarendon took place at the Foreign Office on December 26, and it was the record of this con-versation which became the Clarendon Declaration of December 28, 1868.[69] The Declaration falls naturally into two parts. The first recognizes the object of the Mission: to disabuse European Powers of the impression that China was entering upon a retrograde policy and to "deprecate any intention on the part of European Powers to bring to bear on China any amount of unfriendly pressure to induce her Ruler to enter precipitately on a new system of policy." In the second part Clarendon states the essentials of British policy toward China. On the one hand, Clarendon assures China that "as far as this country is con-cerned, there was neither a desire nor intention to apply unfriendly pres-sure to China to induce her Government to advance more rapidly . . . than was consistent with safety and with due and reasonable regard for the feelings of her subjects." On the other, he points out that this assurance involves an obligation on the part of China for "the faithful observance of the stipulations of existing Treaties" and "the fullest amount of protection to British subjects."

It is important to note that both the bulk and the emphasis of the Clarendon Declaration is addressed to this last point: the obligation and responsibility of China. Cognizant of the growing opposition of British residents in China to the traditional policy of benevolent non-interference, of referring grievances to an impotent Peking, Clarendon is, in effect, stating that this policy can continue only so long as Peking implements its responsibility.

But H.M. Government are, moreover, entitled to expect from China as an indispensable condition of their goodwill the fullest amount of protection to British subjects resorting to her dominions. They are aware that the Provincial Governors are too often in the habit of disregarding the rights of foreigners trusting to impunity as regards the Central Government of Peking, and to the unwillingness of Foreigners to assert the rights of their subjects by local pressure.

H.M. Government feel that they are acting in the interest of the Chinese Empire, when they announce their preference for an appeal rather to the Central Government than to local authorities, for the redress of wrongs done to British subjects. It is with the Central Government . . . that Foreign Powers have entered into Treaties, and it is for the interest of the Central Government that Foreign Powers should recognize its supreme authority over its provincial Governors, and that the Central Government should assume, and . . . be prepared to exercise that authority.[70]

That this was the major consideration in Clarendon's mind is further evident from the fact that it served as the primary subject of discussion in his second interview with Burlinghame.[71] The Foreign Minister again emphasized "that we should henceforth have a right to expect on the part of the Chinese government the faithful fulfillment of treaty engagements, the prompt redress of grievances referred to the Central Government, and friendly treatment of British subjects by the Chinese authorities." Burlinghame put this pledge down on paper in a private letter to Clarendon,[72] and the latter interpreted this as meaning that "he clearly understands that force may be at once employed to protect life and property immediately exposed" with referral to the Minister at Peking and finally to the British Government for decision when "these had been secured."[73] Again, that June when anti-foreign disturbances had led Alcock to doubt the efficacy of the policy of conciliation,[74] Clarendon dispatched a strong note to Burlinghame reminding him that the Declaration had been founded "on your assurance that the Chinese Government had both the will and power to enforce observance of treaty rights and to compel local authorities to protect foreigners from wrong of every description." [75]

This emphasis on Chinese obligation rather than British "conciliation" was never realized by the Old China Hands; to them the Clarendon line appeared as the fatal blow to any aspirations they may have had that treaty revision would prove the occasion for the adoption of a vigorous policy toward China. And the legend arose that Gladstonean Liberalism had reversed Palmerstonian policy and shattered all hopes of extending British interests in China. For this a curious turn in the sequence of the publicity given to recent developments in Anglo-Chinese relations may have been partly to blame. The first public intimation of the "new policy" was neither the announcement of the Clarendon Declaration nor an account of what had actually taken place in the Clarendon-Burlinghame conversations. It was, rather, the publication early in January, 1869, of the instructions to British consuls and naval officers to refrain from applying local pressure and, what was more, to pay due respect, in their dealings, not only to the laws but to "the usages and feelings of the people." This latter, it is safe to assume, was not simply the product of Clarendon's convictions, but stemmed from a minute which Gladstone himself penned on the draft of the Clarendon Declaration: "Caution will be given to British subjects to pay due respect not only to the laws of the empire but as far as may be to the usages and feelings of the Chinese people." [76]

. This sentiment was incorporated into the over-all instructions to British consuls which Hammond drafted early in January and which aroused such indignation in the treaty ports. Even as the Burlinghame honeymoon reached a climax in London, news arrived of three incidents, occurring in rapid succession, in which the gunboat technique had been revived by British consuls. At Taiwan, Formosa, following a series of anti-missionary attacks and the confiscation by the local taotai of a shipment of camphor belonging to Ellis & Co., Consul Gibson used the protection of H.M.S. *Algerine* and H.M.S. *Bustard* to occupy the local port on November 21, 1868. The effect was immediate and Gibson secured not only the payment of indemnities but the abolition of the camphor monopoly. At Swatow, two months later, unidentified native snipers wounded crew members of the *Cockchafer*. Consul Alabaster, enlisting the support of the *Rinaldo* under Commodore Oliver J. Jones, debarked troops at the port and inflicted reprisals on the local population. And, finally, anti-missionary outbreaks at Sharp Peak Island, near Foochow, resulted in disciplinary action by Consul Charles Sinclair with the effective aid of Admiral Keppel of the *Janus*, with results as effective as those enjoyed by Medhurst at Yangchow several months previously.[77]

It was the action of the Foreign Office in response to these consular adventures which originally aroused the ire of the treaty ports. Hammond drafted instructions to Alcock strongly disapproving of the independent actions taken by the Consuls and laying down specific rules for future action. Alabaster was ordered to be removed from Swatow "until that officer's zeal and propensity to violence are moderated"; Sinclair was sharply censured, while condemnation of Gibson's conduct at Taiwan was particularly severe. "You will be careful not to place under his charge the superintendence, even temporarily, of a consulate or vice-consulate for the duties of which judgment, tact, discretion and moderation are essential requisites." [78]

As for the future, Clarendon declared:

You will explain to H.M. Consuls that the special purposes for which H.M. Ships of War are stationed in the Ports of China . . . are to protect the floating commerce of British subjects against piratical attacks in Chinese waters, to support H.M. Consuls in maintaining order and discipline among the crews of British vessels in the ports, and in cases of great emergency, to protect the lives and properties of British subjects. . . .

As regards this last point, H.M. Consuls must constantly bear in mind that the interference of naval force . . . will alone receive the subsequent approval of H.M. Government when it is clearly shown that, without such interference the lives and properties of British subjects would in all probability have been sacrificed. . . .

H.M. Government cannot leave with H.M. Consuls or Naval officers to determine for themselves what redress or reparation for wrong done to British subjects is due, or by what means it should be enforced. They cannot allow them to determine whether coercion is to be applied by blockade, by reprisals by landing armed parties, or by acts of even a more hostile character. All such proceedings bear more or less the character of acts of war and H.M. Government cannot delegate to H.M. servants in foreign countries the power of involving their own country in war. . . .

H.M. Consuls must appeal to H.M. Minister at Peking to obtain redress through the action of the Central Government. . . .[79]

Similar instructions were sent to naval officers. Treaty port opinion was stupefied, overlooking entirely the more measured policy of the Clarendon Declaration in the face of the published consular instructions which Old China Hands regarded as a direct provocation to further anti-foreign outbreaks. Even Alcock exhibited a *volte face;* as a result of the successful local solution of recent crises he had come to regard the judicious employment of gunboats as necessary. He went out of his way to congratulate the commander of the *Janus* on the happy termination of the difficulty at Sharp Peak Island, thus promptly taking off "a long list" "one more grievance otherwise likely to increase and be interminable." [80] Alcock, disillusioned with the progress of revision, had become convinced that the impotent, obstructive Imperial authority at Peking would neither enforce respect for treaty rights nor assume responsibility for redress of grievances in the provinces.

Despite his opposition, however, Alcock recognized that the Clarendon statement was not a repudiation but a formal recognition of "the policy which has been carefully observed since the ratification of the Treaty of Tientsin in 1860." [81] It was treaty port propaganda which created the legend that Clarendon and the Liberal Government of 1868 had effected a complete reversal of British policy toward China; and that this reversal constituted a betrayal of British interests insulting to the recent memory of Lord Palmerston. Thus J. Barr Robertson, after extensive exposure to treaty port atmosphere, wrote a learned article to prove that the arrival of Clarendon and Mr. Otway (Parliamentary Undersecretary) at the Foreign Office had resulted in "an entire change in our policy toward China." [82] He speaks of "the positive dangers of the policy of Lord Clarendon . . . from which the policy that we have just abandoned was comparatively free." All the merchants who in their memorials of 1867 had been bewailing the lack of a positive policy were now convinced that Clarendon had just abandoned it. A. R. Colquhoun, publicist and explorer who nursed ambitions of becoming the Cecil Rhodes of China, was still exclaiming thirty years later of the Clarendon Declaration:

It was the first public pronouncement of the death of the Palmerstonian tradition, and of the relapse of Great Britain into an effeminate, invertebrate, inconsequent policy, swayed by every wind from without and from within, and opposed to the judgment of her own experienced representatives—the policy which has beyond doubt led to the decline of British prestige in Asia.[83]

The legend was perpetuated for scholarly consumption. F. W. Williams' talk of "the change in British policy" and "so manifest a change in the policy of Great Britain as that implied by Lord Clarendon's communication to Mr. Burlinghame" [84] has since been repeated by lesser scholars of Anglo-Chinese relations.

The treaty port press echoed the indignation of local residents when the first news of the consular instructions reached China in March.[85] The *London & China Telegraph's* Tientsin correspondent expressed the "surprise" of port merchants: "Surely this must be a hoax. No Minister with the slightest knowledge of Chinese character . . . would ever agree to such a thing." [86] Old China Hands, he reported, were suggesting a Civil Service Examination making it imperative on Secretaries of the India, Colonial, and Foreign Offices to have "full knowledge of the people and countries they are called on to have dealings with." Rumor was rife that the Burlinghame Mission was intended to lull the suspicions of foreign governments while China built arsenals and gathered ammunition for a war against the foreign devils. The unusual number of outbreaks could only be attributed to "a concerted scheme of Peking to influence the crisis in Chinese foreign affairs and check progress." [87]

The first knowledge of the Foreign Office censure of Consul Gibson reached Hongkong with the arrival of the *London & China Express* of April 9. The Hongkong *China Mail* published the paragraph with a border of deep mourning:

Lord Clarendon has announced that the Government disapproves of the recent retaliatory measures in Formosa. The naval operations are censured, the Vice-Consul who instigated them is to be removed, the indemnity money repaid, and an apology offered to the Chinese. This most disgraceful course is warmly applauded by The Times and the Liberal press, but strongly opposed by all who have any real knowledge of China and are not biased by party prejudices.[88]

Père Osouf, Procureur at Hongkong of the French *Missions Etrangères,* wrote to Paris of the disastrous impression created by Clarendon's action:

La malle anglaise, qui arrive, excite dans la colonie une sorte de tolle contre le Ministre des affaires étrangères á Londres qui vient de casser le Consul anglais de Taiwan à l'occasion des dernières affaires de Formosa, et de charger le Ministre d' Angleterre à Pekin de faire des excuses au Gouvern^t Chinois, et de restituer l'indemnité exigée des Chinois à Formose!—Une pareille manière d'agir avec les Chinois va sans doute créer bien des difficultés à tout ce qui est éuropéen dans ces pays-ci. Et l'Angleterre elle-même pourrait bien avoir à payer plus tard par les frais d'une nouvelle expédition les maladresses politiques de certains de ses agents.[89]

It was not alone the reaffirmation of the official policy of benevolence toward China which disturbed the treaty ports. Even more provoking was the discovery that, despite Old China Hand propaganda, the "Clarendon Policy" was popular at home. It was this support from press and Parliament which strengthened the Government's hand in the face of the vituperative clamor from the Bund. On April 19, Lord Clarendon was emboldened to repeat his instructions to Alcock censuring the gunboat tactics of the Consuls which he viewed in a "serious light," adding the warning that the accounts you will have read in the public papers of the debates in Parliament will leave no doubt in your mind, and it is hoped in the minds of all British subjects in China, whether in the public service or in a private capacity, that it is the intention and desire of this country that the intercourse with China should be maintained by friendly means and should not be subject to interruption by injudicious and rash proceedings on the part of British subjects.[90]

For, even before the release of the consular instructions, the first repercussions of the Yangchow affair in the London press showed the direction in which the wind was blowing. Sir Charles W. Dilke, M.P. for Chelsea and the most vigorous champion of the Burlinghame line in Parliament, in a letter to *The Times* criticized Medhurst's action as indicating a return to the "old system of sending gunboats to discuss diplomatic questions with subordinate officials" and urged the "wise rule" of referring differences to Peking. *The Times* strongly backed Dilke's position, while the Tory *Standard* grumbled that Peking had neither the will nor the power to cause provincial authorities to offer redress.[91]

A week later, publication of the Clarendon-Burlinghame New Year's correspondence (but not of the Declaration) showed a similar party line-up on the China question for the first time since 1858, with an overwhelming leaning, however, toward full approval of the government's course. A survey by the *London & China Telegraph* (January 11, 1869) showed *The Times*, the *Pall Mall Gazette*, and the *Morning Star* favoring the Clarendon move with *The Standard* against. *The Times* warmly praised the "new British policy" as a "welcome departure from the old policy where the instinct of consuls, merchants and naval officers" was to settle matters in the "old high-handed way." The difficulty encountered in opening China was attributed to the "refusal of foreigners to submit to the jurisdiction of native law." *The Standard*, on the other hand, deplored "Clarendon's unilateral fetters" and inquired whether the injunction to "respect usages" included those providing for torture and white slavery. It predicted that the government policy would be productive of "infinite mischief" and throw Anglo-Chinese relations into confusion. As was soon to be evident, however, Old China Hands were to derive little comfort from the *Standard* which opposed mercantile aims as well as the Liberal policy of non-intervention.

Parliamentary opinion, where it was not indifferent, provided even less comfort to Old China Hands than the Liberal press. Occasionally, Charles Magniac of Matheson & Co. or Colonel W. H. Sykes would rise to defend the character of the treaty port resident. But they were invariably faced with the righteous indignation of the majority which insisted on a full implementation of the policy of conciliation. In fact, debate was usually stimulated by interpellations charging the Foreign Office with laxity in carrying out the Clarendon Declaration and the consular instructions; and the Foreign Minister was more than once forced to renew his assurances that "those instructions will be rigidly adhered to by the Government." [92] Under the leadership of Sir Charles Dilke, watchdog of the Clarendon policy in Commons, the pro-China bloc monitored the least deviation by the Foreign Office from the doctrine of self-denial.[93]

Little interest was aroused when the China correspondence was laid on the table. The closest thing to a full-dress debate took place on July 13, 1869, precipitated by Colonel Sykes' motion that the Shanghai Chamber of Commerce memorial and correspondence relating to treaty revision be laid before the House.[94] Sykes deplored the current state of Anglo-Chinese relations which he attributed to the fact that "there is not any permanent security for the persons or property of foreigners in China." He trotted out all the mercantile tenets: the Treaty of Tientsin had never been fulfilled due to Chinese obstruction; illegal inland dues were prevalent; the China trade could be expanded almost without limit if inland residence and other concessions were granted. He repeated the contradictory thesis that the Central Government was powerless to enforce treaty rights but it should be forced to concede mercantile demands. Even Mr. H. G. Liddell, who seconded the motion, did not agree, holding that "it was only just that they should not insist too rigorously and absolutely upon all stipulations." The *London & China Telegraph* confessed that the choice of Colonel Sykes as spokesman had not been fortunate; he tired out the House by recounting the history of China for the past sixteen centuries before coming to the point. Liberal members, led by Dilke, had no difficulty in demolishing his arguments, while Otway had smooth sailing in defending the Clarendon policy. Any other policy, he charged, would lead to war and disorganization from which other nations than Britain would profit.[95] The House was thin; even members connected with the China trade did not attend, regarding their case as hopeless. Both *The Times* and *Pall Mall Gazette* took the occasion to back the Foreign Office.

The Standard, though dissatisfied with all the debate, offered small consolation to the Old China Hands; the policy it advocated was a recasting of objectives in China. If these were limited to protecting commerce "it might fairly be argued that a good deal of what we have already done in the Empire is unjustifiable." Rather, it argued, policy should be pointed toward advancing the material happiness of the natives. British superiority gave her the right and duty to rule inferio races; the Chinese millions, oppressed by a decrepit dynasty, were crying to Her Majesty's Government for light on the path of progress.[96]

This Tory plea for assuming the white man's burden in China, later to become a cardinal point in the folklore of Imperialism, was hardly acceptable to the merchants at that time and explains why Old China Hands neither sought nor found champions along strict party lines. It accounts for their isolation and later efforts to set up their own China bloc in Parliament.

In an attempt to bridge the cleavage between home and treaty port opinion, the mercantile community enlisted the aid of James Barr Robertson, publicist and correspondent for the London *Daily News*, who wrote a series of three letters setting forth the mercantile view in the *North China Herald* during June and July of 1869. These were then reprinted in pamphlet form for home consumption.[97] They met with an indifferent response, but the views set forth are interesting as reflecting the more mature exposition of mercantile opinion. Robertson exposed the "absurd error" made by Clarendon in treating the Chinese Government as a civilized power, with responsibility centered at Peking. Effective power, he maintained, lay in the provinces and only by dealing with the viceroys would Anglo-Chinese relations reflect reality. He attributed the current official line to "that contemptible but unhappily successful imposture, the Burlinghame Mission." In his last contribution, Robertson presented a general review of British policy in China, condemning it for "its utter inconsistency, so manifest that adherence to it is impossible," and suggesting its substitution by Old China Hand doctrine. In reviewing the Robertson pamphlet for its readers, the *London & China Telegraph* called upon England to give up the "degrading Gladstone-worship of the present day" and to revive that "spirit of patriotism that in former times maintained our reputation as a first class power."

Part of the taipan brief was the contention that the program of the Old China Hands was also ardently desired by the common people of China. The death of Consul Gibson provided the treaty ports with a rich opportunity for condemning Clarendon who, it was hinted, was responsible for Gibson's premature demise. Hugh Matheson, dean of Old China Hands in London, wrote to *The Times* [98] that Clarendon had been the dupe of Burlinghame and the reactionary party in Peking. The success of Gibson in obtaining punishment of the "wicked and persecuting mandarins" was appreciated by the Chinese populace as much as by the British merchant, for he had inaugurated a "reign of justice." The tidings of Gibson's recall from Formosa and the severe animadversions upon his conduct made in England had proved the crushing blow. It had stupefied "everyone who has had any acquaintance with the Chinese," all of whom were convinced that "in dealing with Chinese officials nothing can be gained and no progress made without firmness." The same view was repeated by William Muirhead, former missionary and Shanghai resident, who condemned the Foreign Office and upheld the "reasonable demands of our mercantile residents in China." [99]

That these demands were "reasonable" was also the opinion of J. Ross Browne, Burlinghame's successor as American Minister to China. During his short stay in the Far East, Browne developed into an unexpected—he was the only important official to adopt the mercantile stand—and powerful ally of the British resident community in its efforts to combat the Clarendon policy. As early as November, 1868, while engaged in obtaining ratification for the Seward treaty, Browne officially wondered whether its terms were "reconcilable with the efforts of the British Minister to enlarge the scope of foreign intercourse by insisting upon a more liberal interpretation of the British treaty under revision," and, further, whether "the difference between the laws, customs and religion of China and those of Christian nations is so radical as to preclude intercourse upon equal terms." [100] At the same time he approached the Tsungli Yamen with advice to speed reforms, holding that the concessions so far made in British treaty revision were petty and did not show that substantial effort at extended intercourse which Burlinghame claimed was the Chinese policy.[101]

Browne advanced a program for China which paralleled, in every respect, the maximum demands of the merchants. His fame in Shanghai was soon high. Disappointed at the lack of progress in treaty revision and at delay in ratification of the American treaty, Browne had reached a position "revealing a prepossession in favour of the aggressive portion of the foreign community in China." [102] He had become convinced that the object of the Burlinghame mission was "to prevent all progress inconsistent with Chinese isolation; to avoid the execution of treaties, and set aside the foreign Ministers at Peking." He warned that China was playing for time—"time to establish arsenals, build gunboats, poison the minds of the people throughout the provinces, and, in the end . . . make a final attempt to drive every foreigner out of the country." [103] The policy of non-interference had been practiced since 1860 and without result; it was indeed time for a "new policy" that would exact from China those reforms which Peking continued to delay.

The jubilation of the mercantile community at such talk can be imagined. Browne, shortly afterward, resigned his position in protest against disapproval of his policy in Washington. Early in July he passed through Shanghai where he was feted and presented with memorials praising his "opposition to the shining-cross nonsense." The press blossomed out in editorials attempting to persuade home opinion that the entire China community, which obviously knew what was best out there, stood united behind Browne.[104]

Browne's reply (July 17, 1869) to the Shanghai addresses became a classic in mercantile doctrine. Better than the merchants had been able to do in their memorials he put forward the case for a policy of rapid reform and firmness which three generations of Old China Hands held as their own. He argued that the way to handle China was to "deal firmly with her . . . and require her to fulfill every treaty obligation." China was not in fact equal to other civilized powers; and in the relation of superior to inferior force had necessarily to be used in order to open the country. "Having forced obligations upon her, we must compel her to observe them or recede from the position which we have undertaken to maintain." [105]

The Browne incident was the signal for a renewed campaign on the part of Shanghai to convince British public opinion that the merchants had been right all along. The Shanghai Chamber sounded out the London firms in the China trade with a view toward promoting favorable public sentiment by organizing a China Association in London. But the project fell through. Despite the valiant efforts of the London Committee of Merchants, which had been formed to marshal local opinion against the limited reforms of the Alcock Convention and which will be discussed in the following chapter, the home Chambers of Commerce remained indifferent, while the press was hostile. The *Pall Mall Gazette* continued to exhibit what the *London & China Telegraph* termed "its perverse view of the conduct of British residents in China." [106] A survey of press opinion in September showed not only that *The Times* and the radical newspapers were behind the Gladstone policy, but that *The Standard*, though more congenial to China merchants, still insisted on treating the issue as a party question.[107]

The rift between home and overseas opinion was marked. The *Saturday Review* (October 18, 1869) remarked on the great disparity between the "philanthropic doctrine" at home and the "vigorous measures demanded by residents in China," noting that while the Burlinghame démarche had been hailed in England, treaty port opinion was unanimously opposed. How to account for this disparity? The best the *Review* could offer was the quip: "It is interesting to watch the dissolution of cosmopolitan philanthropy as it crosses the Pacific or the Indian Ocean."

At times the disparity achieved peculiar results. *The Times*, while continuing to run leaders supporting the Government's China policy, also published the dispatches of "Our Own Correspondent" in Shanghai enforcing exactly opposite views.[108] At times it became vehement. Sir Charles Dilke, parliamentary champion of the conciliatory policy, wrote a furious letter to *The Times* (January 4, 1870) criticizing the statement of Colonel Knox Gore at a Hongkong dinner in honor of Admiral Keppel which referred to the Chinese as an inferior people and charging the merchants with fabricating telegrams and news unfavorable to the Clarendon policy. The response of the Hongkong *China Mail* was not any milder: "He condemns the whole of the newspaper press of China as scandalously mendacious in matters of fact, and as utterly illogical and unfair in its criticisms and conclusions. Dilke himself is guilty of the misrepresentation with which he charges the European communities of China." Citing the various outrages committed against foreigners in the previous year, the *Mail* rhapsodizes: "What language is too strong for a man who ignores all this and considers the experience of 1869 as showing that China is ready to follow the path of progress, and charges falsehood and want of sense to the press of China and the mercantile men who support that press." [109]

Despite the vituperation, the protagonists were but touching the fringes of the issue which divided mercantile and official opinion. In his letter Dilke, for a brief moment, focused attention on the crux of the issue when he remarked that in the treaty revision which had just been concluded (and which will be discussed in the following chapter) the Chinese "appear to have granted more than the Board of Trade thought it advisable to ask." For the real difference lay in the premises one held as to the potentialities of the China trade. During a quite impromptu debate on China affairs some weeks later, a Mr. P. Rylands, second only to Dilke in opposing the pretensions of the Old China Hands, saw this more clearly. Calling the attention of the House to naval activities in China waters during the recent outrages, Rylands charged merchants and official with sabotaging the consular instructions based on the Burlinghame doctrine. Despite Foreign Office condemnation, the conviction that the Chinese were inferior and had to be handled *vi et armis* animated the residents of the treaty ports. The difficulty, Rylands stressed, derived from the fact that "we were engaged in forcing upon the Chinese goods they did not want." He quoted the Peking correspondent of *The Times*: "The opening of the country is their cry "progress" is their motto, war their object. Trade is slack at present It is necessary to live, and Micawber-like, they hope for something to turn up in the general disruption it would infallibly produce." [110] A judicious policy, he suggested, must recognize the limited nature of the

China trade and seek to concentrate it in certain entrepôts rather than to expand it.

This, too, proved to be the verdict of the Board of Trade; and it was upon this premise that the Foreign Office continued its policy of gradualism and limited objectives in China. For the Old China Hands the failure to enlist the support of home and parliamentary opinion against the Clarendon policy was the first major defeat sustained in the crucial period at the end of the sixties. But exactly what that decision entailed was not yet too apparent. It was to be brought into sharper focus during the struggle over treaty revision.

III

The Verdict of the Board of Trade

"When it is recollected that these results have only been obtained at the cost of three wars—and the constant presence of British Squadrons in Chinese waters for the protection of trade, it is a great question on which side of the national ledger the balance will be found to stand"—Louis Mallet of the Board of Trade, 1869.

DESPITE the defeat suffered by the Old China Hands in their efforts to force a repeal of the Clarendon policy the battle was far from decided. For, by winning acceptance of their maximum program on treaty revision, the substance of their desires could be achieved. At no time during the long period of negotiation was there the least indication that the merchants were prepared to retreat from the position they had adopted in 1867, and which has been outlined in the preceding chapter. Alcock's policy of gradual reforms and the petty concessions which he was able to wring from Peking under a diplomacy limited by the declared policy of conciliation did not begin to meet their demands. And, as they shrewdly realized, their best strategy lay in convincing home opinion that British interests were being sold down the Yangtze by Gladstone's foreign policy.

By the middle of 1868 Alcock was already convinced that no fundamental reforms would result from treaty revision. He was caught between mercantile demands on the one hand and the attitude of Whitehall—that nothing be forced from China which she refused to give freely—on the other. In addition, each of the other treaty powers had peculiar interests for which it pressed during the negotiations. (The most-favored-nation principle meant that whatever arrangements Great Britain arrived at in the new treaty would benefit all other Powers.)

Writing to Sir Robert Hart, who, as Inspector-General of the Maritime Customs, acted as go-between in treaty negotiations, Alcock complained of the difficulties he had encountered.

After our experience with the coolie convention . . . taken in connection with the decided animus and hostile spirit of the Board of Trade, which *must* be consulted by the Foreign Office in such a matter as revision, and add to all this the captious spirit of the merchants and opposition to anything that is done or proposed for them—with the certainty that some main sources of grievance must still remain—and the great disparity between what the memorialists ask, and what they will be offered—we have nothing else or better to look for than abuse and dissatisfaction.[1]

Hart could suggest no better formula "to reconcile the claims of both countries" than the Burlinghame generality that "British interests . . . that they may flourish, require that Chinese interests shall flourish too." [2]

By December (1868) negotiations were sufficiently advanced for Alcock to send to London the minutes of the mixed commission on revision and the correspondence of Prince Kung with the Foreign Ministers at Peking for the information of the Foreign Office. Alcock had failed to persuade his colleagues to support his views on the limited nature of the revision and discovered that, like the merchants who did not have to assume responsibility for the treaty, the foreign Ministers were lined up with the mercantile community in urging major concessions. Alcock did not try to conceal his bitterness.

Your Lordship will see that my colleagues were disposed to treat as comparatively insignificant all concessions which would not open China as completely to Foreigners as any country of Europe while still preserving their rights of exterritoriality. Such unequal and incompatible conditions might possibly be imposed by force upon a conquered nation, but can never be the result of negotiation; nor could they in my opinion be carried into effect without great danger to the existing Government and Empire.[3]

Alcock reiterated his doubt that "in the present state of the country and the government, either as regards their hold on the provinces or their power to assert their own rights where Foreign States are concerned, it is possible for them to admit Foreigners freely to navigate the inland waters with steam vessels, and to take up their residence in the interior, or even to open mines to foreigners without danger to themselves and to us." As against these mercantile demands China had been willing to grant very limited facilities which Alcock thought might be accepted as "road-breakers" but should not be regarded as dividends. "The actual shareholders in the concern, the merchants now in China, of course, look, here as elsewhere, rather to the present than the future, and would probably much prefer dividends in hand to better prospects hereafter, but governments must look to the end." [4]

"Governments must look to the end." And unless they were willing to accept the risk of war and anarchy they must be satisfied with the "minor concessions" which could be obtained through diplomatic means.[5] Memorialists who insisted on maximum reform "seem to assume that nothing more is required to secure all they have asked or desire than the will on the part of H.M. Government to demand." In actual fact, Alcock argues, to adopt this tactic would open the question whether Britain is willing to face the contingency of war.

If it be true that although the policy of absolute non-intervention has been condemned by public opinion in England, the intervention of the future . . . will tend more and more in the direction of efforts enabling each nation to develop itself according to its own inherent nature, it will be difficult to reconcile this with any attempt to impose upon China, against her will, European forms of civilization.[6]

Alcock's plea made little impression at the treaty ports. Old China Hands continued to urge adoption of their maximum program, skirting the issue of whether this could be done without the employment of force. The Shanghai Chamber of Commerce met on January 29, 1869, and recommended the opening of more treaty ports and navigation of inland waters by foreign steamers; but it reiterated the view that nothing short of the complete opening up of China would give satisfaction.[7] The *London & China Telegraph* (March 22, 1869), organ in London of the Old China Hands, enthusiastically supported this sentiment. "This is completely in accordance with our own views. We have been scraping at the outer shell of China long enough and we hail with considerable satisfaction the views thus enunciated by the merchants of Shanghai as the only sure footing on which we can take our stand." The newspaper expressed the hope that Alcock would receive the new Shanghai suggestion in a better spirit than he did the last representations when he was little short of "insulting." Similar renewal of mercantile pleas for major revision came from circles throughout the treaty ports as negotiations proceeded in the spring of 1869.[8]

While Alcock and the Shanghai merchants continued to differ over the wisdom of forcing an industrial revolution upon China, British policy was actually being fashioned in the offices of the Board of Trade in London. The decision there reached in May came to be accepted as the basis of British foreign policy toward China until the end of the century. The author of this policy was Louis Mallet, the influential and vigorous Permanent Under-secretary at the Board of Trade. And although Mallet had strong leanings toward radicalism his observations were based not on a Cobdenite opposition to warlike adventures in

China, but on the ledgers and trade balances of the Board of Trade which showed up the China trade in its true light.

Mallet's letter of May 19, 1869, which runs to forty-five pages in the original hand,[9] was carefully composed in response to Lord Clarendon's request of March 4. From the outset Mallet pointed out that he was not confining himself to the merits of treaty revision but had given "careful consideration" to the "problem of Anglo-Chinese commercial relations" in their broader aspects. Two distinct and conflicting lines of policy are suggested by the occasion of revision, Mallet writes:

1. To insist not only upon effectual execution of existing engagements, but also upon new and important concessions with a view to what is called "opening up" China to Foreign Trade, and introducing Western civilisation into the Empire.

2. To confine the present negotiations to the assertion of admitted Treaty rights essential to the gradual progress of Foreign Trade and to the removal of such defects in the Chinese administration affecting Foreign Trade, as the Chinese Government is willing and able to undertake to remedy and to the acceptance of some spontaneous concessions.

The first alternative, he argues, would involve the exercise of force and the risk of war. "If any doubt existed as to the impossibility of obtaining at the present time, except by force, the larger concessions which are called for by the Mercantile Body in China, such as the right of residence in the interior and of working mines, the introduction of Railroads and Telegraphs and Inland Steam Navigation, such doubts can be no longer entertained." For, after perusing the Alcock correspondence, it is clear that the results of the Mixed Commission are "all that can be obtained by negotiation at the present time, and unless H.M. Government is prepared to face the possibility of war for the attainment of the main points insisted upon by the merchants . . . they must be content with much less and with the vague hope of gradual progress."

Radical reform, such as the merchants demanded, could be secured only by force and, Mallet pointed out, "the responsibility and sacrifices involved in the exercise of force must fall upon the British nation and not upon that section of its people which is engaged in the trade with China." That in pleading for a course which might lead to war, "both merchants and Ministers are urging on a policy in the fruits of which if successful they would largely share, and in which the consequences of failure would fall chiefly upon other interests than those which they represent."

The inference was obvious. Such a policy could be urged only if it was worth the risk, not to the merchants in Shanghai, but to British interests as a whole. But, the Board of Trade emphasized, neither current trade in China nor its future prospect was as important to Britain as the memorialists pretended; certainly it was not worth the risk of war. Although large and powerful interests were connected with it "and the unusual intervention of H.M. Government in its creation and protection have directed to this branch of British commerce an amount of public and political attention which calls for careful scrutiny," a commercial review made by the Board of Trade indicated that both actual and prospective interests in China had been exaggerated. Although the China trade was often referred to as amounting to £100,000,000, accounts for 1866 showed that only £70,500,000 of this was British and at least half that sum consisted of coastal trade. In actual fact, "the highest estimate that can be made of the value of British trade with China is from thirty to forty million pounds per annum." Compared with other markets it was small. Moreover, "it may be further stated that out of a total export of £70,000,000 of cotton goods—the export to China constitutes only £5,000,000."

Nor were prospects for the future more sanguine. The nature of the Chinese economy was such that the trade was always bound to show "relative inferiority" as compared with "more highly civilized countries." Besides opium and specie the China trade was limited to four articles: tea and silk, cottons and woolens, with cottons confined to heavy goods. Both the silk and the tea trade were precarious. As for the prospect of a large development of export trade to China, population figures were misleading. The Chinese consumer was poor and "deficient in desire for the material comforts and elegancies of life." China produces the raw material and has the labor for a large native industry with which even the coarse cotton goods of the United Kingdom cannot hope to compete. "These are not conditions of a healthy and solid trade, and an examination of the records of the China trade will exhibit fluctuations and irregularities which have been the source of great commercial disasters."

"When it is recollected," Mallet continues, "that these results have only been obtained at the cost of three wars—and the constant presence of British Squadrons in Chinese waters for the protection of trade, it is a great question on which side of the national ledger the balance will be found to stand." Again and again Mallet emphasizes this point: "My Lords have dwelt on this to impress on H.M. Government that having regard to past history, the peculiar character of the trade . . . , any attempt to extend by diplomatic pressure would be to enter upon a policy which even in a commercial point of view would be dangerous." There was nothing to gain either imperially or commercially from an aggressive course. For these reasons, and "so long as the conditions of that trade rest on a foundation so limited and insecure," the only "safe course" for the Government to follow is "To confine their efforts to the consolidation of the position already obtained, by patient, moderate, and gradual negotiation, and by bringing to bear as much as possible the moral influences derived from the principles of international equity which regulate and control the intercourse of civilized nations." [10]

Whether or not Mallet's arguments were intrinsically valid is not relevant. The significant fact, historically, is that the letter formed the basis for the premises of British foreign policy toward China. It was the culmination of a long series of consular reports and intelligence from China since the Mitchell Report of 1852, all reinforcing the same conclusion. And it was the Mallet letter which Lord Clarendon consigned to Alcock as a "guide of your conduct in your further negotiations." [11] He was directed to accept whatever advantages "you have induced the Chinese government to express their willingness to concede." These instructions were reinforced on June 4 (1869) in a confidential dispatch authorizing him to accept any arrangement satisfactory to the Chinese.[12] Again he was directed to use the Board of Trade letter as a guide in negotiations. Despite a cool reception from the other treaty powers to the Foreign Office proposal for an interim treaty in line with the Board of Trade recommendation, Alcock was instructed to accept whatever compromise arrangement the Chinese were ready to grant.[13]

Given the Foreign Office decision to proceed on the lines recommended by the Board of Trade, mercantile opposition to the Alcock Convention, signed at Peking on October 23, 1869, was a foregone conclusion. The new Convention [14] fell far short of mercantile demands and, in fact, incorporated certain changes which Old China Hands regarded as retrogressive. Major provisions included: most-favored-nation treatment for Britain on the same conditions as those enjoyed by other Treaty Powers; appointment of Chinese consuls in British territory; foreign goods imported by British merchants to pay tariff and transit dues (a combined charge of about 7 1/2 percent) at the time of import and to be provided with a Transit Pass exempting them from all further charges in *treaty port provinces* only, with commutation no longer optional; native exports purchased by British subjects in the interior to pay inland charges enroute and be entitled to refund of all charges in excess of 2 1/2 percent if export takes place in one year; Wenchow in Chekiang and Wuhu in Anhui opened as treaty ports; import duty on opium to be increased; British subjects in possession of consular passports were permitted to visit non-treaty port provinces in native craft; a steam tug to ply Lake Poyang; coal mines to be opened at two or three places in South China by order of the Imperial Commissioner; an increase which doubled the export duty on silk; and foreign coal and guano to enter duty free. Alcock regarded several of these concessions as substantial. Although the treaty fell far short of mercantile desires as "steam navigation on inland waters, railroads and telegraphs, rights of domicile inland, working of mines by foreigners, have all been refused as impracticable or inexpedient at present," he insisted that "this treaty shows progress." [15]

Apprehensive of the welcome the Alcock Convention would receive at the hands of the mercantile body, the Legation at Peking lost no time in submitting it to the Chambers of Commerce for approval, while the Foreign Office consulted the home Chambers before proceeding to ratification. At its meeting on November 26, 1869, the Shanghai Chamber voted qualified acceptance of the Convention.[16] Its letter to Lord Clarendon, dated December 31, proved to be not only the first expression of mercantile opinion on the treaty, but the only one which could be regarded as granting even grudging approval.[17] In effect, Shanghai's position had not changed. Standing on its declaration of 1867, the Chamber again emphasized the Old China Hand view that the trouble lay not in the inadequate provisions of the Tientsin Treaty but in the failure to assure its observance. "The main purpose of all foreign treaties with China is the extension of trade. It is for this purpose that the Chamber of Commerce exists, and it is presumably for the same purpose that European Governments maintain relations with China." The main obstacles to the growth of trade had been the difficulty and delay in transit, and excessive and irregular inland taxes. Treaty revision had failed to remove these obstacles. The opening of Wenchow and Wuhu was a step in the right direction, but not until the Yangtze above Hankow was opened to navigation and China's inland waters plied by foreign steamers would the problem be solved. On the subject of transit dues, the Chamber welcomed the explicit admission that transit passes should be respected but objected to making commutation compulsory; above all, it italicized, the main difficulty lay in assuring that arrangements be *carried out*. The Chamber protested doubling the duty on silk and the substantial increase in opium tariff. Increased burdens were not offset by concessions. But the Chamber would not commit itself to opposing ratification, merely insisting that the treaty "be made terminable at short notice should the misgivings of the Chamber prove to be well-founded."

Shanghai's position was surprisingly mild. Although the memorial embodied all the detailed objections to the Convention, it was willing to concede qualified assent to ratification. The intensive propaganda campaign against ratification which was organized in London early in

1870 thus appears to have stemmed not from the treaty ports but from the Old China Hands at home. In fact, *The Times* later accused home opinion of outheroding Herod and shaming Shanghai into withdrawing its original approval. Charles Magniac, chairman of the London Committee formed to combat the Alcock Convention, took great pains in a letter to *The Times* (March 19, 1870) to reply to this charge. In any event, sentiment at home and abroad seems to have been formed simultaneously and independently of each other.

In China, mercantile opinion was expressed most forcefully by the Hongkong General Chamber of Commerce, which met in January (1870) under the Chairmanship of William Keswick, a partner in Jardine, Matheson & Co., to express its firm opposition to ratification. In its memorial to Clarendon,[18] the Hongkong Chamber returned to premises and insisted on the necessity for "forcing performance of treaty obligations." The Burlinghame Mission, it emphasized, had been the major cause of Chinese recalcitrance in refusing to grant the mercantile demands. So vigorous was its plea that it found it necessary to protest to Clarendon against the parliamentary canards painting Old China Hands as bellicose. "We are emphatically men of peace; all our avocations are peaceable, as all our interests tend to the preservation of peaceful relations between the two countries." Meanwhile, the "Inhabitants of Hongkong" met on January 3 and sent a separate memorial protesting the provision for establishing a Chinese consulate at Hongkong. This, they argued, would only serve to provide Peking with a spy on wealthy Chinese merchants for "squeeze" purposes. As against the Board of Trade's view, Hongkong advanced the premise that "the end and aim of British diplomacy in China is, without doubt, the ultimate opening up of the whole of the Empire to commerce, and unrestricted intercourse with its people."

In London, meanwhile, an independent movement had been organized by the larger firms in the China trade which proved to be the spearhead behind the concerted mercantile effort to force the Government to scrap the Alcock Convention and substitute for it the mercantile program. The movement was noteworthy as being the first public action taken as a body by Old China Hands returned to the homeland and foreshadowed the vigorous activity of the China Association twenty years later. On January 13, 1870, the most important China merchants met at the Lombard Street offices of Matheson & Co. and organized a London Committee of Merchants to memorialize Clarendon and mobilize home opinion behind a new Anglo-Chinese policy. With Hugh Matheson as chairman and Charles Magniac directing policy, the Committee addressed its propaganda to the home Chambers, calling for a united front both against the Alcock Convention and against the policy of conciliation.

The Committee's memorial to Clarendon boldly urged non-ratification. Major objection was twofold: that the compulsory addition of 2 1/2 percent to the commuted tariff did not afford sufficient guarantee against further inland exactions; and that two additional treaty ports hardly scratched the surface of mercantile demands for an open door. "The object to be aimed at by British diplomacy is less to multiply the number of these fixed resorts, than to obtain a general right of travel and settlement for the peaceful trader." The Committee preferred the Treaty of Tientsin if it were "enforced." The issue was clear. It was not a question of opposition to individual provisions but of hostility to the very basis of British policy toward China. A deputation was organized and on January 21, Hugh Matheson circularized the home Chambers, requesting their support and participation in the deputation.[19]

At the same time Shanghai and Hongkong had also sent copies of their memorials to the Chambers for support. The *London & China Telegraph* throughout January exhibited increasing hostility to the Alcock Convention and on January 24 it bluntly published what others had been whispering—that ratification of the Convention would be regarded as approval of Clarendon's policy of conciliation. "Ratification," it concluded, "would be fatal to British interests."

The Alcock Convention was published in *The Times* of January 11 and was circulated by the Foreign Office to the Chambers of Commerce for comment. Interest in commercial circles proved high and the treaty port propaganda had apparently done its work. In fact, even before publication of the Convention, the Executive Council of the Associated Chambers of Commerce had passed resolutions calling on the Government to accede to Shanghai demands, open the Yangtze and insist on the "loyal execution of the treaty."[20] The sentiments there expressed indicated how far the home Chambers had travelled in accepting the premises of the Old China Hands. Upon receipt of the circular letter from the Foreign Office, the Glasgow, Leith, Edinburgh and Dundee Chambers protested ratification in memorials whose wording revealed the hand of the Committee of London Merchants.[21] The Macclesfield Chamber complained of the practice of Whitehall in framing commercial treaties without prior consultation with commercial bodies.

The public relations pattern which convinced the home Chambers to oppose ratification is best seen by following the process through the Manchester Chamber of Commerce. A special meeting of the Board of

Directors met on January 12 (1870) to hear Sam Mendel, agent of
Jardine, Matheson & Co. in Manchester, explain the reasons for mercantile opposition to the treaty, and a resolution was passed "that in the
opinion of this Board it is undesirable that the Treaty with China should
be ratified until full opportunity is afforded for examining its provisions." [22] The next meeting of the Board was held after the letter from
the Committee of London Merchants had been received. Mr. Bower of
Bower, Bevan & Co., described as "China merchants of London," was
introduced by Mendel and explained at considerable length the nature
of the China trade and the reasons for Old China Hand opposition to the
Alcock Convention.[23] The Board was not yet completely convinced but,
after discussion, passed a resolution "that in acknowledging receipt of
the Foreign Office letter and copy of the Treaty" it hoped confirmation
would be deferred until sufficient time had been allowed for consideration
or until Alcock's return to England to explain his treaty. On February 9,
however, Sir John Bowring addressed the Board and persuaded it to
appoint a committee to draw up a memorial against ratification. Five days
later this committee drew up a memorial which contrasted the stipulations of the Tientsin Treaty, if properly enforced, with the lesser concessions of the Alcock Convention.

   Thus by mid-February the Manchester Chamber, ideologically
closer than any other to the Liberal thesis, had been completely converted to the traditional Old China Hand view. As finally adopted by
the full Chamber,[24] the Manchester memorial failed "to discover in the
Convention advantages for internal intercourse which are not conferred
in a much larger degree under the original treaty" and urged non-
ratification. Few of the home Chambers could resist the bandwagon. At
Bradford a diversity of opinion at the Chamber meeting on February 4
led to postponement of a decision.[25] Liverpool, despite the concerted
campaign of the London Committee, the China Chambers and the East
India & China Association, held out. A special deputation from the
London Committee failed to change the decision of the Chamber's
Council "that it is inexpedient to take any action in the matter." [26] But
Bradford and Liverpool were decidedly in the minority.

   The British press reflected the attitude it had adopted on Clarendon
policy. The Times (January 11, 1870) supported Alcock's view that the
minor concessions gained would prove a wedge to further reform, while
the Pall Mall Gazette,[27] confessing that it had hoped for a "more
limited" treaty, congratulated him on having obtained certain mercantile
advantages without force. The Standard [28] alone believed the treaty un-
satisfactory as it was based on no principle or policy and had lost ground
for Britain's imperial position. Several weeks later, when the first mer-

cantile memorials appeared, *The Times* continued to urge ratification on the ground that the treaty's advantages outweighed the burdens pointed out by the merchants.[29] In fact, the journal accused London merchants of fomenting hostility and changing Shanghai opinion from lukewarm acceptance to outright opposition. Similarly, the *Pall Mall Gazette,* which interpreted the Shanghai memorial as favoring ratification, stated that "merchants in China who approve the treaty show to better advantage than the London merchants who disapprove." The *Gazette* urged that "to prevent transgression of the treaty by Englishmen on the spot" Far East affairs be placed under a separate governor-general who would be placed under the jurisdiction of the Board of Trade!

Overwhelmed by the extent and character of home opposition, and in preparation for the deputation organized by the London Committee for the end of February, the Foreign Office again addressed itself [30] to the Board of Trade for possible reconsideration of its strong views on treaty relations with China. But the Board held firm.[31] It was true that concessions did not approach the claims of the merchants; but that was not unexpected. For the Government had held a "very different opinion from that of the memorialists as to the limits within which it was desirable in the general and permanent interest of our commercial relations with China to confine the recent negotiations." As for detailed criticism, the Board held the increased duties on silk and opium justified and the new arrangement on commutation of inland dues more than fair.

Fortified with this letter, Lord Clarendon received the deputation, organized by the London Committee, on February 28. It was, as the *London & China Telegraph* boasted, a body of "formidable dimensions and influential character," including thirty-four members of Parliament, "several City magnates," and "influential merchants." Hugh Matheson of Matheson & Co. presented the argument that the interests of the country had not been guarded in this revision and that the "further opening up of China" was the concerted desire of London, Shanghai, and Manchester.[32] Charles Magniac, speaking for the London Committee of Merchants, argued that by the Alcock Convention they had been placed in a worse position than before and expressed the belief that if the Government would "firmly and patiently" carry out the Tientsin Treaty the majority of merchants would trust to time for further advantages. Lord Clarendon, denying that the treaty had been negotiated in a spirit hostile to British interests, replied that nothing further could be gained by force and that the Government were of the opinion that the concessions granted were not inconsiderable. He read them the letter which he had just received from the Board of Trade.

The *London & China Telegraph* took Lord Clarendon to task for implying that there were two sides to the question. China merchants, supported by such a brilliant array of financial and parliamentary representatives, could hardly be blind to their own true interests.[33] But the London press generally sided with Clarendon. *The Times* [34] thought the merchants were inclined to take a narrow view of their own business and that the Government knew best. The *Morning Post* [35] declared that the real conflict revolved around Imperial versus Provincial treatment of China, and supported the Government's view as tending to the practical advancement of free trade doctrine. *The Standard* [36] took the occasion to attack Clarendon for his "complete ignorance" of Chinese affairs without, however, backing up the merchants. The *Daily News,*[37] most outspoken in support of Clarendon against the mercantile "policy of bluster," regarded the merchants' demands as unjust and their attempt to interpret the Tientsin Treaty as though their rights coincided with their desires as unworthy of the Liberal age.

Despite press support, the Foreign Office was not unconcerned by the formidable proportions of the mercantile opposition. The strategy of converting the leadership of the mercantile movement was adopted. It was thought that by persuading the respectable heads of the China houses to abandon the "rowdy" elements and to see that their own interests would be advanced by accepting the limited concessions of the treaty the movement would collapse. On March 2, E. Hammond, the Permanent Undersecretary at the Foreign Office, had a three-hour talk with Hugh Matheson and Charles Magniac, leaders of the London Committee, at the end of which Hammond was convinced that he had made some impression. To Shaw Lefevre at the Board of Trade he wrote: "I will not say I convinced them but I do not think they left me as firm in their previous conclusions as they came." [38]

At first talk revolved around the difference over treaty interpretation, with Hammond presenting the Foreign Office view that in respect of inland taxes the Alcock Convention was a step forward because it would protect British goods from further taxation in treaty-port provinces and would not affect their status in non-treaty port provinces. Hammond then proceeded to appeal to their practical interests. Alcock had fought for the Convention long and ably and it was hopeless to expect a substitute for it. To depend on revision by France or Germany, scheduled to take place in several years, would be foolish for merchants, as the Frenchman "would be quite content to sacrifice our commercial interests in hope of gaining something for his religious interests."

But Hammond's major appeal was to the immediate, vested interests of the representatives of Jardine, Matheson & Co. Merchants had demanded the entire opening of the country. But

nothing would be so dangerous or even destructive to trade as to allow free and unrestricted access into the interior. Quarrels would arise, which would lead to consequences that might be destructive of all trade by involving the two nations in war. They knew enough even of their own people . . . to be aware that unrestricted access to the interior was not calculated to improve our relations with the Chinese; and then came the rowdy class who certainly would involve us in difficulty.[39]

When the interview ended, Hammond was left with the impression that he had gained his point. He even reported that Matheson and Magniac "disclaimed any sympathy with the exaggerated demands of the British merchants in China for railways, telegraphs, etc., and indeed did not seem disposed to uphold their general views and practice, but rather to excuse them." There exists no other record of this interview, so that Hammond's judgment cannot be measured against the impressions of the merchants.

I suspect from what dropped from my friends that they find that they have embarked on a crusade which gives them more trouble than they looked for; and that although it was very pleasant to parade at the Foreign Office delegates from manufacturing towns, they are beginning to fear that their friends may prove hard and troublesome auxiliaries.

At the Board of Trade, Shaw Lefevre agreed that the position of the London Committee was destined to undergo a weather change. "I have seen Mr. Magniac since your interview with him and found him very much shaken—I shall be surprised if in the next letter from the merchants we do not find they take a very different view of their rights under the Treaty of Tientsin and also of the provisions under the new Convention. . . ."[40]

Hammond and Lefevre were destined to be disillusioned. Not only did the merchants refuse to retreat from their previous position, but following several meetings in the City at which the governmental attitudes were reviewed, the London Committee sent an even stronger memorial to Lord Clarendon opposing ratification.[41] This time there appeared to be the conviction that by marshalling mercantile opinion and bringing pressure on the Government a dent in the conciliatory policy might be made. In detail, the memorial renewed every criticism that had been levelled against the Alcock Convention and boasted of the unanimity of mercantile opinion hostile to it. At the same time the campaign to enlist the support of home Chambers of Commerce continued to meet with remarkable success. Conversion of the Manchester Chamber had, of course, been a major triumph. And, while Bradford and Liverpool continued indifferent, Halifax had been persuaded to support the London Committee.[42] The following day the East India & China Association of Liverpool passed a resolution concurring in the stand taken by the Matheson forces in London.[43]

More specialized interests were not silent. On March 7 a deputation of property owners in Hongkong called on Lord Granville, the Colonial Secretary, to protest the provision for establishing a Chinese consulate in the colony, a provision which had been agitating Britons in the Straits Settlement as well as Hongkong residents.[44] The Sassoons, chief importers of opium from India, protested the proposed tariff increase of twenty taels per chest on the grounds that it would prove disastrous to British Indian revenue.[45]

By the spring of 1870 mercantile opposition had hardened and public opinion tended to be swayed by the unanimity displayed in commercial circles. The *Saturday Review* [46] in an article on "The London Merchants and the Chinese Treaty" reflected the growing tendency to doubt the wisdom of the Clarendon policy. The reply of the London Merchants, it stated, increased public suspicion of the merits of the Alcock Convention and, while Clarendon might know more of foreign politics than they, it is hard to rival the "special knowledge" of the treaty port residents.

This, of course, was just the result aimed at by mercantile propaganda. On April 11, the *London & China Telegraph* jubilantly predicted that the Convention would not be ratified. In addition to the "thorough exposure" to which the treaty had been subjected, it was understood that the French Government was also opposed. And if ratification were withheld, Old China Hands were convinced that negotiations for a new treaty based on mercantile conceptions of Anglo-Chinese relations would be inaugurated.

Confronted with such pressure, the Foreign Office anxiously awaited the return of Alcock, the one authority who might be able to turn the tide. On March 23 an urgent telegram was sent to the British representative at Alexandria to speed Alcock's journey upon his arrival from India.[47] It was another month before Alcock reached London and was quickly briefed on developments. On May 3 Alcock submitted to the Foreign Office his reconsidered views on revision, reaching the weary conclusion that official differences with the mercantile community were irreconcilable and could not be resolved by minor changes.[48] Nothing had changed, Alcock argued in his Memorandum, for the points raised in London did not differ appreciably from those submitted by Shanghai and Hongkong. Between the official view and the mercantile view there was a cleavage on essentials. "The merchants desired certain great things which however desirable from their point of view or in the interests of commerce, both the Government of Peking and their own negatived, as being either inexpedient or wholly impracticable under present circumstances." In view of the "irreconcilable difference of opinion," was it wise to force even an "advantageous arrangement" upon the merchants against their will? He dumped the question into the lap of the Foreign Office. To Hammond he wrote privately that he had forseen from the start that any Convention entered into under existing circumstances would have little chance against the "want of concurrence of Foreign powers" and the opposition of "our Merchants." He suggested that if the Government decided on non-ratification it should do so on the basis of lack of consent by other Powers. Otherwise, if rejection were attributed to the opposition of the merchants "we must be prepared for a great deal of ill-feeling and distrust at Peking." [49]

While the Foreign Office was considering Alcock's Memorandum, it received a communication from the French Ambassador providing it with an opportunity to refuse ratification on the grounds suggested by Alcock and thus to skirt the issue of mercantile pressure on the formation of its policy. In a confidential memorandum M. de la Valette stated that the French Government would be unable to consent to the Alcock Convention, principally because of the doubling of the export duty on silk.[50] The Foreign Office was now faced with the alternatives of submitting the Alcock Memorandum to the merchants in the remote hope that some compromise might be reached or of deciding on outright non-ratification with the proviso that future treaty revision be taken up with the French upon the majority of the Emperor in 1873. Non-ratification, however, appeared to be a foregone conclusion and the only question that remained was the grounds upon which it would be put and the procedure to be followed. Again the entire issue was submitted to the Board of Trade.

The reply of the Board of Trade, written by Shaw Lefevre, was even more revealing than the Board's letter of the previous year in its analysis of the premises upon which Anglo-Chinese policy must be based.[51] As it has not been previously published, an extensive review is warranted.

1. While it cannot be denied that the representations received from the principal manufacturing centers appear to confirm the adverse opinion entertained by the British merchants engaged in the China trade, these must be discounted because of the intensive campaign of the London Committee and treaty port Chambers which influenced them.

2. Memorialists overlook the fact that China has the same right to prefer claims in treaty revision as does England and that it is no slight advantage to have arrived at an understanding with the sacrifice of so little of vital importance.

3. It must also be recollected that while the opinions and interests of British merchants in the China trade are entitled to "very great consideration" their

importance in this branch of commerce is due in large measure to "the abnormal and artificial character of our relations with China and is diminishing year by year."[!] Recent reports from British Consuls in China upon the tendency of trade to pass into native hands bear "unequivocal testimony to the change which is gradually taking place especially in the Import trade, which is the branch for the benefit of which the provisions of the present convention were principally designed."

4. Under the circumstances, the opinion of the British mercantile class, however apparently unanimous, cannot be considered as conclusive with respect to the probable operation of the Convention. Moreover, it should be recalled that on many recent occasions there had been a "wide divergence of views" between the British Government and the memorialists on the fundamental principles of British policy in China.

5. If, therefore, these had been the only obstacles to ratification, the Board would recommend that the question receive further discussion. But in view of French opposition further discussion is futile.

6. However, non-ratification should not be publicly attributed to mercantile opposition. Such a course could hardly fail to create an impression on the Chinese Government that the merchants, whose attitude towards them has been so often of an unfriendly character, are strong enough to overrule the Government even in a case in which their own convictions are opposed to mercantile views. Rather, the Chinese Government should be informed that "until the concurrence of the other Treaty Powers has been secured it appears useless and undesirable to proceed to ratification." And it would be sufficient to tell the merchants that the Government "did not intend under the present circumstances to ratify the Convention."

Although the Foreign Office agreed that because of difference on principles the Convention would not be ratified the circuitous reasoning of the Board of Trade did not quite appeal to it as diplomatically correct. At first Lord Clarendon agreed to proceed on the lines suggested by the Board of Trade, with the proviso that the Alcock Memorandum be first circulated among the Chambers; Otway, the Parliamentary Undersecretary, was also convinced that it would probably be sufficient to attribute non-ratification to the action of the French.[52] Action was postponed for several days, however, and the sole decision taken was to circulate the Alcock Memorandum to the merchants "without inviting any further controversy but simply to inquire whether it alters or modifies the views they have always expressed." [53]

Before the reactions of the merchants had been received, however, the Foreign Office had decided to reject the Board of Trade's grounds for non-ratification and was prepared to place it squarely on mercantile opposition. Hammond, who prepared the draft of what was later to become the famous circular letter to the China Merchants of July 25, 1870, argued that it would be diplomatically disastrous to attribute rejection to French pressure and that it was preferable to publish openly the differences between Whitehall and the mercantile community which made ratification impossible. Otway was impressed and approved: "It seems to me to put the non-ratification of the convention on the proper ground while it does most ample justice to the endeavors of Sir R. Alcock." Clarendon endorsed this with a brief "I concur" and the decision had been made.[54]

Three days after this decision had been reached the Alcock Memorandum was circulated, more as a tribute to the Minister than because it was expected to reveal any substantial modifications in mercantile views.[55] As the Foreign Office anticipated, the reaction was a unanimous reassertion of mercantile opposition. Following a meeting on June 15 at the offices of Matheson & Co., the London Committee informed the Foreign Office that Alcock's Memorandum did not modify their views and added proudly that "it is satisfactory to them to know that, so far as time has admitted of information being received, the mercantile bodies throughout the country have arrived at a similar conclusion."[56] The Manchester Chamber similarly passed a resolution that the memorandum "in no way alters the opinions that they have expressed on the inexpediency of the convention being carried into effect in its present form."[57] Edinburgh and the East India & China Association of Liverpool agreed. Macclesfield submitted a long memorial which emphasized that "the opinions of the mercantile communities in China and Great Britain cannot be too often repeated until they shall have had their desired effect upon the mind of H.M. Government at home and representatives abroad."[58] More fanatic even than the China merchants, the Macclesfield Chamber vigorously dissented from Alcock's view that trade privileges in China had been extorted under pressure; nor would they agree that the sole British interests involved were that "small body of European merchants located at the open ports" but rather that "every manufacturer as well as every merchant in this country" had an interest in exploitation of the China market. So important was the subject that the Chamber urged an inquiry by a Parliamentary committee!

Macclesfield hit close to the center of the issue. It was obvious from the tenor of the London merchants' meeting that with non-ratification practically assured the Old China Hands were aiming at reopening negotiations on their own premises.[59] In a larger sense they were aiming at a complete reversal of the official attitude, as stated by the Board of Trade, on British policy toward China. The interest they had succeeded in stirring up would be dissipated if non-ratification were not followed by a new course leading toward a Chinese industrial and commercial revolution. They were soon to be disillusioned.

For the Foreign Office, the decision which had been taken on June 6 was a painful admission of defeat in the battle over the Alcock Convention. But it was no more than that. At no time, documentary sources indicate, was a reversal of the Clarendon line ever contemplated. What it did mean was stated by Hammond in a private letter to Sir Thomas Wade (Alcock's successor at Peking) which reaffirmed British policy.

We wish above all things while holding our own with China, not to keep up those perpetual bickerings in which our merchants so much delight and which, so far from leading to good, merely embitter our relations and render the Chinese suspicious and distrustful of us.

I fear that non-ratification of Alcock's convention, which is inevitable, may produce a bad impression at Pekin. Practically, however, it signifies little whether we ratify or not, for the French will not come into it, and therefore they would make it a dead instrument. However it would never do to assign as a reason for not ratifying the objection of France; we should have refused on our own ground; tho' when we have refused it may serve to allay any feelings of irritation on the part of the Chinese to know that tho' direct action of England caused the treaty to fall thro', the indirect action of others who would have refused to ratify it would have led to the same result. The worst feature in the present state of things is that it tends to shut the door to all progress; for the French will probably now and hereafter thwart any arrangement which does not promote their religious views, & we certainly shall not be disposed to fight the Chinese on the missionary ground.

. . . We probably shall direct you to announce the non-ratification of the Treaty in the most concise tho' courteous terms; but this renunciation need not prevent you from endeavoring to induce the Chinese Govt by their own spontaneous and unilateral action to carry out some of the measures which the Treaty would have provided. . . . I am not sure indeed that our best chance of doing good is not to let the French get involved in some missionary squabble, and so realize the difficulties of the situation they have made for themselves.[60]

Official policy, Hammond concluded, continued to be that "mild but continuous pressure will do much more than violence of acts or words." It was a conclusion from which Old China Hands could draw small comfort. Nor did the death of Lord Clarendon on June 27 change matters. In a memorandum summing up the course of China affairs for Lord Granville, the new Foreign Secretary, Hammond emphasized that the decision to attribute non-ratification to mercantile opposition stemmed not from a change in policy but that "the refusal must be placed on British grounds alone; for it would never do to allow the Chinese to suppose that our action in China might be paralyzed by that of the French." [61] The final draft of the letter to the merchants, agreeing to non-ratification of the Alcock Convention on these grounds, was considered at a Cabinet meeting in mid-July [62] and the letter published on July 25, 1870.

It is a remarkable document. While placing non-ratification squarely on the grounds of mercantile opposition, it emphasizes that the Government had reached this decision "with much regret" as it had been hoped that the Alcock Convention "might secure at an inconsiderable sacrifice on the part of England, great immediate, and still greater prospective, advantages. It would, in their judgment, have promoted the Textile Industry of the Manufacturing Districts by facilitating the importation of its products into the most important provinces of China." [63] And though doubting that the decision was calculated "to promote the real interests of the commercial and industrial classes" the Government had, nevertheless, "determined to defer to the wishes expressed by the Commercial bodies who have so urgently appealed to them and have accordingly advised Her Majesty to withhold her Ratification." At the same time, Wade was advised to convey the decision to the Peking government and to sound out the possibility of inducing the Chinese to make spontaneously the concessions for improvement of commercial relations contained in the treaty.[64]

Thus the struggle between merchant and official over treaty revision, which had lasted for almost three years, ended in an initial triumph for the Old China Hands.[65] For it was their publicity campaign which had mobilized commercial opinion at home. But the major battle—that concerning basic policy in Anglo-Chinese relations—was still in the balance. The main issue was still unresolved and the victory in treaty revision would prove empty if it resulted in the perpetuation of the status quo. Without repudiation of the Clarendon policy nothing basic would have been gained. Of this, Old China Hands were well aware. Writing from Shanghai, a resident assails the Convention not for its commercial failings but because it perpetuates the Clarendon doctrine: [66]

Another feature of the present Government's patent mode of treating China is the meek, Christian, non-resistance principle. They say—Dear Children in China, if you get killed any time, do not cry out angrily or lose your tempers, but wait a few months till we have officially laid the matter before the Peking authorities, and all will be well. Let me give one piece of advice to H.M. Government if they mean to carry out this policy. Let them station as many gunboats in China waters as they like, but on no account trust them with powder and shot. When an Englishman, with these dangerous remedies handy, sees his countrymen massacred or his flag insulted, his first impulse is certainly not to write a letter to Peking. . . .

Unless the foundations of the Clarendon policy were destroyed, commercial development, in the view of Old China Hands, would never make headway. Yet there was no indication that official retreat on this score was imminent. On the contrary, in April (1870) Clarendon had taken the occasion of an incident involving French missionaries at Nganking (in Anhui) to restate British policy as follows: (a) "That nothing is further from the wish of H.M. Government than to impose humiliating conditions on China, or to exact anything from her beyond what they are, by Treaty, entitled to demand"; (b) That Britain would continue to strengthen the Central Government "by appealing to it for the fulfillment of international duties rather than by attempting to enforce the observance of them by direct pressure and violent action on the local authorities"; and (c) That Britain would continue to hold Peking responsible "for the protection of British interests and the redress of British wrongs." [67] In conclusion Clarendon succinctly stated the official view:

You cannot too strongly point out that British interests in China are strictly commercial, or, at all events, only so far political as they may be for the protection of commerce and of British subjects in their lawful pursuits. The British Government have neither the desire nor the intention to interfere with the internal administration of China, neither do they wish to employ any other action than that of friendly representation upon the Imperial Government for the defence of British subjects or for the redress of wrongs done to them.

In the light of this restatement of the Clarendon policy and of the urgent need on the part of Old China Hands to capitalize on the partial triumph scored on treaty revision, the reaction to the Tientsin Massacre is significant. It was, for mercantile agitators, a heaven-sent opportunity for keeping alive the propaganda they had initiated when Burlinghame first reached London and, what is more, perhaps the last opportunity for forcing a change in British policy. The facts of the Tientsin Massacre resemble those of many another xenophobic pogrom. Throughout the month of June (1870) sinister rumors were current among the native population at Tientsin that the Sisters of the French Catholic "Asile de la Sainte-Enfance" were guilty of kidnapping native children for conversion; to these rumors were soon added the canards, of a kind not uncommon in the history of human prejudice, that the Sisters had put to death thirty to forty new-born infants after having torn out the eyes and hearts to use in the manufacture of a special kind of Christian medicine.

Agitation was intensified throughout the month and violent action by the French Consul in an attempt to induce the local governor to control the mob led to his own assassination and aggravation of the situation. On June 21 the mob broke loose, pillaging and burning the Lazarist Mission and killing several priests and native converts. Ten Sisters of the Order St. Vincent-de-Paul were massacred and few French residents escaped the day with their lives.[68]

Although no British subjects were seriously harmed, it was evident that agitation had been directed against British missionaries as well, the London Mission having been the scene of anti-foreign demonstrations two days previously and its leaders stoned. W. H. Lay, the British Consul, immediately assumed responsibility for French interests while two British merchant vessels evacuated the European refugees. On the 29th the British gunboat *Avon* arrived, reinforced on July 2 by the *Dwarf*. A joint note of the Diplomatic Corps on June 24 called upon Prince Kung for redress, indemnity and the assertion of Imperial authority to assure the safety of foreigners.[69] Prince Kung immediately gave the required assurances and on June 26 assumed responsibility for the punishment of the criminals involved, payment of compensation, issuance of an edict deploring the massacre and the dispatch of Chung How of the Imperial household to Paris as special commissioner for settling the issue and making amends.

First news of the massacre did not reach London until the end of July and the French Ambassador immediately enlisted the support of the Foreign Office in presenting a common front to Peking. On August 25 Lord Granville officially replied that Wade would be instructed to co-operate with the French Minister in pressing for appropriate measures of punishment.[69a] Meanwhile in Peking the delay in meting out punishment led the French Chargé to issue an ultimatum demanding the execution of the measures promised. Despite support from the other Ministers, Kung's tactics of procrastination continued and a satisfactory settlement was delayed.

For the mercantile community the Tientsin Massacre was an unexpected opportunity: here was proof of what they had been crying for years, that a policy of conciliation would never work. On July 4 a Correspondent wrote to the *London & China Telegraph* [70]:

Good may arise out of the evil in this case if the Foreign Governments avail themselves of this opportunity to really open China, and give railways, telegraphs, coal-mining, and internal steam-navigation to the people, who are only too ready to adopt them, if untrammeled by their Government. As we have the power, it seems childish not to take those privileges, and do away with any distinction between natives and foreigners. The absence of a gunboat at Tientsin no doubt led to the massacre being perpetrated, the worst that has been known since the commencement of foreign intercourse.

This was the mercantile case in a paragraph. In Shanghai, as Wade himself reported, the British Minister was being reproached for inaction even before the details of diplomatic action were known. "What we fear most from him," wrote the Hongkong *Daily Press,* "is that he may send home icy accounts of the whole affair and so give a very false impression concerning the events which have lately blackened the page of history." [71] Ominously, the *Daily Press* concluded: "When is China to come under foreign rule? That seems to be the great question at present and the inevitable result is only a question of time." The *North China Herald* [72] warned that any further disaster would be the signal for a general anti-foreign outbreak and cautioned foreign chancelleries to look to their prestige. Wade, on the other hand, was telegraphing the Foreign Office to persuade Paris to moderate de Rochechouart's excessive zeal.[73]

The Foreign Office was faced with the problem of finding a formula which would appease the merchants without appearing to abandon expressed Anglo-Chinese policy, and, at the same time, not to give the appearance of pulling France's chestnuts out of the Tientsin fire. Aside from a non-committal expression of assurance to cooperate in demanding punishment for the malefactors,[74] the Foreign Office awaited details from Wade. It was not until September 15 that fuller instructions, drafted by Hammond and seen by Gladstone (but not by Lord Granville) were dispatched to Wade. Strategy was left to Wade who was furnished with a set of principles.

H.M. Government would exert whatever moral influence it may possess to induce the Chinese Government to satisfy any reasonable demand which France may take. It is quite clear that the only policy which can be pursued is one of an expectant character though that should not preclude every attempt that can be made without compromising future liberty of action—to impress upon the Chinese government the necessity of anticipating demands that may possibly be made upon them for redress. . . .[75]

Thus, neither the substance nor the temperature of official policy had been affected by the Tientsin affair. One day earlier (September 14, 1870), the London Committee of Merchants led a deputation to Lord Granville to express mercantile apprehensions over the results of the Tientsin affair. Alexander Matheson, as spokesman, pointed to the all-inclusive character of the anti-foreign agitation and revealed information from merchants in China showing that it was part of a concerted plan to wipe out the foreign devils. He inquired as to the steps which had been taken "for more effectual protection of the Lives and property of British subjects in China." He then proceeded to unveil the real objective of mercantile agitation:

We cannot conceal from Your Lordship that the anxiety of our friends, in which we share, has been largely increased by a regard to the policy which in recent years H.M. Government has adopted in its dealings with the Government of China,—a yielding and complacent policy, as opposed to a policy of firmness which should exact the due fulfillment of Treaty obligations and be prepared to demand reparation for injustice and injury.[76]

The shade of Consul Gibson was called upon to testify:

The instance of the able settlement effected two years ago in the Island of Formosa by the prompt action of the late Mr. Consul Gibson cannot be forgotten by us. That officer was severely blamed and degraded instead of being thanked and rewarded for his services. Desirous as we are and have ever been that all grounds and causes for a rupture with China may be avoided, as being most detrimental to every interest concerned, we would earnestly press upon Your Lordship's attention the desirableness of a firm policy, rather than one of yielding and concession of which the Chinese invariably take an unworthy advantage and which as they uniformly attribute it to weakness on our part, is calculated in our opinion to lead to aggressions which H.M. Government would be unable to overlook.[77]

Finally, the deputation brought up the matter reported in that day's issue of *The Times* that naval officers in China stations "are forbidden by instructions from the Admiralty to land their men under any circumstances, even to protect life when it is threatened" and are to confine assistance to receiving refugees on board.

The instructions were correct though reported out of context. Otway, in replying for Lord Granville, stated that Wade would cooperate with the French in securing punishment for the Tientsin malefactors. As for *The Times* report, standing instructions to consuls and naval officers as to employment of war vessels are "in cases of great emergency to protect the lives and property of British subjects if placed in peril by wanton attacks directed against them." [78]

The London Committee decided to go to the country. While interest on China affairs was still alive, as a result of the agitation attending the Alcock Convention, support of commercial circles was again solicited. Accounts of the deputation and copies of recent correspondence with the Foreign Office were circulated and the Chambers of Commerce asked for aid in the fight. The response, though far from unanimous, was heartening. Bradford held a rally on September 29 which called for decisive action on the part of the government.[79] Bradford even approached Liverpool, pointing out the urgency of the case, but the latter hedged, replying that the Foreign Office response to Matheson appeared adequate.[80] Manchester also appears to have been indifferent, but the Halifax Chamber on October 18 wrote a strong letter to Lord Granville urging prompt redress and guarantees for the future. The peroration is instructive. "What the Chinese merchants, our fellow-countrymen resident in China, ask is not war but firmness in our diplomatic intercourse with the Chinese authorities and above all the practical recognition of the principle that no European shall be subject to gross outrage without the intervention of European governments for the protection of their subjects." [81]

Similar sentiment in the treaty ports was compounded by an active fear of anti-foreign outbreaks. In September, Jardine, Matheson & Co. and the Shanghai Chamber of Commerce wrote to Consul Medhurst for governmental assurance that they would not be left helpless in the face of growing anti-foreign manifestations.[82] The Shanghai Chamber was particularly concerned about the renewed instructions to naval officers to restrict the use of gunboats to affording asylum to British subjects in actual danger.[83] Despite this agitation, the *London & China Telegraph* [84] bewailed the lack of interest in the country and appealed to the Government to save the British position in China which was seriously endangered. The press, it noted, showed little concern. While the *Standard, Globe* and *Morning Post* endorsed their views calling for firm action, the Liberal papers were "flippant or reticent." The *Telegraph* urged the formation of local committees at home and abroad to acquaint the public with the danger. Actually, the home press did speak seriously of the imminent prospect of war with China, but interest soon died down.

Not insensitive to mercantile opinion, the Foreign Office was nevertheless far from contemplating a major change in policy nor did it regard the situation as acute. On September 26 the Foreign Office telegraphed Wade to "urge on the Chinese government the absolute necessity, if they wished to avoid a serious difference with England, of providing adequate protection for the British subjects and their property at Tientsin and other places where during the winter season the protection afforded by Her Majesty's ships will not longer be available." At the same time, however, Wade was instructed to refrain from giving any provocation: "I trust in your absolute fairness and avoidance of unnecessarily irritating language. . . . You will on no account sanction a British occupation of the Taku forts without orders from home." [85] In a more extensive dispatch on October 6 this view was repeated with the added caution that where British lives were in danger Wade would offer them the means of withdrawing to a place of safety.

At the same time Hammond prepared a memorandum on policy to be pursued in the Tientsin crisis, which served as final instructions to Wade.[86] Great Britain, Hammond pointed out, was not the principal party concerned. Wade had already been told to give "moral support" to the French in their demand for "reasonable redress." Now, if that demand were refused, it will be a matter of further consideration for the Government whether any (Gladstone here minuted "and if at all") and how far material assistance may be given the French. In any event, the British Government was prepared to provide sufficient naval protection to protect lives and property "but not so great as to alarm the Chinese into assuming British hostility." Three hundred Marines were being sent out to protect Shanghai, to be reinforced by infantry from Japan if needed. Gladstone added that Wade should try to moderate the action of the French, who might be tempted to take high-handed action in China in consequence of disasters suffered in Europe.[87]

Wade's position was difficult; the Foreign Office formula was not easy of application. His own view was that though the Central Government was "false and timid," it must be upheld if British interests were to be protected—"unless we would govern the country." [88] In a private letter to Hammond, he outlined his difficulties:

It was in the interest of all of us to press the government to make the people understand that it, the government, recognises its duty by the foreigners without distinction of nationality. We have not been very successful, but we have had against us a French war and a most uncontrollable French colleague. . . . I have had to urge, yea to goad, the Chinese to do something that would satisfy the French . . . and I have had to try and keep my French colleague within bounds. . . . I hope the Government will speak rather sternly to China and yet uphold me in my much condemned indifference.[89]

As for immediate policy, Wade suggested that the British Government speak out "gravely" against Chinese delay in affording redress for the Tientsin outrage and, at the same time, support its Minister at Peking, who was trying to "ensure a continuance of peace by *pacifically* exacting satisfaction of treaty obligations."

Wade's suggestion was taken and a note prepared by Hammond criticizing the Chinese for their "tardy and reluctant consent . . . to do justice in a case in which the feelings of all Christian nations were so enlisted" and warning of "the serious consequences which any interruption of friendship between the two countries would involve." [90] At the same time, the Foreign Office made a placating gesture to the Shanghai Community, assuring the Chamber there that the recent naval instructions had been misunderstood.

It is to be inferred from the tenour of the instructions that it would be consistent with their spirit and with the policy of H.M. Government that the Senior Naval Officer on the spot, if satisfied that an attack on a British settlement at any port is imminent, should disembark and maintain on shore till the danger was passed a body of marines, which, however, it would be desirable to relieve daily or frequently from the ships.[91]

Placating as this was, it involved no change either in the restrictions on employment of gunboats or in basic policy toward China. In reply to a question from Charles Magniac as to the measures being taken to protect British interests and whether it was true that troops were being sent from Madras to China, Hammond replied that he had no knowledge of any change in the situation.[92] He added, however, that a battalion of marines was being placed at the disposal of the Admiral at Shanghai which "might be landed for purposes of protection" in emergencies. This reply the *London & China Telegraph*,[93] which invariably reflected the views of the London Committee, called a "complete disappointment" for all who had hoped that the Government was at last beginning to understand its duty. Despite evidence of Chinese war preparations, the journal continued, the Government "still clings to delusions concerning China which it cherished before the Tientsin affair. . . . Our trade with China may slip from our grasp, all hopes of improving our position in the country are melting away, but our Government will not see any danger or lift a finger to save the interests at stake." How differently things were arranged in Palmerston's day!

Now that the Tientsin storm had been weathered, policy was becoming crystallized: moderation, support of the Central Government, and the promotion of gradual reforms which would not endanger the stability of China. Not only was the Foreign Office convinced that it was unwise to fish in the troubled waters of China; Whitehall was determined to pour oil on those waters. Succeeding dispatches from the Foreign Office to Peking at the end of 1870 made it clear that, despite the fiasco of the Alcock Convention and the mercantile propaganda which agitated home opinion during the Tientsin affair, Old China Hands had not succeeded in making any impression on the foundations of policy. These remained what they had been since 1860, as reaffirmed by Clarendon; the Liberal Government was solidly behind this policy and no strong parliamentary or public movement had arisen to challenge it. The flurry caused in the mercantile circles of London and Manchester by recent events was dying down.

On December 12, 1870, the *London & China Telegraph* began to admit defeat. Perpetuating the legend that Palmerston had been repudiated in 1870 and not in 1860, the journal of the Old China Hands editorialized that the denouement of the Tientsin affair indicated the decline of British prestige in China. Ministers who had "inaugurated the vigorous policy of 1860" had been succeeded in 1870 by men "whose mild diplomacy, during momentous times, is bringing the nations which they represent into contempt." Wade had been "cajoled" by the Chinese Government to report that no military force would be required to protect British lives and property. "Under these circumstances, it behoves our Government to accredit a Minister to Peking who will restore the prestige we have lost by inaugurating a dignified and vigorous policy."

This opinion was the final gasp of mercantile resentment, reflecting murmurs in Shanghai that Wade, the Sinologue, had fallen under the spell of the mandarins and was responsible for misleading the Foreign Office as to the serious nature of the crisis. At Peking, meanwhile, after "long, humiliating and painful negotiations," France obtained with the support of Wade, "the mediocre conditions" of settlement calling for punishment of Tientsin officials responsible for the massacre and the payment of indemnities.[94] For the residents of the treaty ports the settlement was hardly satisfactory; and talk of Britain's loss of prestige became the order of the day. Wade's telegram of November 26 told London that all was quiet, but to the Old China Hands it was the quiet of a truce.

Toward the end of this period of crisis, marked by the Burlinghame Mission, the battle over treaty revision, and the Tientsin affair, the *Pall Mall Gazette* ran two articles on "Our Policy and Prestige in China" [95] which attempted to analyze the reasons for the stalemate in the struggle between Old China Hands and the Foreign Office. Granting that the Tientsin settlement was a "travesty of justice" and that British residents had cause for feeling insecure, the journal blamed the merchants themselves for the failure of their propaganda and the lack of appeal in their program. No doubt the English nation acknowledged the importance of the China trade for what it was worth; and that the China communities had "great influence" with the Government was evident from the rejection of the Alcock Convention. Why then did they "always assume a position of antagonism to their own Government as though the latter were their natural enemies?"

Old China Hands, the *Gazette* charged, completely misinterpreted the tenor of the country.

Aware as they must be of the strong feeling which prevails in this country in favour of peace and moderation—and especially against any spirit of aggression in Eastern affairs whether for commercial or any other objects—why do they and their local press harp only on one string, and in the most absolute spirit of Philistinism demand a policy of gunboats and coercion as the sole means of securing the trade and themselves from molestation?

A commercial policy based on menace and compulsion and only to be carried out by resort to acts of war will find few supporters these days, the journal continued. As an example of crude mercantile thought on the subject it cited the recently published work of Dr. George Thin,[96] former medical missionary, who suggested that China was not ready to be admitted to the comity of nations and should be placed under a modified British suzerainty in which local mandarins would be responsible to the nearest consul for the safety of foreigners. To home opinion this was a policy of "absurdity and impracticability" typical of recent mercantile expression. By adopting this intransigent attitude, accompanied by the "constant deprecation" of British officialdom, they were alienating the British public. "If it be in hope of creating public opinion on the Chinese question which may influence the Government they go about it in the worst possible way. . . . If prestige has really declined who is responsible if not the Anglo-Chinese community which has constantly abused the authority of their Government, and the Anglo-Chinese press which now proclaims it as the result of a bad policy."

The *Pall Mall Gazette* spoke a half-truth. For, to attribute the failure of mercantile propaganda to the bad public manners of the Old China Hands did not explain the almost universal popularity of the Clarendon policy, even in such communities as Manchester, where the textile industry looked to the China market as an outlet for excess production. The *Edinburgh Review* [97] came much closer to reflecting home opinion. After paying tribute to the increasing importance of the China trade to Indian and British revenue and to the cotton industry, the journal denied that obstacles to that trade were political and could be abolished by forcing China to accept mercantile demands. To do so would lead to the collapse of China, it argued. To resolve the main grievance of the merchants—excessive and irregular inland taxation—would involve modification of the entire Chinese fiscal system. Equally unreasonable were the "imperious demands" for the immediate adoption of railroads, telegraphs, coal mining and steam navigation, as well as the basic demand for inland residence. Would the British people feel justified in going to war in order to bring about a new order in China? Of course not, nor would this remove the main obstacles to China's development which came from *without* and consisted of the importunities of all types of foreigners. Policy for the future, the *Edinburgh Review* maintained, must accept the premise that the halcyon days of rapid fortunes had passed; trade was passing into native hands and foreign merchants, except at the larger ports, would disappear. Retrenchment must be the keynote; that was the basis of the Government's policy; it was accepted by the country as the only reasonable approach.

Old China Hands were beginning to see the handwriting on the wall. The *London & China Telegraph* (January 23, 1871) was sorrowed by the *Edinburgh Review* analysis, which, it had hoped, would "scatter the platitudes of the Foreign Office and the sophistries of the Pall Mall Gazette." Instead, it was distinguished by "rancorous ill-will against commercial men in China." But, behind it all there was an even more devastating argument which accounted for the failure of mercantile propaganda. Writing to the *Pall Mall Gazette* (January 25, 1871), a correspondent, referring to the "reasonable" article in the *Review* which had attracted considerable attention, yet took issue with its tribute to the "increased importance" of the China trade. It was a delusion to argue that the stoppage of that trade would mean that "our workmen would have to starve and pinch." The loss of tea imports would not result in one English spindle the less at work, for the amount of trade was relatively so small that it could easily be transferred to Ceylon or Brazil in exchange for tobacco or coffee.

This, of course, was the basic argument of the Board of Trade. It accounts for the relative indifference to China affairs displayed even during critical periods; and for the failure of Shanghai to wean Manchester from its fundamental adherence to the Clarendon policy. It was the verdict not only of the Board of Trade but of commercial England. What was more, this economic judgment lubricated acceptance of the Radical policy toward China, the moral conscience which Cobden had introduced into the Parliamentary discussions during the Arrow affair.[98] Englishmen would again become exercised over the China dream but rarely to the detriment of their moral sense—until the end of the century. For, as the *Gazette* correspondent concluded, the nature of the China trade was such that "we may really use mercy and justice towards the Chinese without incurring the slightest danger of starving or pinching our workmen."

The Tientsin affair had been weathered by the Government and, to the consternation of the Old China Hands, that change in policy for which they had propagandized had not come. The Queen's Speech promised a continuance of the "conciliatory and forbearing spirit" in Anglo-Chinese relations.[99] To the *London & China Telegraph* this spelled disaster.

So far, it is a mere political euphemism for allowing injuries and insults to pass without redress, and for leaving our countrymen and their trade in a position of growing insecurity. Our energetic and thoughtful merchants cannot surely sit down patiently under the insulting disregard of their just claims, while every interest dear to them as men and citizens is menaced with ruin.[100]

It was a cry in the wilderness as the *Telegraph* itself was aware. For whither could it turn for that mobilization of public and parliamentary opinion which, it argued, was needed to clear up the situation.

Nor could it gain much comfort from the China debate in the House of Lords on the Tientsin affair.[101] Attendance of peers was small. Opening the debate, the Earl of Carnarvon, after describing the Tientsin outrages, charged that Government policy and statements on naval protection to British subjects were vague and inadequate. The Government had no difficulty in defending its action. Lord Granville pointed out the simple historical truth (which ran counter to current mercantile legend) that the instructions against local use of force and referral of grievances to the Central Government at Peking were not new but a continuance of the policy inaugurated by Elgin and Bruce and followed ever since. Earl Grey asked an unpleasant, rhetorical question: if foreign action by taking redress of grievances into its own hands so weakened Peking authority as to reduce China to a state of anarchy, were their Lordships "prepared to set up any authority in its place?"

Despite the vigorous attack of Lord Salisbury, who rebuked Lord Granville for speaking of the weakness of British consuls for the bunting of a man-of-war in front of their dwellings and called for a decisive policy in place of the ambiguity of orders recently sent to British representatives; despite the ranting of the Anglo-Chinese press and the continued alarmist reports which Shanghai merchants were sending to the China firms in London—there was never any question of a serious challenge to the China policy of the Foreign Office. The country was convinced that the China trade was not worth another war. The Shanghai correspondent of the *London & China Telegraph* [102] might warn London that the "Chinese government is persistently preparing for War," while Wade, "paid to protect our interests," telegraphs home that there is no danger. Intermittent questions might be asked in Parliament,[103] by Lord Carnarvon and Charles Magniac, about alarming rumors of Chinese attempts to abolish the independence of foreign missions in China. There would be no change. The battle was lost.

Some final efforts were made to revive interest in the China question. Of these the most striking was a very provocative petition by the Edinburgh Chamber of Commerce in May (1871), asking the House of Commons to institute a thorough inquiry into Anglo-Chinese relations. Noting that there had been, during the Alcock Convention affair and in other matters, "a great divergence of opinion between the official representative of Great Britain at Peking and the body of British residents at the various ports"; that the series of outrages at Formosa, Chefoo, Yangchow and Tientsin has led to a feeling of insecurity; and that the trade was still insignificant considering the number of port merchants and "their industrious and mercantile disposition," the Chamber petitioned for a Select Committee of the House of Commons to inquire into the following startling charges: (a) Whether the Legation at Peking has on the whole been beneficial to British interests, and whether the British representative should not spend some time visiting the treaty ports? (b) Whether it was advisable for H.M. Representative to be received in China as the representative of a Sovereign, equal in dignity to the Emperor? (c) Whether the various anti-foreign outbreaks were not connected with the declared Foreign Office policy of referring grievances to the Central Government? (d) Whether the avowed policy of forbearance towards the Chinese had tended to lessen or increase occasion for complaints by British subjects? (e) Whether the Government had instructed their representatives to discourage the introduction of appliances of Western science and to restrict points of contact? (f) Whether there was a disposition on the part of the Chinese to trade? And, finally, whether the constitution of the Foreign Office and its agencies is such as to admit of Chinese affairs being dealt with in satisfactory manner? [104]

This petition aroused no particular interest except in the Anglo-Chinese press. Nor, as the London & China Telegraph [105] sadly remarked, was there that much chance of success for the Hongkong proposal that a Royal Commission inquire into the present insecurity to life and property in China. With the exception of Lord Derby, the Telegraph [106] mourned, not one of "our recent Foreign Secretaries has regarded the Far East as of importance." Agitation along similar lines continued throughout 1871,[107] but in a lost cause.

The strategy of the Foreign Office, to continue the policy of conciliation and gradualism, was predicated not only on the thesis that there was a definite limit to the stake which Britain had in the Chinese venture. Hammond, particularly, was convinced that pressure carried to the point of China's collapse would play into the hands of foreign powers, particularly France. To give the Chinese no reason to suspect that a policy of forbearance meant a policy of weakness and, at the same time, to protect this "false and timid" government against French ambitions, while maintaining the form of international cooperation, was the formula which he counselled Wade to adopt.

You must keep the Chinese as far as you can in their present uneasy frame of mind as regards the future, taking care however, not to use language which might eventually compromise the government. We have too much at stake in China to admit of our running amuck against the people or government in association with others who have little to gain or lose. . . . It is, of course, most important that all the Christian powers should pull together in China, and support each other in any discussion with the Chinese which may not involve principles incompatible with the public feeling in this country, and likely if pushed to extremity to bring us into collision with the Chinese.[108]

During the interlude which was to follow, this policy came to involve the strategy of never making claims or pushing demands on the Chinese Government which might lead to its weakening. It meant supporting it against signs of internal disturbance. It meant, above all, abandoning all ambitions for fundamental administrative and industrial reform. As such it continued to embody the very opposite of mercantile politics. For the Old China Hands, therefore, the campaign against Clarendon ended in outright defeat despite the partial victory in the battle of treaty revision. Their ultimate objective had not been gained and they were forced to retire to previous positions. A resentful truce ensued for the next twenty years.

PART 2

The Interlude, 1872-1890

IV

The Period of Apathy

> *"What was done in India can be repeated in China.
> . . . More than once it has seemed that the Chinese Empire was going to pieces, and that, in spite
> of ourselves, we might be forced to give a perilous
> extension to the Sovereignty which has already begun to grow in the Treaty Ports. Now, it is well for
> our countrymen in China to understand once for
> all that we are not in the mood to undertake the responsibilities of another India"—The Times,* September 15, 1875.

O N THE occasion of the publication of the Consular Reports for 1870, which breathed a subdued note of optimism, the *London & China Telegraph* [1] was led to editorialize that the time had come for the Far East to get that attention from the home front "so long withheld." "Let but the facts be brought before Parliament and the public and we shall soon cease to hear the cuckoo cry about the apathy of the English with regard to their interests in the Far East." But the cuckoo was destined to sing his refrain for the next two decades as Old China Hands failed to make any headway against the continued "apathy" at home. Even in their own ranks, the fervor attending the struggle over treaty revision and the Tientsin affair was considerably dampened. The London Committee of Merchants was dissolved and the cold reception accorded its *ad hoc* successor, the London Committee of the Shanghai Chamber of Commerce, during the agitation against ratification of the Chefoo Convention in 1876, was an adequate index of home sentiment toward China affairs. Even when the Powers commenced nibbling at the edges of the Chinese Empire in the eighties, little concern was demonstrated by the mercantile community. Only in the remarkable interest displayed by the home Chambers in the project for constructing an overland railway from Rangoon to Yunnan, as a back door to the fabulous markets of southwestern China, was the ancient folklore, the

"China dream," kept alive. But that was a side issue, and it was not until the 1890s that a China Association was formed in London to marshal opinion in the new age which was dawn in Anglo-Chinese relations.

The apathy displayed toward China affairs in this period is all the more curious when it is noted that the issues current in the sixties were still alive in the seventies and eighties. Occasionally, and particularly in the early seventies, these issues would be revived, as feeble attempts were made to gain the concessions denied in 1869. But they were soon dropped. The questions of *likin* and the confused situation respecting inland taxation, of railways and mining concessions, of steam navigation on inland waters (particularly the Yangtze), of anticipating the French in securing a shorter route to Yunnan and Szechuen and guarding against Russian encroachment from the North, in short of realizing the old China dream, remained as unresolved in 1875 and 1885 and 1890 as they had been in 1865. The questions remained; but interest, where not entirely lacking, is intermittent and lukewarm. Mercantile documents of the period reveal an almost embarrassing emptiness with regard to China affairs. Like Sherlock Holmes' dog that failed to bark in the night, it is the lack of evidence that is the most striking evidence.

The year 1872 is the significant point of demarcation, both in trade figures and in political interest. It was the high point in the China trade, the year when British representatives sent back the last glowing accounts of the potentialities latent in the China market.[2] M. Lemmonier of the French Missions Etrangères wrote home from Shanghai that "le commerce . . . s'agite avec une activité vraiment fièvreuse," and that tremendous developments were expected from the opening of the Suez Canal.[3] Commercial commentators were more cautious. Even while noting with pride the increase in piece-goods imports in 1872, the *North China Herald* remarked that "the hopes of improvement so frequently indulged in with regard to this branch of our trade with China seem doomed to constant disappointment."[4] "Great and beneficial results were expected from the establishment of direct telegraphic communication with Great Britain and from the opening of the Suez Canal, but at the beginning of 1873 it is not too much to say that many of them have yet to be realized." Quick returns and profitable employment of capital had not materialized. Even in this good year Manchester manufacturers were "making arrangements to curtail the production of shirtings adapted to the East, as they find them more unprofitable than other goods."[5] Jardine, Matheson & Co. noted that instability continued to characterize the market.[6]

The year 1873 which ushered in the Great Depression in Europe resulting in that "numbness in the industrial and commercial life of the country which marked the years of falling prices and quickened international competition" [7] had its special meaning for the Far East. For, despite the added urgency for markets during this period, the China trade exhibited first a decline and then a stagnation which lasted until the nineties. What was more, the ills which affected it proved to be aggravated developments of a chronic condition. From a high of slightly more than nine millions sterling in 1872, there was a gradual decline in British exports to China leveling out to a figure of seven to eight millions until the end of the eighties. Averages, in millions sterling, of British imports to China follow: 1869 to 1872, 9.35; 1873 to 1876, 8.22; 1877 to 1880, 7.74; 1881 to 1884, 7.93; 1885 to 1888, 8.57; 1889 to 1892, 8.23.[8] Cotton goods exports during the period averaged slightly over five millions sterling.

The opening of the Suez Canal in 1869 and the completion of telegraphic communication the following year only served to accentuate the twin weaknesses of the mercantile position in China—overtrading and native competition. The tendency toward overtrading and glutting of markets, of which Jardine, Matheson & Co, had grumbled throughout the sixties, was intensified as British produce could be poured into the treaty ports at an accelerated rate while distribution over the interior was as difficult as ever and the internal market was not being tapped.[9] Similarly the tendency of trade to pass into native hands, while the foreign merchant was reduced to the status of a commission-agent, became more marked as credit facilities for operating on small capital were extended and the telegraph made commission work feasible.[10]

Consular reports confirmed the gloomy picture. At Shanghai, the consul noted, statistical statements seemed to suggest progress and prosperity. But actually mercantile losses had been on a large scale due to overtrading: "the extent of business has been in excess of the requirements of consumption." [11] Even the optimistic Edward Malet, Secretary of Legation, in his trade report for 1872, concluded that a dispassionate review leads "to a fear that the increase of trade noticeable in 1872 arises rather from feverish competition on the part of mercantile firms in stocking the markets than from a rise in demand." [12] How to increase demand? The consul at Shanghai, reporting on the disastrous trade situation of 1873, tended to agree with the Shanghai Chamber that the "real obstruction" to trade consisted "in an irregular and excessive taxation imposed on the movements of commerce and the want of speedy and cheap means of internal transit." [13] Consul Robertson at Canton did not agree. Writing privately to Hammond, he maintains that "there can be no question that the days of European supremacy in trade have passed away forever in this country and the foreign merchant finds his field of action being gradually circumscribed and limited by those who but a few years ago kowtowed to him for his patronage." [14] He draws the conclusion, comforting to the Foreign Office, that "all I have seen in China strengthens my conviction that our true policy is, not to force Western civilisation upon her, but to let her alone."

Without departing from this premise, the Foreign Office was convinced that by a gradual approach and inconspicuous diplomacy some of the more vexing commercial questions, such as *likin* and the navigation of the Upper Yangtze, could be solved. This was the task set Wade in the early seventies. With a full knowledge of the difficulties involved Wade addressed himself to a solution of the *likin* question, while cautioning the merchants that they had made things particularly troublesome by their propaganda during treaty revision. Again and again he reverts to the fact that "it is beyond dispute that the difficulties of the Legation are infinitely multiplied by the rejection of the Convention of 1869." [15] Wensiang, the negotiator on the Chinese side, was "thirsting for revenge because of the discredit and inconvenience our rejection of the Convention has occasioned," and threw the charge of untrustworthiness at England when negotiation became tight. "I beg that this may be borne in mind when people at home are clamorous for the opening of fresh ports, the working of mines and the like privileges; all of great advantage to the Chinese, did they but know it, but to which they are doubly opposed because they see that we are eager to obtain them." [16]

As an aftermath of the interest aroused in China affairs during treaty revision and the Tientsin massacre, agitation for concessions, with respect to *likin* and other matters, continued among Old China Hands for another year or so, prodding the Foreign Office to exhibit more enthusiasm for commercial progress in China. Hammond, suffering from the gout, is probably being more petulant than the occasion warrants but he does reveal that the Government's show of activity with respect to the transit dues question was not entirely spontaneous.

I wish you could realize to yourself the active correspondence that takes place between the residents in China and their friends in this country. The former, it is true, systematically indulge in absurd speculations, misstatements and misrepresentations, but they find implicit credence with their friends in this country both in and out of Parliament. Of course, no one can expect that you should furnish the F.O. by anticipation with the means of refuting all such nonsense, but in all matters in which you yourself take a part in China, such as the Missionary Circular—Transit arrangement—Redress of grievances, etc. you should not leave us while waiting to make a full report, in ignorance of what you are doing. . . .[17]

The date of this letter is instructive—January, 1872. Within a year, certainly in two, no one would speak of an "active correspondence" on China affairs. The attempt to solve the most vexing questions, particularly that of "transit arrangement," spurred by mercantile agitation, was the last gasp of interest until the nineties.

Though Wade labored for three years, no satisfactory solution was found. In July, 1871 he addressed a circular letter to the Consuls asking for a report on *likin* and other forms of "abnormal taxation." [18] The replies varied, but the consensus appeared to be that while the tax was applied in an irregular and arbitrary manner in few instances did it reach prohibitive levels. At Canton, Consul Hughes pointed out that precise information was lacking as native merchants made purchases at Hongkong and Canton on their own account and then arranged for distribution inland. With the connivance of officials short quantities were reported at *likin* stations, the trader paying less than the legal amount; but the delays and exactions were burdensome as something like forty stations might be passed before the goods reached destination. *Likin* was not levied in undue proportion on foreign goods. At Swatow, W. M. Cooper reported that *likin* was collected only at the port. C. A. Sinclair at Foochow dryly commented that while all merchants complained of the oppression of *likin* few were prepared to specify the nature of the burden. Major complaint was that the transit pass covered British goods only so long as they remained in British hands but was not respected when held by a Chinese dealer. In Formosa only opium was subjected to *likin*. Davenport at Shanghai made a general survey and found that the incidence of *likin* varied with the province through which goods passed. The levy was often dishonest and discriminatory; in addition a local or octroi tax was imposed in the city and suburbs. The practice had grown up of Chinese merchants taking out transit passes in the name of foreign hongs. In all, foreign piece goods, when passing from Shanghai to Soochow, might pay a maximum of 9 percent ad valorem. He judged that such a rate might tend to check consumption of British textiles.[19]

What the merchants demanded was the total abolition of *likin* (as well as all other forms of transit and destination levies) on foreign goods, whether in native or foreign hands, when covered by a transit pass which showed that the 2 1/2 percent commutation tax had been paid to the Imperial Customs. The issue was one of respect for transit passes on the part of provincial authorities. And, as all recognized, the difficulty lay in the fiscal and administrative set-up which made no provision for reimbursing provincial treasuries for this lost revenue. Old China Hands played up the seriousness of *likin* as a trade obstacle not only for intrinsic reasons; it was a good talking point in agitation for inland residence and the cry for internal reform.

By the fall of 1871, Wade was optimistic that the Foreign Office formula of quietly securing commercial concessions without full treaty revision would work. Particularly, he writes, "I am convinced that the Transit duty question will now be settled more satisfactorily than heretofore, and in the purely commercial part of the treaty we shall not have much to complain of." [20] Meanwhile, Hart had proceeded to Shanghai to look into the transit dues question. On the basis of his report, the Yamen at the end of January, 1872, proposed a set of rules regulating drawbacks and the transport of imports into the interior, the most significant aspect of which was the declaration that the native merchant would be authorized to take out transit certificates covering foreign goods.[21] Wade was sanguine: "If these Transit rules are adhered to and the new Rule affecting Chinese carriers of produce is brought into operation, there will be little to revise in any commercial treaties." Three months later he was still optimistic that the new transit rules "might secure that wider distribution of imports which is the foremost object of British trade." [22]

Hammond not only approved of these negotiations but hoped that solution of the transit dues questions would also resolve basic political issues, as it is "one of the utmost importance to the British manufacturing interest, as involving facilities for distributing by native agency alone, articles of British industry throughout the Provinces of the Empire, and so relieving British authorities from discussions and dispute on the subject." Lord Granville's optimism ran even higher: "If this is effected in a satisfactory manner, one of the great points sought to be obtained through the unratified treaty of 1869 will have been indirectly accomplished, and it may be that by a similar indirect process . . . another very important point, that of opening the Upper Yangtze to British trade, may be obtained." [23]

Conscious of the suspicion with which he was regarded by the mercantile community, Wade was determined to accept no transit arrangement until it met their approval. In July he had received a conciliatory letter from F. B. Johnson, Chairman of the Shanghai Chamber of Commerce, outlining mercantile complaints on *likin* and recommending, as a permanent arrangement, that a first and final payment of a commuted tax should free foreign goods from all further inland taxes, whether in foreign or native hands. Under such conditions, he believed, even an increased tariff might be acceptable to the merchants. Wade was jubilant and dispatched Edward B. Malet, Legation Secretary, to Shanghai to arrive at an accord.

Reporting on his conversations with Johnson (which were kept confidential and out of the press as "the Chinese get ideas of resistance from them"), Malet was optimistic. Provided guarantees were given that the transit pass would be respected in native as in foreign hands, the merchants were prepared to sanction the levy of strictly local *likin* at destination. Johnson's notes on Malet's dispatch to Wade [24] indicate that there was no such meeting of the minds as Malet pretended. The formal recognition of native right to transit certificates, contemplated in the new regulations, was so significant that Johnson was willing to give them a try provided (and this was the crux of the issue) the levy of destination *likin* was clearly defined and schedules of transit dues published with guarantees of enforcement. It was the uncertainty of the tax which made it obnoxious.

On September 8 Johnson talked with the leading merchants of Hongkong, who declared themselves ready to follow his lead.[25] A month later he wrote a cordial letter to Wade expressing satisfaction with the interest displayed by the legation in the question, but emphasizing that the new regulations were not acceptable, as they might be a Chinese trick for raising *likin* dues, and that without the sanctions suggested by Shanghai (publication of inland dues, etc.) the new code should be rejected.[26] The issues of "guarantees" had again become the obstacle and Wade was becoming convinced that no fundamental change would be effected so long as Britain continued its policy of self-denial.

That this was still policy was evident from Foreign Office reaction to France's preliminary negotiations on treaty revision taken up in 1873. Granville reiterated the views expressed in the Board of Trade letter of May, 1869. Specifically, he pointed out that the right of residence in the interior ought not to be pressed; and that while navigation of inland waters in foreign steamers was desirable, "H.M. Government would not feel justified in forcing it on China until the natives are more familiar with such agencies and Chinese merchants themselves are prepared to adopt it." [27] Even on transit dues the Government was not prepared to go beyond concessions which China would freely make. In forwarding this dispatch to Wade as a guide toward cooperation with his French colleague, Granville reminded him that

H.M. Government are firmly persuaded that those objects will be best attained by a policy of compromise and conciliation, and they believe that any attempt prematurely to force upon the Chinese government reforms and innovations for which they are not prepared, would be likely to lead not only to war, but to such a political and social disorganization of China as would more than counterbalance any nominal advantages that might be obtained.[28]

Given this attitude Wade was unable to make any further progress on transit arrangements in line with the Shanghai recommendations. The new regulations were published and variously enforced in the provinces; but foreign merchants would assume no obligations under them. Wade, like Alcock before him, could but cry out against the sisyphean difficulties of a Minister at Peking.

He may . . . be certain that unless the Chinese government believes that in one form or another coercion will be applied to it, his most reasonable requests will, as a rule, be met with delays and puerile explanations in which fact goes for little. The local press meanwhile, merchant and missionary alike feeding the cry, is clamorous for energetic action, its denunciations of ministerial inactivity being in turn denounced by the home press as inconsiderate and unchristian.[29]

The *likin* question dragged on throughout 1873 and 1874 without solution. The Foreign Office plan of obtaining mercantile concessions by "slow degrees" and cajoling was not working out. The optimistic Minister of 1872 was reporting two years later that "in commercial relations there is a going back. Sometimes in one province, sometimes in another. There are continually recurring attempts to bring the Import trade under the weight of abnormal taxation."[30]

As with *likin,* so with inland navigation. In January, 1872, the Associated Chambers of Commerce again memorialized for the opening of the Upper Yangtze to foreign steamers in order that "the richest and most industrious province of China (Szechuen) may be brought into almost direct communication with Europe."[31] Wade having reported progress on the *likin* negotiations at that time, the Foreign Office urged him to take up and dispose of this question as well.[32] He found the going hard. In September, 1872, Wade reported that the real objection to the opening of new ports and of introducing foreign steamers on the Upper Yangtze came from provincial authorities who feared diversion of revenues to the Imperial Customs.[33] Alternately, he exhibited optimism and dejection over the possibility of obtaining the desired concessions through quiet diplomacy. But by the end of 1873 he was convinced that he had been rolling stones uphill without the support either of the Foreign Office or of the mercantile community. Continued disappointment led him to repeated outbursts like the following in which he reveals the unique relation of Peking diplomacy to mercantile agitation:

The difficulty is simply this, that while it is rarely possible to get by negotiation from Chinese government any fresh concession, it will constantly tolerate the imposition of a change if this be not too rudely forced on their attention. . .

This indifference so long as a fact is hid and uncompromisingness whenever it is brought to light, are very embarrassing to a foreign minister whose countrymen, inspiring and inspired by a local press, are very ready to maintain that but for our government they could do much to their advantage in China that they are now hindered from doing.[34]

Nor was it possible, under that type of diplomacy, to secure the other major concessions—particularly in mining and railways—for which merchants had agitated during the Alcock treaty revision. Opportunities for investment in China were very limited, and, with the continued stagnation in trade, mercantile capital sought few outlets. In 1873, the Shanghai Share Market listed no more than two dozen stocks: one in banking (Hongkong and Shanghai Banking Corporation), four in steamship companies, two in dock companies, three in gas companies, and the remainder divided between insurance and miscellaneous, such as wharfs and tugs.[35]

The major mercantile ambition was to see the inauguration of the railway age in China, partly as a field for investment and partly as a means of penetrating internal markets. All overtures proved unsuccessful. An ambitious scheme to make railways popular by presenting the Emperor with a short line as a wedding gift got nowhere. Conceived by the engineering firm of Ransoness & Rapier and backed by the Duke of Sutherland and a long list of notables who subscribed fifty thousand pounds to the project [36] the "nuptial railway" gained more publicity than success. Great things were at first anticipated from the scheme. The Manchester Chamber of Commerce, invited to participate, resolved that "the successful carrying out of the scheme would be very advantageous to the commerce of the world." [37] Wade was given the delicate task of sounding out the Imperial household and found it "embarrassing, for it is all but certain that nothing can be done." [38] To the Duke of Sutherland Wade confided, after unofficial investigation, that the government of China would be "exceedingly unwilling to appear discourteous in the rejection of the very handsome offer made it, but it would prefer to wait its own time, and to use its own method in regard to any such undertaking as that contemplated." [39] And although Wade tried to console the prospective investors by intimating that the Chinese were already contemplating a line from Shanghai to Woosung, the subsequent history of this railway fiasco indicated that the period of concessions was not at hand.

Jardine, Matheson & Co. had quietly proceeded to buy up land between Shanghai and Woosung without revealing to the Chinese authorities that they proposed to lay a railway line on the route. The line was

completed as far as Kangwan in June, 1876; the following August a
Chinese was run over by the locomotive, the local authorities protested,
and the Chinese Government took over the railway only to tear up the
rails and remove them, along with the rolling stock, to rust on a Formosa beach. It was a disheartening affair.[40]

Similarly, an attempt to reopen the mining question made little headway. In February, 1873, Mr. Edward Ackroyd, President of the Hali-
fax Chamber of Commerce, asked the Foreign Office whether the
Government would do anything to provide for the safe investment of
English capital and scientific appliances for the working of mines in
China.[41] The joker, of course, was "safe"; and, as the *London & China
Telegraph* ruefully remarked, any such concessions required the "judicious use of that diplomacy which has been described as being pressure
without force." Sir Rutherford Alcock, now retired, wrote to *The
Times* [42] that where concessions were not now embodied in treaties
"obstacles have been insurmountable and not to be overcome by any
diplomacy without force in the background"; and that since the Tientsin
Treaty was ratified no force had been brought to bear on the Peking
court except in isolated cases of local coercion. He blamed the impasse
on failure to accept the minor concessions of the Alcock Convention
and mercantile impatience.

> But one of the greatest obstacles to any satisfactory negotiations in China
> whether as regards the working of coal mines or any other advantages, lies in
> the impatience of the British merchant to obtain everything he desires from the
> Chinese and all that at once. He assumes that the advantages conferred on the
> Chinese by foreign trade are sufficient in themselves to entitle it to exemption
> from any fiscal burdens or limitations in an administrative sense beyond pay-
> ment of the low tariff rate. . . .

It was, he concluded, a day of "small results" favorable only to gradual
reform.

In reply, William Davison, formerly agent of the P & O Steamship
Co. at Shanghai, asserted that "unless pressure is put upon the Chinese
officials they will not give way; that pressure should be applied, and war
threatened in case of refusal. . . . A war with China would not stop our
trade. I was a resident in that country during several wars, and the
general opinion among the merchants was that trade was better then
than at any other time." [43] It was, of course, the old dispute warmed
over. Wade, realizing that he could make little headway, had "declined
to invite the Yamen to consider the various propositions" of private
firms for coal mining concessions.[44] The issue of coal mining, like that of

railways and steam navigation and transit dues arrangement, gradually faded from diplomatic consideration after 1873.

A strange apathy, lasting for almost twenty years, descended upon China affairs after that time. The major issue, to which all minor disputes returned, was whether the Government could be induced to abandon the policy of self-denial in the use of pressure and that, in turn, was dependent on repudiation of the Board of Trade verdict. Though Wade was vilified by the mercantile press, it was evident that he was but carrying out home policy. With the fall of Gladstone and the accession of the "Ministry of All the Opportunities" under Disraeli in 1874, there was a renascent hope that vigor in foreign affairs would return to Downing Street. "Shanghai" wrote to the *London & China Express* [45] that the advent of the new Government should be the occasion for a change in Anglo-Chinese policy. The last Government had been deaf to pleas for a "real opening of China" and the redress of grievances. Concessions should be pressed with the understanding that 'it is useless for an English Minister or Envoy to attempt negotiation with the Chinese unless he is backed by a respectable naval force." He expressed the silent thought of the treaty ports that "the English government is a greater hindrance to the opening of China . . . than the Chinese government. . . . Remove the English authorities, and I would undertake to navigate any of the inland waters by steam without molestation." But hopes of a change in policy were to prove illusory. Lord Derby's tenure at the Foreign Office saw no departure from the policy of Clarendon and Granville.

At Peking, France and Germany postponed treaty revision, while Wade became reconciled to the policy of outwaiting the patient Chinese. Only the mercantile press would sometimes grumble, unheard. Discussing the transit dues question on March 8, 1875, the *London & China Telegraph* recalled that the transit pass system had once been regarded as the infallible means of pushing goods into the interior. And it would have been if given a fair trial; but thanks to the evasion of treaty obligations by the Chinese and the "supineness of that officer who in bitter mockery is called the Chief Superintendent of Trade," the British merchant had been deprived of his opportunities. The transit question was again being used as a scapegoat.

From 1874 depression and stagnation in the China trade appeared to be no longer temporary. In the autumn of 1874 the Hongkong and Shanghai Banking Corporation reported a loss to its shareholders and in 1875 passed its dividend for the second time in Shanghai history. Press and shareholders were indignant, demanding a radical change in

bank management. That same year reports of fraud and embezzlement
by "trusted servants" of the larger commercial firms were becoming
alarmingly frequent.[46] Due to close social relations between Europeans
in China peculation was often hushed but cases were becoming too frequent to escape notice. Particularly shocking was the reported embezzlement by A. F. Chambers of a large sum from Jardine, Matheson &
Co. This "epidemic of failures" spread to home firms in the China trade,
the failure of Collie & Co. of Manchester being the most outstanding.

Was this, then, the end of the China dream? Why had the mercantile
promise remained unfulfilled? Economists might argue that "the economic self-sufficiency of China was perhaps the most formidable barrier which we had as yet encountered in our carrier of industrial and
commercial expansion." [47] But to the Old China Hands it was still those
political obstacles which a Foreign Office, misled and uninformed, refused to remove by the sword.

In the summer of 1875 the *London & China Telegraph* [48] ran a series
of articles reviewing the causes which have reduced a traffic "once most
profitable to a position of unsoundness, speculativeness and unprofitable-
ness." The argument was familiar. The Treaty of Tientsin had failed
to remove internal barriers to trade and the Alcock Convention had been
rejected for the same reason. The China trade had never been overesti-
mated! It had been strangled by *likin* and practical exclusion from the
interior. In contrast to external developments, such as the opening of
the Suez Canal and increased capital, stood internal restrictions. As
a result, the trade was overdone, leading to failures.

As a result, too, capital was driven back upon itself, leading to over-
investment—and unprofitability—in local enterprises such as docks,
banks, and wharves. "Were it possible, as in other countries, to make
investments in roads, canals, mines, redundant capital would find an
outlet and would not be forced to seek investment in a few limited articles
of trade, or be a loss to the banks and the merchants." Improvement
could only come with the removal of restrictions. Given the vast potentialities of the China market for trade and enterprise, the *Telegraph*
urged the Chambers of Commerce in Great Britain to agitate for a real
revision of treaties by 1878. But the Chambers remained apathetic and
the Government gave no sign of being ready to embark on an imperialist
policy in China.

The apathy of home opinion was broken only by the phenomenal
interest of British commercial circles in various schemes for opening
a back door into China by means of an overland railway from Rangoon
to Yunnan. Bare of almost all other references to China affairs from

1870 to 1890, the records of the principal Chambers exhibit continued interest in tapping the southwestern China trade through such a project. By 1880, about one hundred memorials, some of staggering proportions, had been submitted to the Government, principally in favor of the Sprye route. Nor was there a slackening of interest in the eighties, when Archibald Colquhoun and Holt S. Hallett took over where Captain Richard Sprye had left off. Partly this phenomenal interest is due to the convincing efforts of their sponsors, the explorer-publicists who foresaw Anglo-French rivalry in southwestern China years before it became an issue in international affairs. But, principally, it is safe to conclude from the evidence in mercantile documents, the Chambers saw in these projects another China vision, a substitute for the China dream which spoke of the vast opportunities hidden in Yunnan and Szechuen. It was through the back door that Eldorado would be tapped.

This interest, it should be noted, antedated by a dozen years the first French attempts to explore the Red River route into Yunnan. It was on April 10, 1858, that Captain Richard Sprye, retired Indian Army officer, having received no response to his first letter, addressed Lord Malmesbury for the second time on "the benefit and expediency of your now obtaining, by treaty with China, freedom, at all times, of overland trade and travel with the interior of that country, across its Burman frontier." [49] It was not French, but Russian and American, competition which he feared; Russia from the northwest, America across the Pacific.

Now, My Lord, while those our rivals for the *future* trade with China, are thus making their approaches towards China's interior at a point by which *our* commerce can never travel to it, I appeal to your Lordship, as England's Foreign Minister . . . not to neglect in any present treaty with China, the route which I bring to your notice in the southwestern extremity of that empire, by which *our* commerce can be made successfully to compete for all future in the interior of that country.

His scheme envisaged survey of a railway route from Rangoon to Shuey-guen, along the Salween River to Takau Ferry, thence through Kiang-tung and Kiang-hung (in the semi-independent Shan States) to Esmok (Szumao) on the Yunnan frontier.

In reply, the Foreign Office acknowledged Sprye's interest, adding the caustic comment that the China trade is sufficient to employ all nations without any cause for jealousy.[50] But Sprye was not to be dismissed in his fashion. A long, voluminous, and, for the Foreign Office, aggravating correspondence ensued. And, with the enlistment of mercantile support in 1860, Sprye forced Whitehall to take him seriously. His early arguments are striking, for they anticipated almost everything that was later to appear in the Blue Books. On May 8, 1858, he wrote "on the necessity of a British-Pegue and Central China Railway to compete with the short route the United States now possess of 18 days only from their Pacific Ocean Ports"; his route, he argued, would be instrumental in securing to "our Manufacturers and Merchants, who *are* the main source of our prosperity in peace as our power in war, a continuous fair share of general commerce with Eastern Asiatic countries." [51] In this letter the main rival was "America's monopolising intent" bent on "realising Columbus' dream of reaching China by a western route." On June 7 he stressed the need for reaching the Yangtze, "for the river once so commercially attained by an unbroken iron road from our port of Rangoon would give us a position over the interior of the celestial Empire which would be, both in commercial and military points of view, in all but its proximity to Pekin, equal to the commanding position into which Russia is working herself on the North of China." [52]

In an attempt to escape Sprye's fulminations the Foreign Office moved to transfer his correspondence first to the Board of Trade and then to the India Office, but without avail. Sprye kept bombarding the Foreign Office with warnings of Russian designs in the North and pointing out the military importance of his railway as well as its "commercial wisdom." [53] Meanwhile he approached the Chambers of Commerce, several members of Parliament, and Baring Brothers, all of whom exhibited some interest. With this promised support he again addressed the Foreign Office at the end of 1858, emphasizing that he and his sons, who had organized the project, were not "railway projectors" backed by capitalists but were interested in a Burma railway as *a great national work.* [54]

To enlist the aid of the commercial public, Sprye published a pamphlet on "The British and China Railway" addressed to the "manufacturers and merchants" and containing a reprint of his letters to the Foreign Office. Interest was building up, but the Foreign Office remained cool. With the advent of Lord John Russell, Sprye renewed his plea for quick action, adding the suggestion that the overland route and the opening of Esmok (Szumao), its terminus, be incorporated in the Chinese treaty. Again, he called upon British predominance in Yunnan to redress the balance of Russian gains in the North and French designs in the South.[55] The Foreign Office remained quietly irritated, while the India Office was definitely hostile. For the benefit of the new Foreign Secretary, an unidentified hand in the Foreign Office prepared a précis of the Sprye correspondence, followed by the minute: "Capt. Sprye is a

visionary who indulges in the wildest notions and consumes an enormous
quantity of Foolscap—there is a certain degree of interest attaching to
his schemes but they are impracticable." [56] Captain Sprye and son, however, continued to pour their polemics and warnings into the dispatch
cases; the letters piled up with only formal acknowledgment from the
Foreign Office.[57]

Meanwhile, Sprye's pamphlet had attracted the attention of press and
commercial bodies. A leader in the Glasgow *Daily Mail* (January 11,
1860) and another in the *Sheffield Independent* advocated the Sprye
route as a means of opening China at a point where Peking would find
it difficult to interfere. And, despite Foreign Office irritation,[58] Sprye
captured a real lion when *The Times* gave him not only its notice but
its approval.[59] Sprye circulated the press notices along with his pamphlets. Finally, in the summer of 1860, some of the most prominent
Chambers of Commerce in England adopted the Sprye route as their
own and flooded Lord Palmerston and the Foreign Office with lengthy
memorials favoring an overland route through Burma. It was an interest
destined to endure throughout the century; even in the days of widespread apathy to China affairs, mercantile ambitions turned to the
Burma route as the vivid hope of realizing the China dream.

The Manchester Chamber of Commerce memorial of July 12, 1860,
was the first of a long series favoring the Sprye route and urging that its
terminus at Esmok be made a treaty port.[60] The Huddersfield Chamber,
assuming leadership of the Sprye movement, emphasized the important
commercial advantages expected from the opening of a road or railway
through Burma to Yunnan.[61] Leeds, Liverpool, Bradford and Halifax
sent memorials in the same vein. On the advice of the India Office, the
Foreign Office curtly replied that the project "does not seem feasible."
Hammond, irritated, added the minute: "This is evidently got up by
Capt. Sprye." When the Leeds Chamber, not to be put off, suggested
that the plan to open Esmok as a treaty port be pressed, Hammond demurred, suggesting to the Foreign Secretary that "it seems to me that as
we could not protect trade at the City of Esmok, it would not be expedient to raise any question on this subject with the Chinese Govt." [62]

Hammond prepared an extensive reply to the Leeds Chamber in this
sense, stating that "much inconvenience might arise from introducing
so novel a question as that of access to a city on the Western frontier of
China; even if the Chinese Government acquiesced, it would be impossible to afford adequate protection to British trade at so inland a city or
to exercise due control over British subjects." [63] To Lord Russell he
suggested that this reply be published so as to "put a stop to the agita-

tion which the Spryes are getting up in furtherance of their long cherished scheme to get employment," but the Foreign Secretary demurred,
regarding the agitation as "harmless."

Backed by *The Times* and the Chambers, Sprye also enlisted the support of the *London & China Telegraph* [64] and ran a series of articles in
which the opposition of the Government of India to his plan was first exposed as the major obstacle. For political reasons the Government of
India favored the alternate route to Yunnan, running through Bhamo
and Momein (Tangyueh) to Talifu, which later came to be known
popularly as the Bhamo route. An expedition under Dr. Clement Williams from Rangoon to Upper Burma in 1862 was the first of several
expeditions in the Bhamo and Salween areas—all, the merchants
charged, pointedly ignoring the Sprye route. By December, 1862, the
India Office informed the Foreign Office that the Sprye route was not
feasible and that if communication were to be established it would probably follow an alternate road. The Foreign Office concurred.[65]

But they were reckoning without the tenacity of Sprye and the exuberance of mercantile circles in Britain. Memorials kept pouring in
throughout the next several years, the Chambers bitterly charging the
India Office with failure to include the full story in the papers presented to Parliament. Sprye claimed that the Chief Commissioner,
Phayre, favored his scheme,[66] while the Government of India maintained
that the Williams expedition of 1864 up the Salween had demonstrated
that the Sprye route was both geographically and politically not feasible.
The official view maintained that the best route to be explored would
be that already known and employed by traders—up the Irrawaddy
River and then the land route from Bhamo, the route later followed by
the Burma Road.

Mercantile agitation was renewed in 1866 with some success, led by
the Huddersfield and Liverpool Chambers. Huddersfield emphasized
the importance of taking up the matter at that time.

The activity and recent development of French commerce and the growing competition of French with English Manufactures in Neutral Markets render this
consideration at present one of greatly increased importance. . . . The dis-
locations which have taken place in existing markets through continental and
American disturbances impress your memorialists with the conviction that it is
more than ever necessary to encourage and provide for new markets for the
productions of British industry and that as regards our Eastern Empire
the policy of development by means of new roads and communications in lieu of
the ancient policy of war and annexations becomes constantly more manifest
as the true policy of the country.[67]

Lord Stanley succeeded in shifting the matter to the India Office,[68] which was to prove fortunate for the proponents of the scheme. For with the advent of Lord Cranborne to the India Office the original bitter hostility ceased despite the continued opposition of the Government of India. On September 29, 1866, Cranborne forwarded the fourth memorial of the Liverpool East India and China Association to the Government of India and, impressed by recent mercantile deputations, ordered an immediate survey "to ascertain the best route for a road or railway between the frontier of British Burma and Western China," with particular reference to the Sprye route.[69]

Despite objections from India, on official and political grounds, Lord Cranborne pressed the survey, citing the "strong opinion, also, expressed by the manufacturing and mercantile population of the North." Early in 1867 a surveying party, under Captains J. M. Williams and Luard of the Calcutta Railway Department, surveyed two routes, including that proposed by Sprye, up to the limits of British territory, a distance of 250 miles, half way to Kiang-hung.[70] The results were variously interpreted, but that was destined to be the last official action on the Sprye route. Cranborne, so the merchants claimed, had been prepared to go ahead with the survey beyond the frontier but his successor, Sir Stafford Northcote, dropped the project.

While home opinion was concentrating on the Sprye route, the mercantile press of the treaty ports was more closely concerned with the possibilities of the Bhamo route. It was hoped that this would encourage the opening of the upper waters of the Yangtze, while the more direct route from Rangoon was discouraged as tending to compete with the coast. With Government support and the concurrence of the Indian authorities, an exploration of the Bhamo trade route under Major E.B. Sladen, Political Agent at Mandalay, was organized to proceed from Bhamo to Yunnan and, if possible, continue on to Canton. Alcock was afraid that the Mahometan Insurgents (Panthays) would create difficulties and although he succeeded in obtaining the approval of Peking for the expedition he realized how little authority the Central Government exercised in its outlying provinces.[71] He was opposed to the whole idea and differed bitterly with the Hongkong *China Mail* (July 1, 1868) which accused him of putting obstacles in the path of the Sladen mission. Alcock believed that "by nothing short of force will such a trade route be maintained open." [72] The Sladen expedition achieved a limited success, reaching Talifu [73] but being forced to turn back, owing to native hostility.

In sober fact, the British Government was largely indifferent to the entire matter of opening a back door to China, for it could create nothing but difficulties and trade benefits were doubtful. Whatever action was taken was due almost exclusively to mercantile agitation at home. Almost—for the Government of India was also interested in the strategic possibilities of joining India with China through Bhamo, a route with far less commercial value than that from Rangoon to Yunnan. The number of Parliamentary Papers on the subject grew throughout the sixties, stimulated by mercantile demands. And the memorials favoring the Sprye route kept piling up. A note of resentment at government inaction began to creep into them.

In April, 1869, the Huddersfield Chamber submitted a memorial of staggering proportions to Gladstone reviewing the history of the Sprye route and charging previous Governments with criminal neglect of commercial interests. In effect, Huddersfield maintained that British goods had failed to reach the vast markets of the Western provinces through Canton and Shanghai; and that these could be reached only by an overland railway from Rangoon. It was charged that political opposition was sabotaging the only practicable route, that of Sprye. Huddersfield complained that its woolens were losing the American and European markets, and that the potential markets of Western China must be called in to redress the balance.[74]

An excerpt from the Liverpool Chamber of Commerce Semi-Annual Report of August, 1869 provides a contemporary account of mercantile interest in the Sprye route:

At sundry times within the last nine years this Chamber, in common with many other commercial bodies of the country, has addressed by memorial various departments of the Government in favour of a survey of the direct route through the Shan States, from Rangoon to Kiang-hung, in Western China, on the upper Kamboja river. . . .

Whether Capt. Sprye be right or wrong as to the particular route which should be followed, the object he has in view is recognized very generally to be worthy of earnest consideration and your council continue to watch the question, therefore, with unabated interest. They have, for the eighth time, memorialized the Government in favour of the enterprise, praying that orders may be given for the resumption of the survey of the route from Rangoon from the point at which it left off in 1867 to . . . Kiang-hung; that conduct of the survey be entrusted to the direction of a railway engineer of eminence in England; that the Government of India be instructed to aid him; that an envoy be sent to the King of Burmah to give him assurance that peaceful commerce with the West of China is the sole object of the expedition and to obtain his cooperation; and drawing attention to the representations made by the Chambers at Wakefield and Huddersfield in their memorials of November 1868 and April 1869, respectively.[75]

Despite this pressure, neither the Sprye route nor the Bhamo route made much headway. The *North China Herald*,[76] which favored the latter, castigated the Gladstone Government for its failure to take steps "to push the Burmese way" to Yunnan. "We presume Mr. Gladstone's Cabinet finds relaxation from the strain of intense Liberalism at Home, in the profound respect they pay to conservatism in China." Indifference would have been a more accurate word than conservatism.

By the end of 1870, when interest in other aspects of China affairs had begun to wane (as noted above), mercantile circles again concentrated their attention on promoting the Burma-Yunnan railway project. At a special Council meeting of the Associated Chambers of Commerce [77] Thomas Ormerod, representing the Halifax Chamber, moved that a deputation be sent to urge on the Duke of Argyll, Secretary for India, "the immediate completion of the survey of the route from Rangoon to Kiang-hung, already partly surveyed and reported on." Ormerod pointed out that during the past ten years more than sixty memorials had been presented by British Chambers favoring the Sprye project, but that the situation had become even more pressing due to the need for "new markets for our productions" which could only be found in the vast Empire of China. The Bradford Chamber had already prepared an elaborate report on Szechuen and Yunnan which concluded that this market could not be tapped from Shanghai. Only the Sprye route appeared feasible. The resolution was seconded by William Morris, also of Halifax, who referred to the hundred million customers of Western China as the largest untapped market. W. R. Haigh of Huddersfield pointed out that the Bhamo route, favored by official quarters, involved more political complications and greater physical hazards than the one Sprye proposed. Opposition was vocally expressed only by Jacob Behrens of Bradford who inquired whether Halifax wished "to push our trade at the point of the bayonet?" Because of the slim majority favoring the deputation, the chairman ruled that action would be postponed.

The difference, as was evident from subsequent meetings, was not over the vast potentialities of the market in Western China, but solely over the route by which it could be tapped. Under the leadership of the Bradford Chamber, the Associated Chambers turned its attention to opening the upper waters of the Yangtze [78] but a strong minority reiterated the view that a Rangoon-Yunnan railway was still the sole practicable route, with which the "crumbs of a few added miles on the Yangtze" could not be compared. Sprye, who was present at the meeting, recounted his discouraging path since 1858, and insisted that his route was the only way of gaining the fabulous markets of China and of countering American and Russian designs.

Through the, pressure of Halifax and Huddersfield, the Associated Chambers of Commerce were soon won over to public espousal of the Sprye project. Halifax, in the summer of 1872, had directly petitioned the House of Commons for a Select Committee to examine the whole question, a move which the *London & China Telegraph* wrote "ought to make Earl Granville blush at Osborne, and even Mr. Gladstone's ears tingle in far Harwarden." [79] The petition did not appear to move the Government but continued agitation had its effect on the other Chambers. Finally, at a special meeting of the Associated Chambers of Commerce held on September 25, 1872 [80] the resolution was voted that "the Association memorialize H.M. Government to complete the survey from Rangoon to Kiang-hung and to ascertain generally the best means of opening up communications for the purpose of establishing commercial relations with Southwestern China." It was carried unanimously. An elaborate memorial was prepared, addressed to Gladstone,[81] and presented to the Duke of Argyll by personal deputation at the India Office on February 28, 1873. Its premise is instructive, for it indicates the drive behind sustained mercantile interest in a Burma route throughout the century.

That although Great Britain has had commercial intercourse with China for a very long period, yet British goods have only been exported to that Empire in very limited quantities compared with its vast extent and numerous population, because those goods have only been sent through the ports of a very distant seaboard of China.

It was a new twist to the ancient folklore. The Duke of Argyll, while admitting a *prima facie* case, nevertheless contended that the Sprye scheme faced difficulties "much greater than the merchants of England supposed" and in any event objected to treating it as an Indian question. He revealed that he had the previous week received application from some "London men" who contemplated a railway from Rangoon to China, but via Mandalay, and intimated that the Government might prefer the Irrawaddy route, a prediction which was to bear fruit twenty years later. The delegation, dissatisfied, approached Gladstone personally several days later, but received no encouragement. The merchants then took the advice of Halifax and appealed directly to Parliament. At the Cardiff meeting on September 23, 1873, the Associated Chambers voted Ormerod's resolution that a Select Committee of the Commons inquire into the various trade routes on the southwestern approach. The Yunnan rebellion (Panthays) having been crushed and rumors of French encroachment in the south and Russian in the northwest having become disquieting, Ormerod insisted that delay would be fatal. "Were we to stand and allow these two nations to take from us what was our own?" [82]

Mercantile agitation would have continued to run its fruitless course had it not been for the advent of Lord Salisbury to the India Office in Disraeli's Ministry of 1874. For Lord Salisbury was the same Lord Cranborne who had sparked the partial survey of the Sprye route in 1867 and the only official ever to exhibit favorable interest. It was, therefore, with great rejoicing that the Halifax Chamber was able to report to the other Chambers that Lord Salisbury had, on April 18, 1874, instructed the Government of India to complete the survey. Huddersfield enjoined the Government to entrust the job to "engineers of repute"; while the Associated Chambers exchanged congratulations, the Chairman, Sampson S. Lloyd, remarking that "we seem to be reaping some benefit from Sir Louis Mallet's presence at the India Office; it shows the advantage of having someone to represent the interests of commerce there." [83]

It was all a sad misunderstanding, and the proponents of the Sprye route were in for a rude awakening. Salisbury's instructions, though they mentioned the Rangoon-Yunnan route, were sufficiently flexible to allow the Government of India to disregard the Sprye alternative entirely and proceed with its own pet project, the exploration and survey of the Bhamo route, now that the Panthay rebellion had been crushed. In fact, even before the end of the rebellion, the Government of India (whether or not influenced by Calcutta merchants as British merchants charged) was so eager to continue where the Sladen Mission had left off that they flirted with the idea of extending recognition to the Panthays.[84] T. T. Cooper, the explorer, was even dispatched to Talifu to investigate the situation.

In any event, as the Panthay troubles were being resolved in 1873, the Government of India approached Wade to ascertain whether Peking could be induced to open the Bhamo-Yunnan route when Talifu was recaptured, nor were they discouraged by Wade's lack of enthusiasm.[85] The first concrete suggestion for a British exploratory mission to Yunnan via the Bhamo route was made by the Political Agent at Mandalay on June 23, 1873, and taken up by the Chief Commissioner of British Burma, who pointed out that the French appear to have "entered upon a career of direct rivalry" with the British and were attempting to supplant Burmese peddlers (carrying British goods) with Annamese peddlers (carrying French goods) along the Mekong valley.[86] The province of Tonking bordering on the Shan State of Kiang-hung, tributary of the King of Burma, French intrigue to counter the British position in Burma was to be anticipated. Imperial interests thus coincided with strictly commercial ambitions in pressing for the Burma road; the Government of India, however, opted for the Bhamo route.

In London Lord Salisbury took up the matter more on the lines desired by the Associated Chambers, stressing that the opening of a Burma route to the "populous districts" of Western China appeared to offer most favorable prospects for the introduction of British manufactures.[87] The Foreign Office was asked to instruct Wade to cooperate in a prospective Anglo-Burmese Mission to Talifu. Neither the Foreign Office nor Wade was too enthusiastic but agreed to obtain Peking's consent and assurances of protection for the mission.

At the same time Lord Salisbury sent instructions to the Government of India to adopt measures for reopening commercial intercourse between China and Burma by means of a continued survey of the Sprye route to Kiang-hung. But it was left to the discretion of that Government to choose an alternate route or conduct an entirely different survey. The Government of India took advantage of the discretionary nature of these instructions, shelved the Sprye project, and proceeded with its own plans for an Anglo-Burmese Mission from Bhamo to Talifu.

On June 13, 1874, the Viceroy telegraphed the Foreign Office that the mission was to start in November and asked for passports from the Peking Government: the proposed route was from Mandalay to Bhamo to Momein to Talifu, with the mission consisting of three English officers accompanied by a Burmese agent.[88] Wade, so instructed, admitted that "something can be done to secure the expedition admission under Passports within the frontier of China" but reiterated his skepticism as to the commercial possibilities flowing from the mission.[89] In fact, Wade found to his surprise that Peking was not only willing to grant passports to the mission entering from Burma, but would agree to the proposition that a British consul, Augustus Margary, be allowed to journey up the Yangtze and meet the mission from the Chinese side.[90] Arrangements were so made. On the 17th of January, 1875, Margary arrived in Bhamo to await the delayed Anglo-Burmese mission under Colonel Horace A. Browne. His return journey was to prove fatal to himself and postpone Burma road projects for years. Scouting ahead of the mission as it approached the Chinese frontier, Margary and his party were ambushed and massacred at Manwyne, near Momein, on February 21, 1875.[91]

The "apathy" toward China affairs of which treaty port residents complained nowhere manifested itself in more striking fashion than in the almost lukewarm reception on the part of home opinion toward the Margary murder. Old China Hands could well feel betrayed. For the Margary affair, on the face of it, was a natural talking point for a reversal of the policy of conciliation. What better proof that the bellicose merchants had been right, that China would never reform through gradualism? Where public opinion might not be aroused over the prosaic questions of commercial revision or of the massacre of Frenchmen at Tientsin, the murder of a British Representative by unruly natives should not have failed to stir the hearts of Englishmen. What was more, all the ambitions of Manchester and Halifax and Huddersfield to penetrate the fabulous markets of Yunnan had been dealt a shattering blow: and would not even Cobdenites be driven to cry for a gunboat? Moreover, it was not Clarendon and the pacifist Gladstone with whom one now had to deal; Disraeli at No. 10, Derby at the Foreign Office, and Salisbury at the India Office could surely be trusted to be jealous of British prestige. Could not all these forces be mobilized to force a reversal of policy and could not the occasion be employed to capture all the concessions which had been denied in 1869?

Nothing of the kind happened. Even the strong stand taken by Wade in the early negotiations over the Margary affair failed to satisfy the Old China Hands. At one time Wade spoke of withdrawing the Legation from Peking if satisfaction were not given—and quickly. Throughout, he warned Prince Kung that not only indemnity and a speedy trial for the criminals was at issue, but the very basis of the Chinese Government's authority in the provinces. If Peking could not or would not act, foreign powers would be compelled to take things into their own hands in everything ranging from redress of grievances to enforcement of *likin* regulations.[92] He won his main points and future negotiation proceeded without major obstacles, resulting in the solution embodied in the Chefoo Convention, which foreigners regarded as high-handed and mercantile circles as another betrayal. It was not at all what the latter had hoped.

"Shanghai" told the local newspaper readers on April 24 that the Margary murder had been instigated in Peking, that nothing could be expected from Wade, and that the entire affair was a "just retribution" for disgraceful British conduct at the time of Tientsin. "How long are we to endure this state of things and treat China as though she were civilized?"[93] His was a voice crying in the wilderness, despite the general belief in the treaty ports that "Disraeli will uphold the honor of his country." For, from the very start, Old China Hands were disappointed in Disraeli's placid assurance that Wade had been instructed "to call upon the Chinese Government to make a strict investigation into the circumstances."[94] Was that all? If so, mourned the *London & China Telegraph,* it was "an answer fraught with serious danger to our prestige in the East."[95] How different, it sighed, would Palmerston's reply have been. While *The Times*[96] hoped that the Margary affair would not result in abandonment of efforts to reach China from Burma, the *London & China Telegraph* [97] suggested that the occasion warranted an armed reconnaissance from the Chinese side with the Shan States and the King of Burma being brought "under our control." In fact, the organ of the China merchants charged, it was the "laisser-faire, masterly inactivity policy and refusal of public opinion to countenance annexation" which had worsened the British position in the Far East.

Public opinion, indeed, remained singularly undisturbed. An anonymous letter even reached the *Telegraph* [98] containing a plea for tolerance of Chinese weaknesses. Alcock told the Royal Geographical Society at its meeting on March 22, 1875, that political difficulties stood in the way of trade routes to Western China and that it was not the duty of H.M. Government to "open roads for trade to these places." When Mr. T. G. Grosvenor was sent on a mission to Yunnan to investigate and insure the punishment of officials responsible for the Margary murder,[99] British opinion was content that honor had been satisfied. The *Pall Mall Gazette* [100] was certain that the inquiry would be conducted in good faith, but insisted that the "total removal of impediments on the Chinese frontier to Yunnan to the passage of our traders" should be secured. "It may cost us some display of force to obtain all that we may rightly exact; but we had better exact this alternative than lower ourselves in the eyes of an arrogant and treacherous government."

This was unusually strong talk at home as was the passage in the Queen's Speech [101] promising that "no effort shall be spared to secure the punishment" of those implicated in the Margary affair. But, as everyone realized, there was more rhetoric than policy implied. For, as the *London & China Telegraph,* in its discussion of "Prestige and the Margary Murder," [102] inquired: "Is H.M. Government prepared to go to war with China to secure this?" It feared not; and yet nothing short of "one of our 'little wars'—so much ridiculed, but which nevertheless are indispensable—will suffice," since British prestige had fallen so low in the East.

The true temper of the country was revealed in *The Times'* leader on September 15, 1875. Welcoming the first news of a full settlement at Peking—providing for indemnity, opening of western trade routes and regulation of inland taxes—*The Times* proceeded to scold those Englishmen residing in China who, in this as in other affairs, had been far from impartial. Too often they go to China with a mind that would exasperate a people less vain than the Chinese, acting as if the chief end of the native was to minister to the demands of British commerce. "Our traders and even our diplomatists too often sum up all the resources of negotiations with the Chinese in one word—firmness. That word . . . is

often merely another name for undisguised dictation." Some had urged
the sending of a military force to cut the Gordian knot of the Margary
affair; but the consequences were not acceptable to the British people.
For, "if we shatter Chinese authority we shall have the responsibility
of setting up a substitute. . . . We are not in the mood to undertake
. . . another India."

In actual fact, although the merchants were not satisfied with the
Chefoo settlement of the Margary affair, British diplomacy exhibited
more "firmness," even impatience, with Chinese dilatoriness during its
negotiation than had been the practice since before the days of Elgin.
With the full approval of the Foreign Office, Wade not only secured
rigorous conditions of indemnity and punishment of offenders but seized
the occasion to clear up some of the outstanding commercial problems,
particularly *likin,* and Lord Derby expressed his belief that the draft
Chefoo Convention "will not only secure a full and searching inquiry
into the attack on the Browne mission but will lead to improvement of
Anglo-Chinese relations." [103] It had taken more persuasion than usual
to secure these results and the Foreign Office excused this limited withdrawal from traditional policy by pointing out that

H.M. Government in their anxiety not to press too hardly on the Chinese
Government or endanger its stability have in many instances abstained from
insisting on the full satisfaction of their claims, and, although possessing the
means of enforcing them to the fullest extent have forborne from using these
means, in the hope that the Government of China would gradually awake to a
clearer sense of its duties towards foreign powers.

This hope had not been realized and certain guarantees had therefore
been demanded on this occasion.

The Chefoo Convention of September 13, 1876 [104] was Britain's
second attempt at treaty revision in seven years, and encountered a
reaction remarkably parallel but far less intense than that which had
defeated the Alcock Convention. In accordance with Foreign Office
instructions, which Wade had followed in the extensive negotiations lasting more than a year, the Chefoo Convention addressed itself not only to
settlement of the Yunnan affair (Section I), but to the conditions of
diplomatic intercourse between China and Britain (Section II) and the
solution of certain commercial questions, particularly *likin* (Section III).
Section I called for issuance of a Memorial expressing apology for the
outrage, payment of an indemnity, and promotion of frontier trade between Burma and Yunnan. The Section on official intercourse required
China to issue a "code of etiquette" on treatment of foreign officials,

including relations between consular officers and Chinese officials at the ports, and defined procedure in mixed cases (without, however, setting up a mixed court).

Mercantile interest, of course, concentrated on Section III, for which Wade had labored so long. Under it, foreign settlements were defined as areas of exemption from *likin* (with the implication that it could be levied outside this area); as *quid pro quo*, Ichang, Wuhu, Wenchow, and Pakhoi were opened as treaty ports, with Chungking to follow when steamers had access to it (implemented in 1890), and six landing places on the Yangtze were made ports of call for native craft only. A new opium regime was set up under which *likin* would be collected by the Customs Inspectorate at the same time as the tariff in order to stop smuggling and ensure some measure of control. Finally, China agreed that transit duty certificates covering imports would be respected in native as in foreign hands; but that on exports certificates would commute inland taxes only for bona fide British-owned property. *Likin*, as such, was not declared illegal.

The opposition of the other Powers to the Chefoo Convention was even more widespread than had been the case during revision in 1869. The representatives of Russia, Germany, France, the United States and Spain united in a joint memorandum objecting to Britain's unilateral action on the settlement of diplomatic relations, particularly as it affected relations between foreign consuls and provincial officials.[105] It was charged that Britain had split previous foreign cooperation at Peking. In addition, France backed the British mercantile view that the commercial concessions granted did not balance the disadvantages to be expected from the new *likin* arrangement.

Ratification was again held up and opportunity was offered for another mercantile campaign to defeat "partial revision." But, although opposition reached respectable proportions, it did not match, either in unanimity or enthusiasm, the experience of 1870. Again it was London which served as the center of agitation. A London Committee of the Shanghai Chamber of Commerce was formed under the chairmanship of Alexander Michie, formerly a partner of Lindsay & Co., and included representatives of Matheson & Co. and Dent, Palmer & Co., as well as F. D. Barnes, who had for years been active in mercantile politics in Shanghai. By previous arrangement the Shanghai Chamber of Commerce sent its London Committee a letter, dated June 15, 1877,[106] opposing the Chefoo Convention both on political and economic grounds. Politically, settlement of the Yunnan affair was termed "inadequate" because it provided no guarantees against future anti-foreign action by mandarins. But the principal objection was to Section III. While welcoming the opening of new ports as a retraction of the Board of Trade policy limiting points of contact ("this ill-advised policy has been responsible for trouble of late years"), the Shanghai Chamber contended that the *likin* and transit provisions were unacceptable as they failed to recognize the principle of origin rather than ownership of foreign goods and goods purchased for foreign account as determining exemption from inland taxation; or, for that matter, that *likin* itself was illegal. It opposed restriction of *likin* exemption at Treaty Ports to the foreign settlements and the added burden placed on the opium trade. In sum, the Shanghai objections were none too serious, for they failed to bring up either the question of "guarantees" for enforcement of inland dues regulations or the wider issue of railway, mining and other concessions. As Hugh Fraser (Chargé d'affaires) pointed out to the Foreign Office, Shanghai had overlooked the fact that origin of goods did determine exemption in the case of imports and as for exports it would never be practical. The political question he regarded as none of their concern.

In London, however, the Committee adopted the Shanghai letter as a point of departure for a campaign against ratification which attempted to duplicate the experience of 1870. But without much success. Michie forwarded the Shanghai letter to Lord Derby with the suggestion that it be considered before ratification.[107] At the same time, however, he wrote privately to Pauncefote, the Assistant Undersecretary, asking for an interview in which Lord Derby might explain to them "the actual position of the affair" as it might "simplify the communication we are instructed to make to the various Chambers of Commerce," and "prove a convenience all around." This was one of the first instances of an attempt by the more respectable Old China Hands to establish personal relations with the Foreign Office and practice the diplomacy of intimacy which was to become the mainstay of the China Association two decades later. It constituted an attempt to supplement, and at the same time temper, public pressure in alliance with home commercial opinion, and was to come under passionate criticism from the treaty ports. After a further exchange of notes, in which Michie held out the threat of a mercantile campaign if no satisfaction was forthcoming from the Foreign Office, consent for the interview was given.[108] On October 24, Lord Derby and Lord Tenterden received Michie and F. D. Barnes and promised to give weight to the Shanghai memorial. However, there was as yet no indication that ratification might be withheld.

There was to be no repetition of 1870. In fact, so limited was commercial interest in the China market that it was the conflict over the opium clauses in the Chefoo Convention which attracted the attention it was able to muster and which proved most decisive in determining its fate. Consideration of ratification was held up pending referral to the Government of India, which raised the complaint that the Chefoo agreement had been reached without taking into account its effect on Indian revenue. What the India officials were objecting to was brought out in the memorial from D. Sassoon & Co. protesting that the new treaty provision for simultaneous payment of import and *likin* duties on opium at the port of entry would in effect double the tariff, "for provincial governments will continue to exact their squeezes when opium reaches their provinces," and therefore was a measure "calculated to do serious injury to a very important branch of British commerce." [109] Higher tariff would reduce the traffic and Indian revenue derived from that traffic.

The opium issue soon became dominant. The "Society for Suppression of the Opium Trade" mobilized British conscience in support of the very clauses to which objection had been raised. And to add to the complication, the opium provisions were contained in clause three of Section III of the Convention, constituting an integral part of the commercial provisions to which the Shanghai Chamber's London Committee was raising objections.[110] The Anti-Opium Society received widespread support. Lord Shaftesbury forwarded a memorial signed by 350 notables supporting its position, and for the next several years an intensive campaign was conducted among the Chambers of Commerce urging them to recommend ratification.

The Chambers, caught between the opposing forces of the London Committee and the Anti-Opium Society, adopted either an indifferent or neutral position for some time. The London Committee, now reinforced by a Committee of London Merchants representing the China firms,[111] directed its major attack against a Memorandum drawn up by Wade to counter the Shanghai memorial. In a long letter to the Foreign Office, Michie expanded the arguments advanced in the interview of the previous month.[112] Wade's contention that the settlement of the Yunnan affair was a strictly political matter was rejected; for, political or not, it was definitely of interest to "commercial men" because "our security in China is to be found in our *prestige*—in other words the full conviction on the part of the Chinese that 'no one can harm us with impunity.' " Prestige, which might also be defined as "a form of cheap protection," had been dissipated in the Tientsin affair, while the Grosvenor mission had turned into a fiasco as far as getting at the real criminals was concerned. As for the trade section (Section III), though they approved of the new ports ("doubly welcome as some modification of Lord Russell's dictum that the fewer open ports the better"), Michie nevertheless emphasized: "The Shanghai Chamber would, however, go still further, and would urge the desirability of the whole of China being thrown open for the establishment of trading points, wherever it may be found worthwhile for the Chinese Government to place a Custom House, and the European Governments, Consular Stations." Main concern, however, was still the inadequate solution of the *likin* question: exemption should attach to foreign goods, not ownership, and exemption in the port areas should not be restricted to foreign settlements. Above all, commutation of *likin* by payment at the port of entry of one-half tariff rates should exempt goods from all further inland taxes whatever and such goods covered by transit passes should be guaranteed respect. The basic attitude was expressed in the conclusion: that it would be better to revert to the "clear and simple provisions of the Tientsin Treaty" and insist on their being carried out without evasion! Shanghai hands remained orthodox.

The home Chambers, subjected to agitation from the London Committee on the one hand and the anti-opium movement on the other, split ranks; none of them, however, was stirred to take the firm stand adopted in 1870. Bradford, in general supporting the Shanghai objections especially with regard to inland dues, urged "reconsideration" of the commercial sections of the Convention before ratification.[113] Halifax assumed the most decided stand, concurring "entirely" in the Michie-Barnes letter and urging that its recommendations be adopted.[114] The Glasgow Chamber of Commerce and Manufactures remained neutral: on the assumption that the Government was "definitely committed to the Convention and without expressing views on details" it urged ratification for the "good faith of Great Britain." Liverpool took a similar view, holding that as the Convention had already been in operation for eighteen months, ratification would not be withheld without a breach of faith on the part of the British Government.[115]

The Manchester Chamber of Commerce refused to hedge and came out boldly in favor of ratification. Nor was this step taken without full consideration. Several meetings were held in September and November (1877) at which the problem was discussed and the letters from both sides read. The secretary, after conferring with Mr. Holliday of Farbridge, Holliday & Co. on the commercial aspects of the Chefoo Convention, drafted the memorial which was amended and approved at a special meeting of the Board on November 30.[116]

With home opinion thus divided, the Government adopted an unusual course. No formal ratifications were exchanged, but the Chefoo Convention was allowed silently to enter into force, except for two provisions: that concerned with the collection of *likin* taxes on opium by the

Imperial Customs and the clause defining foreign settlements as the area of *likin* exemption. Nothing further was heard concerning the latter, but agitation for ratification of the opium clauses continued for years. In October, 1878, a deputation of the Anglo-Oriental Society for the Suppression of the Opium Trade, led by Thomas Hanbury and the Reverend F. Storrs Turner, visited Liverpool and Manchester, urging the Chambers of Commerce to memorialize the Government for ratification of the Chefoo opium clause. Liverpool declined to take action,[117] as did Manchester, although considerable interest was aroused.[118] The *Manchester Guardian* [119] gave particular prominence to the meeting. The major argument which weighed against ratification was its serious effect on Indian revenue: a committee set up by nine private bankers the following year to investigate the possibility of discovering a substitute for the opium revenue met with little success.[120] Two years later the Liverpool Chamber did petition the House of Commons to stop Indian exports of opium to China in order "to free this country from complicity in that trade," [121] but the issue failed to attract attention in other commercial circles. Over this, as over other issues in China affairs, apathy reigned.

V

The Shadow of Foreign Competition

> *"Other foreign Rep^{es} do not keep within the lim-
> its observed by the British Minister, but actually
> negotiate Loans and Contracts for their nationals
> and bluster and machinate on their behalf and the
> complaint of the British community is that their
> efforts to compete are not supported."*—Baron
> Pauncefote, the Foreign Office, 1884.

FOR years Parliamentary debate on China was confined, almost
exclusively, to a discussion of the opium question, which was not
only a tribute to the vigor of Victorian conscience, but a sad commentary on the stagnation of Anglo-Chinese commerce.[1] Despite sincere and overwhelming public indignation at British complicity in the
traffic, as evidenced by the numerous signatures to petitions circulated
on this subject, the vast annual revenue which the Indian Government
derived from the traffic proved the insurmountable obstacle. The amount
was far from insignificant; British exports to China in 1880 were only
one and one half times the sum.

There were some who, in frantic search for the causes of Anglo-
Chinese trade stagnation, tried to relate the two issues. In one of the rare
fulldress debates on China, on April 3, 1883, a speaker argued that British suppression of the opium traffic would so impress the Chinese with
friendly feelings as to lead them to hunger for British goods. It was a new
open sesame to Eldorado.

Our trade with China has been miserably small hitherto. On examining the
Board of Trade returns for last year, I find that we only sent to China
£7,500,000 worth of British products as against £29,000,000 worth sent to
India. Now, China has a much larger and more industrious population than
India; we have almost free trade with China; so there is no reason whatsoever
why we should send so little produce there as compared with that sent to India.
As a matter of fact, last year we only sent to China, with its 300,000,000 to

400,000,000 of people, as much of our products as we sent to South Africa. We exported less than we sent to Belgium, and less than half of what we sent to Australia. On the Manchester exchange, there is nothing excites so much astonishment as the little elasticity of our trade with China. . . .

The reason is obvious. It is because, in the first place, the resources of the people of China are wasted upon opium; and, in the second place, because the hostility of the Chinese to the opium trade excites hostility to all foreign trade. These are the two reasons why our trade with China is so poor and so languid." [2]

Neither trade nor enterprise showed improvement in the early eighties. Trade figures exhibited two outstanding factors, as always: stagnation at a comparatively low level and British predominance, in both commerce and shipping, at about seventy percent of the total. Consular reports for 1880 proved the trade stagnant.[3] Moreover, the consul at Kiukiang emphasized once again that "it is impossible to disguise the fact . . . that the trade of the port is yearly passing more and more into Chinese hands." Import of foreign goods into the treaty ports in 1878 was not too impressive: a total of less than seventy million taels, or twenty million pounds sterling. And, of this total, thirty-eight percent was accounted for by the import of opium. Imports of British goods stood at less than eight millions sterling.

Merchants might continue to grumble that this thin result could be attributed to political obstacles and the burden of *likin;* but, as Consul Bullock of Chinkiang pointed out, there had been far too long an overemphasis of their effects. *Likin,* in fact, acted as the convenient whipping boy of mercantile resentment. "The assertion," Bullock noted, "that if it were not for artificial impediments (heavy and arbitrary taxation) the demand in China for English cottons would become practically limitless . . . [is] . . . without foundation." [4] Goods paid a five percent import duty, a transit duty of half that sum, and "perhaps" one to two percent destination tax when separated from the transit pass, he reported. The outside total was ten percent ad valorem; on such terms foreign goods should be able to compete fairly with native goods which are themselves "not lightly taxed." The truth is, Bullock concluded, that in order to increase the demand for British goods, "we must discover how to make and lay down in China, as cheaply as the Chinese can, a very strong and durable article," and this, there seems little doubt, "the prices of raw cotton and freight will not allow us to do." An observation made by Mitchell a generation before! But the *likin* issue continued to exercise the merchants and even to infect the officials. Cases and complaints were not wanting; [5] but no fundamental change took place. The issue was still a burning one when the China Association was

formed at the end of the eighties and it constituted a prominent part of
its agenda throughout the nineties.

As in the matter of *likin,* so in the matter of other concessions which
merchants had hoped to secure in 1869; throughout the interlude, the
story was one of a series of frustrations. Much had been anticipated
from German treaty revision and the blood-and-iron sentiments of von
Brandt.[6] But after postponement and intermittent labor for ten years'
the German treaty of 1881 proved a tragic disappointment to Shanghai.
The *North China Herald* [7] found that it contained no concessions and
defined things (regarding *likin* collection) better left undefined. The
Herald was so disillusioned that it gave up all hope of progress until the
Chinese internal renascence would show the heathen the light.

When Shanghai residents took time out from their favorite pastime,
the Saturday Paper Hunt, to consider the state of foreign interests in
China, the picture appeared none too promising. A census taken in 1879
showed the total foreign population at the treaty ports at 3,814; the number of commercial firms at 351. Of the foreign residents, 1,953 were
British, with 420 Americans and 384 Germans. Of the firms, 220 were
British, 49 German and 35 American, with 9 French and 2 Danish; the
Japanese had nine and the rest were listed as "sundry uncertain." [8] The
North China *Daily News* might conclude that while "the besetting
sin of the British merchants on China during recent years has been
apathy, . . . there are signs of reviving animation and energy"; but it
was evident that the China vision had dimmed. By 1885 Britain had
299 firms in the treaty ports, with 2,070 nationals; [9] still none too
promising. Even as late as 1897 there were fewer than 5,000 British
residents in the ports. Intermittently, merchants would grumble that
British interests and prestige were "dwindling" and that representatives
were needed who would use "every nerve and effort to establish, uphold,
promote and push prominently into existence these very interests." [10]
But the old spark was gone.

As restricted as the commercial field were opportunities for investment. The speaker in the opium debate, noted above, concluded that "at
the present time the outlets for British capital seem almost choked up.
There is nothing that the country needs so much as a large field for the
investment of its capital. What field in the world would equal China?" [11]
It was, of course, a constant mercantile grievance. The failure of the
Government to press for railway concessions and other investment
facilities was regarded as of a piece with its reluctance to sponsor particular ventures, as some of the other powers were not above doing.[12]

There was actually little distinction between strictly commercial capital and "enterprise capital" in China. The chief financial institution in Shanghai, the Hongkong and Shanghai Banking Corporation, formed and "owned" by the merchants,[13] was also the chief agency for floating both governmental and concessionaire loans. The larger mercantile houses themselves, aside from their direct interest in the banks, were the major investors in capital enterprises, from sugar refining to shipping. What is more, it was Jardine, Matheson & Co., the leading British commercial firm, which negotiated with the native authorities for the first Chinese loan in 1874, and it was only their refusal to advance the first installment without guarantees which "enabled the Hongkong & Shanghai Bank to slip [in?] & secure their loan of $2,000,000." [14]

Capital was never a factor. When the Hongkong and Shanghai Bank floated this loan in January, 1875, it was oversubscribed locally by more than two million pounds! And, although the *North China Herald* cautioned that this did not necessarily mean that "the money market out here is prepared to devote £2 million to one investment on a few weeks notice," [15] rumors of a later and larger Chinese loan that year did not find bids shy. In fact, there was never any lack of interest or means of capital investment in the treaty ports; it was opportunity which was lacking, as well as government support.

Although merchants claimed that the right to set up industries in treaty ports had been granted by treaty, Peking challenged this interpretation and the Foreign Office never pressed the point.[16] Some development was tacitly permitted by local authorities, who taxed it heavily; Peking generally discountenanced all industrial development. The Shanghai Share Market in 1880 still quoted less than twenty enterprises, mainly in shipping, docks, and insurance.[17] Kiernan cites a list of fifteen foreign establishments in Shanghai, of which eleven were British, manufacturing matches, paper, and gas in 1882; [18] but it was not until 1890 that the first cotton mill was set up. Even so, it was only by drawing Chinese capital, both private and official, into the enterprises that they were allowed to operate without obstruction. By 1885 sugar cultivation and tin mining shares had appeared on the Shanghai market.[19] The latter were smelting companies. Mining itself was not open to foreigners, the Kaiping coal mines having been developed in 1880 by a Chinese company under Li Hung-chang, while the Kelung, using foreign machinery was a state mine.

Overshadowing everything, however, were dreams of a railway age providing outlets for capital and means of penetrating the interior. Since 1863 when Li had refused the petition of Shanghai merchants to build a railway to Soochow,[20] various attempts were made to seduce the Chinese into accepting the inevitability of railways. But without suc

cess. Two of these were noted above, the nuptial railway and the Woosung line; another was attempted in 1875 by a Mr. Thomas Fergusson,
who had been doing business in Chefoo for fourteen years, and had
visions of a line into the interior of Shantung to Tsinanfu.[21] The Foreign
Office was as discouraging as it had been to mercantile demands for
railway concessions in 1869. Indeed, Alcock had been the first to throw
cold water on Fergusson's scheme, holding that there was "no proximate
probability of permission being granted." In 1875, the Foreign Office
again refused official support for the scheme; as for the Chinese, their
attitude became clear—if it was ever in doubt—the following year in
their active opposition to the Woosung project.[22]

This was the last effort by foreigners to introduce railways into China
until the end of the century. Under native sponsorship, a short line was
built in 1881 from the collieries of the Kaiping district of Chihli to the
wharf at Lutai [23] a scheme which the British Legation warmly welcomed
on the wedge principle.[24] The China Railway Company had been born,
and in 1887, the line was extended to Tientsin, a total distance of eighty-
one miles. At about the same time, "great syndicates had been formed in
Europe in anticipation of a China boom after the French war," [25] but the
Chinese refused to hand out the contracts. As a field for investment,
railways did not enter the picture during the interlude.

Nor was the situation much improved as regards the issue of Government loans—"the most sought-for, most lucrative business of the
banks." [26] It was a business from which the Foreign Office could not
entirely divorce itself. By 1880, the Hongkong & Shanghai Bank had
floated three Chinese Imperial Loans: in 1874 for £627,615, in 1877 for
£1,604,276, and the following year for two million taels (about
£600,000), all at 8 percent.[27] The position of the Foreign Office with
regard to foreign loans had been stated in 1871 in a confidential circular
to British diplomatic agents, setting forth the following principles: (a)
that it was undesirable to encourage hazardous loans to foreign countries,
and (b) that political power would not be pledged for the enforcement of
obligations under them. "The policy of H.M. Government with regard
to the general question of the assistance to be given to foreign bondholders who fail to obtain their rights has always been and will continue to be limited to unofficial support and friendly remonstrance with
such foreign states as from time to time fail to meet their obligations." [28]
Experience in China soon revealed how difficult it would be to enforce
this self-denying formula.

The first effort by the Hongkong and Shanghai Bank to enlist official
support for a Chinese loan so disturbed the British representative in

Peking—Hugh Fraser, the Chargé d'affaires—that his reaction must be regarded as an accurate reflection of Foreign Office sentiment. Fraser did not conceal his distaste for the role of official broker. In July, 1877, Ewen Cameron, manager of the Hongkong and Shanghai Bank at Shanghai, concluded an agreement with Hu, a banker of Soochow acting on behalf of the Imperial Government, for a loan of 5,000,000 Haikwan taels (£1,604,276) to finance Tso Tsung-tang's armies fighting to recapture Kashgar, on the northwest frontier, from rebel bands. An Imperial Decree was to be issued authorizing the loan and Customs bonds given to the Bank as security. The first Decree published was not satisfactory to the Bank as it failed to provide for payment in sterling; Peking claimed that Hu had acted for Tso Tsung-tang and would be responsible for converting the sycee to sterling.[29] Fraser first heard of the loan unofficially from Consul Davenport of Shanghai in July and upon inquiry at Peking learned that the first Decree was about to be issued. He did not feel quite comfortable about the entire affair and tried desperately to steer clear. When difficulties arose over the Decree he telegraphed the Foreign Office the first news of the loan adding: "there is, I am glad to say, a slight difficulty in the matter at present, for the Imperial Decree sanctioning the loan is not drawn up in terms satisfactory to the Bank." [30]

The same day he wrote a long account of the affair, in which he pointed out that he had not become involved, even boasting of his ignorance of details: "I do not know what the points of difference are, for I have not examined the question, not caring, in any count, to be concerned with it." Cameron, however, informed Davenport of the difficulties he had encountered and asked for Fraser's influence in securing a satisfactory Decree. Davenport, "aware that the matter was not one in which a diplomatic agent could be properly asked to intervene, demurred, and Mr. Cameron finally limited himself to requesting me [Fraser] to inform the Chinese Ministers that the Bank could not make any advances to the Imperial Government under the Edict actually issued." Fraser conveyed the message; but informed Cameron that "he must not look for assistance from me in the matter." The Chinese Government's reply he merely "forwarded" to the banker. When Peking issued a new Imperial Rescript ordering that effect be given to its Decree and requested Fraser to "direct" the Bank to act on it, he took pains to "leave no room for doubt as to my own position in the matter," and warned Cameron of "the absolute and individual nature of the Bank's responsibility for its own transactions." [31] To Davenport he reiterated: "I do not wish to take any part in the negotiations that lead to this loan. It is not a matter in which a diplomatic agent ought to be concerned. . . . The Bank alone is responsible for its affairs. A diplomatic agent has no business to be concerned in negotiations for any loan, however regular." The matter was finally straightened out with the Bank accepting the procedure insisted upon by the Chinese Government.

This first quasi-political loan to China is instructive for several reasons. Throughout, Fraser discouraged the Bank's appeal for assistance on the ground that a diplomatic representative must be careful not to involve his Government in such loans—a position far different from that which obtained at the end of the century. The Foreign Office approved of his procedure. Moreover, it was the first loan secured on the foreign Customs, setting a precedent for later loans. And, it is interesting to remark that it was the Chinese, not foreigners, who felt even at that time that such loans might prove a menace to the integrity of the Empire. Pointing out the necessity of coming to "some arrangement for the repayment of the enormous sums of money that have been borrowed from foreign merchants for defraying the expenses of war in the West," a Memorial from the Chinese Board of Revenue in 1881 cautioned against further borrowing from foreigners. Terming foreign borrowing a "ruinous policy" the Memorial proceeded to emphasize the imperative need for repaying the sums out of provincial contributions to military expenses and warned against further borrowing "no matter how urgent the need for funds." [32]

The disturbing issue of official assistance in loan negotiations confronted the Foreign Office even more starkly during the loan affair of 1884. In March, 1884, Mr. de Bovis, Tientsin Agent of the Hongkong and Shanghai Bank, called on Sir Harry Parkes, the British Minister in Peking, to ask for his assistance in obtaining the sanction of the Imperial Government for the loan negotiated by the Bank with Canton provincial authorities. Security for this loan of 2,000,000 taels at 9 percent was the salt revenue of Canton and general revenue of Kwangtung; but the Bank would not proceed without an Imperial Decree. Parkes talked to the Yamen several times and finally succeeded in having the Decree issued. [33]

When the dispatch describing the transaction reached the Foreign Office in May (1884), it created quite a stir. Childers, the Parliamentary Undersecretary, felt very strongly that Parkes' intervention was uncalled for and that the transaction should be repudiated. To this, Pauncefote, the Assistant Undersecretary, minuted apologetically:

It is no doubt undesirable that our Reprs. shd. mix themselves up with Loans by English Banks to Foreign Govts. But in the present case the Loan had already been agreed upon before Sir H. Parkes moved in the matter—& the only action he took after having been officially apprized by Prince Kung of the Loan, was to request that its approval . . . be signified as usual. . . . Foreigners have no access to the Chinese Govt. except through the diplomatic Channel and on that acct. Foreign Ministers in China have necessarily become the medium of communication with the Sup. Govt. in matters of this kind—on behalf of their countrymen in China, and such assistance has never been considered to involve any undertaking or guarantee or responsibility of any kind.

The peculiar state of things in China, create an exception to the sound rule advocated by Mr. Childers, but of course the action of the British repr. should not extend to any negotiation; but be limited to the protection of the just rights of the parties concerned— This has been the practice in China in all cases of Loans . . . and if the good offices of H.M. Repr to that extent were to cease it would cause very great dissatisfaction in commercial circles.[34]

It is a most interesting view, adumbrating the newer diplomacy which recognized "the peculiar state of things in China." Granville noted that "Pauncefote's minute appears to be sound." But Childers violently disagreed, concluding

I cannot but think that China ought not to be an exception to the general rule. If the Chinese Government should fail to fulfill their engagement to the Bank, our intervention will be insisted on, and I do not see how it can be refused.

I don't (on other grounds) think that any encouragement should be given to English Cos. becoming mixed up with semi-barbarous governments.[35]

The issue was not resolved but it served to state the dilemma with which the Foreign Office would be faced ten years later. Pauncefote, in reply to Childers, noted with some sympathy the complaint of the merchants: "Other foreign Rep[es] do not keep within the limits observed by the British Minister, but actually negotiate Loans and Contracts for their nationals and bluster and machinate on their behalf and the complaint of the British community is that their efforts to compete are not supported."[36]

Pauncefote's observation touched on a point which was beginning to exercise the mercantile community. During the period of the interlude, and particularly after 1880, the challenge which Russian and French encroachment on the fringes of the Chinese Empire offered to British predominance in the East began to modify the nature of the Chinese Question. Later problems were being posed in embryonic form and, although the concern later displayed in mercantile circles was not yet prominent, the factor of international rivalry for the Manchu legacy was already beginning to affect mercantile attitudes.

There was, during the interlude, no widespread movement in the treaty ports or among the home Chambers to counter Russian and French ambitions in China. On the contrary, interest was sporadic and inchoate:

this is the primary fact which strikes one in surveying contemporary documents. It was the publicists, men like Archibald R. Colquhoun, explorer and Special Correspondent for *The Times,* who called for the great awakening. "Two great markets, China and Indo-China, still remain open to our energies, and we may yet possess ourselves of them. Success seems to have enfeebled and robbed us of that commercial enterprise which made us the nation we are." [37] Deploring the apathy of British manufacturers at home and of the treaty port merchant who "looks only to the immediate present," [38] Colquhoun warned that a struggle for empire had commenced, with the ambitious powers "usurping or carving away at the enormous monopoly which England has by her energy and foresight, but still more by her opportunities in the past, gradually built up." [39] He called for a "Greater Britain policy," concluding that "upon the political supremacy of England in the East, upon the possession and defence of India and our Eastern possessions, depends the continuance of her commercial prosperity."

Except in the fostering of their pet scheme, the Burma-Yunnan road (which will be noted later), mercantile circles were not roused to political action by Colquhoun's alarmist dispatches from China. Nor, as Kiernan has pointed out, was parliamentary opinion less reticent during the Franco-Chinese crisis of the eighties.[40] Widespread interest in the Chinese Question, as it was to be called, was ten years away.

But no matter how reticent and sporadic, the expression of mercantile attitudes toward the Kashgar Crisis and the Tongking Affair must be noted, not so much for its intrinsic significance as for the light it sheds on Old China Hand opinion in the nineties. Mercantile sentiment does not appear clear-cut because of the contradictory pressures involved: a blockade of Shanghai or war's interference with established trade might be vigorously opposed, but there was the contrary appeal of breaking down Chinese trade restrictions through whatever new deal might arise from war's settlement; the expenses of war would increase *likin* and other taxes, but there was the opposite pressure derived from the fact that British capital, through the Hongkong and Shanghai Bank loans, was financing Peking in both crises. But these factors, although often given prominence, were not, as such, decisive.

The decisive fact was that the challenge of international rivalry to British commercial predominance in the Far East was added to, or rather *superimposed* on, the existing, traditional ambition of opening China. In mercantile thought, at this period and even more forcefully in the nineties, there were two enemies, two obstacles, two challenges to be met: Chinese exclusion and backwardness on the one hand, and on the other, international competition for commercial and political advantages in China which threatened to undermine Britain's position.

These pressures were contradictory, confusing mercantile attitudes, and resulting in a marked ambivalence in mercantile policy. For, while Russian and French (and later Japanese) trade competition was a menace not to be overlooked, was it not also true that Count Witte and M. Jules Ferry might succeed in doing what Clarendon and Derby and even Salisbury had failed to do—open China to the profit of established British merchants and entrepreneurs? Sometimes the one, sometimes the other would weigh more heavily in the balance. In general, during the early stages of a crisis, Old China Hands opposed British official mediation for peace, hoping that the crisis would help to break down Chinese trade barriers; or that the consequent settlement, as in 1895, would widen commercial opportunities. On the other hand, as in the later stages of the Tongking crisis, the fear that France would establish a preferential trade regime and monopolize trade routes in the territory which came under its political control would predominate in mercantile attitudes. It is this ambivalence which is the key to an understanding of both British policy and mercantile pressures. Officially, British policy was to mediate differences and protect, without risking anything overt, the integrity of China; at the same time, should any exclusive rights be granted to other Powers, "compensation" from Peking was in order. Mercantile opinion rarely supported the first and always pressed for the second.

The Kashgar crisis first raised these issues. While in London in 1877 Wade first proposed to mediate differences between Yakoub Khan, leader of the Kashgar rebels, and the Chinese Government. Tso Tsungtang, commander of the Northwest, was committed to war and the Chinese Minister in London pointed out that a formula must be found to save face. Wade thought Yakoub Khan might be willing to accept the position of a tributary, thus ending a civil war which "would be of some importance to us; for the war is costing China three million pounds per annum, defrayed out of *likin* which falls heavily on foreign trade." [41] In this document Wade emphasized British interest in peace in China against Russian and German hopes for war:

It may be urged, as M. von Bradt urged after the misunderstanding with Japan in 1874, that in these states open wounds of the kind are of advantage to us. He could have cried with vexation, he told me, when he heard in Japan that I had brought about pacification. I believe our policy in China is to aid her in securing herself, which she cannot do without peace. . . . On the Indian side they are very anxious to see Yakoub let alone by Russia, believing that if Russia absorbs Kashgaria she will trouble our trade to the north.

He feared Russia and Germany working together to drive both sides to intransigence.

With the reconquest of Chinese Turkestan by Tso in 1878, the question arose whether Russia would be allowed to retain the Kuldja province in western Sinkiang, which she occupied temporarily during the crisis. Chung How, China's envoy to France during the Tientsin affair, was sent to St. Petersburg to attempt a settlement.[42] Chung signed a treaty at Livadia (Yalta of later fame) in September of 1879, the terms of which were so unfavorable to China that he was arrested upon his return. There was talk of war and the possibility that England might be drawn in was seriously discussed.[43] Wade was desirous of avoiding war in China if only for the reasons he had mentioned in 1877, and exerted his efforts toward mediation despite Russian attempts to convince him that Chinese resistance was a manifestation of general anti-foreign sentiment.[44] In view of Britain's trade superiority and interests even an alliance with China might be contemplated in order to prevent the breaking up of the Middle Kingdom.[45] The Foreign Office did not become as exercised as Wade over the seriousness of the crisis, but fully approved his efforts at mediation, and urged him to uphold the "peace party" at Peking.

Treaty port opinion vigorously opposed this policy, holding it "impolitic to interfere between Russia and China" unless a direct threat to Shanghai were involved; war, so long as it was localized, would not prove injurious to British trade.[46] Mercantile motives were none too clear; editorials sometimes stressed the civilizing influence of Russia in remote Chinese provinces, at other times implied that Russian involvement in war would strengthen a neutral Britain. Again there was a marked difference between Liberal journals at home and the treaty port press, with the former backing the Foreign Office. Wade continued to exert all his efforts toward arranging a peaceful settlement, which involved a diplomatic retreat by Peking; Chung was reprieved and Russia appeased on Wade's warning that "if China would not yield and could not resist, there would be many Powers eager to advance real or imaginary claims." [47]

The *North China Herald*, however, reiterated mercantile criticism of Wade's "ill-timed display of desire to intermeddle," and hinted strongly that Russian occupation of Kuldja might not prove injurious to British interests.[48] It was sufficient for the British Minister to state to both parties that "we will not permit the quarrel about Kuldja to be made a pretext for interfering with our trade with the Far East." The central attitude in mercantile circles was one of indifference. The most significant aspect is the total absence of anti-Russian sentiment, coupled with an undercurrent of satisfaction that the reactionary mandarins of Peking were in trouble. Wade, however, labored for a peaceful settlement, convinced that any disturbance was bound to menace established British interests. On his urging, the Marquis Tseng, Chinese Minister in London, was dispatched to St. Petersburg to effect a new settlement. In September the Shanghai press was reporting that the crisis was over and that Russia would retain Ili and receive an indemnity.[49] Though noncommittal about the treaty, the *North China Herald* remarked that "it will be interesting to see whether the Russians succeed in getting from the Chinese a Pacific port farther south than Vladivostock." If so, it concluded, it was doubtful whether England would have any right to complain, for so long as she holds Hongkong England "could not refuse any other nation a similar foothold."

On the whole, then, mercantile opinion was none too concerned about Russian designs at this time, nor did it share Wade's fear of the effect which a dissolution of Chinese authority would have on trade. For there was always the possibility that something profitable might result from a new deal. When the settlement of the crisis by the Treaty of Ili was finally confirmed in May, 1881, it appeared that Russia had given up most of its territorial gains in return for a larger indemnity and overland trade advantages. This caused some uneasiness in mercantile circles in England,[50] but treaty port residents were not disturbed. There was no threat to coastal trade nor was Russian competition feared; not half so much as Chinese exclusiveness.

Appreciably more concern was displayed over the Tongking affair, in which mercantile reaction went through more than one phase. The comparative indifference to French ambitions coupled with the rejoicing at war orders which Colquhoun found prevalent among Hongkong traders [51] soon turned to pressure for mediation. Partly this was due to the proximity of treaty ports to the scene of action and resultant trade disturbances caused by the war; partly, too, it was due to fear of French annexation of Chusan on the approaches to the Yangtze. Even more French penetration up the Red River valley was regarded as the chief threat to British projects for reaching Yunnan by ascending the Canton River or, more important to home opinion, by a railway route through Burma. But overshadowing everything was the fear that French conquest meant the establishment of a preferential system in which British interests would suffer prejudice or exclusion. It was this above all which exercised both official and mercantile circles.

French ambitions in Indo-China, dating back to the time of Loui

XIV, had by 1874 succeeded, through the Treaty of Saigon, in establishing an undefined protectorate over Annam; China, which regarded Annam as tributary, looked on in resentful silence. Nor did Britain welcome the move. Wade had during the seventies been calling attention to French ambitions in that area, and was particularly aroused by the journey of M. Dupuis to Szechuen and Yunnan in 1872, the first of many such missions.[52] But, above all, the Saigon Treaty had aroused the commercial suspicions of the Foreign Office. Previous to its publication, extensive conversations were held in Paris, and despite protestations by the Duc de Decazes, Lord Lyons was convinced that special commercial privileges had been accorded to France, as the newspapers reported. Official copies later received proved his suspicions correct. "It is in fact plain that special privileges are secured to France by these treaties and that the stipulations are far from being so strictly confined as the Duke supposed to opening the commerce of Annam to all nations on equal terms." [53]

In fact, France had established customs control, trade preferences, and travel under French Consular passport. Wade attributed French designs on the region loosely styled as Cochin-China to two causes: the hope of reestablishing French prestige in Asia, "so disturbed by British ascendancy in India," and a desire for monopoly of enterprise to French merchants.[54] He might have added: the ambition of securing the first overland route to Yunnan. Lord Derby pointed out that Britain's chief objection to France's action, as well as to the Treaty, derived from the exclusive privileges which the latter granted to the French,[55] a point equally stressed by the Colonial Secretary, who noted that "these treaties would make Annam for all political and commercial purposes a French province." [56] The point was incorporated in the memorandum submitted to the French on November 15, 1874; the latter emphasized their peculiar position with reference to Annam, acquired at such great sacrifices, and maintained that foreign interests were better off than before. There the matter rested.

Consul Robertson at Canton expressed the real attitude of residents at that time, showing the ambivalence which manifested itself whenever Western pressure forced concessions out of China:

Assuming the protectorate to be a fait accompli, I think it exceedingly doubtful that any but France will benefit thereby . . . but there is no question that if the French would liberally throw open these countries they would be a magnificent field for English enterprise and open new sources for trade, besides, I think, settling the *vexatia questio* of opening Western China to foreign trade, which has so long been mooted via the Burma route. . . .[57]

It was obvious, as the Chairman of the Saigon Chamber of Commerce pointed out, that Annam was important only as a stepping-stone to Tongking which "would assure to our commerce a sound future" and serve as a base for penetration of Yunnan.[58] In 1880, the Shanghai press was reporting the imminent occupation of Tongking by French troops as a result of disturbance in the province. In June a new French Minister arrived in Peking "avec un plan arrêté à Paris" to occupy the Red River valley while China was occupied with the Kashgar crisis, establish "order," and render unnecessary any further appeals by Tongking to Peking.[59] France took the position that Tongking was a vassal of Annam which in turn was under French protection; China did not recognize the Treaty of Saigon. The issue was thus defined.[60]

The Tongking affair, which later developed into an undeclared and undefined war, dragged on for the next five years, raising issues and producing incidents which affected mercantile interests. When the French started moving up the Red River in 1881, native Canton opinion which was behind the rebel Tu Duc threatened to develop into a general antiforeign movement. At the same time reports that the Chinese were taking steps to blockade the river at Shanghai in case of war aroused mercantile suspicions. The Manchester Chamber of Commerce appealed to Lord Granville to protect British commerce against such an eventuality and, as a result, the Chinese were advised to delay any such action.[61] Hostilities seemed imminent in 1882 as the French dispatched the Rivière expedition up the Red River to Hanoi, which was taken, and then continued its penetration into Tongking. Chinese troops moved southward, and Peking hinted that British intervention would be welcomed.[62] To the surprise of everyone, however, an agreement was reached in December by Li and the French Minister Bourée, calling for the opening of Yunnan, recognition of the French protectorate over Tongking except for a frontier strip, and French respect for the "territorial sovereignty" of Annam.[63]

Despite these favorable terms, Paris rejected the Li-Bourée agreement; M. Jules Ferry had become Premier in February, 1883, at the head of a bellicose cabinet. Bourée was recalled,[64] and both sides became more intransigent. Popular feeling in China was so threatening that Grosvenor wanted a gunboat placed at Tientsin for the winter, which the Admiral opposed because it would be frozen in.[65] Except for possible anti-foreign disturbances and threats by both sides of blockading Shanghai British opinion was not yet aroused. Lord Granville, requested to mediate, put off the Chinese Minister. Grosvenor, echoing mercantile opinion, was writing at this time that French annexation of

Tongking might not be an evil, for it might result in the opening of the Red River to all.[66] Britain engaged in watchful waiting.

This sentiment soon changed. On August 9, 1883, France announced a blockade of Annamese ports, the first of a series of blockades affecting mainly British commerce. An article appeared in *The Times* predicting that England would be drawn into any war which might develop from the Tongking situation. Later in September, Granville made a half-hearted attempt to use his good offices to bring France and China to settlement, but withdrew when he could discover no common ground; [67] it was evident that the pressure exerted was directed toward persuading China to give in. But the Chinese balked and attempts at reaching a peaceful settlement broke down. Grosvenor wrote in October, 1883 that "should war between the two countries be the result of the present state of feeling, the losses of British merchants engaged in the Far East will be enormous." [68]

But it is safe to conclude that this was not a major consideration, for trade had not been appreciably affected by the crisis and war might provide its own opportunities. More important, as is evident from the Shanghai mercantile press, was concern over the general anti-foreign sentiment aroused and the realization that the bellicose party at Peking was none too favorable to foreign interests. While a show of neutrality was made, the *North China Herald* admitted that during the crisis of 1883 mercantile sympathies were not with China.[69] Opinion turned only when suspicions were aroused that France meant to occupy and later annex Chusan (which in the Davis Convention of 1846 China had promised England would "never be ceded to any other foreign power"); and the Hongkong Chamber of Commerce memorialized Sir Harry Parkes, the new Minister at Peking.[70] At the same time, upon the instigation of Hongkong, the London Chamber of Commerce addressed Lord Granville in support of this démarche.[71] The Law Officers concluded that the Davis Convention was still binding; but the Foreign Office thought the time was not ripe for warning the Chinese Government.[72]

Both these factors—the fear of anti-foreign outbreaks and uncertainty about French designs—along with the adverse effect on the volume of trade tended to strengthen the section of mercantile opinion which regretted the Franco-Chinese disturbance and called for English mediation. The Li-Fournier Convention of May 11, 1884, which was the last attempt to reach a settlement before active hostilities broke out, was warmly welcomed in mercantile circles despite its preferential provisions for French trade. Its rejection by Peking and the surprise attack by Chinese irregulars on French occupation troops at Langson led to an outbreak of anti-Chinese sentiment in the treaty ports.[73] The Hongkong

Chamber of Commerce appealed to the Powers to mediate in the interests of peace; a copy of the resolution was sent to the home Chambers, but the latter refused to act in support of a purely diplomatic measure.[74]

~ In sum, then, the most striking thing about treaty port sentiment in 1883 and 1884 was the almost total absence of anti-French feeling or suspicion of French designs. The only exceptions were the mild flurry aroused by the Chusan incident (which was never publicized) and the alarmist views of publicists like Colquhoun. The latter attributed Hongkong's complacency in the face of French penetration of Tongking to sheer ignorance.

The renewal of the crisis in the summer of 1884, as has been noted, merely served to make the French cause more popular, not out of love for the French but out of impatience with Chinese intransigence which appeared to make war inevitable.[75] Some hint of the motive is indicated by the *North China Herald's* consistent reference to the "war party" in Peking as the "anti-Foreign Party" and the "anti-Li Party," the latter referring to Li Hung-chang's reputed pacifist and reformist views.[76] Merchants who had campaigned vigorously against the Alcock Convention were citing Peking's repudiation of the Li-Fournier agreement as evidence of China's untrustworthiness, and of her fundamental antiforeign bias. The *North China Herald* even went out of its way to defend the special privileges for French trade included in the agreement.[77] The sense of community among foreigners against the obstinacy of Peking was still strong among Old China Hands.

Incidents and a series of ultimata by the French developed into a state of war, which was regarded as dating from August 22 after the French attack on the Formosan port of Keelung. "Peace though not expected is universally desired by the business community," wrote Consul Hughes from Shanghai [78] but when war came, the mercantile community, far from blaming the French, congratulated them on their long-suffering patience.[79] The North China *Daily News* even criticized them for the delay in taking "prompt action," principally because of the "languishing" effect it had had on trade.[80] Shanghai's major concern was still for a rapid settlement,[81] and its major fear the threatened blockade of the river by the local taotai. To this was added the anxiety over possible anti-foreign riots.[82]

Such was mercantile attitude through most of 1884. It is difficult to state with exactness when sentiment changed and suspicion of French designs began to outweigh earlier fears. As early as October 22, 1884, the *North China Herald* warned that French occupation might be more than a military maneuver: could annexation be regarded with equanimity? "Is France fighting simply to avenge the wound her honour received at Langson, or is there a bigger policy altogether in the background?" Was there in "the international courtesies of France and Russia at the present juncture a deeper meaning than may appear at first sight?" The ambivalence of Old China Hand attitude is manifested nowhere more clearly than in the following passage:

What would be the effect on trade and upon the interests of foreigners generally were France the mistress of Formosa? Were she to strangle its trade by protection and other forms of official interference, as she has done in all her colonies hitherto, there can be but one reply. But supposing she were to adopt, for once, a liberal and far-sighted policy, throw open the Island to free trade: would the results be good or evil? Hongkong might possibly be injured: and it is for foreign Powers to decide how much they would relish the possession, by France, of the virtual command of the whole of the coast of China. It is possible that that which might injure a certain section of British interests would have beneficial results to China and the world generally. . . . It is possible that some such measure is actually necessary to ensure the opening up of China. That the task should have been left to a country whose colonial policy has been frequently and somewhat severely criticized . . . and which has no trade to speak of in the Far East, may be regretted; but that the task itself is one of the "eternal necessities" of the world there can be no doubt.[83]

It was the existence of such mixed motives which accounts for the almost schizophrenic attitude of the treaty ports toward the French adventure. But anxiety over French ambitions tended to overshadow earlier views that "some such measure is actually necessary to ensure the opening up of China." Partly this growing hostility was due to revulsion by the home press over the French bombardment of the unfortified port of Foochow; to a large extent it was created by French measures of blockade during the active phase of hostilities.[84] But principally it derived from the growing conviction that the real danger to British interests would come from the commercial provisions of the peace terms which France would dictate.

By March, 1885, when French columns were within striking distance of the Tongking-Yunnan frontier and negotiations were proceeding both in Paris and China, Nicholas O'Conor, who had succeeded Sir Harry Parkes upon the latter's death, wrote to Granville: "I do not feel quite at ease as regards the exceptional commercial advantages which it is believed France will ask in lieu of the indemnity. It is not easy to see what she can get without injuring us." [85] O'Conor warned the Yamen against any concessions injurious to British interests, such as any French monopoly of railway construction in the region under dispute. On April 9 he expressed the opinion that "I think we can work the West River from Canton being opened to our trade as against any commercial frontier advantages France may claim and I shall do all that lies in my power to prevent any privileges being granted to France contrary to our interests." [86] At the end of April he warned again that France was aiming at two things: railway priority and a frontier tariff one-third lower than that at the ports; again he suggested the opening of the West River as compensation.[87] In the treaty ports France was being stigmatized as intransigent, and correspondents were accusing the French of war-guilt, with no dissenters.[88] Nor did the *North China Herald* bother to hide its satisfaction at the news of reverses suffered by the French at Lungchow.[89] In May the same journal ran a leader urging the creation of a firm alliance between England, China, and Japan to counter the "Franco-China Indian Empire" which threatened the peace of Asia and, especially, the independence of Siam.[90]

The Franco-Chinese treaty of peace (Li-Patenôtre), signed at Tientsin on June 9, 1885, served to justify these suspicions. China accepted the French position in Annam and undertook not to interfere with the work of "pacification" in Tongking. The frontier was opened to trade on conditions favoring French subjects and French "proteges" and tariff rates on the overland route to Kwangtung, Kwangsi, and Yunnan were to be set at a reduced figure. France was to construct roads and railways in Tongking and an undefined priority was granted to French industry and personnel in the construction of railways on Chinese initiative. This clause, however, was not to be considered "an exclusive privilege in favor of France." [91]

The treaty was submitted to the British Board of Trade for observations at the end of July, and the Board concurred in the instructions already sent to O'Conor by the Foreign Office to claim most-favored-nation treatment with respect to lower overland duties and any other privileges granted to French nationals on the land frontier.[92] The Board suggested that O'Conor's attention be drawn especially to those provisions which appeared to grant French nationals exclusive right of access to China under consular passport, to establish themselves along certain frontier points, and to enjoy lower tariff rates on foreign trade with Kwangsi and Yunnan. Mercantile susceptibilities were particularly aroused by the conclusion of the Cogordan Treaty the following year, which gave effect to the commercial clauses of the peace treaty.[93] The Glasgow Chamber of Commerce took the initiative in attempting to mobilize the home Chambers, but no concerted action was taken. Manchester debated the issue but decided to refrain from memorializing the Foreign Office.[94] Instead, a speaker at the Chamber meeting on October 27, 1886, suggested that they agitate for the opening of the West River, "in which case British commerce would have a very much easier mode of approach to Tonkin than that possessed by the French." This would have been the only adequate response in mercantile eyes. But British diplomacy entered hesitantly on a policy of counterconcessions (ten years later to become the mainstay of British action in the Far East) and contented itself with the treaty signed on July 24, 1886, defining the Burmese frontier and promising to "encourage" overland commerce to Yunnan.[95]

Of all the aspects of the Tongking settlement, what excited mercantile circles most was the suspicion that France had stolen a march on them in the overland race for Yunnan and Szechuen. The immediate gain of tariff preference on the frontier stations was not so frightening as the anxiety over leadership in reaching the vast, fabulous territory of southwestern China. Sprye, as has been noted, had stressed the factor of foreign competition in his very earliest propaganda; and the more successful publicity expert and explorer, Archibald Ross Colquhoun, who succeeded to Sprye's favored position in mercantile circles during the eighties, beat the same drum even more vigorously. The routes they recommended differed, but the intent and propaganda was the same.

As we have seen, Lord Salisbury's instructions to the Government of India to continue the Sprye survey from the point where it had been suddenly halted in 1867 had been disregarded; and when the Bhamo expedition ended in the Margary disaster, the chances of undertaking the even more hazardous venture of surveying the Salween route through the Shan States became even slimmer. At its annual meeting in February 1877, the Associated Chambers of Commerce was again urged by the Halifax and Huddersfield champions of the Sprye route to memorialize the Government to complete the survey to the Kiang-hung. At no time was it more important to open a direct route to the markets of southwestern China than at present "when excessive competition, hostile tariffs and a general depression of trade" existed.[96] The Halifax representative recalled that more than one hundred memorials had already been addressed to Whitehall by the Chambers of Commerce favoring the Sprye route, despite which the Indian Government favored the Bhamo approach with the "disastrous results" shown by the Sladen Mission in 1868, which had been forced to retreat "with diminished forces and plundered baggage," and by the fatal outcome of the Browne-Margary expedition in 1875. The Wakefield representative, adding his warm support, stressed the imperative need for anticipating the French. The motion was carried that memorials be sent to the Prime Minister, the Foreign Office and the India Office. But representatives charged with preparing the document met with a blank wall at the India Office when they inquired for correspondence to support their argument, and the subject was apparently dropped.[97]

What Sprye had failed to accomplish in the sixties and seventies, Archibald R. Colquhoun, with the assistance of another explorer and publicist, Holt S. Hallett, attempted with more success in the eighties. Colquhoun had journeyed from Canton to Yunnan (the last leg was from Szumao to Tali) early in 1882 [98] and during a subsequent stay in Burma had become convinced that an overland route, paralleling Sprye's but farther to the east, was feasible. Colquhoun's route ran through the Siamese Shan States: starting at Martaban, rather than Rangoon, thence to Zimme (Kiangmai) and through the Shan States to Kiang-hung to Szumao. He also proposed an alternate route from Bangkok to Zimme. Aside from meeting French competition, he was convinced that the commercial value of such a road would so impress the Chinese that it would "in all probability, give the necessary impetus to railway construction in China." He was convinced that the venture would prove more successful if conducted under non-official auspices, and approached the London and Manchester Chambers for aid.

It was the London Chamber, then reorganized under the chairmanship of the distinguished China Hand, Charles Magniac of Matheson & Co., which took the initiative in offering publicity and financial backing. The Chamber's *Journal* reprinted Colquhoun's first speech to the Royal Geographical Society as a Special Supplement.[99] In it Colquhoun, who fancied himself the Cecil Rhodes of China, reflected that in India British rule had brought peace and good government to a people who would otherwise have been torn by dissension and oppressed by the princes; besides, it had been good for trade. Now a new India was needed to meet the growing threat of international competition. Industry and international trade were no longer English monopolies; new markets were vitally necessary. A private venture, backed by the Chambers, to open such a route through the "friendly and trade-eager" Shan States to the rich Western provinces of China would tap virgin markets.[100]

Colquhoun then approached the Manchester Chamber and on December 12, 1882, addressed a special meeting; his eloquence was impressive. Two weeks later, when the Chamber received an appeal for funds, it was not disregarded. Colquhoun proposed that the four chief Chambers subscribe six hundred pounds each toward his estimated expedition expense of seven thousand pounds, and the Board recommended the subscription to its membership, "the object being in its opinion of great importance to the trade and commerce of this country." [101]

Meanwhile, the *Journal* of the London Chamber of Commerce continued to serve as Colquhoun's publicity organ, warning that British initiative was confronting French competition everywhere, not least in the race for Yunnan. The troubles in Tongking and French designs on Siam made swift implementation of Colquhoun's scheme imperative.[102]

By November, 1883, Colquhoun was able to report that although the Indian Government refused to support him financially it would not object to an unofficial exploration for which the amount to be raised from the Chambers, set at £3500, would suffice. The Manchester Chamber remitted the amount subscribed by its members—£393; £2900 had already been pledged by other sources, including £600 each from the London and Glasgow Chambers, £500 from the Rangoon Chamber, £100 from the Singapore Chamber, and £300 from the Hongkong Chamber. In addition the Singapore Government subscribed £500 and the Hongkong Government £300. Most significant was the substantial interest displayed by Hongkong circles whose previous hostility to the competitive Burma route had melted away in the face of French designs on the Southern Provinces.[103]

By the spring of 1885 Colquhoun and Hallett were back in England after completion of their survey,[104] and were seeking support for their scheme to organize a railway company. The Government of India had been none too cooperative and Colquhoun, like Sprye before him, was convinced that he faced an official conspiracy. Actually, the Indian Government still favored the route from Mandalay, either through Bhamo or by way of Kunlon Ferry on the Salween. At a special meeting of the London Chamber on April 13, Holt Hallett gave an account of the expedition concluded the previous year and the merchants passed a resolution calling on the Government to defray the cost of the projected railway out of the one million pound surplus of the Burmese Administration.[105] A week later Hallett addressed the citizens of Manchester at the Town Hall under the sponsorship of the Chamber of Commerce, which endorsed his railway scheme.[106]

So enthusiastic was the Manchester Chamber that its president headed a delegation to Lord Randolph Churchill at the India Office urging the adoption of the Colquhoun route and implementation of the railway projected through the Siamese Shan States. The first step was to be an engineering survey under Holt Hallett; it was estimated that the portion of the railway passing through British territory would cost one million pounds. Churchill replied that the matter had his careful consideration and that Lord Dufferin had looked through the correspondence before departing for India. He promised to telegraph again, and the delegation was heartened.[107] It appeared, however, that Minister and merchants had been talking at cross-purposes, for Churchill was speaking of no particular route. Lord Dufferin and the Government of India were, in actual fact, giving their serious consideration only to the Mandalay route.

No progress having been made, there was talk of another deputation in September, but Churchill replied that it was unnecessary, as his own views accorded with those of the Chamber. Meanwhile, Colquhoun wrote the Chamber, urging that it put pressure on the Government to annex Upper Burma, but Manchester balked at such an openly imperialist move.[108] However, a resolution was again passed in favor of the Colquhoun-Hallett railway project, to which was appended the desire of Manchester for "putting an end to the Political and Commercial difficulties existing in Upper Burmah" as a result of local disturbances. Representations accordingly were made to the Government.

September, 1885, saw the climax of Colquhoun's publicity campaign. On the 29th he addressed the London Chamber of Commerce on "A National Policy on the East," urging not only support for his railway route to southwestern China but the importance of consolidating and extending British interests in the Far East generally. Free trade and *laisser-aller* no longer sufficed, as markets were being shut and the continent converted into a formidable rival in world trade. Britain must throw herself into the struggle. As colonies took more British goods per head than European states (sic!), and since trade follows the flag, Britain could no longer afford to countenance the anarchy and misrule in Burma and the Shan States which effectively shut out her commerce. But the importance of Burma lay not so much in her own trade as that "it forms for us a portion of our highway to China" which was the real market of the future. The only solution was annexation of Upper Burma as the first step to securing that route.[109]

The London merchants applauded. Along with Liverpool they had already memorialized Lord Kimberley to put the affairs of Burma on a more satisfactory footing. A deputation representing London, Liverpool, and Glasgow called on Kimberley urging that trade routes through Upper Burma be reopened, if necessary by annexation. The Rangoon Chamber of Commerce further urged that the surplus revenues of the Burma Administration be employed "in extending British influence into transfrontier states of Indo-China in which direction there is perhaps a better field for extension of British trade than in any other part of the world." On December 3, 1885, the Liverpool Chamber again sent a resolution to Lord Randolph Churchill favoring annexation of Upper Burma,[110] and on January 1, 1886, Upper Burma became part of British territory.

The year 1885 proved to be the highpoint of mercantile interest in the Colquhoun scheme; and, in fact, there was a general falling off in mercantile agitation for a Burma route to southwestern China.[111] Partly this was due to the impetus which the annexation of Upper Burma had given to the rival Government-sponsored route from Mandalay to Kunlon Ferry; with the growth of official interest it was felt that mercantile pressure was no longer necessary. As Franco-British rivalry in the region became more prominent, the issue came to be considered more and more as a political affair best left in the hands of Whitehall.

Colquhoun, of course, continued to agitate. On November 7, 1887, he addressed the London Chamber, with Hugh Matheson presiding, again expounding his favorite theme. A resolution was passed which is of interest principally because it introduced a note later to become prominent in China affairs—that the Government of India *guarantee* against loss any responsible private entrepreneurs prepared to undertake construction of the Colquhoun railway.[112] But even the London Chamber was soon to desert Archibald Colquhoun; seven months later it was regarding with sympathy suggestions that the Bhamo route might be preferable and that an independent, impartial survey should be undertaken.[113] Similarly, the Associated Chambers of Commerce passed a resolution urging a survey of railway routes through Burma to southwest China in order that railway communication might be opened as rapidly as possible. It was passed unanimously; but an amendment which would have recommended specifically the Colquhoun-Hallett line was rejected. The days of elaborate commercial memorials had passed. Intermittent agitation for the Colquhoun project continued, but was soon dropped. The Burma route became a Government affair, slow though the progress proved to be. By 1892 surveys of the Mandalay-Kunlon line were begun; in 1895 the line was finally authorized and construction commenced. Aside from occasional prodding by some of the Chambers, notably Liverpool, the vision of a highway into the fabulous markets of southwestern China had been converted into a correspondence file at the India Office.

By the end of the eighties, the China Question, in mercantile opinion, had yet to be converted into one of international rivalry for the legacy of the Manchus. Business men still desired to make the best of both worlds; to open the Chinese market wide, but to keep the lion's share for the established firm—Britain. The *Journal* of the London Chamber of Commerce, remarking on an item in the Journal of the French Chambers of Commerce that a struggle was about to begin at Tientsin between rival syndicates for a Chinese loan to finance the construction of the first China railway, made the striking observation that the execution of such a gigantic work, no matter by whom accomplished, would impart fresh life to European industry and would open China to European commerce and ideas.[114] The principal task was still that of "opening China"; who did it was of secondary consideration.

PA3RT

The Revival

VI

Formation of the China Association

> *"There would be no Army and Navy but for Commerce, and the duty of every man in this country was the development of that commerce which, in the words of the late Lord Carnarvon, was 'our life-spring, our vital breath, without which England would be the poorest, discontented, overpopulated isle in the North Sea' "*—Sir V. Hamilton at the Annual Dinner, China Association, 1891.

> *"I do not know, indeed, that it would be good for China to be treated generously; for then the lessons of adversity and of supreme misfortune might be forgotten"*—William Keswick, Chairman of the China Association, 1895.

> *"But what the devil is the B. Govt. about letting everything slip thro' their fingers? Cannot they see the game of Russia and France is to hamper* our *trade? Do they imagine that these countries want to reform China? . . . She is playing into the hands of Russia and France whose sole object is to replace* our *influence, which alone arises from commerce, by* their *own, which is founded on intrigue. . . ."*—Sir Edmund Hornby to R. S. Gundry, Torquay, June 13, 1895.

IN the autumn of 1888, Lord Rosebery addressed the Leeds Chamber of Commerce on "Chambers of Commerce and Government Policy," and emphasized the important political role which such commercial organizations might play if only they would. The Empire, he premised, was founded on commerce; commerce made Britain's colonies, and foreign policy today was mainly concerned with Britain's colonial position. It was, therefore, up to the Chambers to concern themselves with topics of Imperial interest and make their wishes known to the Government.[1]

Chambers of Commerce had, in fact, been operating in Great Britian since the end of the eighteenth century to promote foreign, as well as domestic, trade interests; but in intermittent fashion and apparently without defined political aims. The larger Chambers were reorganized in the middle of the nineteenth century and federated in the Associated Chambers of Commerce in 1860. Their method of operation in the political field is thus described by a commercial agent of the United States Department of Commerce:

British chambers of commerce, in spite of their unofficial character, are frequently consulted by governmental authorities in regard to the commercial interests of local character or matters affecting industries strongly represented in certain localities. They send deputations to Parliament and submit memorials, suggestions, and petitions to the Government. They correspond freely with the Foreign Office, the Colonial Office, the Board of Trade, and the Secretary for Home Affairs.[2]

Chambers underwent further reorganization in the eighties when the growth of foreign competition in world markets, and even the threat of invasion of the domestic market, stimulated a search for political aids to commerce.[3]

China interests in Great Britain had always lacked adequate representation. The East India and China Association of Liverpool had never gained prominence and, as we have seen, the larger London houses assumed the leadership in forming *ad hoc* mercantile committees during critical periods in Anglo-Chinese relations. The London Chamber of Commerce, formed in 1881 and destined to assume a position of leadership, had a strong Far Eastern bias. Such Old China Hands as Charles Magniac and William Keswick not only assisted at its birth but served *in loco parentis* for the first few years of its existence. Its East India and China Section continued to serve for some years as the center of home agitation on China affairs.

But, as more and more taipans and other China hands returned from the Orient in the eighties, pressure for the formation of a powerful and representative body exclusively concerned with Anglo-Chinese affairs gained ground. Not only was there a community of economic interest among them; social cohesion was strong. A profound sentimental attachment drew together those who had gone through the China adventure as it does those who have shared military life. Old China Hands—as they fondly referred to themselves—would gather at the Thatched House Club to exchange nostalgic memories of Hongkong and Shanghai and it was at the Club that the project for a China Association was first broached. Later, indeed, there would be some to complain that the economic aspects of the Association's activities were being neglected for its social functions. But the record, as we shall see, proves otherwise.

In any case, no single event was responsible for the decision to organize the China Association; the time was ripe for its formation because enough returned Old China Hands believed that organization for common interest would prove politically profitable. It was to prove a momentous decision. It is safe to venture the judgment that the China Association carried to a finer point the delicate art of lobbying in foreign affairs than any other mercantile body in the realm. From the start its leadership was assumed by representatives of the larger China houses, that is, the spokesmen for vested interests in commerce, shipping, utilities and banking in the Far East, leavened with members of Parliament from the "China bloc" and retired colonial and military officials who had seen service in the East. From the start, too, it preferred to work with the permanent civil service at the Foreign Office on a friendly, not to say intimate, basis, and to avoid all public manifestations which might embarrass its respectable relations with Downing Street.

Formation of the China Association was first broached at an inaugural dinner organized by "people in London interested in the China trade." On April 11 the Association was launched. Sir Alfred Dent, whose career as a leading China merchant had started twenty-five years before, acted as first Chairman and informed the organizing committee that "he hoped the main object of the Association would be to maintain British interests and British trade, and by so doing obtain the cooperation of the British Foreign Office and of H.M. Minister at Peking." [4] It was an accurate prospectus. A month later an Executive Committee was formed and Richard Simpson Gundry named Honorary Secretary. The "honorary" was a concession to the fact that Gundry received no salary, but concealed the fact that he was to serve not only as the executive secretary but as a major power and influence in the Association. Gundry, a man of fifty at the time, had been editor of the *North China Herald* and *Times* correspondent in China from 1865 to 1878; he was a prolific writer and had been extensively published in the better reviews. In June the Executive Committee invited those interested in the Japan trade to join. [5]

The year 1889 was one of organization and no substantive issues came up for consideration. There were, in any event, none but the chronic issues outstanding in Anglo-Chinese relations. By year's end the membership of the Association stood at over one hundred and was growing. The Association got off to a slow start and, indeed, it was not until the quickening of events in the Far East brought about by the Sino-Japanese war gave promise that a new day in Anglo-Chinese relations was dawning that the China Association was transformed into an active agency in mercantile politics. But even before then, in the few issues that did arise, the Association gave promise of leadership. What was more striking, the leaders of the Association were from the start aware of the fact that they were called upon to deal with the same problems and issues which had faced mercantile circles in the sixties and which had lain dormant for twenty years.

But first a word on organization. The functioning body of the Association was the General Committee (sometimes called the London Committee) which served as a board of directors on matters of policy as well as administration, and submitted its report to the membership at an annual dinner. An Executive Committee, consisting of the nuclear leadership of the General Committee, was chiefly of administrative importance, as the size of the General Committee permitted it to function efficiently. The presidency tended to become an honorary office (until Gundry took over in 1905) and leadership was vested in the Chairman of the General Committee. Sir George Bowen, former Governor of Hongkong, served as chairman when Sir Alfred Dent was elevated to the presidency, but he was soon replaced by William Keswick, who remained the active chairman throughout the period here reviewed. Keswick had become a partner in the firm of Jardine, Matheson & Co. in Hongkong in the early sixties, and returned to London as partner in Matheson & Co. He had also been a director of the Indo-Chinese Steam Navigation Co., as well as Chairman of the Hongkong Chamber of Commerce. In 1899 he was elected member of Parliament for a constituency in Surrey.

The first General Committee boasted the following names: Sir Robert Jardine, of the famous China house; Sir Thomas Wade, retired envoy; Sir Alfred Dent; Sir Edmund Hornby, former Chief Judge of the British Supreme Court in Shanghai; William Keswick; F. D. Barnes; E. F. Duncanson; E. Iveson; J. H. Gwyther; S. Ezekiel; T. Jackson; Thomas Sutherland; J. Whittall; David McLean; J. A. Maitland and C. D. Grant, all prominent in the China trade. Many were former leaders in the Shanghai and Hongkong Chambers and many were directors in the Hongkong & Shanghai Banking Corporation.

By March, 1890, when the first Annual Dinner was held at the Thatched House Club, organization was complete. The keynote speeches indicated that the Association was the spiritual descendant of the Shanghai and Hongkong Chambers; but with one exception. In congratulating Thomas Sutherland on his election to Parliament, Sir Thomas Wade noted that "they might feel assured that whenever there was a question to be brought forward connected with the interest of the China Trade in Parliament that they had an advocate upon whose zeal and ability they might thoroughly rely." He cautioned, however, that it might often be inconvenient ("he might say impossible") for the Foreign Office to pay the attention to their requests which they might desire, and it was incumbent upon them to approach the Foreign Office "in a spirit of cooperation and patience." It was a lesson the Association took to heart.

It was not until the very end of 1891—two and one-half years after its formation—that the China Association had occasion to publish a broad statement of its stand on Anglo-Chinese policy. But several issues which the organization considered in the first two years of its existence afforded a clue as to the direction it would take. The first was in response to a request by the Shanghai Chamber of Commerce that it oppose the ratification of the contemplated agreement between China and the cartel of telegraph companies, the Great Northern, a Danish concern, and the Eastern Extension, a British company headed by Sir John Pender, which aimed at fixing cable rates for fourteen years to combat competition expected from the extension of the Russian line to Kiachta and thence to Peking. The inducement to China was an annual subsidy of Tls. 100,000, but Peking would not ratify without British Government approval. The Shanghai Chamber, representing mercantile interests, strongly opposed the agreement which would have frozen the high cable rates, the burden falling on commercial consumers. Shanghai had already approached the London Chamber of Commerce, and Keswick (who was Chairman of the London Chamber as well as of the China Association) had made representations at the Foreign Office. Though he was given to understand that no decision had yet been taken, Keswick told the General Committee of the China Association that the "British Government appeared to be influenced by the important interests involved in the companies and feared their breakdown in the event of competition by a cheaper system." [6] Sir John Pender, who had the ear of the Foreign Office, was on his way to London to plead his case.

It was a striking conflict of interests. For, while mercantile circles desired low rates, Pender's telegraph cartel had powerful backing, his line from Hongkong to Shanghai to Tientsin being regarded as vital in maintaining the lines of the Empire in British hands. In fact, the Foreign Office had as far back as 1883 taken a deep interest in securing permission for Pender's cable to land at Shanghai.[7] The China Association, however, backed the plea of the Shanghai Chamber on the ground that "all other considerations are overruled by the prospect of a tax on commercial enterprise so onerous and so enduring, and in presence of a relief which the proximity of the Russian and Indo-Burmese lines to the China frontier otherwise promised." [8] The point was pressed by personal interview in Whitehall, with the support of the London Chamber, and Sir Thomas Sanderson [9] finally conceded that negotiations for ratification would be suspended as a result of this agitation.[10] It was the Association's first victory.

The China Association had gained prestige as a result of this victory. From that time no important problem in Anglo-Chinese affairs would be solved without its intervention. But, again in 1891, no outstanding event offered occasion for the assertion of mercantile policy—until the very end of the year. In sterling figures (which interested the Manchester manufacturer) the China trade remained stagnant in the neighborhood of eight million pounds sterling.[11] Treaty port residents became excited about only one issue which was in itself an index of the low state to which China affairs had fallen. In March Shanghai residents held a mass meeting protesting the proposed amalgamation of the offices of Chief Judge and Consul-General. It was an unhappy move on the part of the Foreign Office, dictated by public economy. The China Association was soon up in arms, Keswick writing a strong letter to the Foreign Office, even before the General Committee could meet, associating London with the China protest. It was too late. Sir Alfred Dent called at the Foreign Office to be confronted with the view of Whitehall that the two separate establishments were regarded as too costly and that the reduction had been made in fairness to the home taxpayer. This, of course, was the crowning insult: so low had the China trade fallen. Even Sir Alfred's appeal to prestige fell on deaf ears, but the Foreign Office promised to repeal the measure if it proved unworkable after a year's test.[12] The sole consolation to the China Association was that the Manchester Chamber expressed willingness to support them had they been approached in time.[13]

The incident proved several things to the members of the Association. It was felt that had they moved earlier they might have influenced the decision of the Foreign Office. It proved, as one member suggested, that the Association ought not to wait on Shanghai initiative before taking action on China affairs. Finally, it was the first attempt by the Association to enlist the support of the home Chambers and the result was not unfavorable. This became standard practice. For the first time it was suggested that the China Association, in order not to depend on the Shanghai Chamber, should set up its own committees at Hongkong and the major treaty ports.[14]

The occasion—and it was occasion rather than cause—which led to the first broad statement of policy by the China Association was its reaction to the series of anti-foreign outrages which had broken out in China in the summer of 1891.[15] At a meeting of the General Committee on December 2, 1891, it was proposed that a subcommittee be established to deal with the Foreign Office on the settlement of the issues arising out of this anti-foreign movement, and that information from the Far East be collected and employed as evidence to back up the following program on which future relations between Britain and China would be based: (a) that the mandarins rather than "the poorer classes of Chinese implicated" be held responsible and publicly punished; (b) that in addition to compensation for individual losses, broad guarantees for future protection of person and property be demanded; (c) that the "same privileges be demanded for foreigners in China that are accorded to Chinese in this country," a suggestion apparently advanced in all seriousness; (d) that "entire freedom of manufactures and other forms of enterprises should be accorded to Europeans at all treaty ports"; and (e) that "free communication, for purposes of trade and otherwise with the interior be allowed." [16]

This was, of course, far more than a plan for settling the anti-foreign riots; it was a program of political and commercial policy. Moreover, it was a declaration that the mercantile program of 1869 still had priority. Indeed, it was a plan for repudiation of the Board of Trade position of that year. As one member put it: "The best guarantees of the future consisted in the Chinese getting a better knowledge of foreigners, and this would be accomplished by their being brought into more intimate contact with them." [17] The China Association, however, was not prepared to publish this program as emanating from London. As a matter of strategy, it was decided that the Shanghai Chamber be urged to take the initiative, with London backing up the treaty port residents. Consequently, a letter was sent to Shanghai embodying the proposals suggested by the General Committee but outlining more specifically "the several things which we should like to see conceded" to be put forward in "an official statement." [18]

No formal reply was received from Shanghai, but it was learned that Shanghai did not consider the moment opportune for a broad statement, as the question of protection of foreigners was occupying the exclusive attention of foreign Ministers at Peking. The China Association placed the letter on record and thenceforth assumed the initiative in matters of policy, often disregarding the treaty ports. At the same time, Sir Alfred Dent proposed that the Association proceed with establishing its own committees at the treaty ports, committees which would be purely British and therefore devoted to British interests as against the Shanghai Chamber which was cosmopolitan and had an American chairman at the time. [19] There is no record as to when these bodies were set up, but within a year a Shanghai Committee and a Hongkong Committee had been established, acting as branches of the China Association in London. Henceforth, in all matters affecting Anglo-Chinese relations, these committees, rather than the local Chambers would express British mercantile attitudes.

The policy of the China Association—which was coming to be fashioned more and more by its energetic secretary, R. S. Gundry—had been outlined in the letter of December 4, 1891. The rebuff from Shanghai, however, made it evident that the occasion for pressing this program had not arrived. It was to come three years later under the impetus of the Sino-Japanese War. Meanwhile, the China Association turned its attention to the solution of the outstanding problems resulting from the failure of the Tientsin Treaty to open China in the manner traditionally interpreted by the merchants. As Gundry saw it, the main issue was still that of extending the frontier of commercial opportunity in China. The opening gambit was the attempt in 1892 to force respect for transit passes in the southern provinces. By the end of the eighties, the transit pass system as partially modified by the Chefoo Convention (which had been ratified in amended form in 1886) was working successfully along the Yangtze. The general principle of immunity had been established and, so far as imports were concerned, transit certificates even in the hands of natives were being generally honored. Complaints, however continued to be voiced that no such immunity was enjoyed in the southern provinces of Kwangsi and Kwangtung, traditional centers of anti-foreign sentiment. The issue was closely tied up with that of internal trade and residence and it was out of an incident involving this assumed privilege that the occasion for China Association action arose.

At Fatshan on the West River in Kwangtung, a Mr. Herbert Dent had opened a hong (warehouse) under a native compradore (contrary to the letter of treaty provision); the local authorities, regarding the action as illegal and as a maneuver to evade *likin* dues, confiscated his goods and imprisoned his native employees. Dent appealed to the China Association, asserting his right to establish a hong and claiming further that the native authorities should not have acted except through the British consul. At its meeting of May 25, 1892, the General Committee debated the question. Keswick, leading the moderate faction, asserted that Dent had put himself out of court by opening the hong, while Gundry insisted that Dent had as much right as any missionary, under the treaty, to establish himself in the interior. He urged that it be made a test case, for "it raised the question whether treaties were negotiated for the benefit of missionaries rather than merchants." [20] Action was postponed. Dent later raised further objection to the settlement of the case under which the consul had agreed that on release of his employees and restoration of goods the affair would be closed. He had, he argued, been relying on the immunity granted by the transit pass for his goods and this right would be "extinguished" if the settlement were allowed to ride. Gundry backed up this view, but the Committee decided not to press the matter.[21]

The affair did not end there. Gundry was determined that it be used as the occasion not only for solving the transit issue but as a lever for other concessions.[22] In a letter to Lord Rosebery, dated October 14, 1892, Gundry reasoned that the Fatshan case was an attempt to deal a blow at the whole transit pass system.[23] He elaborated on the importance of the transit arrangement for the extension of British commerce, choked by illegal taxation. But what was needed above all for the adequate expansion of commerce in the southern provinces was the opening of the West River to foreign steamers. For that matter, similar authority to carry goods by steamer up the Yangtze to the far interior was the most effective way of freeing goods from inland taxation.

At the same time Gundry enlisted the strong backing of the home Chambers. Bradford, Glasgow, London, Liverpool and Manchester— all endorsed the Gundry letter, Liverpool going beyond it to demand "steps necessary to ensure observance of the terms of the Treaty of Tientsin." [24] The reply of the Foreign Office, though not entirely favorable, led Gundry to believe that "the question will not be lost sight of by H.M. Minister in his intercourse with the Imperial authorities." [25] Although the China Association did not immediately gain its ends, it had laid the foundation for a strong mercantile policy which the Foreign Office would respect when the occasion arose some years later. Moreover, two further points had been made. The center of mercantile pressure for realization of the demands put forth since ratification of the Treaty of Tientsin had shifted from the Far East to London, and the home Chambers could be counted on for support when given effective leadership by the China Association.

Following the initiative and acting on the suggestion of the China Association, the Hongkong Chamber of Commerce under the chairmanship of J. J. Keswick concentrated throughout 1893 on pressure for the opening of the West River to steam navigation and foreign trade. In a memorial to Lord Rosebery of July 31, 1893, the Hongkong Chamber advanced the traditional mercantile argument that the existing treaty ports of South China had "now" reached their trade limits and "cannot possibly be extended until new fields are opened up by improved means of communication with the interior." [26] Numerous *likin* stations had a restrictive effect on trade, it was argued. The interior markets of Fukien and Kwangtung were scarcely tapped, while the great inland provinces of Kwangsi, Yunnan, and Kweichow had hardly been touched at all from the commercial point of view. In addition, the Chamber stressed the fact that existing traffic was threatened by diversion to the new route opened through Tongking to Yunnan, an overland road on which preferential tariff rates obtained and which the French Government was encouraging "to the detriment of British interests."

The Hongkong Chamber here raised a point which was beginning to concern mercantile as well as official circles. The Anglo-Chinese treaty of July 24, 1886,[27] relating to Burma, had contemplated encouragement of overland trade from Burma to Yunnan (a pledge implemented by the treaty of March 1, 1894 [28]) as a counter to the trade concessions obtained by France after the Tongking War; in addition, Britain obtained by treaty in 1890 and 1893 further rights to overland trade and the residence at Yatung.[28a] But, in British eyes, the only practical competitor to the Red River route was the water route from Canton along the West River.[29] This explains why the merchants became so exercised about opening the West River. For it involved not alone the traditional ambition for penetrating the interior, but also the fear of French competition to existing trade. Hongkong, therefore, pressed Lord Rosebery to "induce" the Chinese to open the West River to foreign steamers and the cities of Wuchow, Sinchow, and Nanning on its course to foreign trade. And it specifically urged that the diplomatic basis for these concessions could be discovered in the recent concession to France of the right to trade at two points in Kwangsi and Yunnan.

Hongkong had thus furnished the Foreign Office not only with substantive demands but with strategy, a strategy to be employed when the occasion presented itself three years later. The China Association backed up the memorial, noting that it embodied some of the demands it had made the previous year.[30] Support also came from the home Chambers. Liverpool fully agreed that the concessions demanded by Hongkong should be pressed as "an equivalent of privileges given the French on the Southwest borders of China," [31] while Manchester reiterated its stand of the previous year in favor of extending the transit pass system throughout the southern provinces.[32]

This was the major direction of China Association activity in the few years of its existence prior to the Sino-Japanese War. Concern with possible foreign competition, despite the noted anxiety over French rivalry in southern China, was peripheral. Study of the Minute Books and correspondence of the China Association indicates that what was later to figure so prominently—that is, the threat to Britain's predominant position in China as a result of international rivalry—played almost no part in mercantile counsels. On the contrary, the major problem was still that of convincing Whitehall that pressure on the effete, inefficient, economically backward Chinese was the sole means of extending the frontier of economic opportunity in China. As one Old China Hand remarked in toasting the officers of the Association at its Annual Dinner in 1893, the thing that struck him most was that they

had evidently acted with a full sense of the importance of the lessons of the past with regard to the Government of China. They saw and felt, he was sure from the tenor of their communication with the Foreign Office, that the old oriental spirit which always had animated the Government of China . . . still pervaded the Chinese Government. That spirit must be kept down and pushed back by a proper insistence.[33]

Nor did the leadership of the China Association see the Sino-Japanese struggle as a turning point in Far Eastern affairs, but rather as the supreme occasion for pressing upon China the traditional program of organized merchants. Indeed, neither the General Committee nor the Executive Committee even considered the implications of that struggle until the very end of 1894 and the attitude then taken was hardly surprising; it will be noted below. Throughout the year, the Association was concerned with only two major issues: whether openly to support the bimetallist convictions held by a majority of its members, and how to combat the new Anglo-Japanese Treaty. The first is significant only as an index of the profound respect paid by its leaders to maintaining the good-will of the Foreign Office. The second indicates that British merchants were seized neither with pro-Japanese nor with pro-Chinese bias during the struggle, but were merely eager to maintain their privileges in the Far East against threats from any quarter.

While the membership of the China Association was overwhelmingly in favor of bimetallism—because depreciated silver had, on the whole, an adverse affect on mercantile profits in silver-using countries like China— its General Committee was nevertheless opposed to becoming identified publicly with the bimetallism movement. Thus, when the Shanghai Committee proposed sending a delegation from the Far East to address meetings and approach influential people to attract attention to the currency question and to the "important volume of Far Eastern trade," the General Committee was unanimously of the opinion that such agitation was uncalled for; unofficial support of the Bimetallic League was regarded as preferable.[34] Actually, the China Association leadership was pursuing a policy of collaboration with Whitehall and opposed the radical publicity methods of the bimetallists. When Gundry, who was also secre-

tary of the China section of the Bimetallic League, proposed that the
China Association participate in organizing a deputation to lobby for
bimetallism, officers of the Association urged caution and succeeded in
tabling the matter.[35] This conservative procedure was to be characteristic of the Association.

The China Association's attitude to Japanese treaty revision, which
was the second major issue considered that year, is even more significant.
Objection by residents at Yokohama to the proposed Anglo-Japanese
commercial treaty of 1894 was taken up by the General Committee,
which throughout the summer brought strong pressure to bear against its
ratification. Major opposition, as evidenced in the letter sent to the
Foreign Office, was to the projected abolition of extraterritoriality in
Japan in 1899; a few voices were also heard opposing the higher tariff
rates in the new treaty.[36] Under the guidance of Gundry, this agitation
spread among the home Chambers with some success. London and Leeds
immediately aligned themselves with the China Association. The Manchester Chamber, however, pointed out that in exchange for abolition
of extraterritoriality foreign merchants had been granted complete
liberty of trade in the interior, and refused to associate itself with the
movement.[37] Residents in the treaty ports failed to see the point and the
Shanghai Committee again urged the parent organization to protest ratification in order "to prevent any assumption on the part of H.M. Government that silence might mean acquiescence in what was considered a
monstrous surrender of British interests." [38]

The affair itself was of small concern but it indicates the direction of
mercantile thought during the summer when the Sino-Japanese war had
already started. The early effort of the British Government to organize
a concert of Powers to prevent the outbreak of hostilities [39] was in line
with early mercantile opinion that war would have an adverse effect on
British trade and shipping. But there is no evidence that the China merchants were appreciably concerned, nor that they shared official indignation at Japan for disturbing the peace.[40] Certainly, there is nothing to
demonstrate mercantile suspicions of Japan as the aggressor. George
Curzon's conclusion that "our interests therefore, whatever our sympathies, lie neither with this nor with that combatant but are undividedly
involved in the restoration as soon as possible of peace" [41] would probably come closest to general opinion at that time.

Even the surprise sinking by the Japanese of the *Kowshing*,[41a] a
British steamer chartered by the Chinese to carry their troops to Korea,
although it aroused some indignation, had no appreciable influence on
mercantile attitude. In fact, the most instructive reaction to that incident
is Gundry's attempt to employ it as a debating point in the China Associ-

ation campaign against the abolition of extraterritoriality in Japan. In a letter to *The Times*,[42] Gundry seized on the "ghastly massacre" attending the *Kowshing* sinking as proof of the mercantile contention that Japan was still unfit for equality of treatment in treaty relations with Western Powers. Aside from this, he did not regard the war itself as of major concern to British interests, unless "complications" set in.[43]

Successful efforts were made by the British Government [44] to maintain the neutrality of the treaty ports during the conflict and mercantile interests apparently did not go beyond that concern in the early months of the war. Nor is there any indication of China Hand interest in the efforts of the Foreign Office in October, 1894, to bring about joint intervention to stop the war.[45] Owing to German opposition and non-cooperation by the United States, the effort failed,[46] and evidence from mercantile sources would indicate insufficient public sentiment for unilateral intervention on the part of Great Britain. If the peace project was dropped by the British Government, it was really never taken up by unofficial circles.

What, then, was the mercantile attitude? Not too concerned with the immediate effect of the war on trade nor with the prospect of the disturbance of the balance of power in the Far East, the China Association turned its attention, toward the end of 1894, to the occasion offered by the war and post-war settlement for pressing upon China that program of reform long sought by Old China Hands. The discomfiture of China meant that the opportunity had finally arrived for securing the concessions, part of which had been adumbrated in the China Association letter of December 4, 1891, and most of which had been inherited from the generation of 1869. No other interpretation can be placed on the evidence available in mercantile sources.

Following a series of discussions at General Committee meetings in November and December, 1894, Gundry was authorized to draft a letter to the Foreign Office outlining the basic position of the China Association in Anglo-Chinese relations; at the same time, it was agreed to coordinate efforts with the Shanghai and Hongkong Committees and their views were invited.[47] In a letter to Lord Kimberley, dated December 15, 1894, the China Association, after noting with approval the "endeavours made to terminate hostilities that cannot but have a serious effect on British trade," advanced the argument that in the postwar settlement Japan would exact terms which would profoundly affect the terms of international trade in China for the future. The true policy of Britain, therefore, was to seize the occasion "to urge upon the Chinese government, with a weight which the circumstances cannot fail to render impressive, the adoption of changes that have been hitherto resisted, but whose urgency will, it is conceived, be now apparent to the more enlightened mandarins themselves." [48]

Without, at that time, particularizing the reforms desired, the Association emphasized that the inefficiency displayed by the Chinese forces was due to "their failure to accept foreign instructions, as well as the exclusiveness which has closed the waterways against modern navigation and the apathy which has delayed the adoption of railways, mines and other forms of progress." As for the "extravagant and doubtless irresponsible" rumor that Japan was about to occupy Shanghai, the Association was convinced that she would hesitate to take such a step by "the pronounced apprehension and dislike with which the appearance of her fleet in the approach to the Yangtze would be unanimously viewed by Foreign Powers." [49]

To its Shanghai and Hongkong Committees the China Association forwarded copies of this letter, noting that "you will perceive that reference is made to the possibility that it may lead to great changes in the condition of trade and residence." It was further suggested that the Shanghai Committee draw up a memorial in the sense suggested in December, 1891, "collating the suggestions that have been made from time to time for the extension of intercourse and general improvement of British relations with China." [50]

It is important to note what the policy thus outlined implied, for it was not an isolated statement but the consistent line pursued by mercantile circles throughout the period immediately following the Sino-Japanese War. Certain modifications were incorporated when foreign rivalries threatened British predominance, but the basic policy of employing the crisis as a means of pressing traditional demands for the opening of China was never abandoned. As Keswick put it to the membership of the China Association, China was being counselled to "put her house in order for the future; otherwise, with the progress of the nations around her . . . she will be torn to pieces. It will become only a matter of time, unless she assimilates modern ideas and makes herself strong as a nation by modern improvement." Japan might not prove moderate in her demands, but that might prove beneficial to China as well as to Western Powers. "I do not know, indeed, that it would be good for China to be treated generously; for then the lessons of adversity and of supreme misfortune might be forgotten." [51]

Or, as it was put somewhat differently by Sir Richard T. Rennie, formerly Chief Judge of the Supreme Court in China, at the dinner that evening: China would probably need a loan after the war and when she "comes into the European markets as a large borrower, European financiers will say 'What security?' " China will then be forced to grant concessions for railways, telegraphs and mines, and it would be a splendid opportunity for pressing those industrial and commercial reforms which business men had always desired. Not the menace of Japanese aggression or Russian rivalry, but the "splendid opportunity" for British trade and investment quickened mercantile hearts in February, 1895.

By this time the China Association had a membership of over four hundred and its General Committee spoke as the recognized representative of British commercial interests in China. According to the *London & China Telegraph*,[52] the Association's leadership was regarded in mercantile circles as so eminently representative and so well in touch with everyone concerned that it would instinctively choose the course its constituents desired.

That the evil times which had fallen on China might prove the splendid opportunity for forcing upon her the maximum demands of the mercantile program was the basic premise of China Association policy. But even early in the crisis there were dissident voices warning the Old China Hands that they might be trading a small but vested business for the menace of foreign competition. It was this added awareness of the danger implicit in international rivalries superimposed on the traditional drive for the opening of China which accounts for the ambivalence of mercantile policy and the compromises which it was later forced to adopt. The Japanese peril to Britain's position in China was noted as early as January, 1895. Writing to *The Standard*,[53] "A Former Resident in China" criticized mercantile adherence to the policy of non-intervention. The opening of China would, in any event, no longer be delayed: but the question was, who would teach the Chinese, the "immature Japs" or "civilising Westerners"? "That the Japanese should never be allowed to control the wealth and men of China is a matter of almost life and death to England, so long as she intends to maintain her position in the East."

This was a dissenting opinion. The *London & China Telegraph* [54] termed such views "alarmist in tone." The Japanese, it held, would not overstep "diplomatic limits" in any settlement imposed on China. Throughout February and March, however, as the Japanese were gaining military successes, this element of a Japanese peril to British interests, so long as the peace terms remained unknown, could not be overlooked. It became a chess game in weighing probabilities. The conversations which commenced at the Foreign Office with Russian and German representatives in February, exploring the wisdom of intervention, were apparently aimed at a solution of this uncertainty.[55] As Joseph puts it: "The British statesmen's desire for intervention between China and Japan was in direct ratio to the scope of Japan's aims in

China." [56] Thus, on February 21, *The Times* cautioned Japan that unless her terms were moderate she was in danger of colliding with the Western Powers, "who also have to think of the relations to be maintained in the future between themselves and China." Two weeks later, however, the same newspaper [57] was reporting "from the highest sources" in Tokyo that "in opening the whole of China to trade, Japan does not seek to obtain for herself better conditions than for any other country."

The same ambivalence prevailed in mercantile circles, and for similar reasons. China Association policy had been stated in a letter of December 15, 1894, [58] but disquieting and contradictory views began to arrive from the treaty ports in March. A telegram from the Shanghai Committee, dated March 21, expressed the apprehension felt on the Bund: "Committee strongly urge British vigilance Chinese-Japanese negotiations; advocate immediate despatch High Commissioner [to] safeguard important British interests involved. British Minister [in] Japan incapacitated [by] illness. Private agreement China-Japan antagonistic England feared." [59] Another telegram was received that day urging the Association to inquire as to the truth of a report that the naval squadron in China waters was being reduced and the Admiral changed, a move vigorously opposed because of "increased Japanese [and] Russian fleets [and] general position affairs." [60] Shanghai was jittery.

The first telegram was forwarded to the Foreign Office with a private note from Sir Alfred Dent to Sir Thomas Sanderson. Dent later called at the Foreign Office and received Sanderson's assurances that Lord Kimberley would look into the matter, but he did not believe the appointment of a special commissioner, desired by Shanghai, practicable. The Foreign Office was fully aware of the issues involved, but was biding its time until treaty provisions were known. Gundry, meanwhile, had approached George Curzon, the Parliamentary Undersecretary, and pointed out the menace involved in the rumored Japanese acquisition of Port Arthur and Formosa. Curzon replied that he doubted Japan would adopt an attitude antagonistic to England, but assured Gundry that he recognized the importance of the Formosan issue and its relation to Britain's position at Hongkong. [61]

The General Committee was uncertain of the position to adopt or where the greater danger lay. While some members supported the Shanghai stand, Sir Cecil Smith (former Governor of the Straits Settlements) expressed the belief that a secret Russo-Chinese treaty existed which would prevent Japanese annexations in the North. Sir Richard T

Rennie also tried to calm the members, suggesting that it would be sufficient to caution the Foreign Office that Formosa and the Pescadores remain unfortified in the event of Japanese annexation.[62] It was, however, decided to address a letter to the Foreign Office (a) voicing apprehension lest the peace terms be injurious to British interests, (b) urging acceptance of the Shanghai proposal that a "strong man" be sent to Tokyo to replace the ailing Trench, and (c) expressing alarm if Japan intended to secure a military or naval base off the southern coast of China.[63] Mr. Bertie, the Assistant Undersecretary, replied that the Government had full confidence in the Secretary of Legation in Tokyo and repeated assurances that no reduction of the naval squadron in China waters was contemplated. The Foreign Office would express no opinion on the Japanese menace.[64]

The Shanghai letter of March 23, 1895, proved even more alarming than their telegram.[65] Underlining the menace involved in Japanese expansion, the Shanghai branch noted that "the belief gains ground that if affairs are left to be settled between the two Eastern nations, without the intervention of the Great Powers of Europe, the result may be prejudicial to . . . the now vast and valuable interests of British subjects in the whole of the Far East." The aims of Japan, Shanghai predicted, were more far-reaching than annexation and indemnity; she intended to reorganize China under her "ambitious and restless" control, "a prospect so grave in its material aspect as to amply justify the appeal of this Committee to H.M. Government to exercise the utmost vigilance over the events which may be expected to follow the mission of Li Hung-Chang to Japan."

This prophetic warning, however, proved to be an historical aberration, and mercantile circles were not to speak of a Japanese menace for another ten years. There was no such abrupt change in British opinion as McCordock suggests,[66] but rather a conviction that the peace terms would be moderate politically and profitable commercially.[67] The famous leader in the *St. James' Gazette* of March 18, 1895, probably best expressed the feeling of the mercantile community:

Japan, for many years to come, will do us no harm. We need not object to her naval strength in the Pacific. No doubt she would menace and alarm Russia; but that is no affair of ours. Let Japan and Russia fight it out if they please. For ourselves, if Japan acts as a counterpoise to the formidable Empire which is stretching one of its long arms round Northern Asia, we are no losers, and if Japan throws open the gigantic territories of China to foreign trade, we of all peoples in the world have most to gain by it, in spite of the competition of Yokohama and Tokio.[68]

The *London & China Telegraph,* which had repeatedly been stressing the view that Japan would act as just such a counterpoise to Russia and had even been suggesting an Anglo-Japanese alliance,[69] fully approved of the *Gazette's* views. By becoming friends with Japan, it noted, Britain could take advantage of her efforts to open China.[70]

This, too, was the decision of the China Association. Even before the peace terms were known, mercantile circles renewed appeals to the British Government to exact from China the traditional reforms and concessions for which Old China Hands had always clamored. In response to the London Committee's gambit of the previous December, the Shanghai branch, in April, 1895, listed the following suggestions "for the improvement and extension of commercial relations";

(a) All British subjects to have the right to reside in any part of China, and trade anywhere under consular regulations.

(b) The British Consul-General at Shanghai and the Chinese Commissioner to form a Board of Control for purposes of regulating commercial relations.

(c) A High Commissioner to be appointed to deal with the current crisis.

(d) A Special Commissioner to be appointed to investigate trade conditions and opportunities.

(e) Additional British consuls to be established at places open to trade.

(f) Improved provisions for inland navigation, for railway construction and the establishment of a national currency.[71]

But, Shanghai concluded, it was hardly necessary to list specific reforms, for they had been contained, not only in the Hongkong memorial of July 31, 1893,[72] but in the memorials submitted by the Chambers of Commerce in 1867 and 1869–70 during the treaty revision discussions of Alcock's day! The mercantile position, they pointed out, had not changed since that day and policy should now consist in securing those concessions which had been refused thirty years before. Similarly, the Hongkong Chamber, in its reply to the Association, pointed to their memorial of 1893 as embodying present policy.[73]

The Shanghai letter was forwarded to the Foreign Office and its provisions privately advocated in an interview with the Permanent Under secretary.[74] British mercantile opinion was not disposed to intervene in favor of China if Japanese peace terms proved acceptable, that is, if they would extend trading opportunities and offer no threat to Shanghai and Hongkong.[75] And so they proved. The Japanese terms as submitted at Shimonoseki the first week in April left little doubt that mercantile opinion would view the settlement not unfavorably. If anything, the "moderation" displayed in watering down original commercial demands was not welcomed in the treaty ports. Japan had demanded the cession of Formosa and the Pescadores, which caused some disquiet in mercantile circles, as we shall see, and of Southern Manchuria, which disturbed them not at all. An indemnity of 200 million taels was to be paid by China. The commercial provisions read like something out of a British Chamber of Commerce memorial: four new ports were opened to "trade, residence, industry and manufactures"; the right to navigate the Upper Yangtze from Ichang to Chungking with steamers was granted (though not of the West River as provided in the original terms); the right to establish warehouses in the interior and to engage in industry in the open ports was also secured.[76] Under most-favored-nation treatment British subjects would enjoy all these privileges. Only the provision that the indemnity be guaranteed by the Customs revenues was designed not to meet mercantile approval.

The original Japanese terms became known on April 4 and were regarded as so favorable to British interests as hardly to warrant British intervention.[77] The one fear, that Japan would organize China into an Asiatic sphere aimed at excluding the Western Powers, had failed to materialize. Lord Kimberley informed the German Ambassador that the cession of the Liaotung peninsula might menace Russian interests but that "English interests are principally concentrated in and about Shanghai," and suggested that the danger to Peking might be avoided by removing the capital to Nanking, a proposal which was later taken up by mercantile circles with determination.[78] On April 8 the British Cabinet met and decided against intervention on the grounds that the peace terms did not harm British interests.[79] The same day The Times stated that the Liaotung territorial cession did not menace British interests, "while by other parts of the agreement they may be possibly advanced." [80] Great Britain, therefore, did not associate herself with the action of the Dreibund, consisting of Russia, France, and Germany, which forced Japan to renounce her claim to any territory on the China mainland.[81] On May 8 the Treaty of Shimonoseki, as modified, was ratified.

In these negotiations, mercantile interests appear to have displayed little concern. The treaty, on the whole, was acceptable. In fact the sole objection to its commercial provisions was that they had not gone far enough. But the cession of Formosa and the Pescadores, which threatened the life-line from Hongkong to Shanghai, was regarded with some suspicion. It was held that "British interests would be affected by the cession of Formosa, as keenly as Russia would be affected by the annexation of Manchuria." [82] For the possession of Formosa would give the Japanese a commanding position off the coasts of Fukien and Kwangtung and "compel a permanent addition to the military and naval strength of Hongkong." Gundry said it was an open secret that China would prefer to transfer the island to England. The immediate interest involved was stressed by the Shanghai firm of Butterfield & Swire in a protesting note to the Minister at Peking. Japanese annexation, they stated, would mean discriminatory duties and regulations favoring Japanese trade and shipping. Before England agreed to it, such conditions should be insisted upon "as will preserve the equality which at present exists and to which we have a right by treaty." [83]

The Shanghai Committee supported this stand, while the China Association in London urged upon the Foreign Office the vital importance of preserving for British trade and shipping conditions of equality if the cession could not be prevented.[84] Sir Nicholas O'Conor, then British Minister in Peking, replied that annexation would probably not interfere with Butterfield & Swire's shipping privileges between Japan and Formosa, but admitted that it is "only too probable that tariff changes will be made, which will severely handicap the British trade competing from Hongkong. But this is a consequence of the cession of territory which it would be difficult to isolate from the results of the war or to prevent by diplomatic action." [85] Without access to Foreign Office documents of the period, the Government's view cannot be stated with certainty; but it apparently coincided with that of O'Conor. Britain was hardly in a position to take action in view of her abstention from the Dreibund démarche on the Liaotung cession. As Gundry reported, after seeing officials at the Foreign Office, it was felt that "political difficulties would best be conciliated by acquiescing in its surrender to a third and friendly power." [86] The incident was thereafter dropped.

The benefits to be derived from the commercial sections of the Treaty of Shimonoseki, however, were pursued. These, in Gundry's words, had been "less drastic than had been anticipated," and it was evident that mercantile demands were far from fulfilled. Keswick told the General Committee (what later was revealed to be a fact) that the original agreement had included the provision for opening the West River, but had been dropped at the time of ratification.[87] It was difficult to approach the Foreign Office to remedy the situation since "political relations in the East are very strained on account of the intervention of the Powers from which England held aloof." China might feel antagonistic and balk at granting concessions. Some members disagreed with Keswick, whose respect for Whitehall sensibilities was not universally shared, and reasoned that China would appreciate that Russia's intervention had hardly been a disinterested one. It was decided to approach the Foreign Office and renew the plea made at the end of 1891 and the program outlined by Shanghai in April.

In the hands of Gundry, the China Association letter to the Foreign Office, dated July 1, 1895, and outlining basic policy to be pursued in Anglo-Chinese relations, was converted into something more than the General Committee had apparently intended.[88] While certain fundamental concessions—such as the right of access by steamer to Chungking and the right to establish industries at the treaty ports—had been secured, the treaty had fallen far short of the commercial progress anticipated. It had been believed that the right to navigate the West River and to reside in the interior would be granted; this hope had proved abortive. But, Gundry argued, the crux of the matter lay not in individual concessions but in securing basic fiscal and administrative reform in China without which British enterprise would be unable to profit from the opportunity offered. The China Association concluded that while the political situation "may be unfavourable to large measures of reform at the present time," it was also true that "Chinese statesmen may in the near future be more willing than in the past to receive advice which may help to extricate them from political and financial embarrassment."

In sum, the China Association was recommending that the British Government might assume leadership in reorganizing Chinese administration in the Egyptian manner. Mark the date: July 1, 1895. The first indemnity loan was just being negotiated, while talk of "the break-up of China" was far from prevalent. But Gundry, at least, was already aware that the mercantile program for opening China could never be attained unless the British Government were willing to assume the responsibility of reforming, reorganizing, and administering China. The suspicion that the other Powers might be unwilling to see England undertake the task was not even breathed.

In addition, the Committee supported Shanghai's proposal for the "appointment of a special High Commissioner to deal with the great questions involved, and to secure for Great Britain continuance of the foremost situation it has long enjoyed." [89] It was the renewal of a request made the previous April, but exactly what Shanghai was aiming at is not clear. To O'Conor, the Shanghai Committee wrote at about the same time that while the Treaty of Shimonoseki rendered superfluous some of the demands made in the April memorial, they were

still impressed with the importance, to their own national commercial interests, of effect being given to certain other suggestions . . . particularly as regards the appointment of a Commissioner authorised to inquire into and report upon the entire state of British trade in China and upon the validity and practicability of reforms suggested by the practical experience of years.[90]

Whether it was a political or a commercial agent which Shanghai desired, whether it was the "continuance of the foremost situation" of
British interests against international rivalry or commercial reforms
which concerned them most, it was quite clear that Shanghai was searching for a policy which would secure both these ends. That was the goal of
British mercantile circles from mid-1895 and Gundry had proposed that
the solution lay in a reform of China under British tutelage.

But a new factor was to enter into mercantile thinking. On May 20,
1895, the *London & China Telegraph,* an accurate sounding-board of
Old China Hand opinion, remarked that now that the treaty was signed
and the Dreibund démarche successful, China would be opened to trade
but that a race for concessions would ensue in which "British capital
and enterprise will have a hard fight to hold its commanding position
in China." Although business had supported the governmental policy
of non-intervention, the suspicion was gaining ground that that policy
might prove inadequate to the situation. The *Daily Graphic* [91] published
the "uneasy impression" of a correspondent that Lord Kimberley's
policy of "masterly abstention" in the rearrangement of the power
balance in the Far East had been neither sound nor farsighted. This
suspicion grew when the negotiations for the first indemnity loan ended
in a triumph for the Franco-Russian bloc, a triumph which first aroused
the mercantile community to the realization that power politics had
entered the Far Eastern scene. It was, from then on, not enough to press
for implementation of the program inherited from the men of '69; the
chief issue was being transmuted from one of opening China to one of
protecting British predominance there. Or rather the one factor was
being superimposed on the other, leading to a marked ambivalence in
mercantile attitudes.

It was, particularly, the loan of 1895 which first projected this new
element onto the scene, leading Sir Edmund Hornby, former Chief Judge
in Shanghai, to interrupt his vacation at Torquay long enough to write
an indignant letter to Gundry:

But what the devil is the B. Govt. about letting everything slip thro' their
fingers? Cannot they see the game of Russia and France is to hamper *our* trade?
Do they imagine that these countries want to reform China? So long as she goes
on in the way she has been going on—she is playing into the hands of Russia
and France whose sole object is to replace *our* influence, which alone arises from
commerce by *their* own, which is founded on intrigue etc. They revel in the
"raw" which China is always keeping open in her relations with *us*. All our
schemes for improving the governmental and Fiscal administration of China
they are thwarting and will thwart. They know that we will *not* fight and they
know that we have no firm policy, or indeed any worthy of the name.

I do hope that you will use all your Press influence to prevent Englishmen subscribing to the Loan. If as nation *we refuse* they *cannot* get the money— brag of their resources as much as they like.[92]

The Treaty of Shimonoseki had exacted an indemnity of 200 million taels, and in addition China was required to pay 30 millions for the retrocession of the Liaotung peninsula. Even before the news broke that a Russo-French bloc had been formed to negotiate the loan for the first indemnity payment, mercantile circles were afloat with all sorts of rumors concerning banking interests which would participate in this first really large Chinese loan to enter the European financial markets.[93] British and German capital had financed China during the war, though on a comparatively minor scale. But it was not the question of the investment as such which stirred the China Association; there is no evidence in its records that this factor was given serious attention. Rather, its primary concern was that a loan guaranteed on the customs revenue might lead to an increase in provincial taxes or tariff rates and impair the administrative integrity of the Imperial Customs.[94]

There was also the fear that the Russian-led bloc would insist on the removal of Sir Robert Hart as Inspector-General of the Customs. The fact that loans were guaranteed in the order in which they were incurred led Gundry to prepare a list of loans outstanding in 1895 compared with the customs revenue for 1894. In pounds sterling these were:

On the 1887 Berlin & Hamburg loan, 5½%	175,000
On the 1894 Hongkong & Shanghai Bank loan, 7% . .	1,635,000
On the 1895 Hongkong & Shanghai Bank loan, 6% . .	3,000,000
On the 1895 Chartered Bank loan, 6%	1,000,000
On the 1895 National Bank of Germany loan, 6%	1,000,000
A total in 1895 of	6,810,000 [95]

All but the first of these had been incurred in connection with the Sino-Japanese War, but the total was still small compared with the 400 million franc (£15,820,000) loan concluded by Franco-Russian interests on July 6, 1895. As against this indebtedness of more than 22 million pounds, Chinese customs receipts in 1894 amounted to £3,750,000, out of which costs of administration and subsidies to provincial governments had to be paid.

When the Russo-French loan was first reported, mercantile circles expressed concern only with its possible effect on the integrity of the customs. If there was any suspicion that "the consummation of this loan resulted in the introduction of a new factor in the politics of the Far East," [96] it was certainly not expressed by the members of the China Association, with the single exception noted above. It was on June 7 that Europe first learned of the proposed loan,[97] excluding German participation. Anglo-German conversations apparently ensued in an attempt to counter the effects of the Russo-French action. In the absence of complete diplomatic records Whitehall's attitude can only be surmised, but opposition apparently centered on the threat to British commerce implicit in the hypothecation of customs revenue and in the rumored political concessions which France and Russia were demanding in compensation for the loan. A joint Anglo-German note was issued to China warning "of the risk involved in accepting a loan guaranteed by Russia," and pressing upon it the alternative of accepting a loan from the Anglo-German syndicate which had been formed for the occasion by the Hongkong & Shanghai Bank and German financiers.[98]

Despite this strong objection, China felt forced to accept the loan and, on July 6, the agreement was concluded. It involved a loan of 400 million gold francs (about 16 million pounds) at four percent, of which French banks supplied 250 millions. Most important from the mercantile standpoint was the fact that this borrowing took its place on the growing list of Chinese obligations secured on the customs revenue. In addition, Russia undertook to guarantee repayment in exchange for certain political privileges which were defined in an attached protocol, under which China promised that in the event of a grant of "any right or privilege under any name whatsoever concerning the supervision or administration of the revenues of the Chinese Empire," the grant would be extended to the Russian Government alone.[99]

The loan, as such, did not profoundly disturb business circles. Its aftermath, however, revealing an apparently concerted Russo-French scheme for penetration of China by means of exclusive commercial and industrial concessions led to a substantial modification in mercantile opinion. The threat to British predominance was real. But the most striking thing about Old China Hand attitude was that, even in the face of this recognized threat from foreign competitors, primary emphasis in mercantile briefs was still placed on the traditional program advanced in Alcock's day. Crises created by foreign pressure were still recognized as opportunities for forcing concessions from China.

The situation in the South first revealed this attitude. As compensation for participation in the Dreibund, France succeeded in extracting from China, during the loan negotiations in June, two treaties designed to strengthen her position in the southern provinces. By the first,[100] the Sino-Annamese frontier was adjusted in France's favor, including the cession of territory along the Mekong river. Despite British objection that this contravened the Anglo-Chinese Treaty of March 1, 1894, under which territory in the Shan States (through which the Sprye route was originally scheduled to pass) was recognized as Chinese, provided it was not ceded to any other nation, French pressure forced China to sign.[101] By the second treaty,[102] China agreed (a) to open three treaty ports along the border, (b) to allow reduction of customs tariff at these points, (c) to grant priority to French manufactures and engineers in "the exploitation of its mines in the provinces of Yunnan, Kwangsi, and Kwangtung," and (d) to permit the continuation on Chinese territory of existing or projected Annamese railways, under mutual agreement.

Treaty port reaction to these developments is instructive. It was felt that French successes afforded renewed opportunity for pressing certain territorial and commercial demands regarding extension of the Hongkong boundary and opening of the West River. For some time the residents of Hongkong, concerned with the exposed position of the colony, had been urging the extension of the Hongkong territory to include Kowloon Bay. The possibility of French or Russian naval action was posed as a not improbable threat.[103] The advent of Lord Salisbury to the Foreign Office was hailed by Old China Hands as assurance of a "firm hand" to counter French designs. His strong action on the Kucheng massacre in Fukien, in which nine Protestant missionaries had been slain by members of a secret society called the "Vegetarians," was marked as a hopeful sign, for Salisbury had insisted on placing the responsibility squarely on the Viceroy of the province.[104] Hongkong agitation was therefore renewed.

On September 20, the Hongkong Committee of the China Association telegraphed to the parent body: "China Association much pleased with position taken by Prime Minister regarding Kucheng massacre. Hope settlement to come will include extension of Hongkong boundaries and opening of West River." [105] At the same time a campaign was opened in Hongkong to secure not only these two concessions but guarantees for transit pass enforcement in Kwangtung and Kwangsi provinces. The action of France had added a strong argument for fulfillment of these demands. Writing again to the Governor on behalf of the Hongkong residents, the Honorable C. P. Chater of the Legislative Council noted that the colony's Chamber of Commerce, as well as the Navy League, favored the annexation and that the China Association had commenced agitation in London. "War has reopened the foreign relations of China," he noted, and the grant of large commercial advantages and frontier adjustments to France furnished a favorable opportunity for counter-concessions to Great Britain. The territory asked for is small and hardly compares with the cession of Formosa to Japan or of Yunnan to France! To rival French pretensions, the opening of the West River was now imperative. As Gundry also emphasized, "these requirements had become more urgent in the presence of territorial and other concessions, and facilities for trade and commerce with Yunnan, which had been exacted by French diplomacy." [106]

At that time the Government was not moved by this agitation, though later it was to bear fruit. The uneasy feeling grew throughout September that while Britain waited the other Powers were gathering the plums. Rumors of Russian projects in the North, of the movements of German warships in the neighborhood of Amoy, together with the announcement in September that Sir Nicholas O'Conor was about to quit Peking at a time when an experienced hand was needed caused growing concern. The removal of O'Conor was particularly disturbing, wrote the *London & China Telegraph*,[107] at a time when British prestige in Peking had fallen so low. From being first in the Chinese capital, England was now last. "Her influence is insufficient not only to bring about the opening of the West River on her own account, but to prevent the concession being eliminated from the Japanese treaty at the bidding of France." Lord Kimberley's policy of inactivity had led to disaster, mourned the same journal which had praised the policy of non-intervention.

Despite the growing uneasiness, the sole overt evidence that a Russo-French program of penetration had commenced was limited to the loan protocol and the Franco-Chinese treaties. Public opinion was, however, profoundly stirred by the "startling announcement" in *The Times* [108] of a Hongkong report that under a secret treaty with China, Russia had obtained the right of anchorage at Port Arthur and the concession "to construct and work under Russian management and administration the Nertchinsk-Tsitsihar-Vladivostok and Tsitsihar-Port Arthur [later the Chinese Eastern and South Manchurian lines] railways, together with other commercial advantages to which the most-favored-nation clause is not applicable." *The Times* called it "a destruction of the existing balance of power almost unparalleled in its audacity" and predicted that for England it would involve "a fundamental revision of the arrangements by which its position and commercial interests are at present secured." It quoted American opinion to the effect that "the action of Russia, if confirmed, assumes a protectorate over China, and can only be intended to overset the existing balance of power in the East." [109] Despite an official denial of the report—Lord Salisbury later branded it "false news" [110]—it was generally accepted as accurate. *Le Temps* even taunted *The Times* for accepting the *démenti*, saying it was convinced of the accuracy of the report and that the concessions Russia had obtained were proper payment for the *Dreibund* action.[111]

Old China Hands were disturbed. At the China Association dinner on November 4, 1895, voices were heard suggesting that if Japan took Formosa, Britain should take the Pescadores, and if Russia entered Port Arthur, Britain should compensate herself with Chusan.[112] The time had arrived for recasting the mercantile attitude toward China events. An "informal meeting" of the General Committee was called for November 6, at which the Chairman, William Keswick, stated that the time had arrived for approaching the Foreign Office regarding clarification of Far Eastern policy. Recent events had brought home the gravity of the situation and he was of the opinion that if they were united and accurately reflected the views of the "China Community" they could make their influence felt.[113]

Realism, argued Keswick, dictated acceptance of the inevitable— and he proceeded to outline for the Committee the concept of what was later called the sphere of influence policy in China. This was the first serious suggestion, coming from a responsible source, that Britain should modify her open door stand in China and accept a sharing of spheres. The date should be marked: November 6, 1895; thus, two years before Whitehall reluctantly accepted the necessity for a "modified open door" stand, leading commercial spokesman were already discussing it. It was inevitable—Keswick proceeded to argue—that Russia should come south to an ice-free port on the Pacific; it would therefore be wise to recognize this and allow Russia a "certain freedom of action" provided the balance were maintained by "taking up for ourselves such a position as to obviate detrimental results from her advance." [114] He suggested the acquisition of Chusan, and believed that the enlargement of Hongkong to embrace Mirs Bay and the Kowloon peninsula would make Britain's position strong enough to regard without fear the presence of Russia at Port Arthur.

The Committee debated this proposition for the next two days. One member (a Mr. Richardson) agreed that an understanding with Russia was imperative, but Chusan was hardly sufficient compensation. What England wanted was control of the Yangtze valley and of Szechuen. Keswick agreed this was desirable but thought that possession of Chusan would prevent any other power from "interfering" in the Yangtze; as for Szechuen, he would also like to see as much activity from the West as from the East and hoped the Government of India would soon push its approaches from that side as the Chambers of Commerce had been urging for years. Several other points were thrown into the debate. French activity in the south must be watched, and another member (a Mr.

Wood) remarked on the importance of renewing agitation for opening the West River. The possible opposition of Germany was set aside as of minor importance. The important thing was to come to some amicable understanding with Russia and press for an extension of Hongkong territory.

Sir Richard Rennie then proposed that a powerful meeting be organized at which opinion would be mobilized and that a deputation to Lord Salisbury should follow, in order to elicit his views. If these were in accord with those of the Association, support to the Government would then be publicly given. Gundry suggested that the deputation join forces with the renewed agitation by Colquhoun urging a railway project from Burma through Siam to Szumao; the action would thus be expanded to embrace the entire situation in the Far East. It was an integral part of the problem that France was trying to draw Szechuen into her sphere "whereas we were agreed that Szechuen should be brought within the sphere of England, by way of the Yangtze valley and approach from the West." An agreement with Russia would diminish the effect of her alliance with France and "the motive for supporting France would disappear." Japan could be conciliated by the neutralization of Korea under international guarantee. The suggestion by another member that the deputation also urge further facilities for trade in the interior was rejected by Gundry on the ground that "British influence at Peking was at present null and impotent to exact any concession." [115]

On the urging of Keswick (who was consistently opposed to mass action of any kind which might embarrass the Government) it was decided to send a small deputation to interview Lord Salisbury, and if views "coincided" a supporting meeting "might follow." Keswick, Rennie and Gundry were deputed to frame resolutions for the meeting the following day. Next day the discussion continued. They were all aware, said Keswick, of "the great and signal collapse of China before Japan," to which the "great interests" they represented could not remain indifferent.

What attitude should be adopted? *The Times* report of Russian designs in the North had alarmed British opinion. Russia could not be stopped; but with her special rights in Manchuria and a naval station at Port Arthur she would dominate Peking. It had, therefore, become "imperatively necessary to take measures for the protection of those interests" by the acquisition of a base of operations "in the event of our having to take action to defend the paramount position and interests we possess in China." [116] Such a position was Chusan in which England had an historical interest (referring to the Davis Convention of 1846) and which was so situated as to dominate Central China and from which "in case of need we could command the approaches to the Yangtze." The Yangtze was the primary concern, for there "the great wealth and industry and capacity for development were to be found" and "however other nations might be inclined to view our action, he thought our Government should be prepared to take possession of Chusan if our position in China and our Imperial and commercial interests were in any way affected by developments and changes requiring them to be permanently and effectually safeguarded." [117]

The question was how to approach the Government? Commercial interests should endeavor to "influence events in the direction of progress and peace," but the first step was to get information: to find out confidentially from the Prime Minister what Government policy would probably be. It would be imprudent to forestall its actions by any hurried suggestions of their own. Should it be decided, for example, that war was necessary to safeguard their interests, much as they would deplore it, it was well to be prepared for the eventuality.

The resolutions which the sub-committee had drawn up were then read and adopted: (a) That the Association views with grave anxiety the present crisis in the Far East, and is persuaded that a solution might be facilitated by a friendly understanding with Russia; (b) That a deputation be sent to Lord Salisbury to lay before him the views of the Association and to elicit some indication of official policy; (c) That Messrs. Keswick, Cameron and Gundry, Sir Alfred Dent and Sir Thomas Sutherland compose the deputation. To this was added, on the urging of Sir Cecil Smith, that "the strongest man we can get" be appointed to replace O'Conor at Peking.

The interview was arranged for November 16. The China Association had definitely opted for a policy of spheres to protect Britain's predominant position and vested interests in China—a significant development in view of the intimate relationship of the Association's leaders with the vested trade and shipping interests in Hongkong and Shanghai. Keswick, who was the major exponent of this view, was not only the outstanding advocate of the policy of asserting a Yangtze sphere and abandoning the North to Russia. He had also committed the Association to the strategy of avoiding mass action and of promoting their influence by establishing close and harmonious relations with the Foreign Office. Both factors were to play a major role in the future orientation of the China Association.

It is not irrelevant to recall that just a week before the China Association interview, Lord Salisbury made his first public statement on the Far Eastern situation since publication of *The Times* report, which he had branded as "false news." The Guildhall speech, in which the Prime

Minister recalled Disraeli's remark that "in Asia there is room for us all," has been variously interpreted. But the most striking thing is that Lord Salisbury dismissed the Far Eastern situation in one paragraph as no longer affording cause for alarm. Most of the speech was devoted to the situation in the Near East and was obviously an attempt to allay fears and court Russian friendship for the concert against the Sultan during the Armenian atrocities.[118] What makes it significant for this story was the fact that Lord Salisbury, while assuring British interests that he would always be their champion, viewed with favor the possibility of an understanding with Russia. In other words, his views accorded closely with those expressed two days before by the leaders of the China Association. For, while he stressed the importance of an Anglo-Russian understanding, he was hardly counselling appeasement.

Depend upon it, whatever may happen in that region, be it in the way of war or in the way of commerce, we are equal to any competition which may be opposed to us. We may look on with absolute equanimity at the action of any persons, if such there be, who think that they can exclude us from any part of that fertile and commercial region, or who imagine that if we are admitted they can beat us in the markets of the world.[119]

The Times might criticize Lord Salisbury for dismissing the Russian menace so lightly,[120] but the *London & China Telegraph* praised his "quiet words of confidence." [121]

What significance is to be attached to the China Association interview of the Foreign Office on November 16, 1895, cannot be accurately gauged, for Lord Salisbury made no commitments. But the China Association was convinced that it had made its influence felt, and it is of historical importance that for the next two years relations between the Association and the Foreign Office were cordial. As no other record of the interview has been published, an extensive paraphrase from the Minute Books of the China Association is here presented: [122]

KESWICK (Chairman of the China Association): The China Association, which represents British interests in China and Japan, had asked for this interview conscious of the gravity of the political situation in the Far East. It was generally felt that if *The Times* report of Russian designs in Manchuria were not now true, it did indicate the inevitable trend of events. Russia will undoubtedly strive for an ice-free port. If so, might it not be wise to acquiesce in her ambitions for an open port; though, of course, fortification of Port Arthur could not be regarded without apprehension.

LORD SALISBURY: You would not say so of a commercial port?

KESWICK: No, there would be no such apprehension of a commercial port, though what had happened at Batoum might happen again.

SALISBURY: We can get at Port Arthur. We couldn't get at Batoum.

KESWICK: In any event, if such a contingency occurred, it was the view of the China Association that British interests might be safeguarded by obtaining control over Chusan which commanded Shanghai and the Yangtze.

SALISBURY: We have certain treaty rights over Chusan, I think.

KESWICK: The Yangtze valley is the important thing. It is the richest and most vulnerable portion of China. It also gives access to the extreme Western provinces, notably Szechuen.

SALISBURY: Would you not preferably approach it from the Indian side, by railway?

KESWICK: It was the Yangtze which formed the natural outlet of that region and whatever might be done by a railway from Burma, the greater facility and cheapness of water transport would always draw a great portion of its commerce toward Shanghai.

The China Association also considered it opportune to ask for the extension of the Kowloon frontier to include Mirs Bay and both sides of the Lyeemon pass.

SALISBURY: Would you not wait till the occasion arose?

KESWICK: There were considerations connected with the Chinese customs which also rendered an extension desirable. This would give greater freedom to local commerce by pushing back the cordon which Chinese revenue cruisers drew around the Colony. There had been frequent complaints of interference in Hongkong waters.

It was also considered that we were entitled to ask for the opening of the West River to steam navigation, giving access to Yunnan.

SALISBURY: That matter is receiving attention.

KESWICK: Such a concession is required for another reason. Commerce is hindered by numerous *likin* stations involving heavy transit taxation, while merchandize is admitted via the Red River from Hanoi on payment of the stipulated treaty rate of $2\frac{1}{2}\%$. The proposition might be carried even further: all the great waterways should be opened to steam navigation.

It might be travelling outside our sphere to allude at this time to the desirability of securing access to Yunnan by railway from the south through Szumao as had been often proposed.

SALISBURY: A railway there would be open to the objection that it would run across territory not our own and which might not always be in friendly hands. There were political as well as physical difficulties to be considered.

KESWICK: It was hoped that Siam would always be friendly. . . . One of the chief reasons why England views with dislike the annexation of territory by other powers is that they invariably impose heavy protective duties in the regions acquired.

SALISBURY: That is true, and the chief sinner in that respect is France.

KESWICK: That was an additional reason why the present situation was looked upon with anxiety. It was felt that we were in the presence of political combinations that might be exerted to the detriment of British interests, but *whose significance might be lessened by a friendly understanding with Russia upon certain points.*

SALISBURY: If we sat with our arms folded, but that is very improbable.

KESWICK: Another consideration by which the Association is impressed is the desirability of our being represented in Peking by a strong man.

SALISBURY: When you say a strong man, that means the strongest man we can get to go there.

KESWICK: It was therefore recommended that the emoluments of the post be sustained at a liberal figure; a reduction had occurred at the time of Sir Harry Parkes.

SALISBURY: Can you point to any other European Power which pays £5,000 a year?

KESWICK: But no other Power has interests approaching ours in magnitude. . . . If necessary one might go outside the diplomatic service. Sir Cecil Smith, who had had experience at Hongkong and been Governor of the Straits Settlements, was regarded with confidence.

A similar consideration was that England's preponderating interests in China made it desirable that the post of Inspector-General of Customs should always be held by an Englishman. This was important in view of the possibility of the retirement of Sir Robert Hart.

SALISBURY: But they have no man so well qualified as we have; would that not prevent the contingency from arising?

KESWICK: It was still important. They might set up one of their own as a figurehead to gain control of the Customs.

Another thought: One of the motives of Japan in the recent war was the reorganization of Korea. It was believed that the proposal to neutralize Korea would be welcome to her and would obviate the danger of a Russo-Japanese war over Korea.

SALISBURY: It was to be doubted whether such neutrality would be respected.

KESWICK: Other European Powers, as well as the United States, seemed well disposed to come to some such arrangement.

SALISBURY: *I have been surprised to hear no apprehension expressed of Japan.*

KESWICK: Upon the question of the military power of Japan, I am of the opinion that it has been exaggerated. Japan would go down before any European Power.

SALISBURY: Even before Russia? You must remember that Japan is fighting on her base, whereas Russia would be fighting from Vladivostok.

KESWICK: During the recent war Japan was pitted against a rabble and the result afforded no test of strength.

SALISBURY: I have heard that opinion expressed before. I should have thought a nation of forty millions situated similarly to ourselves was destined to be an important power.

The interview ended with Lord Salisbury's assurances that the views of the Association would be taken into consideration and that he recognized the importance of British interests in China, which he referred to as "our principal market."

At the meeting of the Executive Committee, held after the interview, it was agreed that Lord Salisbury had not only shown a clear perception of conditions in the Far East but was determined that England would not take a back seat in future settlements. The China Association was agreed that its cause rested in good hands. And, in any event, its own policy had been defined.

VII

The Politics of Economic Concessions: 1896-1897

"The time has arrived when the British merchant in China should receive from Her Majesty's Government a more effective support in a country the government of which will recognize nothing but direct and weighty influence"—Shanghai Committee of the China Association, July 10, 1896.

THE year 1895, when defeat appeared about to precipitate the collapse of the Chinese Empire and foreign rivalries commenced to nibble at British economic predominance in the Far East, is generally taken as the year of decision, marking the dividing point between the old and the new in Far Eastern policy. The battle for concessions is presumed to have started at that time, with imperialist ambitions pressing the respective governments to stake out political and economic claims in China. There is no denying that the Franco-Russian program of penetration unfolded in a very short time after the Dreibund had rescued the Liaotung peninsula from the Japanese. Implementing the treaty of June 20, 1895, M. Gérard, the French Minister to Peking, secured the first railway concession to encroach on Chinese territory, from Langson (in Tongking) to Lungchow (in Kwangsi), on March 31, 1896.[1] It was an obvious move in the direction of asserting the Southern provinces as a French sphere. Three months later the larger ambitions of Count Witte resulted in the conclusion of the Russo-Chinese Treaty of Alliance, which included the concession for the construction and exploitation of a trans-Manchurian railway to Vladivostock, financed by the Russo-Chinese Bank, a camouflaged organ of the Russian Government.[2] And although this treaty was kept secret at the time,[3] rumors of the "Cassini Convention," which was reported to have implemented this scheme, received wide credence in mercantile circles at the end of the year. Moreover, there was no secret as to the existence and hardly less as to the purposes of the Russo-Chinese Bank.

Yet mercantile documents reveal no overwhelming concern with these maneuvers. On the contrary, they reflect a lull, lasting for almost two years, in mercantile suspicions of Franco-Russian designs. Throughout 1896 and most of 1897 the mentality reflected in the proceedings of the China Association is that of 1869 and not of the newer imperialism. Primary concern was still that of breaking down Chinese exclusiveness, of opening China to commercial opportunity. Chinese backwardness and reluctance to embrace Western improvements were more immediate concerns than a threat of foreign competition. Following the interview with Lord Salisbury of November, 1895, the leaders of the China Association were convinced that political questions could safely be left in the hands of the Foreign Office. And the course which they envisaged was that of coming to an accommodation with France and Russia, based on the sharing of concessions and spheres.

The Salisbury-Courcel Agreement with France in January, 1896, which called for a sharing of commercial privileges in Yunnan and Szechuen, appeared to be carrying out this policy, while Mr. Balfour's speech at Bristol on February 3, 1896, indicated that the Government was prepared to follow that policy toward Russia which Keswick had suggested to Lord Salisbury the previous November. Balfour was convinced that Russian acquisition of an ice-free port and commercial outlet in the North would benefit not merely Russia and the world but "British commerce and enterprise." "Let us lay to heart this doctrine that what is good for one is not necessarily bad for the other—surely Asia and Africa are large enough for all of us." [4]

This attitude was perfectly in accord with mercantile policy at the time. Keswick could thus tell the membership of the China Association that while they continued to be concerned with the "new order of things" in which "Russia, Germany and France took up a position from which England was excluded and had attained a status which they had never before possessed," the British Government was now "quite alive" to the importance of recent events and that "so far as it was possible quietly to regain the supremacy of England without straining the relations existing between this country and other Powers, every effort would be made." [5] British concern was still primarily that of forcing open the markets of China, for in free competition the established English merchant was bound to win. And, as Sir Valentine Chirol, always an honored guest at the meetings of the China Association, wrote at the time: "Whether the maintenance of the Chinese Empire itself continues to be in the future, as in the past, a matter of British interest, is a question to which China must be left to furnish the answer by her own acts." [6]

The appropriate answer for China, it was felt, was to fulfill the mercan-

tile demands of 1869 and finally to realize the dream of decades by lift-
ing all trade restrictions and embracing Western economics. "The commerce of China, although it has expanded," complained the Shanghai
Committee to its parent China Association in July, 1896, "is still utterly
insignificant, being 3s. per capita of population for 1895; and its extension is dependent entirely upon a policy which shall open the entire
country to the advantages of unrestricted commercial intercourse." [7]

The nineties had seen some trade expansion, but regarded as a continent, the China market did not begin to compare with India as an outlet for Manchester goods. In 1894, for example, China and Hongkong
took less than 4 million pounds in value of all types of cotton piece
goods, as against almost 20 millions for India and the Straits Settlements. Turkey alone took almost as much as the entire China market.[8]
Chinese imports of all foreign goods averaged 100 million taels an-
nually in the period from 1885 to 1888, as compared with 126 millions
in 1889–1892 and 172 millions in 1893–1896, reaching 222 millions in
1897–1900. But these figures are misleading, for the continued fall in
the gold value of silver (the tael dropped from 5/2 in 1890 to 2/10
in 1898, recovering to 3/1 in 1900) meant that in sterling values no rise in
imports was perceptible. Thus, foreign imports of 134 million taels in
1891 when translated into sterling figures of 34.3 million pounds just
equalled the trade of 211 million taels in 1900.[9] The declared value of
annual British exports to China and Hongkong in terms of millions
sterling exhibited phenomenal stagnation:

1885–1888	8.57
1889–1892	8.23
1893–1896	7.10
1897–1900	8.11 [10]

Although the Sino-Japanese War did not have a disturbing effect on
trade and the total volume showed an increase in 1895, the fall in silver
led to a decrease in expected demand.[11] The Statistical Secretary of the
Imperial Maritime Customs, reporting on China's trade in 1894, noted
that while there had been an increase in the tael value of foreign imports,
actual quantities were not so great, owing to the increased cost of com-
modities in silver prices. (This was particularly true of yarn, metals,
coal, kerosene, matches and sugar, as well as piece goods.) The unparalleled falling off in textile goods imports, which formed so con-
spicuous a feature of the 1893 trade, was just as pronounced in 1894.[12]

According to British representatives, the two obstacles to the expansion of foreign trade were *likin* and growing native competition, with the
latter by far the more serious. In his report on the trade for 1894, Mr.
Beauclerk, the Secretary of Legation at Peking, noting the decline in

imports of cotton goods, granted that *likin* barriers were still serious ("Our British merchants would like to see a British Resident established in each province, whose special duty should be to see that Treaty stipulations are not burked. . . ."), but stressed the greater danger to British manufactures from the growing "industry of the East." [13] The first cotton cloth factory had been established by Li Hung-chang, with native capital, in Shanghai in 1888, and by the end of 1895 five more Chinese-owned cotton mills had been set up.[14] Foreign participation in local industry, a right secured under the Treaty of Shimonoseki, was still a phenomenon of the future.

Consul Jameson's report on the Shanghai trade of 1895 also emphasized the threat of oriental competition. Indian and Japanese yarn and cloth imports, as well as the growth of local manufactures, meant that "China will soon manufacture the greater portion of her cotton goods." However, Jameson endorsed the merchants' view that the growth of British commerce was being strangled by the inland tax system, which he termed the greatest single hindrance to commercial progress. The fear that China would increase *likin* dues to obtain additional revenue for the servicing of foreign loans was also voiced. "No course could be more fatal to trade." [15]

Given these conditions, it is not difficult to understand mercantile attitudes in 1896. While some gain had been scored as the result of the Treaty of Shimonoseki and the Sino-Japanese commercial treaty of July 21, 1896, which implemented its economic clauses,[16] vexatious questions of *likin* barriers, restriction on inland navigation and trade in the interior, as well as the traditional demands for railway and mining concessions, were still outstanding. And the issues were now more pressing because of the fear that foreign interests might anticipate the established British merchant and entrepreneur in securing the first profits. Moreover, without governmental support mercantile ambitions would never be realized. That, at least, was evident from the experience of 1895.

It was agreed that the China Association and its representative committees in Hongkong and Shanghai should now undertake a campaign to realize the program outlined the previous year. But it was soon evident that mercantile chiefs were not unanimous on strategy, particularly as it affected the perennial problem of bringing pressure on the British Government. While in Shanghai and, to a lesser extent, in the lower echelons of the China Association in London, the attitude centered around traditional tactics of pressing the Foreign Office to force the Chinese authorities to make desired concessions, the leadership of the China Association, which had come to be recognized as the spokesman of British business in Anglo-China affairs, had worked out a different tactical pattern. William Keswick and the other representatives of the larger China houses and the Hongkong and Shanghai Banking Corporation who determined policy in the General Committee of the China Association had become convinced that a policy of collaboration, if not intimacy, with the Foreign Office was far preferable. This involved making personal representations at the Foreign Office, avoiding publication of any matter which might embarrass Whitehall and, above all, repudiating anything which smacked of mass pressure or attempts to stir up public opinion. Despite rumblings from the membership and threats of rebellion from Shanghai, the China Association persisted in this strategy.

It was an attitude particularly marked in 1896 and 1897, but exactly when it originated is not known. As was observed in the last chapter, Keswick had championed this line from the very start; it became particularly noticeable after the interview with Lord Salisbury in November, 1895. Among its first fruits was the quasi-political status attained by the Hongkong and Shanghai Bank during the negotiations for the second indemnity loan early in 1896. There is no evidence that members of the China Association were at any time interested in this loan as a business investment. It was, however, welcomed as a counterpoise to Russo-French designs and, above all, as a means of ensuring independence of the administration of the Maritime Customs, in which the mercantile community was so profoundly concerned.

The exact relationship between the Foreign Office and the Bank is unknown, as the pertinent records are not yet available, nor do the records of the China Association mention the matter. Published documents show that it was "in counteraction of the Russian advances" that Great Britain "arranged a joint loan to China of £16,000,000," [17] despite the opposition of the French and Russian Ministers, who "were pressing the claims of their financial interests to be allowed to float the loan." [18] With the blessings if not the encouragement of their respective governments, the Hongkong & Shanghai Bank and the Deutsch-Asiatische Bank formed a syndicate and secured the second indemnity loan, the agreement for which was signed on March 23.[19] From the mercantile standpoint the most significant aspect of the loan was the provision that "the administration of the Imperial Maritime Customs of China shall continue as at present constituted during the currency of this loan." [20]

It was a major triumph and, for a time, the China Association was well satisfied to leave political issues in the hands of the Foreign Office. Even on strictly commercial questions the China Association leadership decided not to press the maximum program which Shanghai had urged in 1895, but to content itself with a gradual solution of outstanding commercial problems in collaboration with the Foreign Office. This became the major task for 1896. Keswick himself was prepared to accept the gains of the Sino-Japanese treaty and, because of Foreign Office opposition, refused to support the Shanghai proposal that a special commissioner be sent to China to report on conditions of trade. He felt that the compromise solution which had been worked out, to send Byron Brenan, one of the most qualified British consuls in China, on a tour of the treaty ports was a handsome concession.[21] If some solution to the transit dues problem could be arrived at by mutual agreement, there was little else the mercantile community could desire in Keswick's view.

The China Association had learned in February, 1896, that on Li Hung-chang's forthcoming visit to Europe he would demand an increase in customs dues in order to meet the burdens placed on Chinese revenue by the service of the indemnity loans. Keswick hinted to the membership that the China Association should agree to accept an over-all customs tax of ten percent provided this would cover immunity from all further inland dues, including the terminal *likin* tax.[22] He even favored compulsory commutation along the lines embodied in the Alcock Convention, and pointed out that the principle had worked in the opium arrangement concluded in 1887. Along these lines Gundry prepared his exhaustive memorandum on *likin* which the General Committee accepted in April [23] and which was forwarded to Hongkong and Shanghai for comment the following month.[24]

Gundry's memorandum and covering letter went beyond Keswick's position in demanding certain concessions and guarantees before acceptance of the increased customs tariff. Pointing out that as early as 1868 a Chinese Memorandum had enjoined respect for transit passes even in the hands of Chinese, Gundry stressed that that was still the issue. In the two important southern provinces of Kwangtung and Kwangsi local authorities had been lax in paying respect to the validity of transit certificates, while in other provinces observance was sporadic. It was thought a solution could be reached by having provincial authorities share in the revenue of the Imperial Maritime Customs; but that an augmented customs tariff would be allowed only if accompanied by substantial trading concessions. For an increase to a ten percent ad valorem rate, the China Association requested the following equivalents: (a) immunity of goods from all inland taxation; (b) improvement of railway communications (but no specific request for concessions was made); (c) opening of waterways, particularly the West River and the Yangtze above Ichang, to steam navigation.[25]

These were moderate demands and hardly calculated to satisfy the residents of the treaty ports. Hongkong had already warned the China Association that Li would request tariff increases and cautioned London not to be caught napping.[26] In June the China Association approached the Foreign Office, asking to be consulted before any tariff increase was agreed to and noting that the question was tied up with that of transit dues. Without being specific, Gundry emphasized that any "revision" would have to be "exhaustive" and accompanied by "guarantees."

The Foreign Office promised to make no changes without consulting the China Association.[27] At the same time Gundry called at the Foreign Office on the invitation of Sir Francis Bertie (the Assistant Undersecretary) and reiterated that one of the conditions of agreement to augmented tariff dues would be immunity from all transit and terminal charges. Bertie suggested that the provincial authorities should retain the transit certificate and be allowed to cash it at the Imperial Customs, a view which Gundry hailed as promising.[28] The General Committee decided to agree to the proposal and to "bargain." In accordance with suggestions made by various members, and in response to pressure from the Far East, the concessions demanded went beyond the position outlined by Gundry in May. In addition to the Bertie formula (that provincial authorities be permitted to cash transit certificates), the China Association informed the Foreign Office that it would agree to an increased tariff up to ten percent on the following conditions: (a) complete immunity from inland and terminal taxation and universal respect for transit passes; (b) access to all provinces and rivers opened to navigation; (c) a general undertaking to facilitate the building of railways. In deference to Sir Cecil Smith, who had begun to take an intense interest in the problem, the right of access for railways from India to Yunnan and Szechuen was added; but it did not appear to interest the other members very much.[29]

This was the plan submitted to the Foreign Office. Despite the fact that this issue constituted the major concern of the China Association that year, no effort was made to secure approval of the program from Hongkong and Shanghai before it was officially presented to the Government. The center of gravity in mercantile politics had definitely shifted to London. Hongkong and Shanghai were informed of the move,[30] and although they gave reluctant consent it was evident that, particularly at Shanghai, dissatisfaction with the restrained policy of the London Committee was widespread. Hongkong, while catering to London opinion, proposed a far more radical program. Increased tariff could be agreed to, stated the Hongkong Committee, only on condition that "the opportunity should certainly not be missed of endeavoring to obtain a more liberal recognition of the status of foreigners in China, together with the opening up of the extensive waterways and the right of travel and residence throughout the Empire.[31] The Hongkong Committee, not exposed to the enervating atmosphere of Whitehall, was thinking in terms of the program of 1895.

It was in Shanghai, however, that dissatisfaction with the policy and tactics of the London Committee—which was to reach the stage of rebellion some years later—had its true source. At a meeting on July 27, called to consider Gundry's *likin* memorandum and the letter of May 15,[32] a resolution was passed that no tariff higher than 7 1/2 percent would be acceptable and that compulsory commutation would be agreed to only with the understanding that this rate would cover "likin, transit dues taxes, and imposts of every kind," that the Imperial Customs would guarantee equitable distribution of revenue to provincial treasuries, and that freedom of navigation would be granted on all Chinese waterways. In addition, Shanghai insisted that the proper strategy, irrespective of tariff revision, was to concentrate on obtaining the right of inland navigation on all waterways and then to agitate for railways as a means of penetrating the China market.[33]

Nor was this all. Profoundly disturbed by the collaborationist policy of the London leadership and its apparent reluctance to press for the maximum mercantile program of the previous year, the Shanghai Committee had several days before dispatched to the General Committee a strong note calling for all-out action on behalf of British commercial interests in China. Their letter of April 10, 1895,[34] had been disregarded and London appeared to be acquiescing in the do-nothing policy of the Foreign Office. Such inactivity at a time when the long-awaited opening of China was at hand and in the face of the designs of the other Powers was regarded as disastrous.

In a long and exhaustive letter, dated July 10, 1896,[35] therefore, the Shanghai Committee again proposed a vigorous British policy toward China. Its more immediate aims, they noted, were the reforms which merchants had demanded as long ago as 1869.

Yet, notwithstanding the lapse of fully twenty-five years, during which efforts have been made by Chambers of Commerce and deputations of London merchants to stimulate interest in the important questions raised, the proposals remained practically unanswered, and the trade of China remains at this date under the control and to a great extent hampered by tradal conventions unsuitable to the existing requirements of a commerce capable of vast extension if proper means are adopted for its enfranchisement.

For Shanghai, despite the Sino-Japanese war and the Franco-Russian menace, the program of 1869 was still relevant. Beyond that the essential requirement was maintenance of British predominance. The original mistake had been made when the British Government had failed to take Shanghai's advice to assume leadership. Britain should have offered monetary assistance to China conditional on "essential commercial reforms." Instead, whatever progress had been made was due to the treaty of Shimonoseki; it was a fact "inconsistent with the dignity of the British nation that the earliest acquired and immeasurably the most important commercial interests in the Far East should be dependent in any degree upon concessions extorted from China by Japan or any other power." This was Britain's prerogative and "it was most desirable, practically and commercially, that this preëminent position should not now be sacrificed."

What then should now be done? As in April, 1895, Shanghai emphasized that British interests could only be benefited, not by dividing up concessions and other piecemeal measures, but by adopting "measures calculated to increase the prosperity of the empire as a whole." Only by internal reform, under British supervision, could China and its fabulous commercial future be saved. To do this Britain would have to face reality; it was not realistic to deal with the provincial authorities through Peking. Instead, Shanghai recommended the appointment of a British official of sufficient rank—with power to command the respect and attention of the Viceroys; in commercial and fiscal matters the local authorities would then be responsible not to Peking but to this special British commissioner.

Shanghai's plan was none too clear; but it envisaged a sort of commercial suzerainty on the Yangtze. "The functions of this commissioner would be principally exercisable among the Viceroys and Governors of the provinces, with whom as well as with his nationals at all the treaty ports he should be in continuous communication." It was only by the adoption of some such system that the "great national reforms, such as the extension of internal communication by means of roads, railways, rivers and canals; the establishment of a coinage system, and equalisation of provincial taxation; opening of rivers to steam transport; systematisation of likin; administration of justice in mixed cases; opening of mines and the development of great national resources" could be effected.

In effect, the Shanghai letter was an appeal to the London Committee to cease its policy of collaboration with the Foreign Office and of accepting piecemeal concessions. It was a call to implement the attitude and policy of the men of '69. Not through deals with Russia to save vested

interests on the Yangtze, but through the assertion of Britain's preeminent position in a scheme to reform and open China would British
interests be served. The main China question, in Shanghai's view, was
not partition or the battle for concessions, but the fact that "the commerce of China . . . is still insignificant" and its expansion "dependent
entirely upon a policy which shall open the entire country to advantages
of unrestricted commercial intercourse." For Shanghai the China problem had not changed as a result of the crisis of 1895; it had merely become more urgent.

Nevertheless, Shanghai could not disregard the impact of foreign
rivalries. Along with its commercial program which "comprehended a
system of reform calculated to strengthen China and simultaneously
promote the welfare of British commerce and British interests," the
Shanghai Committee called on Whitehall to depart from its pose of
neutrality in the competitive struggle for concessions. "The time has
arrived when the British merchant in China should receive from Her
Majesty's Government a more effective support in a country the government of which will recognize nothing but direct and weighty influence."
Conjuring up a picture of the good old days "when British influence in
China was potent" and "the affairs of commerce had much more consideration at H.M. Legation than they receive at present," Shanghai
viewed with alarm "the tendency of the time . . . to make British commercial interests in China entirely subservient to the exigencies of the
diplomatic situation in Europe."

Although the China Association forwarded this stinging Shanghai
letter to the Foreign Office, Gundry rejected it as a basis for action. To
Shanghai he replied:

The political horizon is clouded at this moment in many quarters, and it is
impossible for H.M. Government to deal with British interests in China with a
free hand, irrespective of the rivalry of other Powers. It seems likely, however,
that the question of our relations may be opened up shortly in a way that will
afford an opening for the consideration of questions that you raise.[36]

This was in September, and in that last remark Gundry was referring to
the current tariff revision negotiations. In handing the Shanghai letter
to Bertie at the Foreign Office, however, Gundry took occasion to remark
that the General Committee dissented from the allegation that there was
a tendency in official quarters to treat British interests lightly.[37] The
honeymoon between the China Association and the Foreign Office was
still enduring.

Despite this incipient cleavage between London and the port residents, the Shanghai insurgents did accomplish part of their purpose. In the negotiations for tariff revision, the China Association adopted a firmer stand and expanded its demands. A special committee was appointed to secure the support of the home Chambers,[38] and an exhaustive memorandum circulated outlining the concessions the China Association was demanding as *quid pro quo* in the event of a tariff increase.[39] Replies were universally favorable, with London, Liverpool, Leeds, Bradford, Glasgow, Blackburn, and Manchester supporting the China Association without reservation.[40] London even undertook a campaign of its own among the other Chambers. The Manchester Chamber, for example, was solicited not only by the China Association but independently by the London Chamber of Commerce and by Alexander Michie, who pressed the proposal on local China merchants. Manchester interest was widespread and the Chamber wrote to Lord Salisbury urging not only the fiscal arrangement recommended by the China Association but (a) the opening of all waterways to steam navigation, (b) the opening of more treaty ports, (c) an undertaking to open the country by a widespread railway system acceptable to the Chinese Government, and (d) assimilation of the gauges on Chinese frontier railways to those of the Indian system.[41] The Associated Chambers of Commerce likewise pledged full support to the China Association.[42]

With such strong support from the Chambers and under the prodding of the Shanghai dissidents, Gundry in subsequent conversations with Bertie at the Foreign Office refused to compromise on any of the issues raised. No increase beyond a 10 percent total would be accepted; and for this, basic fiscal reform in which the Maritime Customs secured control of *likin* and concessions, now including not only the right to steam navigation on inland waterways but a pledge that railway building would be pressed, were demanded.[43] By October it was evident that merchants and officials differed not only on individual points but as to the process itself. The former spoke in terms of fundamental tariff revision and reforms, while Bertie intimated that the Foreign Office had narrowed down the entire issue to what blanket surtax increase Britain would accept. The membership, circularized, urged Gundry to stick to his guns; in fact, the Shanghai recommendations were now to be added to the original demands.[44] Gundry was authorized to draft a letter to Lord Salisbury setting forth the new synthesis at which the China Association had arrived.

The China Association letter of November 2, 1896, is a highpoint in the development of mercantile policy on Anglo-Chinese relations, for it served as the summing-up of mercantile opinion at the time and as the final statement of mercantile plans for commercial reform in China. Whether or not it influenced subsequent demands on China by the British Government, as seems likely, it unquestionably made an impression on the Foreign Office. Subsequent developments reveal a remarkable parallel between the Association's program of 1896 and the list of concessions submitted to China during the next two years. A striking commentary on the continuity of mercantile policy exhibited by the Association's letter is Gundry's suggestion that the Foreign Office should address itself primarily to securing the concessions demanded by merchants at the time of the Alcock revision in 1869!

To these were added newer features. The mercantile program now included: (a) the general right of foreigners to construct railways and exploit mines in China, in accordance with the demands of 1869; (b) solution of the *likin* question through acceptance of the principle of compulsory commutation of inland dues, but with guarantees that transit passes would be respected universally and that the Customs would earmark *likin* collections for provincial treasuries; (c) following the pattern of the Franco-Chinese treaty of 1895 reducing tariff rates on overland trade from Tongking, trade between Burma and China to enjoy similar advantages; (d) on the same pattern, in view of France's right to extend railways from Tongking into Yunnan and Kwangsi, Britain to enjoy a similar right to extend its railways from Burma to Yunnan and Szechuen; (e) opening of the West River to steam navigation; and (f) extending the principle incorporated in the loan agreement of 1896 that the administration of the Imperial Maritime Customs remain on its present basis during the currency of the loan, the China Association suggested that the preponderance of British trade called for proportional employment of British subjects by the Customs administration.[45] Whether it was owing to the stringency of these demands, as Gundry suspected,[46] or because the Foreign Office thought the time not opportune for pressing China for treaty revision, the proposal for tariff increase was dropped.

But the mercantile program was not; and occasion was found during the following year to squeeze out of China the major portion of the concessions which the Association letter had foreseen. The first triumph was scored when Sir Claude MacDonald, the new Minister at Peking, who remained a favorite of the China Association, secured the publication in January, 1897, of proclamations by the Governors of Kwangtung and Kwangsi enjoining respect for transit passes within those provinces and specifically recognizing the immunity of foreign goods from "differential taxation" enroute.[47] The China Association was pleased with this "striking success" although they deplored the exclusion of terminal taxes (*tso-ku* or octroi and *loti likin* or destination tax) from the immunity granted.[48]

In any event, it was a step forward and the China Association spent a considerable part of the year in an attempt to solve outstanding *likin* questions.[49] Gundry had several conversations with Mr. Cartwright, acting head of the China Department in the Foreign Office, in an attempt to clear up the question of *likin* exemption areas in the settlements, a problem not solved by the Chefoo Convention because of mercantile opposition to the definition of exempt areas as implying that other areas were not exempt. Cartwright intimated that the Foreign Office no longer held the Board of Trade view that *likin* as such was legal on goods passing out of foreign hands. On his assurance that guarantees against *likin* levies on certificated goods would be forthcoming, Gundry consented to the definition of areas exempt from *likin*.[50] This was later incorporated into the treaty arrangements of February, 1898, which will be noted below. In November Gundry prepared a comprehensive memorandum on *likin* which attempted to prove that it was illegal in all forms, including destination tax, when placed on goods covered by transit pass.[51] The sole apparent result was greater activity on the part of Sir Claude MacDonald in solving some outstanding *likin* cases, and an intimation by the Foreign Office that the Board of Trade ruling in 1869 was no longer accepted. *Likin* thereafter ceased to be the primary issue it had been for forty years but an over-all settlement of the problem was delayed until the treaty revision of 1902.

Far more important, and the first sizable installment on the program outlined by the China Association in November, 1896, was the series of concessions secured in the Anglo-Chinese Agreement of February 4, 1897. This treaty is generally regarded as the British response to the Franco-Chinese Agreement of June 20, 1895, and the subsequent unfolding of French railway schemes in the South.[52] This is undoubtedly so, but it fails to account for the lag of over a year between the first attempt at arrangement—the Salisbury-Courcel Agreement of January, 1896—and the final arrangement in February, 1897. It is a safe hypothesis that it was mercantile dissatisfaction with the first arrangement and subsequent agitation on the part of Old China Hands, culminating in the China Association letter of November 2, 1896, which provides the clue to renewed diplomatic action in the winter of 1896–97. The sequence of events is instructive.

As was pointed out in Chapter Five, the height of mercantile interest in the Colquhoun route from Burma through the Shan States to Yunnan was reached in 1885. Colquhoun continued his agitation and sporadic activity was displayed on the part of the Chambers, but it was not until 1893 that a Burma-Yunnan route again became a major item on the agenda of the home Chambers. The immediate cause was the revelation of French designs in Siam which stirred the Liverpool and Manchester Chambers to caution the Foreign Office not to give up any rights in the territory through which the projected route was to pass. On November 1, 1893, the Liverpool Chamber urged Lord Rosebery to prevent French occupation of the area and proposed the establishment of a buffer state with equal trading rights, a solution incorporated in the Salisbury-Courcel Agreement.[53] Manchester expressed similar fears, but to avoid possible conflict with France withdrew its support from the Colquhoun route and, while favoring the general idea of a Burma road, left the decision as to particular routes to the Government.[54]

Meanwhile, the Government had commenced survey of the Mandalay-Kunlon Ferry route favored by the Indian Government, and mercantile interest switched to its support. In answer to an inquiry by the Liverpool Chamber, the India Office reported on August 8, 1893, that the survey had been completed to the half-way point at Thebaw. The work went slowly owing to unexpected terrain difficulties and on October 14, 1895, the Liverpool Chamber again addressed the India Office and was informed that the survey had been completed but no part of the line actually begun.[55] The Chamber was not satisfied and urged the importance of reaching the China frontier ahead of the French. Manchester, too, broke with the Yorkshire Chambers in the Associated Chambers of Commerce on the question of continuing support for the Colquhoun route and joined Liverpool in pressing for completion of the Mandalay route.[56] Whatever the route, Chambers were agreed on the importance of reaching the Yunnan market first. It was in the fall of 1895, also, that Hongkong became disturbed by French designs in Kwangtung and Kwangsi and called for counter-measures, including the opening of the West River, a move taken up by the China Association, as was noted above.

Interest in southwest China was thus intense, but at the same time the China Association had been urging that some accord be reached with the Franco-Russian bloc. It was against this background that the Salisbury-Courcel Agreement was reached in London on January 15, 1896. It was strictly a protective measure, involving the neutralization of the border regions of Siam and renunciation of any special privileges or advantages in that area. With respect to Yunnan and Szechuen, France and Britain agreed that "all commercial and other privileges" conceded or to be conceded in those provinces would "be extended and rendered common to both Powers, and to their Nationals and dependents." [57]

The Agreement was received without too much enthusiasm in mercantile circles and pressure for positive implementation of the Burma-Yunnan route did not slacken. It was a subject of intermittent debate at meetings of the China Association. The Associated Chambers of Commerce, in March, 1896, memorialized the Government to survey the Colquhoun route.[58] Response from Whitehall was lukewarm and the Associated Chambers organized a deputation to Lord Salisbury on June 12, 1896, urging that the Government sponsor or at least guarantee a Burma-Yunnan railway. It was the first time that the issue of governmental guarantee of a railway in non-British territory had arisen. Lord Salisbury, always a master at handling business men, showed sympathy, uttering his classic remark—"I think other governments, if they seek trade, it is in order that they may obtain territory; if the English government seeks for territory it is in order that it may obtain trade"—but stood adamant against a government guarantee of railways in foreign territory. The best he could offer was the suggestion that a powerful private company be formed, bringing the railway to the edge of British territory and "I have not the slightest doubt that we shall be able to penetrate into foreign territory when we think it is desirable to do so." [59] Agitation continued and it centered around the argument that without governmental support the Burma railway would never be built and French interests would anticipate Britain in the rich markets of southern China. It was this agitation, along with treaty port cries for the opening of the West River, which added strength to the China Association letter of November 2, 1896.

That winter Sir Claude opened negotiations in Peking which led to the Anglo-Chinese Agreement of February 4, 1897.[60] Ostensibly on the ground that its violation by the French treaty of June, 1895, required modification of the Anglo-Chinese treaty of 1894 relative to Burma,[61] Britain secured the following concessions: (a) rectification of the Burma-China frontier and an undertaking by China not to cede to any other nation the Shan territory around Kiang Hung (through which the Colquhoun route was planned); (b) "in the event of their construction," railways built in Yunnan to be connected with any Burma railway reaching the frontier; (c) British consulates to be established at Momein (on the Bhamo route) and Szumao (terminus of the Colquhoun and Sprye routes); (d) the West River to be opened to foreign navigation from Canton to Wuchow.

The Agreement thus incorporated part of the mercantile demands, but only a part. Even the concessions granted were of a limited nature: the West River had been opened, but only to Wuchow and not by steamers; the Burma-Yunnan railway was still a promise contingent on Chinese initiative. As Gundry noted, the problem of meeting French competition had been only partially solved. "The rivalry will doubtless continue, and the desirability of meeting it by establishing British agencies at Nanning has been urged. The contest is for the trade of Southwest China, which the French are trying to attract to Tongking by the Red River and the Langson-Lungchow line, but which may conceivably prefer the West River. . . ." [62]

Nevertheless, the China Association continued its policy of collaboration with the Foreign Office, of leaving strictly political issues to the government. It concentrated on the gradual adoption of its commercial program, on the solution of *likin* and sustained pressure for the removal of restrictions to the Chinese market. What is most striking is the almost total unconcern in mercantile circles with the political questions raised by activities of Russia and France in China throughout 1896 and most of 1897.

Indicative is the reaction to publication of the so-called Cassini Convention in December, 1896, which lent substance to earlier rumors of a Russo-Chinese Alliance and the contract for the Chinese Eastern Railway. It was now almost universally accepted as a fact, yet the *London & China Telegraph*,[63] which reprinted the text of the Convention, cautioned its readers to be "hesitant" in drawing conclusions. It was, without doubt, a blow to the Japanese, but as for England, so long as she was not excluded commercially, there was nothing to fear.

There was a mild disturbance at the China Association and Gundry prepared a memorandum for the Foreign Office listing the compensatory demands which the Association had suggested in November, 1895, but on Keswick's urging no official protest was made and the memorandum was pigeon-holed. The China Association was not yet disturbed by *hochpolitik* in the Far East; *likin* still bothered it more than international rivalries. Even the signing of the contract for the Peking-Hankow railway concession with Belgian interests, behind whom stood the Russians and French as everyone knew,[64] in the summer of 1897, did not find a place on the agenda of the London Committee.

Nor did parliamentary opinion exhibit any greater interest. Not a single debate on China affairs occurred in the sessions of 1896 and 1897, and Mr. George N. Curzon, the Parliamentary Undersecretary for Foreign Affairs, was called upon but five times in that period to reply to questions on Anglo-Chinese relations. The first time was when he stated that the Government had no intention of appointing a commercial attache at Peking,[65] the second was in response to pressure by R. A. Yerburgh, leader of the China bloc in the Commons, that the Burma-Yunnan arrangement be expedited.[66] Twice thereafter Curzon denied rumors that the Russians planned to build the trans-Manchurian rail-way.[67] The lone mention in the session of 1897 was a request for copies of the Anglo-Chinese treaty on the Burmese frontier adjustment.[68]

~ Sometime in 1897 emphasis changed, and the threat to British pre-dominance implicit in the policies being pursued by the foreign Powers modified the entire outlook of mercantile opinion on Anglo-Chinese rela-tions. It was this realization and not the Sino-Japanese war as such that marked the turning point. Exactly when it occurred cannot be measured with accuracy, but by mid-year (1897) suspicions had been aroused on a marked scale. The China Association began to concern itself with the future of Kiaochow on which both Germany and Russia were said to have designs. This will be examined shortly. But the first really alarming note was sounded by Shanghai on June 17, adumbrating the struggle which was to take place around the issue of the loan. "Position is critical at Peking in consequence of preponderance of Russian influence. We urge upon you the necessity of objecting [to] Russia securing next in-demnity loan as Customs control is in danger." [69] It was an accurate summary both of the position and of the danger.

Gundry immediately communicated with the Foreign Office and the Hongkong & Shanghai Bank and was assured in both quarters that the alarm was unfounded.[70] Shanghai refused to be reassured and wired again that "private sources" in Peking which had furnished the in-formation were "reliable." The General Committee of the China Asso-ciation felt that such matters could be left securely in the capable hands of the Foreign Office and the Bank. But in a more pointed letter of June 11, the Shanghai Committee warned that Russia was on the move and that England did not appear to realize "the importance of recent events." Gundry replied that there appeared to be no anxiety on the part of Russia to obtain the loan and that the rumor had apparently originated with the visit of the Chairman of the Russo-Chinese Bank to Peking and the distinction there shown him.[71] Shanghai followed up later that sum-mer with another warning that Russia intended to secure the loan in order to gain control of the Customs. Bertie assured the China Associa-tion that there was nothing in it.[72]

Whether Foreign Office pretense at unconcern with the loan in the summer of 1897 was genuine is not known. That the China Association accepted these assurances may have been due to Keswick's knowledge that the Anglo-German syndicate, led by the Hongkong & Shanghai Bank, was actually engaged in negotiations for the loan.[73] The first in-timations of the larger design in Russia's policy reached British official circles in August, when Sir Claude MacDonald learned that Russia had demanded the removal of Mr. Kinder, a British subject, as Engineer-in-chief on the Tientsin-Shanhaikwan line of the Chinese Imperial Rail-ways.[74] MacDonald's protest prevented the move, but the Russian Chargé made no secret of the fact "that the Russian Government in-tended that the provinces of China bordering on the Russian frontier must not come under the influence of any nation except Russia." [75] Russia had embarked on a policy of spheres as was to become evident before many months had passed.

But here we are concerned with the sequence of the development of mercantile attitude. The Kinder affair had not yet become known and evidence that Russia was building the trans-Manchurian was not re-garded as a threat. As has been pointed out, as early as November, 1895, the leadership of the China Association had been content to come to some understanding with Russia on the sharing of what later came to be called "spheres of preponderance." Only Shanghai marked the serious-ness of rumors that Russia was moving on the Customs administration via the third indemnity loan.

It was not until the Kiaochow affair that issues of *Hochpolitik* came to assume importance in the counsels of the China Association. Germany's desire for a coaling station and *point d'appui* on the Chinese coast, first broached during the Sino-Japanese war,[76] centered on Kiaochow as the most feasible point in September, 1895.[77] A visit the following year led Admiral von Tirpitz to confirm the choice.[78] Germany waited im-patiently for the incident which would allow her to take action,[79] and meanwhile busied herself with securing the consent of Russia.[80] Rumors of Germany's designs on Kiaochow (in collaboration with Russia, it was thought) led the China Association to suggest to the Foreign Office in June, 1897, that the move might be forestalled by having it declared a treaty port.[81]

The idea was new to Bertie, who inquired as to the commercial pos-sibilities of the port, and remarked that the Admiralty thought it "some-what exposed." [82] However, he suggested that the proposal be put in writing. At the meeting of the General Committee some members began to discuss seriously the commercial potentialities of Kiaochow, but Kes-wick pointed out that they were interested in the political aspects more than the commercial; primarily the object was to keep it out of the hands of Germany and Russia. "As a treaty port it would certainly be less liable to foreign occupation." The suggestion was officially communi-cated to Lord Salisbury. The Foreign Office forwarded it to MacDonald for comment, but the Minister also seemed to have missed the point, noting that Kiaochow had little commercial or strategical value and would not be worth the expense of a consular establishment. He agreed, however, almost as an afterthought, that to open it as a treaty port would be a good method of protecting it against aggressive designs.[83]

Whether the Foreign Office was seriously considering some such action is not known, for before the British Government could decide to move, German warships had entered the harbor of Kiaochow on November 14, following the massacre of two German Catholic missionaries in southwestern Shantung.[84] Despite Russian opposition,[85] Germany proceeded with her plans for a station on the China coast. The German Ambassador in London received the impression from a conversation with Lord Salisbury that Britain would not object to German occupation.[86] But Germany's original demands did not mention occupation; in addition to punishment of local officials and indemnity, she demanded preferential railway rights in Shantung.[87]

Despite British protests, China consented to grant this latter concession provided Germany would evacuate Kiaochow.[88] Germany insisted on holding the port as security and early in December revealed that her true purpose was to keep it as a station.[89] Ignoring the territorial question, Lord Salisbury continued to protest against special commercial privileges in Shantung and hinted that England would be forced to demand compensation.[90] Early in January, 1898, nevertheless, China agreed to Germany's demands and on March 6 a convention was signed ceding Kiaochow to Germany on a 99-year lease, sanctioning the construction of two railway lines in Shantung and giving Germany preferential status in any future industrial undertakings in the province.[91] This action, as the Russian press predicted, was bound to "form a starting-point for a decision in the Far Eastern question," from which "Russia especially can learn a lesson." [92]

The Kiaochow affair was also the turning point in mercantile attitudes. The Shanghai Committee, already piqued at London's neglect of its warning over Russian plans for securing the third loan, telegraphed in November accurately outlining the German plans. The China Association was finally aroused and at its meeting on November 30, 1897, the General Committee held its first debate on political issues in two years.[93] Keswick noted that Germany's action raised a very serious question, as Kiaochow commanded the approaches to Peking; he invited expressions of opinion as to the stand the Association ought to adopt. Lord Loch, President of the China Association, held that permanent occupation would give Germany great influence at Peking which might be used in detriment to British interests. If Germany was acting with the consent of Russia, as appeared likely, it looked like an anti-British move. Russia would now take Port Arthur and Talienwan, and probably insist on a Russian successor to Sir Robert Hart as head of the Maritime Customs.

Sir Cecil Smith pointed out that it was the first instance of a seizure of Chinese territory without war. He was certain Russia was partner to the deal. Despite recognition of the danger, the Association hesitated. It was decided to inquire by letter for clarification of the Government's stand.

To this inquiry the Foreign Office replied that Lord Salisbury knew practically no more than had appeared in the press, and in private conference Bertie told Gundry that no further information was available.[94] It was not a reply that the Association could accept with equanimity, for events were moving rapidly. In mid-December the Russian fleet sailed into Port Arthur, ostensibly as a temporary measure. Alarming telegrams from the Far East reached the China Association that month. Hongkong wired on the 3rd suggesting that "in the event of Germany or any other power acquiring Chinese territory hope Great Britain will obtain extension of Hongkong boundaries. Is of greatest importance France should not obtain a footing in Kwangtung or south China generally." [95] This advice was repeated on the 21st, and Gundry pressed the issue at the Foreign Office.

Shanghai telegraphed three times, hardly able to conceal its indignation at the failure of the London Committee to anticipate the situation. The first, dated December 2, noted:

It is reported Russia trying to get possession of Manchuria, Chihli and Korea; Germany of Shantung; France of Fukien. Strongly recommend, if true, that the British Government offer to protect Yangtze in order to secure British influence in that region, in addition to whatever course is best to protect our interests in Gulf of Pechili.[96]

On the 24th the Shanghai Committee warned that Russia was endeavoring to force dismissal of Mr. Kinder as Engineer-in-chief of the Imperial Chinese Railway system, and three days later reverted to the question it had raised in June:

It is reported and generally believed that the Russian Government has offered to guarantee the Chinese Government sterling loan conditionally on controlling the Imperial Maritime Customs, railway from Tientsin to Peking, and railway prospects in China generally. It is necessary Great Britain improve the position without delay. We strongly urge you to urge Secretary of State Foreign Affairs to make an offer same as Russia. Press the matter.[97]

The China Association was now faced with the twofold problem of adopting a political attitude in the face of these developments and of bringing pressure on the Foreign Office without departing from its previous policy of collaboration. Relations with the latter were cordial, a relationship resulting from the tacit understanding that the China Association would not inject itself into political issues; even in the matter of loans the Association had refrained from attempting to influence the government stand. The Association's commercial program was clear and comprehensive; in such matters the Foreign Office was accommodating. Appreciable gains had already been made and the demands of November 2, 1896, appeared to have been accepted as a desirable program. It was aimed at opening China, but now a new series of issues had arisen centering around the need for maintaining British predominance. There was little point in agitating for the loosening of trade restrictions while other Powers roped off exclusive spheres and threatened established British interests.

Moreover, whatever the London Committee might think, Old China Hands in the treaty ports were insisting on a reappraisal of policy. Hongkong regarded the occasion made to order for its long-standing ambition to see the boundaries of the colony extended and was becoming jittery about French designs in the southern provinces. The opening of the West River and of Nanning as a treaty port was being pressed with unprecedented urgency. Shanghai had raised three important points. If spheres of interest and influence were being carved out, it was imperative that England secure the commercial heart of China. Secondly, were Britons prepared to acquiesce in the Russian process of squeezing all British interests out of the North? And, finally, was the Russian effort at capturing control of the Customs administration through the third indemnity loan to be countered?

The Russian fleet had sailed into Port Arthur, and on December 22 MacDonald reported that Russia had offered to guarantee the third indemnity loan, at the attractive figure of 93 and at only 4 percent interest, on the security of the land tax and *likin* revenue, and as a *quid pro quo* had asked for control of all railways in Manchuria and North China, and "that a Russian should be appointed Inspector-General of Customs when that post becomes vacant." [98] China had been prepared to accept the previous offer from the Anglo-German syndicate provided it did not entail foreign control of the revenues pledged as additional security. The Bank was apparently willing to grant the loan with a guarantee from the British Government.[99] Salisbury's reply was that the British Government was still considering how far it could go in guaranteeing the loan and inquired as to "what you think we might fairly ask for if we could offer entire or partial guarantee, or advance the money ourselves." [100] MacDonald listed the following concessions as desirable: requisite control of revenue, "railway from Burmese frontier to Yangtze Valley," guarantee against cession of territory in the

Yangtze valley to any other Power, Talienwan to be made a treaty port, greater freedom of internal trade, and *likin* exemption for foreign goods in treaty ports.[101] It is striking how closely this list resembled the mercantile program.

It was in this atmosphere that the China Association on December 29, 1897, held a full-dress policy debate.[102] Lord Loch, President of the Association, opened the discussion by pointing out that any communication to the Foreign Office must state what injury the Association conceived would be done to British interests by the occupation of Kiaochow and Port Arthur. His own view was that British interest lay in assisting China to maintain her integrity, in not allowing other Powers to interfere "beyond a certain limit," and not to pursue a policy of permanent annexation herself. Except for extending the Hongkong boundary and perhaps taking Chusan, he thought that entering upon a policy of territorial aggrandizement would be interpreted as condoning what others had done.

Ewen Cameron of the Hongkong and Shanghai Bank argued that they should start with the assumption that Germany and Russia were in Kiaochow and Port Arthur to stay, and that some agreement should be arrived at. Gundry noted that he had prepared a memorandum at the time of the Cassini Convention rumor a year before and that several of the consequences then foreseen had been realized. He could hardly conceal his bitterness at the fact that the leaders of the Association had seen fit not to present it to the Foreign Office. Gwyther, another member, held that maintenance of China's territorial integrity was no longer possible and that to resist the encroachment of other Powers might involve war. Lord Loch doubted that things would be pushed to the point of war, and suggested that if the Dreibund continued to act in opposition to Britain, an Anglo-Japanese alliance might be indicated. "We do not want more territory and should warn others that we would not allow them to take more." [103]

The discussion appeared to be leading nowhere and it was obvious that the more respectable Old China Hands had arrived at no determined policy except that something ought to be done. Their position crystallized, however, when the discussion passed on to the loan negotiations. Gundry recalled that he had suggested to Bertie several months before that the Government guarantee the loan (this had been in response to the alarming telegram from Shanghai noted above) or offer to make it outright on the precedent of the Suez shares. It was agreed that strong measures were warranted to prevent Russian encroachment on the Customs administration and any further territorial advances. Lord Loch again advised an alliance with Japan, noting that "our interests and those of Japan were similar and we should not lose any opportunity of cooperating with her." As an alternative he proposed an Anglo-Chinese alliance aimed at protecting the Yangtze valley. It was agreed that Britain should forestall Russia by offering to lend the money on easy terms.

From this debate several points were clear. The China Association was determined to counter Russian encroachment, particularly on the Customs, and wanted the loan kept in British hands at any cost. Although maintenance of China's territorial integrity was regarded as the happiest solution, an agreement whereby Britain's primary interest in the Yangtze was protected would be acceptable. For the first time, too, the possibility of an Anglo-Japanese alliance appeared desirable. The actual communication sent to the Foreign Office touched only on the first point, suggesting that it would be "a politic and most advantageous act if the British Government would give the guarantee necessary to enable the Chinese Government to raise the loan" and that "an act of this kind would change materially the present trend of events in China . . . and enormously safeguard British interests." [104]

At the same time this view was pressed upon the Government in a confidential interview between Lord Loch and George Curzon, the Parliamentary Undersecretary, at the Foreign Office.[105] An account of the interview is here paraphrased from the Minute Book of the China Association:

LOCH: The China Association is of the opinion that a Russian-guaranteed loan would give Russia tremendous influence at Peking and be injurious to British interests. It was therefore desired that the Government step in and either advance or guarantee the money itself.

CURZON: No loan has as yet been completed, as the Chinese Government was waiting to hear the views of England. Presuming that the Government did step in, which would the Committee prefer, that the Government raise the loan or guarantee it?

LOCH: The former, as in that case we should be entitled to demand certain concessions such as extension of the Hongkong boundary, the occupation of Chusan and possibly a port or naval station further north. [Later Lord Loch reported to the Committee that he had not listed other concessions as he thought it would drive China into the arms of Russia.]

(Curzon did not commit himself on this point.)

LOCH: Another issue concerns the Committee. We fear the contingency of some Power occupying a position in the vicinity of the Yangtze or even of any territory south of Shantung or north of the present Franco-Chinese border.

CURZON: I cannot speak on behalf of the Government, but at the same time do not see how we could allow any interference within those regions.

LOCH: I suggest that Britain might guarantee the independence of China over a certain area.

CURZON: This might be dangerous as it would constitute an invitation to other Powers to annex territory up to the boundary of the area defined.

In giving an account of the interview to the General Committee, Lord Loch remarked that he had gained the impression that "it is evidently the policy of the Government to resist any action of Russia or Germany that would injure our interests." [106] The Committee, however, decided that the loan matter was so urgent that a deputation would be sent to Lord Salisbury emphasizing the importance attached to it by the Association. A telegram had just been received from China through the Hongkong and Shanghai Bank (if not with its active encouragement) which sounded ominous: "Impress upon Gundry advisable moderate demand [regarding loan] in order to compete effectively with Russian offer." The Committee was unanimously in favor of lending the money to China on any terms required to place England in the position of influence which a creditor Power would enjoy. Pointing up its importance, one member expressed fear of what might happen if Russia organized the "Manchurian hordes" into an army; and what was true of Russia in that respect was also suspected of Germany. A deputation was consequently organized and an interview arranged for the following month. The purpose of the China Association in asking for the interview was to impress on the Government the importance of guaranteeing the loan, without regard to any specific concessions as a *quid pro quo*.

Before the interview could be held, however, "the motives which had prompted the request were no longer urgent enough to bother Lord Salisbury." [107] In fact, so rapid had been the pace of events that the demands of the China Association were outdated before they could be presented. Nor does there appear to have been any direct influence brought to bear during the negotiations of January and February, 1898. But before the General Committee had met again toward the end of February an appreciable portion of the traditional mercantile program had been realized, and private advices from the Hongkong and Shanghai Bank indicated that the loan (and the Maritime Customs) would be safe in British hands.

By the first week in January Government policy was apparently set. It involved the decision to undertake the loan on reasonable terms,[108] at the same time forestalling Russia and advancing a program designed to protect the British position in the Maritime Customs and to secure more extended opportunities for trade. In effect, the concessions demanded constituted what the mercantile community had been demanding since 1869, and particularly since 1895. On January 8, Lord Salisbury indicated Britain's readiness to undertake the loan "on complete acceptance of conditions" named at the end of December [109] and British control of the revenues pledged. Two days later, Arthur Balfour, then First Lord of the Treasury, stated Britain's policy in China. "Our interests in China are not territorial; they are commercial," and because of her trade preponderance Britain had a "special claim to see that the policy of that country is not directed towards the discouragement of foreign trade." [110] That was the purpose of the concessions Britain had requested. British efforts, Balfour observed, would be directed toward preventing any Power from interfering with "equality of opportunity which is all that we claim," and would combat any attempt to set up preferential trade regimes in China.

A week later, the Chancellor of the Exchequer, Sir Michael Hicks-Beach, told the Swansea Chamber of Commerce even more emphatically that

> We do not regard China as a place of conquest or acquisition by any European or other Power. We look upon it as the most hopeful place of the future for the commerce of our country and the commerce of the world at large, and the Government was absolutely determined . . . if necessary, at the cost of war, that the door should not be shut against us.[111]

While negotiations for the British loan to China were proceeding in Peking, the Foreign Office turned its attention toward arriving at some understanding with Russia on the Far East. Lord Salisbury, while refusing to countenance impairment of Chinese territorial integrity, offered Russia a "partition of preponderance" in China; [112] there was some undefined talk about defining spheres, and even a suggestion that the loan be shared.[113] But Lord Salisbury thought St. Petersburg "insincere and their language ambiguous" [114] and the matter was dropped. Meanwhile, Russian opposition to the British loan "on the ground that it would disturb the balance of influence in China" [115] and particularly to the proposal to make Talienwan an open port led China to decide to borrow neither from England nor from Russia, "in consequence of threat of rupture by the latter power." [116]

Lord Salisbury's immediate response was the warning to Peking that "if the Chinese Government enter into negotiations for obtaining a loan from European financiers, Her Majesty's Government must insist on at least an adequate share being assigned to British banks." [117] His purpose was indicated by the stress placed on avoiding "any appearance of excluding this country." But while continuing to guard against the exclusion of the Syndicate from a share in the loan, MacDonald was also instructed to press for fulfillment of the concessions which had originally been demanded as compensation for the loan. By the end of January, the British loan terms had included the following concessions and privileges, embodying a major portion of the mercantile program advanced by the China Association:

1. Nanning and Hsiangtan to be opened. Yamen to give assurance that Talienwan will be opened if railway is constructed.
2. British subjects to be allowed to use steamers wherever they are by Treaty at present allowed to use native boats.
3. On the application of any British Consul, Provincial authorities are to supply details of all inland tariffs on merchandize from Treaty Ports to any specified place in interior, and China to consider what other steps can be taken to improve internal trade.
4. When railway reaches Burmah frontier China agrees to its extension by a British Company into Chinese territory to a point and under Regulations to be arranged by the two Governments.
5. Guarantee against any alienation of Yangtze Valley to any other Power.
6. China agrees to come to an arrangement with regard to *likin* exemption area beyond foreign concessions.[118]

In addition MacDonald informed the Yamen that quite irrespective of the loan Britain was determined that the post of Inspector-General should always be held by an Englishman: "They gave me positive assurances to this effect."

In effect, this *was* the mercantile program as expressed by the China Association, first in 1891 and again in 1895 and November, 1896, as pointed out above. It should be emphasized again that the loan as such, either as investment or as a means of gaining influence, never played an important role in mercantile or official schemes. Rather, it was to serve as a lever for prying loose desirable commercial concessions from China and as a protection against the exclusionary designs of the other Powers. When the loan was turned down, therefore, MacDonald was instructed to demand the concessions as "compensation" and when these were secured "both the loan and the understanding with Russia became matters of comparative indifference to Her Majesty's Government and the negotiations dropped." [119] Some of the original demands were dropped, but those that were retained were pressed with unusual vigor against Chinese objection.

Britain demanded a non-alienation declaration with regard to the Yangtze; that the Inspector-General of Customs "should always be British"; that internal waterways be opened to steam navigation; and that Nanning (on the West River route) and Hsiangtan (in Hunan) be opened as treaty ports.[120] On February 11, in reply to a British note, China issued a declaration on non-alienation of the Yangtze region, obligating herself not to mortgage, lease or cede territory in that area to another Power, including England.[121] Two days later a compromise was reached on the Customs Inspectorate with China consenting that the post would be held by an Englishman so long as British trade was preponderant.[122] Due to French opposition China refused to open Nanning at that time and because Hunan was still a closed province would not consider the opening of Hsiangtan within less than two years. But China did agree that "wherever the use of native boats is now by Treaty permitted to Foreigners, they shall equally be permitted to employ steamers"; [123] the arrangement would come into effect in June, 1898.

These were by no means minor concessions, and on February 19, MacDonald was also able to report the conclusion of a preliminary agreement between the Hongkong and Shanghai Bank and the Chinese Government for a £16,000,000 loan, secured on the *likin* and other revenues to be placed under Customs control.[124] The Hongkong and Shanghai Bank was acting on behalf of the Anglo-German syndicate, and a final agreement was signed on March 1, 1898.[125] The crux of the agreement, so far as the commercial interests were concerned, lay in the provision placing the *likin* revenues pledged as security under control of the Maritime Customs, a move which the China Association had been urging as the basis of fiscal reform in China. In addition, *likin* tolls could now be neither increased nor decreased without prior arrangement with the Bank. And to make the recent Chinese declaration on the Inspectorate even more binding, a provision was added to the loan agreement "that the administration of the Chinese Imperial Maritime Customs Service shall remain as at present constituted during the currency of this loan," [126] that is, a period of forty-five years.

It was this series of events which had led the China Association to conclude that a deputation to Lord Salisbury was no longer necessary. The Association was jubilant and the General Committee meeting on February 23, 1898, was an occasion for exchange of congratulations all around.[127] Although the preliminary loan agreement had not yet been published, Gundry reported that he had that morning learned from Ewen Cameron at the Hongkong and Shanghai Bank that the loan would go through and the *likin* pledged was being placed under the Customs Inspectorate. He had also seen Bertie at the Foreign Office, who had inquired as to whether the recent concessions were satisfactory to the China Association. Gundry had replied that they were "cordially satisfactory." As he pointed out to the General Committee: "It might be remarked that every point taken up—the project of a guaranteed loan; the retention of a British subject as Inspector-General; the opening of inland waterways to steam, and a British protectorate over the Yangtze valley—had been advocated by the Association." [128] To the Foreign Office the Chairman conveyed the "general wish" of the Committee that recognition be expressed for a job well done.

In the Annual Report for 1897–98, submitted to the membership at the annual dinner in March, the China Association listed with satisfaction the concessions that had been gained: a satisfactory loan agreement, *likin* revenues placed under the supervision of the Maritime Customs, which implied "a promise of reform in the method of collection which may have a far-reaching effect," the Inspectorate-General to remain in British hands, a non-alienation declaration with respect to the Yangtze valley, a port to be opened in Hunan within two years, and inland waterways opened to foreign steamers. Well might the Chairman remark, in praise of Sir Claude MacDonald, that "paragraph after paragraph of the report contained a record of some step . . . in the direction of greater facility for commerce, which he had gained. It is scarcely an exaggeration to say that he had accomplished more in two years than his predecessors during the previous twenty." [129]

It was to prove the highpoint in the China Association's honeymoon with the Foreign Office. During the past two years, the London Committee, which acted as the spokesman of the British interests in China, had pursued a policy of collaboration with Whitehall which had apparently paid off. A large part of the mercantile program for the opening of China had been accomplished. Thus far all serious threats to exclude British trade and enterprise from the vaguely-defined spheres had been frustrated. Government spokesmen, including Balfour and the Chancellor of the Exchequer, had enunciated a British policy of insistence on keeping the China door open, in a manner calculated to win the approval of Old China Hands.

But the honeymoon was not destined to last. For, toward the end of the period here reviewed, the suspicion arose that what had been gained from China in terms of commercial reforms for which generations of Old China Hands had been agitating might be lost to international rivalry. A new China Question, whether the market could be saved from break-up into exclusive spheres, was placed on the agenda of the China Association, and a shift in emphasis—from opening China to guarding British predominance against foreign encroachment—can be noted in its debates.

The China Association had not made up its mind when the events of March and April, 1898, forced it to consider its attitude on partition. The

few times that the question had been raised in previous years, majority
sentiment favored the British policy of maintaining China's integrity
But, as early as 1895, Keswick and the leadership of the Committee had
been eager to come to an arrangement with Russia defining spheres of
influence or interest or preference, while in March, 1898, Gundry could
speak of the non-alienation agreement as a "British protectorate over
the Yangtze valley." Besides, the mercantile dream that Britain would
undertake the administrative and fiscal reform of China to the greater
profit of British interests was never absent.

Despite Lord Salisbury's flirtation with Russia looking toward a
"partition of preponderance" in China, parliamentary opinion was
solidly behind the motion introduced on March 1, 1898, "that it is of
vital importance for British commerce and influence that the Independence of Chinese Territory should be maintained." [130] It was admittedly introduced as a counter to suspected Russian designs,[131] but as
Curzon pointed out, maintenance of the integrity and independence of
China had always been the "cardinal bases of our policy." [132] This was
axiomatic but not too helpful in the light of recent events. What Britain
was aiming at was "equality of treatment and opportunity as the principal basis of our relations." [133]

The dilemma was probably best stated by Mr. T. W. Gibson-Bowles
who seconded the motion for maintaining China's territorial integrity
Reviving the China dream, he recalled that China was the last great
potential market for British manufactures. British trade there "is not
one-tenth of what could be, should be, or will be, carried on with China
if only her independence is maintained, and adequate pressure is put
upon the Chinese to remove those barriers which alone impede the commerce." That was the traditional complaint and the traditional remedy
as seen by Old China Hands. But a new factor had arisen which made
it obsolete. "Sir, if once Germany, Russia, and France take possession
of portions of China . . . a system far more exclusive than any Chinese
system ever was will be imposed, and imposed mainly against the commerce of this country." [134]

What was now sought, therefore, in official circles as well as among
the representatives of British interests in the China Association, was a
formula which by "adequate pressure" on China would complete the
mercantile program of opening the entire country to commerce and, at
the same time, secure it against the competition and preferential designs
of the Continental Powers. It was a formula never discovered. For
given the assertion of spheres of interest, by Germany in Shantung, by
Russia in North China, and by France in the South, it was far too late to
insist on the maintenance of territorial integrity without recourse to

war. Accepting the inevitability of the break-up, the China Association
recommended the policy of desperation: a vigorous scramble for concessions and the assertion of a British protectorate over the choicest
sphere—the Yangtze.

VIII

The Struggle for a Yangtze Protectorate, 1898-1899

> *"Our interests in the Yangtze Region should be asserted more decisively if only in preparation for a débâcle"*—R. S. Gundry to Francis Bertie, July 5, 1898.
>
> *"British enterprise in China must be independent, individual and self-reliant. The moment it ceases to be this and leans too much on State assistance, it ceases to be enterprise, indeed I may say it ceases to be British"*—Sir Claude MacDonald, Sept. 28, 1899.

THE jubilation among Old China Hands following the concessions of February, 1898, turned into apprehension the following month. If the Battle of Concessions had resulted in the first major victory for British diplomacy, it also raised the first major threat to British predominance in China. On March 6 the lease of Kiaochow to Germany was confirmed. The concessions granted to Britain and the conclusion of the loan agreement with the Anglo-German syndicate on March 1 led both Russia and France to demand compensation in a manner calculated to give the impression that the break-up of China would be precipitated. On March 9 Russia confirmed the rumor that she had demanded the lease of Port Arthur and Talienwan and the right to construct a railway from Harbin through Mukden to Port Arthur. Count Muraviev assured Britain that Talienwan (later christened Dalny by the Russians and Dairen by the Japanese) would be "open to foreign trade like the other ports of China." [1]

Britain's interest in the matter was immediately expressed by Lord Salisbury as a desire that Manchuria "should remain open to British trade like other ports of China . . . and that no strategical position which would threaten the independence of the Chinese Government shall be established by a foreign country." [2] Sir Nicholas O'Conor informed the Russians that British commercial interests would be menaced by their "possession of a very strong military position like Port Arthur," nor would he grant Count Muraviev's contention that because British interests were principally concentrated in the Yangtze valley events further north remained a matter of disinterest to London.[3] British apprehensions were aroused not alone because of the menace of a fortified Port Arthur, but because of "ultimate intentions."

When they have obtained a lease of Talienwan and Port Arthur under the promise of opening one or both ports to foreign trade they will proceed to re-fortify Port Arthur and to erect fortifications in one of the three harbours of Talienwan. . . . There is no doubt that the Russian Government think that before the expiration of their lease of the two ports Manchuria will be in their possession and Pechili if not actually in their possession virtually at their mercy.

Before this stage is reached and if the effete government of Peking is not, as seems probable, upset by a revolution in the country which will precipitate Russian action, I believe Russian influence in Peking will be so great as to enable them to nullify the assurance given to Her Majesty's Government by the Chinese Government respecting the Inspectorate-General.[4]

Despite strong British objection,[5] Russia proceeded with her plans and on March 27 secured the lease and railway concession. By a further Russo-Chinese agreement on May 7 Russia acquired the right to veto the grant of any railway, industrial or commercial concession to any other Power in the Liaotung sphere.[6] France, meanwhile, had pressed her own demands and by an exchange of notes early in April obtained the following concessions: (a) lease of a bay on the south coast of China, later determined to be Kwangchowan; (b) concession of a railway connecting Tongking with Yunnan by way of the Red River; (c) an engagement by China not to alienate the provinces bordering Tongking, nor to cede the island of Hainan to any other power; and (d) appointment of a Frenchman to head the Chinese Postal Service.[7]

Whitehall's early indecisiveness as to how to meet these developments was matched by mercantile alarm that they were aimed at neutralizing the concessions recently secured. The Reuters report that Lord Salisbury had ordered British ships from Port Arthur under Russian pressure was disturbing.[8] The Shanghai Committee telegraphed early in March in terms which left no doubt that they expected London to counter Russian designs in North China. "We confirm our views. There is great necessity for protecting our interests Gulf of Pechili in view of Russian project Port Arthur."[9] A week later Shanghai renewed the alarm. "Russian occupation Port Arthur threatens all commercial interests. Proposed guarantee open port considered useless. Urge retain also railway construction North ports of China and Manchuria in hands of China not Russia." [10] Hongkong's warning of December that French encroachment on the southern provinces would menace British interests in Kwangtung was repeated in March, and the importance of extending the colony's boundary for strategic purposes was again pressed.[11]

Without having reached a decision on policy, the China Association communicated these expressions of alarm to the Foreign Office. Just as significant was Gundry's determination to gain the backing of the British mercantile community in whatever action might be taken. From March, 1898, the home Chambers were kept informed of developments. Gundry had become persuaded that it might become necessary for the China Association to enter politics and to mobilize public opinion in order to counter Russia's move at Port Arthur. To the membership of the Association he suggested more frequent general meetings not only for "social purposes," as had been the custom at annual dinners, but to give members an opportunity of "getting in touch with groups of M.P.'s." Granting that the China Association had succeeded in large measure in its strictly commercial program, Gundry pointed out that this would be of little value if the political aspect of Anglo-Chinese relations was disregarded by merchants.

There were commercial and politico-commercial questions with which the Association concerned itself; and there were the higher politics which were engaging the attention not only of England, but of Europe and America, at the present moment. There was full confidence in MacDonald but he must have the support of the Government which he is not getting in these critical questions. He would like to ask them the blunt question: Were they in favor of allowing Russia to occupy a fortified Port Arthur? [12]

On matters of "higher politics," however, the Foreign Office was not taking the China Association into its confidence. Nor did the China Association immediately attempt to influence British official policy, aside from endorsing the alarmist telegrams emanating from the Far East. Port Arthur did not effect such a distinct modification in British policy as is generally supposed. For the ultimate response to the Russo-French drive was but an extension of the policy of "compensation" and counter-concessions expressed in the negotiations of February. Curzon's statement in the House of Commons on March 1 that Britain would insist both on China's territorial integrity and "equality of treatment and opportunity" had been accompanied by the qualification that "our policy is and must be to prevent her disruption as long as we can." [13] And he had foreseen the possibility "of circumstances arising in the future, circumstances gravely affecting, and perhaps seriously imperilling, our interests in China, which might tempt us, and even compel us, to depart from that attitude of reserve." [14]

During the Anglo-Russian conversations in January the prospect of recognizing "spheres of preponderance" while maintaining equality of commercial opportunity had been seriously discussed.[15] In Parliament members taxed the Government with having subscribed to an inconsistent position by adopting the March 1 resolution calling for maintenance of Chinese independence and at the same time being prepared to countenance a Russian port in the Liaotung peninsula, so long as it remained unfortified.[16] The Opposition, calling for an understanding with Russia, mocked "this absurd doctrine of the so-called 'open door.' " [17]

There was to be no outright departure from this "absurd doctrine" but rather a reluctant retreat characterized by a policy of compensatory advantages. Whether this policy of counter-concessions involved acceptance of the doctrine of spheres of influence was a problem which the Government left to Mr. Balfour to explain away. As O'Conor put it, Britain could counter Russian designs either by organizing a "combination of Powers" (an alternative hardly likely to be successful in view of Britain's failure to elicit a favorable response to her overtures for an alliance with Russia and Germany in the spring of 1898), or by "proceeding to safeguard British interests and prestige by insisting upon a cession of a port in Chusan, and perhaps Silver Island in the Yangtze, to redress the balance of power." [18] This, as he confessed, was "tantamount at the very least to accepting spheres of influence for which Her Majesty's Government had shown no proclivity." The Foreign Office, however, considered any such move as unwise. Chusan and Silver Island could, in any event, be taken "whenever some other Power moves that way" and there was no point in forcing the scramble for spheres. Instead, Bertie recommended a policy of securing "some counterpoise to the preponderance of Russian and German influences at Peking" by occupying "some point of advantage in the north." He urged Weihaiwei.[19]

The alternatives, as they appeared to the British Cabinet, were either to stand up to Russia, demanding that the latter refrain from leasing Port Arthur, with England engaging "not to intervene in Manchuria," or to accept the occupation of Port Arthur as a *fait accompli* "subject to engagements to preserve existing treaty rights" and take a lease of Weihaiwei as a "make-weight." [20] Reluctantly, the latter alternative was chosen. The British fleet was ordered to Weihaiwei and, on March 25, MacDonald was instructed to obtain "in the manner you think most efficacious and speedy, the refusal of Weihaiwei on the departure of the

Japanese. The terms should be similar to those granted to Russia for Port Arthur." [21]

~ The policy thus pursued was well expressed in the terms "makeweight" and "counterpoise." It was a continuance of the policy of compensation and counter-concessions, an attempt to neutralize the effect of the special rights obtained by the other Powers. Despite the fact that Britain was forced to recognize Germany's "rights and interests" in Shantung as a condition of acquiescence in the lease of Weihaiwei,[22] there had been no outright admission of the existence of spheres. As Balfour explained to the House, Britain's policy had not changed since January. It was still based on limited liability with respect to her interests in China. She sought no responsibility for populations, but a base from which to counter Russian prestige at Peking. Her interests were still commercial, expressed in the concessions obtained in February and aimed merely at preventing the establishment of preferential regimes.[23]

Before the month was out, Balfour would be forced to admit that Britain's action implied more than this, that it came close to a recognition of "spheres of interest." But there was no conscious acceptance of the premise of partition or departure from the "equality of opportunity" formula. In the game of counter-concessions, the Government turned next to the neutralization of the privileges obtained by France early in April. The concessions demanded followed the line advocated by the Hongkong Committee of the China Association and the Hongkong Chamber of Commerce, with the addition of a specific railway concession as compensation for the similar privilege granted to France. These included: (a) extension of the boundary of Hongkong to include part of Kowloon and Mirs Bay; (b) concession to a British syndicate for the construction of a railway from Shanghai to Nanking; (c) Nanning to be opened as a treaty port; (d) declaration of non-alienation of Kwangtung and Yunnan to any foreign Power; and (e) "an assurance in writing that the Chinese Government has not yielded to France any exclusive privileges with respect to railways and mining." [24] After protracted negotiations, China agreed to all the demands except that concerning the opening of Nanning, which was strongly opposed by the French.[25]

Mercantile reaction to these events was marked by a growing concern that Britain's predominant position in China was being lost just as a new age for commerce and enterprise was dawning. For the first time the China Association concentrated its attention on what some members scorned as "political questions" and the suggestion that the Old China Hands go to the country for support gained ground. There was an uneasy feeling that Britain was losing her position of leadership and prestige at Peking. Criticism, from the Far East especially, took the form less of specific recommendation than of noting with alarm. While counterpoises and counter-concessions were welcomed, it was felt that the assertion of a bold, basic policy not dependent on countering the initiative of Russia and France was imperative. It was, above all, a cry against Whitehall's policy of limited liability and a demand that Britain assume the responsibility of her greatness and commercial predominance in the Far East. And, as the battle of railway concessions followed close upon earlier encroachments, it became crystallized around the twofold thesis that Britain should establish a protectorate over the Yangtze while insisting on the maintenance of equal rights in the rest of China. Nor would Old China Hands admit that this policy involved any inconsistency.

Shanghai, which had been alarmed since Russia made her first move at Port Arthur, telegraphed again to the China Association on March 25 the gratuitous cry that "in view of following Russian demands having been conceded; viz., permission to fortify Port Arthur and Russian construction of railways, it is utterly impossible for China to observe treaties. Unless Great Britain intervenes at once [her] influence and prestige totally lost." [26] Another wire, on the 4th of April, warned that there was a concerted effort to "destroy British supremacy at Shanghai." Hongkong again warned that France should not be allowed "to occupy or lease any territory in the four southern provinces or adjacent islands or obtain any exclusive privilege therein," [27] an assurance which, as was noted above, the Foreign Office later incorporated in the April counter-concessions.

The General Committee of the China Association met on April 6 to consider what policy to adopt in the face of these developments. The usual reluctance to interfere in matters of higher politics had been reinforced by the gratitude felt at Foreign Office diligence in extracting the latest concessions from China. But the pressure from the Far Eastern mercantile communities was strong and a growing interest among the home Chambers, itself stimulated by the China Association, made it imperative that the Association assume leadership in mobilizing mercantile opinion behind what Lord Loch termed a "definite stand on policy." [28]

The mercantile temper of the country had recently been indicated at the annual meeting of the Associated Chambers of Commerce.[29] A resolution had been introduced regarding "the absorption of Chinese territory by Russia, France or Germany with great concern as injurious to the interests of British commerce, seeing those Powers exact the prohibitive duties of their respective countries in all their Colonies and Dependencies." [30] Its sponsor, T. F. Firth of Heckmondwike, took care to point out that his resolution was strictly "commercial" and had "no political object"; he advocated a policy aimed at upholding "the great and populous Chinese Empire . . . as a sphere for the trade of the world," if necessary at the cost of an Anglo-Japanese alliance or even of war. Hardly had Firth finished when he was assailed from all sides as a moderate! Members countered with the suggestion that England engage in a war of tariffs to oppose Continental designs on the China market or engage more vigorously in the battle of concessions. But the most striking aspect of the debate was the enthusiasm aroused by the suggestion of the Warrington representative that by adhering to the open door doctrine Britain was weakening her own chances in the current struggle. "While we strain after the shibboleth, we forfeit other advantages," he warned. Assurances of respect for the open door from Russia and France were worthless. The "safer policy for this country," he argued, was "to create an open door of our own." Far from proclaiming that Britain sought no territory, he advocated a division of China "on a fair and equitable basis." It was better to be sure of a province than to be excluded from the Empire.

The membership contented itself with passing the original resolution (which called for no specific action) amended to include the suggestion that Britain press for railway concessions leading to the Yangtze. The remarkable thing was that the open call for a British sphere had been seriously considered by the representatives of the leading chambers in Britain. London and Liverpool were soon to follow this lead. Manchester alone, though it urged a vigorous Far Eastern policy on the Government, called for forthright support of the open door. Following an exchange of correspondence with the China Association, and a special meeting of the Board of Directors on April 27,[31] the Manchester Chamber wrote to the Foreign Office advancing a policy which put it in a minority in mercantile ranks. Manchester expressed satisfaction with the recent official declarations to the effect that "the preservation of an open market throughout the whole of China with equal opportunities of trading for all" was regarded as of the highest importance; urged the Government, in the face of foreign encroachments, to "strenuously contend for the maintenance of British interests in China by insisting upon the continuance throughout the Empire of uninterrupted access on equal terms to the trade of the world"; and advocated international action to attain this policy.[32] No mention was made of Britain's special interest in the Yangtze valley and it was this feature which labelled Manchester as unique.

The China Association was undecided. The Chairman noted that recent French demands "could only be regarded as a direct menace to our position in South China and Canton" and that some stand had to be taken.[33] Sir William Des Voeux, former Governor of Hongkong, pointed out that France had asked not for concessions but for a declaration of non-alienation to which Britain could take no exception. But "what we had to fear was the gradual extension of influence until we find our commercial prospects injured and the country closed." He therefore suggested a resolution demanding that nothing given to France should be taken to mean the "slightest exclusiveness" as regards trade. As for Russia, the policy of counterpoise through the occupation of Weihaiwei was a "monument of failure." It was too late to do anything about that. "If we were not going to oppose Russia taking Port Arthur it would have been better not to object at all. An objection not intended to be backed up by force had better not be made." And the Government "seemed unable to come to the point of war."

Lord Loch dissented from this pessimism. There was still time for the China Association to take a "definite stand on policy." While Weihaiwei was not the equal of Port Arthur, its occupation was meant to "restore our prestige at Peking" and nothing had been lost. He suggested that Gundry draw up a "connected statement of policy" recommending that Britain implement the Yangtze non-alienation agreement by declaring that any encroachment in that region would be regarded as a *casus belli* and "take steps" to safeguard British trade in the South if France went ahead with her demands.

Keswick opposed any action which might be interpreted as criticism of the Foreign Office. The Government was well aware of mercantile opinion and a letter would do no good. Weihaiwei had been a wise move aimed at reestablishing British prestige. If any suggestions were to be advanced, however, he favored a policy aimed at keeping the Russians north of the Great Wall; the Yangtze was a region without definite boundaries. Michie pointed out that it was a question not of territory but of the assertion of prestige.

It was evident from the discussion that while the leadership of the China Association was agreed that the situation was menacing there was no consensus on the direction which they desired the Foreign Office to take. They agreed that the Government should back up the Hongkong and Shanghai Bank in its current negotiations with the German interests over the division of participation in the Tientsin-Chinkiang railway concession negotiations. They were agreed that the Government should somehow oppose French claims and reassert Britain's special interest in the Yangtze without giving up any rights south of the Great Wall. But what form that assertion should take was not defined. In conclusion, a special resolution was prepared respecting the activity of France in south China and Gundry was instructed to gather the sentiments which had been expressed into a connected statement of policy.

The resolution, forwarded to the Foreign Office, is of importance because it probably influenced the later British demands for compensation to balance French claims in South China.[34]

That this Association views with great apprehension the published statement that China has agreed to the demands by France implying a measure of special interest and influence on her part in Yunnan, Kwangsi and Kwangtung, giving her a naval base in the Lienchau Peninsula, and the appointment of a Frenchman to a position of authority in the Imperial Postal department.

That the Association desires to emphasise the protests raised in the telegram from the Hongkong branch of the 3rd and 21st December, and the 29th March, against the admission of any special French privileges in the Southern provinces of China.

That the Association is of the opinion that the principle cannot be too absolutely laid down that no special or exclusive privileges can be recognised in any portion of the maritime provinces the trade of which is preponderantly British.

That the Association desires especially to remark that the province of Kwangtung with its great riverine port of Canton constitutes the hinterland of the British colony of Hongkong, and has for more than a century past been a principal field of British trade; and that a clear and decisive resistance would be opposed to the admission in that province of any external influence.[35]

The principle laid down in this resolution—"that no special or exclusive privileges can be recognized in any portion of the maritime provinces the trade of which is preponderantly British"—went beyond official concern for equality of opportunity and non-alienation of territory. British preponderance in trade was itself advanced as giving title to a special British interest. Kwangtung, the "hinterland" of Hongkong, must be protected from "external"—that is, non-British—influence.

In the letter to the Foreign Office, dated April 14, Gundry went even further.[36] Accepting the more concrete proposals made at the General Committee meeting on April 6, and adding to them his own firm conviction that Britain's future in China depended on Whitehall's readiness to assume the responsibility of leading China on the path of reform, Gundry criticized the weak line of counter-concessions and called for a new departure in British policy. The features of this policy would be the following:

(a) While paying respect to the principle of territorial integrity, Britain could not rely on Russian and French assurances of maintaining the open door.

Under no circumstances should the vast British interests in North China and the even more important interests in Yunnan, Kwangsi and Kwangtung be written off.

(b) "Equality of opportunity in commercial and industrial enterprise" in the southern provinces must be maintained. This involved the opening of Nanning against French objection and demand for railway concessions on the Pakhoi-Nanning and Canton-Kowloon line. As for Kwangtung, "a clear and decisive resistance should be opposed, at all hazards, to the recognition of any alien interest or influence in that great and important province." [For alien, read French.]

(c) Without minimizing British interests elsewhere, Britain should assert "in explicit terms" her preponderance in the Yangtze region, which must be defined as stretching from Chusan to Burma and incorporating all provinces bordering on the Great River.

(d) But such assertion is not enough. The essence of the matter lay in influence at Peking. It must therefore "be followed by an endeavour to reanimate the Chinese Government if Russian pressure is to be withstood." China must be reformed with foreign aid, under the leadership of Britain. And such aid must include not merely control of revenue and fiscal reform, but the military reorganization of China under British tutelage.

(e) In this total reorganization of China, "a measure of control corresponding to the preponderance of British interests should be retained at all hazards in British hands."

The China Association thus went far beyond the policy of counterpoise and concessions. British preponderance was to be the basis for the assertion of leadership in a foreign protectorate of China; while the Yangtze region was to be recognized as a special British sphere. Within a year, mercantile agitation was to concentrate on implementing this assertion of a sphere through "effective occupation."

Under mercantile pressure, the Government was prepared to go part of the way toward an implementation of this program. But it was still a policy of limited liability and an extension of the doctrine of counter-concessions. Balfour had admitted that England considered the Yangtze her "sphere of interest" but not her "sphere of influence." The idea was left deliberately vague. Its first concrete assertion had taken the form of demanding the right to construct the Shanghai-Nanking railway as a "political concession." [37] Subsequent assertions were to be limited by two factors: priority in the Yangtze sphere was claimed only for railway concessions, while commercial opportunities and industrial enterprise were to be extended on the basis of the open-door; above all, no political claims of any kind were attached to recognition of spheres. Secondly, enterprise was to remain private and no measure of Government finance and control, not even government-guarantee, was to be admitted. Despite mercantile urging, Whitehall refused to depart from these two principles. There was to be neither a protectorate nor a British version of the Russo-Chinese Bank.

For the implementation of this policy, the Foreign Office recognized the Hongkong and Shanghai Bank, particularly in its manifestation as the British & Chinese Corporation (in which it was associated with Jardine, Matheson & Co.), as its chosen instrument. The Government was to aid the Bank in obtaining railway concessions and then withdraw from the picture. The idea of a national instrument arose when Germany objected to the Bank's participation in the Tientsin-Chinkiang line running through Shantung, while insisting on the participation of the Deutsche-Asiatische Bank and the German Syndicate (representing all important German financial interests and having the support of the German Government) in the Shanghai-Nanking line. The Hongkong and Shanghai Bank, after terminating its relationship with its German affiliate, "decided to form a strong representative and influential Syndicate to deal with railway construction in China," and arranged with Jardine, Matheson & Co. to form the British & Chinese Corporation to handle railway concessions.[38] This Syndicate thereafter served as the chosen instrument of the British Government. Its existence introduced a new element in the policy of the China Association, for the leadership of the latter was closely identified with the Syndicate.

Four separate conflicts during the battle for railway concessions which followed Port Arthur sharpened mercantile apprehensions. The first followed hard upon the "sudden withdrawal" at the end of March of the Hongkong and Shanghai Bank from the Anglo-German Syndicate and the formation of the British Syndicate.[39] British requests that German interests withdraw from competition for the Shanghai-Nanking concession in return for a free hand in Shantung were rejected by Berlin on the ground that Germany would never recognize the Yangtze as a British sphere.[40] Nor would they admit Britain's right, pressed by the Foreign Office on behalf of the Hongkong and Shanghai Bank, to participate in the Tientsin-Chinkiang line which passed through Shantung.[41]

The China Association backed the Bank [42] in demanding Government support for recognition of the Shanghai-Nanking concession as lying in the Yangtze sphere and in pressing for an agreement with German interests on the Tientsin-Chinkiang line. Lord Salisbury's suggestion that the entire matter be left to private negotiations between the respective banking interests was rejected by the German Ambassador on the ground that the demand for the Shanghai-Nanking line had been made as a "political concession," and could therefore be solved only by agreement between the two governments.[43] An ensuing conference be-

tween the financial groups, at which both the Foreign Office and the
German Embassy assisted, broke down because of German insistence
on limiting the discussion to the question of sharing the Shanghai-
Nanking concession, while British interests were equally insistent on
including the Tientsin-Chinkiang line and the question of Britain's
special rights in the Yangtze valley.[44] Lord Salisbury, emphasizing that
"England's position in the Yangtze valley was similar to [Germany's]
in Shantung," [45] then pressed MacDonald to insist on the Shanghai-
Nanking concession at Peking. Although a preliminary agreement between China and the Hongkong and Shanghai Bank was signed on May
13,[46] German opposition continued. The China Association refrained
from further agitation on Keswick's assurance that the Chinese "had
been loyal to their pledge," but approved of a question being set down
in Parliament in order to admonish the Foreign Office to hold firm.[47]

The crux of the issue, from the mercantile viewpoint, was the Government's reluctance to implement assertion of a Yangtze sphere. The German contention that Shantung differed from the Yangtze because
Kiaochow had been occupied while Britain, not having occupied any
place in the Yangtze region, had set up no special claims,[48] was regarded
as well taken. Salisbury was finally persuaded to ask China for recognition of her preferential position in the Yangtze by the declaration that
"other things being equal, railways in the Yangtze Kiang region should
be conceded to English companies, and in the Province of Shantung
should be conceded to German companies." [49] The Chinese Government refused to make the declaration, nor would Britain take unilateral
action. It was this stalemate which persuaded the China Association
that Britain must pattern her behavior on that of the Continental
Powers—occupy the Yangtze and provide State finance to back the
British Syndicate.

The second trouble spot developed in the South. Rumors that France
had requested the concession of a railway from Pakhoi to Nanning led
the Foreign Office to inquire privately of Gundry as to the reaction of
the General Committee to such a development. Though some members
were alarmed, Ewen Cameron of the Hongkong and Shanghai Bank was
in favor of acquiescence in the French concession. This may have been
due to his belief that the current difficulties with Germany over the
Shanghai-Nanking concession required soft-pedalling of opposition to
French interests. But Keswick and Scott were opposed and the Association voiced its strong opposition to the proposed concession. Keswick
pointed out that in French hands such a railway would prove strong
competition to Hongkong. The General Committee concurred, with the
proviso that if the concession were made, Nanning should be opened as

a treaty port and a Canton-Kowloon line granted to a British company as a counter-concession.[50] China denied the rumor but on June 8 Paris announced that the Pakhoi-Nanning concession had been obtained to complete "the network of commercial roads penetrating South China from Tongking." [51] Although it was never confirmed and construction never undertaken, the China Association was disturbed. As compensation, Britain demanded the opening of Nanning, but without immediate success.[52]

More important than the difficulties over the Shanghai-Nanking line and the French concession, however, was the report in May that negotiations had been reopened with the Belgian syndicate, backed by Russia and France, for construction of a trunk railway from Peking to Hankow, thus penetrating into the heart of the Yangtze.[53] MacDonald confirmed the report, forwarding the Yamen's assurances that "the Chinese Director of Railways still maintains the control in his hands." [54] But both Shanghai and the China Association were profoundly disturbed. Gundry again arranged through R. A. Yerburgh to have a question asked in the House and the suggestion was advanced that a British syndicate be formed to take the concession out of Belgian hands.[55] Keswick noted that Russia appeared to have the intention of controlling the hinterland of Shantung, while Gundry regretted that there was no Anglo-American combination to occupy the regions where British interests were so great. This last was a reference to the report that an American concessionaire still held an option on the Hankow line.

For an unexplained reason, it was not suggested that the chosen instrument, the British & Chinese Corporation, should compete for the concession. The China Association, at that time, took no further action than to bring the seriousness of the matter to the attention of the Foreign Office. Lord Salisbury agreed that the issue was vital and instructed MacDonald to object in terms which came closest to the assertion of a Yangtze sphere as interpreted by the China Association. Noting that the Government had entertained objection to the Peking-Hankow line when originally granted to a Belgian syndicate, Salisbury stressed the fact that

When there is likelihood of Russo-Chinese Bank, which is tantamount to Russian Government, financing southern section of that railway, that objection is greatly increased.

A concession of this nature is no longer a commercial or industrial enterprise, and becomes a political movement against British interests in the region of the Yang-tzse.

You should inform the Tsungli Yamen that Her Majesty's Government cannot possibly continue to cooperate in a friendly manner in matters of interest to China if, while preferential advantages are conceded to Russia in Manchuria and to Germany in Shantung, these or other foreign Powers should also be offered special openings or privileges in the region of the Yang-tzse. Satisfactory proposals will be forthcoming if the Chinese Government will invite the employment of British capital in the development of those provinces.[56]

China, however, refused to yield and on June 26 the Peking-Hankow agreement, consisting of a loan contract and a working agreement, was signed.[57] "In Paris no secret was made of the part played in the transaction by French diplomacy," [58] while despite Chinese assurances that the Russo-Chinese Bank was not involved, its principal role was later admitted.[59] On August 12 the agreement was ratified.

It was this blow, more than any other development, which stimulated mercantile dissatisfaction with British diplomacy in China. Meanwhile, to the three sorespots in railway politics which concerned the China Association, was added a fourth when Russia protested the inclusion of an agreement between the Chinese Government and the Hongkong and Shanghai Bank, on June 15, providing a loan for extension of the Tientsin-Shanhaikwan line (of the Chinese Imperial Railways) to Newchwang. The principal basis of the Russian objection pertained to the provision of the agreement securing the loan by a mortgage on the Shanhaikwan-Newchwang section of the line and providing for foreign control and management in case of default.[60] The Hongkong and Shanghai Bank appealed to the Foreign Office for help, claiming that "if the mortgage of the Northern Extension Railway is prohibited in deference to Russian demands, the security now offered for the loan is insufficient." [61] Russian pressure, on the ground that the concession was an infringement on her sphere, led China to inform the Bank of her inability to abide by the provisions of the preliminary agreement. Lord Salisbury's protest was of no avail and MacDonald could only suggest that he be allowed to take a strong line with the Yamen.[62]

These four developments in the struggle for domination of China by means of railway concessions led mercantile circles, in the summer of 1898, to urge the adoption by the British Government of a major modification in its China policy. Counter-concessions and vague assertions of a position of priority in the Yangtze were insufficient. Recommendations varied, though all were agreed that some steps reestablishing British prestige and protecting British predominance were imperative. A more active participation by the Government in the financial struggle was unanimously recommended. Except for the dissidents in Shanghai, Old China Hands demanded the frank recognition and immediate implementation of Britain's Yangtze sphere. And between the lines lay the

recommendation, first suggested in the China Association's letter of
April 14, that British preponderance entitled her to establish a protectorate over all of China south of the Great Wall. These ideas did not
spring full-blown in the summer of 1898, but developed in the course
of the next year.

On June 24, the Shanghai Branch of the China Association warned
London that the "persistent activity" of the Continental Powers in promoting their own railway projects and blocking British efforts leads to
the conclusion that "there is a definite policy on foot which has for its
object the exclusion of Great Britain from any participation in the railway development of the country, a policy illustrative of what Mr.
Chamberlain termed "a combined assault by the nations of the world
upon the commercial supremacy of Great Britain." [63] There was, said
Chairman Dudgeon on behalf of the Shanghai merchants, but one solution: "the necessity for the protection of British enterprise by our Government." Government must assume its new responsibility. "Private
enterprise cannot succeed unaided, and unless our Government will give
the same active support to British schemes as is being so eagerly accorded by the Continental Governments to the schemes of our op-
ponents, all British effort is . . . vain." [64]

This demand for a policy of economic nationalism also underlay the
démarche of the Associated Chambers of Commerce at about the same
time. An imposing delegation, led by Sir Stafford Northcote and a large
parliamentary representation, called on Lord Salisbury on June 14 in
support of the following resolutions:

(a) That these Chambers regard the absorption of Chinese territory by
Russia, France and Germany with great concern, as injurious to the interests of
British commerce, seeing those Powers exact the prohibitive duties of their
respective countries in all their colonies and dependencies.

(b) That this Association views with satisfaction the announcement that
China will permit no annexation in the Yangtze valley, and earnestly hopes that
the British Government will support China in this resolution.

(c) Having regard to the fact that all these Powers have obtained concessions
from the Chinese Government enabling them to construct railways within the
Chinese Empire, the Associated Chambers consider it imperative in the interests
of British trade, that Her Majesty's Government should press for a concession
authorising the construction of a railway to connect British Burma with the
Upper Valley of the Yangtze.[65]

These resolutions came close to expressing the official view. But the
interview which followed soon demonstrated the direction in which mercantile thought was moving. The delegation emphasized the fact that

concessions were meaningless without official support in the shape of guarantees or actual financial support and control by the Government. Enterprise could no longer be regarded as a strictly private affair in China. Lord Salisbury strongly demurred, pointing out that the Government had never yet undertaken a railway not situated in British territory; such a step would constitute a "very grave departure from policy" which Parliament would not support. Nor would he concede that other nations had obtained concessions "when we have been unable to do so." Britain could not stop these railways, but only insist "that our claims be considered with due equity and justice." Whitehall was thus continuing to think in terms of sharing concessions and preventing the exercise of preferential measures. "The best way of obtaining the construction of railways in China is for independent English companies to produce the capital and ask for a concession," said Salisbury. In any event, he thought the pace of events in China would soon slow down.[66] This exchange of views was striking. Government insisted that the situation called for private enterprise and business insisted that only state finance could meet the need.

There was more to it than that, of course. Basically the difference lay in governmental reluctance to assume the responsibility of a forward policy, in terms of a Yangtze protectorate or financial struggle in which officialdom was implicated, and mercantile desire for all-out support in the battle not only for concessions but for the future China market. Mercantile talk was still in terms of potentialities latent in the fabulous territory of the Manchu Kingdom. The ultimate question was still: how much was China worth? Was it worth a war?

The China Association, considering the situation in the critical month of June, 1898, felt that Whitehall lacked both vigor and understanding of what the situation required. To its letter objecting to the Pakhoi-Nanning railway concession the Foreign Office had not bothered to reply. Gundry learned privately that there was no hope of thwarting the French move and that MacDonald had been instructed to demand the opening of Nanning as a counter-concession.[67] To the initiative of the other Powers Britain could do no better than play the game of counters. The General Committee met on June 21 to review the crisis created by recent defeats in railway politics: in all four critical spots described above Britain had lost a battle. Russian activity was now so marked that she must be regarded as predominant in North China, Gundry pointed out. Additional projects were imminent for construction of a Peking-Chengting line with extension to Taiyuan, the capital city of Shansi.[68] The Lu-Han (Peking-Hankow) project under Russo-French influence was about to be consummated, bisecting the Yangtze.

Yet, while intruding in "the British sphere of influence," Gundry noted, Russia objected to the proposed Hongkong and Shanghai Bank loan for the Shanhaikwan-Newchwang extension in the North. What was wrong with British policy?

What was wrong, said Keswick, was British reluctance to enter the game of spheres. Only by marking out her own preserve in the Yangtze could Britain match Russia's treaty rights in North China. Moreover, on what grounds could China deny to Russia and France concessions on lines leading to the Yangtze? She could not say that these were reserved for Great Britain, if the latter was not even putting forward a claim. The only alternative was for England to say what Russia had: this is our sphere of interest and we will allow no alien interest to intrude.

This suggestion was warmly welcomed by the Committee. That was the correct solution! In terms of railway politics, Great Britain would assert that all lines leading to the Yangtze or through the valley itself would be reserved for British capital. The China Association had voted for a frank assertion of a British sphere in the Yangtze; but there was as yet no suggestion as to how this policy should be activated.

There is no indication that this conclusion was at that time communicated to the Foreign Office. However, it formed the center of the policy advocated by the Association in its famous letter of July 8, 1898. That letter was not a spontaneous move on the part of the Association, but was a response to an invitation from Whitehall. Growing dissatisfaction "with the attitude of the Government in the Far East" had been brought to the attention of the Foreign Office by the delegation of the Associated Chambers and private advices from the China Association, and Lord Salisbury, early in July, invited the "definite expression of City opinion" as the basis for a reformulation of British policy.[69]

The General Committee of the China Association undertook the task on July 7.[70] The crux of the issue, as the Association saw it, was the refusal of the Powers to recognize the Yangtze as a British sphere. Railway politics were sphere politics and the Russo-French capture of the Peking-Hankow contract was the most flagrant example of this encroachment. Railway concessions now had a national and political character and were designed to mark out areas of political interest. To retrieve the situation Britain must demand that the Peking-Hankow concession be turned over to herself as recognition of her special right to Yangtze railways. If it were objected that the contract was already signed, rebuttal was simple. For Russia had objected to the Hongkong and Shanghai Bank loan contract for the Shanhaikwan-Newchwang line and had succeeded in getting it "hung up." MacDonald should be instructed to protest against the Russo-French contract on similar grounds (that it impinged on Britain's sphere) and get it "hung up." There would then be opportunity for a deal.

Without including it in the published letter, therefore, the China Association privately recommended to the Foreign Office that Britain consent to withdraw from Manchuria and the North China Railway loan with the understanding that the Russo-French allies withdraw from the Yangtze and make over their contract to the Hongkong and Shanghai Bank.[71]

The doctrinal basis underlying this proposed deal with Russia was stated fully by the China Association in its letter of July 8, 1898.[72] In his usual manner, Gundry recapitulated the current status of outstanding issues. Commercial questions were no longer the major problem. There was "no need for radical change" as the Treaty of Tientsin "continues broadly applicable to foreign trade and intercourse today." The modifications required by "the altered conditions of modern intercourse" had been stated in the Association's letter of November 2, 1896,[73] and most of this program had been attained by "the solicitude of Her Majesty's Government, seconded by the ability and energy of Her Majesty's Minister at Peking." The boundaries of Hongkong had been extended, the West River opened to Wuchow, and the opening of inland waterways to steam navigation had been assured in principle. Most important, the Inspectorate-General was secure.

But the situation was far otherwise with respect to political issues. The "question of supreme moment" was the international rivalry arising out of railway development which, because of China's weakness, led to "the apprehension that railways constructed by Foreign States, under State auspices, with State aid, may be held in the near future to constitute territorial claims." Under the circumstances, two alternatives were possible: to encourage China to "reassert her right of sovereignty" or to define spheres of national interest from which alien enterprise would be excluded. The first was theoretically preferable, as "the maintenance of Chinese integrity appears to the Association to consist best with the interests of British commerce." Foresight would have dictated creation of a Chinese Railway Bureau, under foreign supervision, modelled on the Maritime Customs. British capital could then have participated and her dominant commercial interests thus ensured. But the alternative was no longer feasible. "The political element in these concessions cannot be ignored and circumstances are conceivable in which preferential freight and differential rates might be made to subserve national ends."

A major threat was the Peking-Hankow line, which encroached on the British sphere, and the Association suggested that this trunk line be transferred to British hands under official guarantee. "The proposition is based, of course, on the assumption that England is interested in maintaining the Yangtsze region intact and that the control of its approaches is a matter of Imperial concern. It is based on the further assumption that the Russo-Chinese Bank is a Russian State bank, and that an enterprise executed by a State Bank has a political aim." Gundry then proceeded to state the theoretical basis for the twofold proposition: that Britain assert her "Imperial concern" with protection of her sphere and that this could be done only by wedding politics to finance, making the latter official.

Commercial enterprise may be left to compete with commercial enterprise; private capital may be left to compete with private capital, but the operations of a great State bank cannot be rivalled by private finance. . . . State finance must be opposed by State finance, and the Association ventures to suggest that a great trunk line leading from North China into the heart of the Yang-tzse Valley is an enterprise too pregnant with political importance to be disregarded.

This was now the essence of China Association policy. To implement the British assertion of a Yangtze sphere by retrieving the Peking-Hankow through officially backed finance was the first step. In addition, Gundry repeated the suggestions of the previous April, that in order to counter French designs in South China, Nanning be opened as a treaty port and the Mandalay-Kunlon Ferry line pushed into Yunnan. But more significant was Gundry's suggestion, apparently as an afterthought, that Britain concern itself with the extension of foreign customs collectorates in the interior and press for fiscal reform, "for a pass has been reached when the Chinese Government must adapt itself to modern surroundings or collapse, and the requirements of modern administration cannot be met by a medieval system of finance." A British protectorate over Chinese administration was the ultimate solution.

Under mercantile pressure the Government was forced to extend the frontier of its limited liability policy. But it refused to go all the way. The distinction between what the more radical Old China Hands wanted and what the Foreign Office was prepared to concede did not become clear until the following year. In essence, the former were demanding implementation of a British sphere in the Yangtze valley through "effective occupation" if necessary, but certainly through some overt sign that Britain would protect its predominant position there; in addition, mercantile circles were unanimous in insisting that British finance be backed by Government guarantee, by "State finance." This came to be interpreted in various ways. Circles identified with the Hongkong and Shanghai Bank desired the full power of the State to back the "chosen instrument" of British financial interest in China whenever it came into conflict with Peking or with foreign financial interests. Others objected to this monopoly and hinted at the desirability of a State bank, patterned on the Russo-Chinese Bank, which would act as a political guarantor for British investors. This the Government refused to contemplate. It was prepared to demand a fair share of railway and industrial concessions for British interests, but without official implication. And it labored to arrive at international agreements which would recognize the Yangtze region as a British railway sphere. But it was still a negative policy, based on the doctrine of counterpoise and of "me too." Nor would it consider the establishment of a protectorate at which the merchants constantly hinted.

To ensure German acquiescence in the Weihaiwei move Britain had been forced to recognize "the rights and interests of Germany in the Province of Shantung," without obtaining a similar assurance respecting the Yangtze. All attempts at securing German and Russian recognition of Britain's "sphere of interest" had failed. Berlin refused to recognize Britain's exclusive interest in the Shanghai-Nanking line, while under Russian pressure China proceeded to ratify the original terms of the Lu-Han contract. On August 10, the British Government announced acceptance of a modified version of the China Association plan.

But it was still to be a policy of limited liability. Arthur James Balfour, master of the art of juggling fine metaphysical distinctions, told the House that without abandoning the open door doctrine Britain was now putting a new interpretation (though he claimed it was not new) on its pronounced policy of equality of opportunity and enterprise in China. Repudiating any intentions of forcing the partition of China or of assuming the political responsibilities of a protectorate, Balfour nevertheless insisted that reality demanded the recognition of "spheres of concessions or enterprise." Britain, he announced, was asserting such a sphere over the Yangtze, a region which he did not further define. The open door policy, which he reaffirmed, was interpreted as being limited to (a) equality of trading opportunities, (b) freedom of British goods from "hostile tariffs" or preferential tariff rates, and (c) equality of treatment on transport and other commercial facilities. But it no longer included equality in seeking and securing railway and industrial concessions; a condition which Balfour defended on the specious argument that a concession once obtained is necessarily a monopoly and therefore "inequality [is] inseparable from the nature of the concession." [74] The Opposition stormed that this was no longer the open door.[75]

The Government had made a partial capitulation to mercantile pres-

sure and proceeded to implement this policy. Without insisting on a
transfer of the Lu-Han contract to British interests, as the China Association had recommended, and leaving the Newchwang affair for
later settlement with the Russians, Balfour instructed Sir Claude Mac-
Donald to demand the grant of railway concessions, for which British
syndicates were then negotiating, "on terms identical with those contained in the Contract for the Peking-Hankow line," and that "unless
they agreed at once, we shall regard their breach of faith concerning the
Peking-Hankow Railway as an act of deliberate hostility against this
country, and shall act accordingly." [76] The lines concerned were:
the Tientsin-Chinkiang, to be shared if desired by American and German
interests; from Honan and Shansi to the Yangtze, lines requested by the
Peking Syndicate; from Kowloon to Canton; from Pukow (across the
river from Nanking) to Sinyang (in southern Honan), paralleling
the Yangtze; and from Soochow to Hangchow, with a possible extension
to Ningpo.[77] The Tientsin-Chinkiang concession was left for later negotiation, and early in September the Yamen agreed to the other demands.
With the exception of the Honan-Shansi line, desired by the (Anglo-
Italian) Peking Syndicate in connection with its mining operations in
these provinces, all the concessions were negotiated on behalf of the
British & Chinese Corporation.

Officially, Britain had nothing further to do with these concessions.
But they were immediately employed as counters in efforts which followed to arrive at understandings with Germany and Russia on delimitation of railway spheres and interests. Negotiations with Germany were
reopened at the end of August and it was agreed that the conflicting
German and British interests with regard to the Tientsin-Chinkiang line
should be reconciled. Balfour thought the best solution "the joint construction of the line by British and German Syndicates" but "if the
Germans wish specially to provide that the part passing through the
Province of Shantung, if any, is to be constructed by German capital
. . . I see no great objection." [78] Berlin, too, favored combined action
but without too close a delimitation of spheres of influence.[79]

With the blessings of their respective governments, the Hongkong and
Shanghai Bank Syndicate met with representatives of German financial
interests (led by the Deutsch-Asiatische Bank) in London early in
September, 1898, and arrived at an agreement not only on the sharing
of the Tientsin-Chinkiang concession and withdrawal of German opposition to the Shanghai-Nanking, but on a general delimitation of
spheres for the future. With the approval of their governments,[80] the
German Syndicate on the one hand and the Hongkong and Shanghai
Bank, together with the British & Chinese Corporation, on the other,

defined the following "spheres of interest for applications for Railway Concessions in China";

1. BRITISH sphere of interest, viz.:—

The Yang-tsze Valley subject to the connection of the Shantung lines to the Yang-tsze at Chinkiang; the provinces south of the Yang-tsze; the Province of Shansi with connection to the Peking-Hankow line at a point south of Cheng-ting and a connecting line to the Yangtsze Valley, crossing the Hoangho Valley.

2. GERMAN sphere of interest, viz.:—

The province of Shantung and the Hoangho Valley with connection to Tientsin and Chengting, or other point of the Peking-Hankow line in the south with connection to the Yang-tsze at Chinkiang or Nanking. The Hoangho Valley is understood to be subject to the connecting lines in Shansi forming part of the British sphere of interest, and to the connecting line to the Yangtsze Valley, also belonging to the said sphere of interest.[81]

It is of interest to note that William Keswick, Chairman of the China Association, signed on behalf of the British & Chinese Corporation.

Conversations with Russia looking toward a similar delimitation of railway spheres were opened in August.[82] The difficulty lay in Russian objection to a British mortgage on and management of the Newchwang line; Count Muraviev suggested that if the Hongkong and Shanghai Bank were willing to grant the loan without the mortgage security, an agreement on delimitation of railway spheres might be reached.[83] The Czar agreed.[84] A draft agreement on this basis was concluded on September 26, 1898; [85] and the following month the Newchwang loan was completed calling for security limited to the existing lines and "the freight and earnings of the new lines when constructed." [86] The Bank, however, refused to proceed with the loan except with a government guarantee upholding the contract and making the non-alienation of the line to a foreign Power a condition of the agreement.[87]

Despite these assurances the Bank was never entirely satisfied and felt that too great a concession had been made to Russia. Negotiations for final conclusion of the railway agreement dragged through the winter, but were finally successful in April, 1899. By an exchange of notes (known as the Scott-Muraviev Agreement) on April 28, 1899, the two countries agreed:

1. Russia engages not to seek for her own account or for Russian subjects any railway concessions in the basin of the Yangtsze, nor to obstruct, directly or indirectly, in that region any applications for railway Concessions supported by the British Government.

2. Great Britain, on her part, engages not to seek for her own account or for British subjects any railway concessions north of the Great Wall of China, or

to obstruct, directly or indirectly, in that region any applications for railway concessions supported by the Russian Government.[88]

At the same time, Russia recognized the Newchwang loan as binding, with the understanding that "this fact cannot be taken as constituting a right of property or foreign control, and that the line in question is to remain a Chinese line under control of the Chinese Government."

Mercantile reaction to these developments was not as favorable as might have been anticipated. This was particularly true as regards the Anglo-Russian agreement, where it was felt that too great a concession had been made, as will be noted later. But, even earlier, following the success of the Anglo-German negotiations, not all Old China Hands were agreed that this was the implementation of the Yangtze sphere they had contemplated. With its conclusion, the Government appeared to have withdrawn from the scene and then left everything to its chosen instrument. Britain's position did not appear to be any more secure than previously. And, most significant, acquiescence in the construction of the Peking-Hankow line could only be regarded as an admission of failure. Not all of them felt that way, of course. The leaders of the China Association, with William Keswick of the British & Chinese Corporation at its head, congratulated themselves on the outcome of events in August and September. At the annual dinner on November 1, 1898, the government was commended for having voiced a "more determined and definite policy in regard to the Far East."

The China Association would ever be active in supporting such a policy, as upon its success depended not only the interests of all who were especially concerned in the affairs of the Far East, but the happiness and welfare of millions in England who scarcely knew China except by name.[89]

But even then, when British diplomatic success in Anglo-Chinese relations was most evident, strong dissenting views were being expressed. Archibald Little, merchant and Yangtze explorer, told the Quarterly Meeting of the Manchester Chamber of Commerce that only "effective occupation" of the Yangtze region "which was supposed to be our sphere of influence" would secure the British position in China. The problem of China, Little maintained, was what it had been when he had attempted to ascend the Yangtze River in his steamer twelve years before; the opening of the China market to Manchester goods. Vested interests, he charged, were concerned with consolidating their own positions rather than opening opportunities for British trade in general. To do this Britain must assert her predominance in China, occupy the

Yangtze and force commercial and industrial reforms on the Chinese. He accused Lord Salisbury of having been engaged in appeasing the other Powers. Every Britisher in China had been "humiliated" by the way things had been managed in the past two years. The Foreign Office should be strengthened to foster foreign trade and in its China policy should take advice not only from diplomats but from merchants and Chambers of Commerce "who are keenly alive to the designs of rival Powers to undermine our trade." If necessary, Great Britain should be prepared to go to war in order to maintain her predominant position in China.[90]

This refrain was repeated by Little at a special meeting called by the Liverpool Chamber of Commerce,[91] attended by representatives of other Lancashire Chambers, to marshal support for the more radical wing of Old China Hands, led by R. A. Yerburgh, leader of the China bloc in the House of Commons. This program of the radicals, never clearly defined, called for all-out Government support of British interests in China. It involved the reassertion of British prestige at Peking, the "effective occupation" of the Yangtze, the opening up of China to foreign commerce and industry, and the fiscal and administrative reform of China under British tutelage.

The meeting was well attended, leading Little to remark that he could now return to China confident that Englishmen there would not be forgotten as they had been for the last "twenty or thirty years" owing to Government indifference. Recounting his personal history, Little touched on the essence of the problem. When he had first gone out to China, England was the sole large possessor of foreign interests. Then she might have done what she liked; she might have taken China under her protection, for the Chinese were like children—"they had only to be firm to get anything they liked out of the Chinese." But they had let things drift and were now beset by international rivalry. Whatever they did, it must be on a grand scale, for China was still the greatest potential neutral market left in the world.

Yerburgh, who was dissatisfied with the collaborationist policy of the China Association, was the driving force behind this attempt to marshal public opinion. His address, entitled "The China Question as Affecting Commerce," was a turning point in the development of mercantile attitude, for it refused to accept the Foreign Office policy of counterconcessions and railway agreements as adequate. His theme, compounded of the newer imperialism and the Old China dream, came to be labelled "nationalist." "What is to be the future of the swarms of children in Lancashire towns if the great neutral markets are to be closed by their being occupied either practically, or in other ways, by protectionist powers?" he thundered. "I think I may say this," Yerburgh continued, "that the country as a whole sympathised with and applauded the utterance of the Chancellor of Exchequer last year when he said that we must be prepared to go to the last resort of war in defence of the open door for our trade." [92] But the open door meant that British predominance—which in 1897 accounted for 65 percent of both trade and shipping in China—must be maintained at all costs. For it was not only the actual trade which lay in the balance, but the potential trade which could be expanded almost tenfold, according to Yerburgh's calculations.

But, he argued, this cannot be done so long as the Chinese remain backward, held down by a fossil government. Only through foreign tutelage, led by Britain, could China be commercially awakened. That was one necessary reform. Another change must come about in the relations of the Foreign Office to the British merchant. The latter had been reluctant to risk his capital because, as Consul Brenan had pointed out, "misgivings . . . filled the minds of British merchants lest they should not receive adequate support and protection from their own authorities. It was this sense of insecurity that had discouraged the pioneers in the Treaty Ports."

I think that amply bears out the contention . . . that it is through want of care on the part of our Governments and want of foresight, and neglect to recognise their opportunities, that our interests have suffered in China, and our position changed so much for the worse.

What could now be done? Britain had neglected the opportunity of becoming the recognized protector of China, but she could still play the part in her own sphere. Britain must lay claim to the Yangtze, which included all the provinces drained by that river as well as Kwangtung ("the hinterland of Hongkong"), as a modified protectorate. In this sphere the following conditions would rule: (a) Government would guarantee interest on capital sunk into railways and industrial enterprises; (b) all waterways would be open to steam navigation and the Yangtze route made effective by Government survey; (c) *likin* and other forms of inland taxation would be collected by a British officer; and (d) the open door for trade in general would prevail. He introduced a resolution to that effect.

Seconding the resolution, Sir J. A. Willcox, M.P., stated the problem somewhat differently. England had hitherto enjoyed predominance in China, and the problem was "how that predominance could be maintained." They must take care that, whatever happened, England came out uppermost, and this required energetic governmental support backed by "an authoritative strong arm." The resolution as finally passed by Liverpool was the first frank abandonment by Lancashire of the open door and private enterprise in this connection. It was resolved that (a) "Her Majesty's Government will give every possible assistance to British merchants and capitalists who are engaged in business in that country and prepared to invest money in it," and (b) "especially in the matter of railway construction, will secure for British enterprise in the Yangtze region similar preferential rights to those which Germany, Russia and France have already claimed in the regions of China which those Powers respectively regard as their special Spheres of Influence; and the Chamber assures Her Majesty's Government of its strenuous support in the pursuit of the policy thus indicated." [93]

Nor was this an isolated action. The Liverpool resolution received wide publicity in official and commercial circles. It was immediately endorsed by the following Chambers of Commerce: Glasgow, Oldham, Bury, Leeds, Huddersfield, Batley, Halifax, Morley, Lincoln, Birmingham, Dudley, Walsall, Newport, Portsmouth, Plymouth, Hull, and Belfast. The London Chamber, still under the influence of the Keswick faction, was not approached by Yerburgh and maintained silence. Only the Manchester Chamber held out, explicitly refusing to repudiate the stand it had taken in April which had urged the Government to contend for "the preservation, throughout China, of an open market with equal opportunities of trading for all nations; and for this purpose to see the cooperation of the Governments of other countries having important commercial relations with that Empire."

In refusing to endorse the Liverpool resolution, the Manchester Chamber pointed out the inconsistency between a claim to preferential rights in the Yangtze sphere and the open door doctrine.[94] To the annual meeting on February 1, 1899, the President of the Manchester Chamber reaffirmed the all-out support of the open door doctrine advanced in April and noted that because of its stand "they had had to decline cooperation with other commercial bodies who had been urging a different policy upon the Government." [95]

The Liverpool resolution, calling for an assertion of an effective sphere, was basically the policy which the China Association was advocating. It became the premise of mercantile agitation for the next two years, tempered by Keswick's insistence that results could be obtained only through continued collaboration with the Foreign Office. For the British & Chinese Corporation at any rate, such collaboration had proved profitable. And for some months Keswick was able to keep the other Old China Hands in line by interpreting the Anglo-German private financial agreement of September and the Anglo-Russian railway agreement of April, 1899, as at least the first steps toward an effective assertion of a British sphere.

In Shanghai, however, rebellion was brewing. There, Old China Hands not affiliated with the vested interests which had the ear of the Foreign Office regarded acquiescence in railway sphere politics as an admission of defeat. The Shanghai insurgents in the local branch of the China Association insisted that the sole adequate solution was a return to their traditional maximalist program. The ultimate aim was the total opening of China and the maintenance of British predominance in that vast market of the future. As always, this could be attained not through the fatal admission that partition was inevitable, but only through a thorough-going reform of China's government and economy under foreign tutelage. Britain must lead that reform, asserting her strength and preponderance not only against other Powers but, more important in the long run, against the effete, backward government at Peking. In effect, the Shanghai insurgents saw the solution of the Chinese Question in some form of British protectorate, with or without the consent of the other Powers. If this meant war, they were willing to make the most of it.

Rumors that the awakening of China was coming from within, that the reform party had taken over at Peking, were scorned by Shanghai. "It can hardly be believed," wrote Dudgeon, "that the reactionary old fossils in the Tsungli Yamen are capable of realising the new order that has set in—things are going too fast for them, and in my humble opinion are already too much on the rush to be checked by such tardy measures of reform as *they* may introduce." [96]

To make clear its position, the Shanghai Committee early in 1899 prepared a memorandum "On the Present Conditions of Foreign Trade in China," for submission to the home Chambers and to the Foreign Office.[97] There had been, Shanghai noted, "a want of expansive vitality in our trade with China" which some attributed to the shortcomings of the British trader. But Shanghai thought otherwise.

We unhesitatingly attribute the slow progress made in the development of foreign trade with China to three main reasons:

(a) The entire absence of good faith on the part of China in the matter of Treaty obligations.

(b) The absence of security for the investment of foreign capital in China outside the Treaty ports.

(c) The general apathy, and want of knowledge, which has been displayed at home regarding Chinese affairs.

This allegation, and the arguments upon which it was based, reflected Shanghai's belief that neither the Sino-Japanese war nor the battle for concessions which followed had changed the basic issues in Anglo-Chinese relations. Chinese backwardness and the undependability of its government were still the major obstacles to British prosperity in China. And the solution lay, as always, in the assumption by the British Government of responsibility for trade and security. The argument followed in logical sequence. Illegal inland dues were still being exacted and Ministers and Consuls had failed, despite all efforts, to attain respect for transit passes. Why?

The failure of their attempts can only be attributed to want of support at home, which, it may be suggested, arises from the fact that those interested at home have been content to rely upon the reasonable and equitable terms of our Treaties with China, and have failed to realise that the complaints of residents here are not directed against the Treaties, but against the gross and scandalous disregard of them by every Chinese official.

Principally, the Government was to blame, for while French and German pressure had resulted in Chinese respect for transit passes in the regions in which those Powers were interested, British officials had not been so successful. "If other nations are able to enforce respect for Treaty rights, why do we who hold about 70% of the trade fail?" The answer lay in British reluctance to apply pressure and to treat directly with provincial officials due to over-sensibility for the authority of Peking. "The only effective policy in China," advised Shanghai, "is that which we employed in our earlier relations with this country, namely to deal with abuses where they occur, and to face Peking with the fact of grievances already redressed."

In addition to a return to Palmerstonian tactics Shanghai advocated the solution of trade problems through inland residence (another echo of 1869). The key to inland residence, in turn, lay in "security" and "such security can only be found in the entire reform of the present corrupt system of Chinese Government." Similarly, the need for security explained the hesitancy of capitalists to invest in railway and mining enterprises. Fundamentally, then, this could be accomplished only by the establishment of a "strong" Peking government "under strong foreign influence" with Great Britain "fostering and guiding" this movement.

Nothing has ever been gained from China except through pressure backed by force and nothing will ever be gained from her except by the same means. Great Britain is today looking with some anxiety for new fields for her export; no finer field in the world exists than in China. Let the nations whose aims are not territorial aggrandisement join together in exerting the necessary pressure for reform through which alone the required security for trade can be found, the integrity of the Empire maintained, and the door of trade kept open to all on equal terms.

In conclusion, the Shanghai Committee made the following somewhat cryptic statement regarding its position on the sphere policy which mercantile circles in England were so strongly advocating:

We do not wish to concern ourselves with any imperfectly understood catch phrases such as "open door" or "sphere of influence," further than to say that Great Britain's sphere of influence should be wherever British trade preponderates, with the door open for equal trading opportunity for all.

This was the position adopted by the Shanghai Committee in January, 1899, and it foreshadowed an impending struggle not only within official circles but with the policy then advocated by the home Chambers under the leadership of the China Association. It was the first move toward that insurgency in mercantile ranks which troubled the China Association for the next five years. The Shanghai Memorandum itself raised a minor tempest when Sir Claude MacDonald protested that its treatment of British diplomacy in China was unjust. The London Committee apologized, terming Shanghai criticism as "less than just to Sir Claude MacDonald in respect of his services to British commerce in China." [98] The General Committee had its members write privately to friends in the Shanghai branch, severely criticizing the independent action that had been taken.[99]

The difference was fundamental. While Shanghai and London might agree that the Government had failed to adopt a bold policy, the radical plan of Shanghai did not appeal to the leadership of the China Association. Instead, the latter proceeded with its campaign to influence Whitehall to strengthen its commitments in the game of spheres. The Liverpool resolution, as was noted above, had the endorsement of the overwhelming majority of Chambers. Under Keswick's influence, the London Chamber of Commerce adopted a similar stand, with an important reservation expressing approval of the recent course taken by the Government. At the annual meeting of the Associated Chambers on March 14, 1899, William Keswick, representing the London Chamber, moved a similar resolution:

That this Association desires to express its satisfaction with the action taken by Her Majesty's Government for the protection of British commercial interests in

China and urges Her Majesty's Government to vigorously maintain (a) the policy of the "open door" for commerce throughout the entire Chinese Empire, and (b) the prior British rights in the Yangtze Valley and its watershed, and at those Ports and Settlements in Chinese territory where British interests and business have been established and have predominated for many years.[100]

About the substance of the resolution there was little dispute, only the representatives of the Manchester Chamber objecting that the two parts were inconsistent. As Keswick pointed out, the time had arrived for Britain to stake her claim. Dismemberment of China was inevitable and "it became important that those spheres in which British trade had been carried on for a considerable period should be preserved as a British sphere of influence." It was the purpose of this resolution to "let it be known that we had prior and special rights in some way, not clearly defined, but still understood, in the Yangtze basin." In seconding the resolution, the representative of Worcester interpreted it as meaning "that though we do not occupy the field, it was intermedially to be kept open for the future of British enterprise. When the inevitable day came in which China fell to pieces—it would be clear what Britain's share would be; we should have a free communication from the Bay of Bengal to Shanghai."

The intent of the resolution was thus clear, and its substance was passed with little further comment. The mercantile position was set. Of striking importance, however, is the fact that Keswick's preamble, approving of the Government's course, was dropped. Keswick attempted to defend the Foreign Office on the ground that while "there might have been some mistakes at the initiatory period, the subsequent policy of Her Majesty's Government had been in accord with the public opinion of this country." It was not convincing to the mercantile "public opinion" there assembled. John Walton, representing Middlesburgh and the China bloc in the House of Commons, branded the Government's failure to prevent concession of the Peking-Hankow line to the enemy as a "serious blunder" and its acquiescence under Russian pressure in the "adverse terms" of the British loan for the Newchwang line as an exhibition of a weak-kneed surrender. In addition he criticized the failure to remove all trade restrictions in the recent concessions opening Nanning and the West River. Under this barrage, Keswick was forced to withdraw his endorsement of government policy.

Despite Keswick's attempt to absolve the Government, growing opinion in the China Association itself expressed dissatisfaction with the ultimate result of recent events. The battle of the Peking-Hankow had been lost. The very limited recognition of a British sphere through the Anglo-Russian railway agreement had been purchased only at the price of surrender on the Newchwang loan settlement. Dr. Joseph's contention that by this agreement "Britain had finally won the recognition of Russia that the Yangtze was a British sphere of interest" [101] was not shared by contemporary mercantile opinion. Moreover, the prospectus of the Peking-Hankow line stated that the Belgian Syndicate held priority for the construction of the Canton-Hankow line on which American interests held an option, while Chinese reluctance to grant further lines to foreign concessionaires was held to be aimed particularly at British interests.[102] Even more serious was the general impression that with the signing of the counter-concessions of August, 1898, and the subsequent railway agreements with Germany and Russia, the Foreign Office appeared ready to retire from its labors. Certainly there was no evidence that a recommendation for "effective occupation" of the Yangtze or for the assumption of a bolder policy toward China would gain a hearing. By the spring of 1899 interest in China affairs seems to have waned. Old China Hands were frantic.

Contrary to the accepted historical thesis that official circles and mercantile interests were in accord, if not in intimate unanimity, at this time, the spring of 1899 marks the beginning of a renewed attack by Old China Hands on the Government's policy of refusing any further commitments in Anglo-Chinese relations. Insofar as there was a happy relationship between Downing Street and Lombard Street, it was limited to the intimacy between the Foreign Office and the Hongkong and Shanghai Bank (allied with Jardine, Matheson & Co. interests in the British & Chinese Corporation) which had captured all except one of the railway concessions labelled "British." The situation was ideal, too, from the point of view of the Foreign Office: for the Bank could now act as the chosen instrument of British imperial policy, and the clamor of business interests for a more forward policy in China would be stilled. Actually, a revolt against the vested interests was precipitated.

On May 4, 1899, T. H. Whitehead wrote to the Secretary of the Hongkong Committee of the China Association, F. Henderson, noting the gravity of the situation in China. He recommended that Hongkong telegraph as follows to the London Committee:

Growing unrest seething mass discontent throughout China, impossible indefinitely avert serious outbreak, position urgently requires the presence of a mobile column of British troops at Weihaiwei or Hongkong to promptly support Navy when crisis arises, otherwise and despite Anglo-Russian agreement Russian troops instantly available protect Foreigners and Foreign property within British sphere of influence Yangtze region.[103]

Whitehead himself did not feel it would be more than a gesture as "people at home will for the present be congratulating themselves on Lord Salisbury's agreement with the Tzar to *uphold the integrity and independence of China*' which is practically impossible unless the other Powers acquiesce in the use of force." The only way to maintain Britain's position, Whitehead emphasized, was to follow the advice of Count Hatzfeldt (German Ambassador in London) and occupy the Yangtze. "While there is no 'effective occupation' of the Yangtze region there can be no British sphere." Such occupation might not be immediately feasible but "the least however that England should now do is to be prepared and to make every provision whereby she will be able to cope with any eventuality which may arise. . . . Should there be a strong revolt in the Yangtze region British gunboats, torpedo boats and small craft would render good service, but for effective occupation a military force would be absolutely indispensable." Otherwise Russia would take over in the Yangtze region and France in Kwangtung and Kwangsi.

Whitehead's slogan became mercantile gospel, propagated throughout 1899 and pressed with renewed force during the Boxer troubles. Even Shanghai, which regarded the strongest of sphere politics as itself a capitulation, wired in May urging opposition to the Russian request for a line from Mukden to Peking (which would tie up with the Peking-Hankow) and that Britain "make a claim for the Yangtze Kiang river [sic!] valley control rights similar to what has been conceded Russian sphere." [104] Shanghai also feared Russian intrigue aimed at removing the Chinese capital to Sianfu and French designs on the mining concessions in Szechuen.[105]

So exercised was Gundry over these alarming telegrams that he interrupted his vacation at Boulogne to write a hasty letter to Campbell, head of the Far Eastern Department at the Foreign Office. Most interesting is his revival of the suggestion that the Chinese capital be removed to Nanking, in the Yangtze sphere.

> I came across here yesterday, and am of course pursued by a telegram. Keswick has doubtless sent in a copy of my absence, but I write to make sure. The matter of it is far too pregnant for irresponsible comment, and there is not much use in making an effort to elicit and formulate any other comment in the presence of Peace Congresses and Paper agreements to let Russia have her way. . . .
> It isn't the first hint, as you know, of migration to Si-ngan. . . . The Chinese motive would be of course to escape from a capital too accessible to foreign pressure. Nanking might be inviting in some respects but it is open to the same objection, besides Russia would object. It would not be surprising if the Reactionary element thought it a fine thing to withdraw right inland to one of the

oldest and finest cities . . . of China. But Russia would be "afther them. . . ."
The best way would be to find a Ming claimant and set him up "counter" at
Nanking.[106]

Gundry returned to London and held a long conversation with Bertie
at the Foreign Office, urging that Britain take a stand against both
Russian and French pretensions. But, as he later reported to the General
Committee, there was little hope that the Government would take any
strong stand. "The situation had been given away in the Anglo-Russian
agreement." [107] Under the circumstances, he felt no basis for complaint
could be entered. "He thought Bertie's views were the same as his own,
that the time to resist Russia was at Port Arthur; and that in retreating
before her then, we had thrown up the game." It was impossible now to
stop her drive to Peking except by war and "the country showed no
inclination to push matters to that point." [108]

At the same interview Gundry had submitted to Bertie the view of the
China Association on the need for asserting the British sphere more
effectively. As he put it, the time had come "to accentuate our position
in the Yangtze region" by aiding the local Viceroys "both against
Peking and the foreign Powers" on condition that they introduce reforms under the supervision of British advisers. It was time to establish a British protectorate over the Yangtze. Bertie would not commit
himself.[109] Nor was the General Committee agreed as to the best course.
To the suggestion of one member that the Association should protest
against the Anglo-Russian agreement, Gundry remarked wearily that
it was no use. "The voice of the Association was listened to in matters
affecting commerce. Everything MacDonald had obtained had been
suggested by the Association; but it would not be listened to in matters
of high policy." The country had desired an understanding with Russia, and Lord Salisbury had presumably secured the best terms possible.

Keswick, the collaborationist and representative of "the Bank,"
sensed that a revolt was brewing and attempted to soothe the membership by pointing out that the Anglo-Russian agreement was a starting
point. It involved acceptance of the Russian position at Peking, that
was true. But the German wedge in Shantung was actually a blessing,
and what was now required was a more explicit recognition by the other
Powers of "our position in the Yangtze." Gundry, voicing the sentiment
of the dissidents, would not agree. The danger was that Russia, after
consolidating her position in Manchuria, would enter North China and
"we should retreat and make another agreement." He opposed what a
later age was to term "appeasement." In its place he advised a firm policy

by Britain, occupation of the Yangtze, and removal of the Emperor to Nanking.

No consensus having been reached, a more definite statement of policy was postponed to the next meeting of the General Committee. Meanwhile, there had been no change in the situation. The Foreign Office appeared to have retired from further activity in the Far East, while the resentment of treaty port residents mounted. There was opposition not merely to the Government's policy of appeasing Russia but to its complacency in the face of China's continued refusal to reopen the market for concessions. To Old China Hands the sole solution remained that of a British protectorate. When the General Committee of the China Association reconvened in June, Gundry submitted the draft of a fifteen-page memorandum [110] on Anglo-Chinese relations which was to be presented to the Foreign Office as a statement of policy and recommendation for future action. Behind it all, as Gundry remarked, was the conviction that "the time had come when British interests in the Yangtze valley should be more decisively affirmed." [111] He had therefore suggested in his memorandum the "effective occupation" of certain points: Chusan as representing Chekiang, Kiangyin for the Viceroyalty of the Two Kiang (Kiangsi and Kiangsu), and a third point to represent the Two Hu (Hunan and Hupeh). Secondly, as regards the assertion of a protectorate, it was suggested that "we should place ourselves cordially alongside the Viceroys and promise to sustain them on condition that they accepted our cooperation in promoting police and fiscal reform."

This was the essence of the Gundry scheme. In explaining the second of the two recommendations, Gundry noted that

he had always entertained a belief that we had created difficulties for ourselves in referring solely to the Imperial Government and ignoring the large measure of independence the provincial authorities enjoy. He would suggest a modification of that attitude, and conciliation of the Viceroys and provincial governments, with whom we should keep in touch through the medium of a commercial attaché whose position and salary and dignity should be on a sufficient level. It was useless to ignore the forces, both external and internal, that are working for disintegration; and it was the part of wisdom to prepare.[112]

The Gundry scheme was approved by the General Committee. Keswick was prepared to go further and claim the maritime provinces as "our sphere" because of British predominance on sea. "We had the might, therefore, and we had the right." If China broke up and Britain commanded the maritime provinces, "we should command the trade." Shantung was Germany's and "a portion of Kwangtung might have to be yielded to France," but Britain's share would include the rest. Japan had enough in Formosa and "it would be doing them a service to keep them off the mainland." Sir Edward Sassoon agreed that they should claim the southern maritime coast, while Mr. Jamieson, former Consul, thought the valleys of the Yangtze and West Rivers would cover the ground adequately. Timidly, one voice was raised against this apparent orgy of annexation as involving the disintegration of China. But it was quieted by Gundry's withering reply that they were intending to do no more than finish what Russia and Germany had started. "Unless we established a real foothold, our occupation was not politically speaking effective," Keswick concluded. It was unanimously decided to send the letter to the Foreign Office.

Meanwhile Gundry had communicated with Sir Cecil Smith, Sir Valentine Chirol, Alexander Michie, and Ewen Cameron of the Hongkong and Shanghai Bank. All of them were favorable to "the drift of the letter," though Cameron opposed some of the fiscal reforms proposed and "was a little apprehensive lest interference should affect the *lekin* appropriated to the service of the Anglo-German loan." The draft letter as approved by the General Committee started with the premise that it was necessary to affirm British interests in the Yangtze region beyond the railway agreements. "Railway concessions in China have been accepted by common accord as significant of political interests and pregnant with ultimate claims." This had been the assumption behind the China Association letter of July 8, 1898,[113] protesting the Peking-Hankow concession to Russo-French interests. Failure was due to British reluctance to recognize the political implications of spheres. As Hatzfeldt had hinted, what was lacking in British policy was "effective occupation."

Another reason for occupation lay in the decentralized administration of China, which must be recognized if any further headway were to be made with the commercial program outlined in the Association's letter of November, 1896. The crux of commercial restrictions was the chaotic state of fiscal and administrative arrangements in the provinces. But fiscal and administrative reform would never come from Peking. It must be applied locally under foreign supervision and control. The British Government must assume that responsibility in the Yangtze provinces, working through the local Viceroys. Appointment of a commercial attaché with a roving assignment in the provinces, effective occupation of certain strategic points, and the assignment of British advisers to the Viceroys were the three specific recommendations advanced by the China Association. The last of these was to come in due time.

British officials would be placed alongside the Viceroys and Governors of the provinces which British policy has earmarked, for the purpose of rendering in these regions the services that have been rendered in Egypt. It is possible that in the evolution of events the time for such an arrangement may come. The contingency is . . . sufficiently probable to make it desirable that the way should be prepared; and no better method of doing this suggests itself than the inauguration of closer relations with the great provincial authorities through whom it will be necessary to act.[114]

Thus, in the summer of 1899, the China Association, representative of British interests in China, boldly urged the establishment of a British protectorate over the Yangtze. There was some delay in sending the letter to the Foreign Office; it was not actually communicated to Lord Salisbury until July 13.[115] Meanwhile, receipt of a letter from the Hongkong branch, embodying the views of T. H. Whitehead, strengthened the hands of the London Committee.[116]

Shanghai alone refused to be persuaded. Just as exercised as London about the intrusion of Russo-French interests into the Yangtze region by means of the Peking-Hankow, a strong faction in the Shanghai Committee led by Leonard Kerr nevertheless insisted that an overt move of occupation by Britain would precipitate partition to the detriment of British commercial interests. While approving the increased garrison advocated by Hongkong, Kerr voiced the opinion that "such additional or other forces should under no circumstances be employed within the territories of the Yangtze Valley until the policy of maintaining the integrity of this Empire is abandoned as hopeless, until in fact the integrity of China no longer exists." [117]

The Shanghai appeal went unheard; the London Committee proceeded with its original plan. Gundry forwarded the draft letter to Bertie early in July, giving as its motive "the strong feeling that our interests in the Yangtze Region should be asserted more decisively, if only in preparation for the débâcle." [118] Bertie's reaction, expressed in a long conversation with Gundry several days later, was not too sanguine. The proposal, he was convinced, "contemplated a tremendous responsibility" which the Government would probably not be prepared to undertake. To Gundry's suggestion that the Association was not necessarily insisting on "the complete, immediate execution of the entire plan," Bertie countered that though he considered the plan "on the whole" intelligent, the Association would probably receive a reply indicating the difficulties in the way. The one point he criticized strongly was "effective occupation"; which was, of course, the center, as it had been the inspiration, of the entire plan.[119]

Despite this warning that the plan would encounter a cold reception in Downing Street, it was formally submitted to Lord Salisbury on July 13, 1899. The Foreign Office failed to reply. Gundry again called on Bertie and the latter again objected to the recommendation for "effective occupation." Never would the Government consent to such action. August passed, and September. Interest in China affairs was waning. Gundry made several further attempts to enlist the support of the Foreign Office but received no encouragement. A request for permission to release the letter to the press was refused. "The feeling at the Foreign Office was that publication of such a document would alarm the Chinese and excite the jealousy of the Continental Powers; the time was not opportune for running the risk." [120] The honeymoon between Old China Hands and the Foreign Office was at an end.

The spirit that had prevailed in 1869 was revived. Little, then editor of the *North China Herald,* published an article on "The Hopelessness of the British Position in Peking" which reverberated in London. It was, in effect, an attack on the Foreign Office.

We are glad to know that the China Association is not trusting entirely to Mr. Dudgeon's being at home and reminding the Foreign Office now and then that there are British interests in China which are in danger. . . . Lord Salisbury's neglect of our interest and our prestige in China is becoming a scandal. To Britishers in Peking it seems that their Government has entirely abandoned them. . . . They are being left to defend the position as best they can with no aid from the Foreign Office; and Great Britain and the British—distasteful as it is to have to confess it—are positively an open laughing-stock in the Tsungli Yamen and the Foreign Legations at Peking.[121]

There was more in the same vein indicating that the Foreign Office had abandoned China to Russia; there was, Little concluded, need for a Cecil Rhodes in China. Dudgeon, Chairman of the Shanghai Committee, forwarding the article to Gundry, remarked that

Little undoubtedly voices the feeling in Shanghai that we are being "left," and I cannot wonder at the irritation that is felt. It is not only in big matters that we fail to assert ourselves, but it is the neglect of smaller matters that I believe is fully as much the cause of our loss of prestige.[122]

Even Gundry, forwarding this correspondence to Campbell at the China desk of the Foreign Office in what was meant to be an apologetic letter, could not refrain from remarking

I dislike the form of expression [in the article] but it undoubtedly voices a feeling that our prestige is at a very low ebb. I am assured that even at Shanghai it is no use making any representation to the Chinese Authorities—no matter

how well founded; and that Bax-Ironside [the Chargé d'affaires] might as well
be a shadow for all the hearing he can command at Peking. Let us hope that an
early squampashment of the Boers will leave us free to put might into Mac-
Donald's right arm![123]

But it was not only the necessity for "an early squampashment of
the Boers" which convinced the Government to refuse to undertake any
further commitments in China. The policy of retrenchment, of accepting no further responsibility for the protection and extension of British
interests in the direction demanded by the Old China Hands, was now
set. At a dinner given by the China Association to Sir Claude Mac-
Donald, who was personally very popular with the Old China Hands,
Sir Cecil Smith enumerated the recent concessions obtained through
the efforts of the Minister, but mourned the retreat marked by the
Anglo-Russian agreement, which was regarded as a measure of appeasement. The basic failure, Sir Cecil remarked, lay in the failure of the
Foreign Office, as well as of the general public, to appreciate the importance of British trade with China. The China Association had attempted to persuade the country to this realization; but without success.
"The British Government had for years neglected the trade of China";
in fact, it had shown an indifference to it that was perfectly appalling.
Whatever trade there had been developed by the merchant, despite the
obstacles placed in his path by the Government.[124] It was the age-old
complaint.

Sir Claude defended the Government by insisting that trade was a
private venture and should not depend on governmental promotion.
"British enterprise in China must be independent, individual, and self-
reliant. The moment it ceases to be this and leans too much on State
assistance, it ceases to be enterprise, indeed I may say it ceases to be
British." But Old China Hands were not convinced. The country
seemed to be sinking back into the apathy of the period of interlude in
Anglo-Chinese relations. Sir Richard Rennie bewailed the fact that
Parliament spent so little time debating China issues, and that the Association had but one member in the Lords (Lord Loch), and but six in
the Commons, the latest of whom was Keswick.

The circle had come full, with mercantile opinion complaining in
1899 as it had thirty years previously that the Government and country
failed to realize the importance of the China trade; that merchants were
left isolated and unprotected at the outposts of the Empire in Shanghai
and Hongkong; that British prestige was waning at Peking while Russia
threatened to take over China; and that without an implementation of
the British sphere through effective occupation and some form of pro-

tectorate, British predominance in China, let alone dreams of a fabulous future in trade and enterprise, would disappear.

It was Foreign Office rejection of their scheme of July, 1899, which convinced the China Association that this was true and that their influence in Downing Street had come to an end. The policy of limited liability, of retrenchment, of appeasement (as Old China Hands saw it) had come in the summer of 1899, and Lord Salisbury's eager acceptance of the Hay Note was but a confirmation of this policy. On June 9, 1899, the Government openly repudiated the suggestion of the China Association: "We cannot make the Yangtze Valley a province like Shantung or Manchuria, first, because it is infinitely larger, and secondly, we are not prepared to undertake the immense responsibility of governing what is practically a third of China." [125]

Acceptance of the Hay Note, itself of at least remote British inspiration,[126] by the British Government in November, 1899, allowed it to freeze policy on the basis of the Balfour formula, ensuring equality of trade opportunity throughout China, but recognizing preferential rights (though not rates) in the respective spheres. The Open Door Note of September 6, 1899, did not, of course, refuse to recognize spheres of interest but merely ensured that the Powers (a) would not "interfere with any treaty port or any vested interest" within them, (b) that the treaty tariff would continue to be collected within the spheres of leased areas on a non-preferential basis and by Chinese officials, and (c) that harbor dues and railway charges within such spheres would also be on a non-preferential basis.[127]

Far from regarding the Hay Note as a turning point in Far Eastern relations, the China Association failed to take any marked notice of it. First apprized of the Hay Note and its acceptance by the Powers in a Foreign Office communication in January, 1900, the General Committee did not consider it of sufficient importance to warrant debate. When, in the summer of 1900, the China Association again communicated to the Government its recommendation for the implementation of the Yangtze sphere, one member, a Mr. Rutherford, demurred on the ground that this might now appear to the Foreign Office to conflict with the declared policy of the open door. The Chairman set his mind at rest. The policy of the open door, he remarked, "was now held to mean 'spheres of influence' and an open 'commercial' door." This, said Gundry, was "clearly set out" in Lord Salisbury's reply to Mr. Choate, the American Ambassador.[128]

The Hay Note, therefore, made no difference in China Association policy. Its program of July, 1899, was still relevant and paramount. The battle to put it into effect continued. Even before the Boxer troubles renewed interest in China affairs, Old China Hands were planning the campaign which would arouse the country to the urgency of establishing a British protectorate.

Within the ranks of the Old China Hands, however, a fundamental split on strategy occurred. Agreed though they might be on objectives, conflicting business interests made agreement on tactics impossible. For the leadership of the China Association, controlled by representatives of the vested interests which had captured the bulk of concessions with Foreign Office assistance—in short, the representatives of the Hongkong & Shanghai Bank and Jardine, Matheson & Co.—insisted that progress could only be made through collaboration with the Foreign Office. On the other side were ranged Shanghai residents and the dissident element in the Association which held such action futile. Only through mass pressure on the Government, brought about by an aroused public opinion was there any chance of a fundamental change in British policy toward China. It was, therefore, imperative that they go to the country. Through press and Parliament, through Chambers of Commerce and provincial meetings, through pulpit and pamphlet the British people must be aroused to demand of their Government that "forward" policy which would finally implement the China dream. For the next few years, the struggle over China policy was fought on two fronts: added to the traditional dispute between merchant and official was the internecine conflict between Collaborationist and Insurgent among the Old China Hands.

PA**4**RT

End of an Era

IX

Old China Hands:
Defeat of the Insurgents

*"It is impossible to divorce commerce from poli-
tics in China"*—R. S. Gundry, September 27, 1900.

*"Here in England, as well as in the Far East, those
who have realised the gradual undermining of our
position, the loss of our opportunities, and the surrender of our natural advantages to our Continental rivals, recognise the fact that our Government,
for lack of that pressure of public opinion which
is absolutely necessary, fails today, as it has failed
in the past, to appreciate the national importance
of our interests in the Far East"*—J. O. P. Bland
to China Association, 1905.

OR Old China Hands the central issue at the turn of the century
was what it had always been: how to bring about a fiscal and
administrative revolution in China under British tutelage. Agitation for a Yangtze protectorate was but corollary, a measure whereby
this program might be extended to the most promising section of the
Empire; but it was never regarded as more than a policy of *sauve qui
peut*. In this campaign the China Association did not appear to be making much headway. Its letter of July 13, 1899, had been pigeon-holed, its
political advice ignored. In strictly commercial aspects of Anglo-
Chinese relations, its voice was supreme. But without fundamental
political changes, commercial treaty revision could mean no more than
an extension of the process of nibbling at the outer fringes of the China
market.

On the morning of December 11, 1899, Gundry called at the Foreign
Office and was informed that Sir Claude MacDonald, recently returned
from Peking, was expecting Chinese proposals for revision of the tariff
and the commercial articles of the Treaty of Tientsin. What stand would
the China Association take? The General Committee referred to the
letter of November 2, 1896, which was still regarded as applicable and

reiterated the stand it had taken at the time of the rumored revision in 1896.[1] No increase of tariff rates without "most ample guarantees in regard to inland taxation" and fulfillment of reforms desired.[2] But the Foreign Office had made no mention of the fundamental issues raised in the China Association letter of July 13. When a member of the Committee smugly remarked that despite obstacles trade did appear to be increasing,[3] Gundry countered with the bitter observation that its total was "scarcely larger than that of Japan, which barely exceeds a single Chinese province in population and area." The problem, he noted, was still the same as it had been a generation before, and so was the danger:

There was danger lest popular opinion in this country be misled as it was at the time of the Burlinghame mission, thirty years ago. The feeling had come home to him at a dinner given by the Article Club where the Chinese Minister made a clever speech which was applauded to the echo, whereas a speech by Mr. Brenan tending to put things in their true light was coldly received. This was being repeated at all the great industrial centers in England; and public opinion was very likely to be misled by the spectacle of a well-educated Chinaman professing to gather information for the advancement of his country. . . . It might become necessary to place matters in their true light.[4]

The "true light," of course, was that the China trade, capable of fabulous expansion, was being strangled by the backwardness of Peking, as always. And that the British Government failed to realize either the potentialities of the China market or the need for bringing about reform under its suzerainty. If Britain failed, was there any doubt that Russia would take over? Seen under the "true light," the sole solution lay in large-scale fiscal and administrative reform under British guidance. British responsibility not only for administrative efficiency but for internal security was a prerequisite for trade expansion and financial investment. Without it the coming railway age in China could not become a reality for British investors.

The remarkable fact was—a fact which must be emphasized because it is contrary to the accepted legend—that the concessions gained in 1898 were not being implemented. British capital was not seeking investment in the flotations of the Hongkong and Shanghai Bank. J. W. Jamieson, the newly appointed Commercial Attaché, suggested "with reference to railways . . . that the Association should devote attention to getting permission for capitalists to construct railways in China as limited companies, instead of by means only of loans."[5] Thus far the railway concessions were merely contracts for loans; and the money had not been forthcoming on the London market. The reason given by the British & Chinese Corporation for not proceeding with their concessions was that the moment was "not propitious" for floating further loans; the security did not appear adequate. Jamieson's solution, however, could not be met without that large-scale reform urged by the Association. As Gundry pointed out: "If an English company made a railway in France, they would have to make it under French law. This was another instance of the necessity for judicial reform which the Association had urged. All the concessionaires now got was the privilege of lending the Chinese Government money." [6]

Extraterritoriality, therefore, was not enough. What had been done for Egypt must be done for China before large-scale investment would be feasible. The Foreign Office, however, appeared to be adamant. A year had passed since the China Association had advanced its scheme for reform in the summer of 1899. Keswick's strategy of collaboration did not appear to be bearing fruit, and the conviction was growing in the radical wing of the Association itself and particularly among the Shanghai members that the Government would not be moved without pressure from public opinion. Was it not time to foster that public opinion? The agitation commenced by Little and Yerburgh among the Chambers in the fall of 1898 [7] had been continued on a limited scale; Yerburgh was not prepared to challenge the China Association leadership; but some headway had been made. Under the urging of the Leeds Chamber of Commerce, the Fourth Congress of Chambers of the Empire passed the following resolution in the summer of 1900:

That in view of the steps now being taken by the various countries to open out the interior of China to trade and commerce, it is the opinion of this Congress that the Government should endeavour by every means in its power to protect the interests of the British trader, to assist him in obtaining concessions, and to afford him all reasonable security against disturbance from the Chinese Government or aggression from foreign powers.[8]

It was significant not merely as a repudiation of *laissez-faire* but as an open plea that the Government extend the frontiers of its limited liability policy in China.

It was evident that with proper leadership this mercantile public opinion could be marshalled into a formidable political weapon. Mr. Yerburgh had more than once urged the China Association to furnish this leadership, but the General Committee, led by Keswick, thought the move unwise. The major fear was that the Association would lose its position of prestige at the Foreign Office by engaging in political tactics. Consequently, an insurgency movement had emerged at Shanghai and among the Shanghai hands returned to London who had formed a cabal around Yerburgh. Ideologically, Gundry was closer to this group than to the Keswick faction, though personal loyalty prevented him from open espousal of the insurgent cause. At Lord Beresford's request, he had provided a parliamentary delegation to Shanghai, led by Mr. E. F. Hatch, with letters of introduction. This initial contact had ripened into a correspondence between Hatch and F. Anderson, the Chairman of the Shanghai Committee, aimed at expanding the work of the Association into a more popular league possessed of mercantile, parliamentary and public support.

On June 7, 1900, the General Committee for the first time took official cognizance of this movement.[9] Gundry presented the issue as follows:

Experience had shown that, although the Foreign Office had been most willing to do anything the Association advocated that lay within its power as a department, when it came to questions of high policy like Port Arthur or the Lu-Han Railway, we failed. Those were Government questions and the Government would not move without a mandate from the electorate.

Sir Edward Ackroyd, who spoke as a representative of the northern Chambers of Commerce, presented the view of the insurgents with great persuasiveness. While it was admitted that the China Association had great success in maintaining contact with the Foreign Office and presenting it with "the opinions and views of practical men—men of experience well versed in the China question," Ackroyd insisted that that was insufficient.

It was suggested that the Association should extend its scope and field of work with the object of instructing the British public on the subject of China and of the great facilities and opportunities for trade which China offered with its teeming millions of industrious people and mineral wealth. He thought that if the public ever realised the importance of China in that respect even the Boer War and the South African problems would not have relegated this question to the background. There were vast opportunities in China for immense expansion of trade if free from exactions and security to life and property.[10]

Ackroyd suggested that the Association reorganize into a League (comparable to the British Empire League) as a means of marshalling public opinion.

The split in the General Committee on this proposal was not unexpected. While there was general agreement on policy, such a departure in strategy did not appeal to the top leadership, particularly to those representatives of the vested interests—principally those concentrated in the British & Chinese Corporation—who had a stake in collaboration. Thus, Keswick, Sir Thomas Sutherland, Lord Loch, Sir Alfred Dent,

Ewen Cameron and E. Iveson, who were all identified with the chosen
financial instrument of British policy, shied away from Ackroyd's suggestion. Prominent among the insurgents were the "professional Chinamen" in the House of Commons led by Yerburgh and J. Walton, representatives of Lancashire interests of whom Ackroyd was the most
notable, and, above all, the insurgents of Shanghai, represented in London by Michie and Dudgeon and later to be reinforced by F. Anderson,
all of whom were allied with the hopeful commercial interests for whom
the China dream had never matured. This struggle between Collaborationist and Insurgent was waged for close upon ten years.

Keswick, as outstanding spokesman for the former, rejected Ackroyd's plea with the argument that "it would be a mistake to interfere
with the existing form of the China Association." The most he would
concede was the formation, outside of the Association, of a parliamentary bloc "to push an inert Government into action." As for the
China Association, its strength lay in its representation of "direct British
interests" in China, in its unanimity which might be shattered by the introduction of political issues, and in its prestige value at the Foreign
Office. Sir Cecil Smith agreed on the ground that "the China Association had succeeded in establishing friendly and even confidential relations with the Foreign Office which had had and which might have far-
reaching effects in the future." By taking in outsiders, he emphasized,
the China Association would "lose influence in official quarters." Several
other members spoke in agreement, Mr. Gwyther charging that the insurgent movement had been instigated by "the young China party in the
House of Commons" who "desired to capture the Association in furtherance of their political ambitions."

Speaking for the insurgents, Michie granted that being "in touch"
with the Foreign Office was a splendid asset, but getting "in touch" with
the electorate was just as important. "This was required to complete
the circuit." Without this pressure the Government's do-nothing policy
in China would continue. "If there was no impulse given it there would be
no policy. Great events were pending in that region, and it was desirable
that the attention of the public should be awakened, otherwise ir-
revocable steps might be taken which would be deplored when too late."

Sir Richard Rennie, himself an old Shanghai hand, backed up this
view, holding that Keswick had "exaggerated our influence with the
Foreign Office." Their proposals met "a polite acknowledgment" and
their tactics of lying low had been "singularly unproductive." Gundry
disagreed that their action had been futile, pointing to the following
gains brought about by their influence: the final separation of the offices of Chief Judge and Consul General in Shanghai, opening of the

West River to Nanning, opening of a treaty port in Hunan, and of inland waterways to steam. They had asked for a Commercial Attaché and after digging £100 a year out of the Treasury had eventually worked it up to £1000 and got their man. But Gundry would not commit himself on the large political issues on which, he felt, the China Association had no influence. Under the overwhelming resistance of the collaborationists, the proposal for widening the scope of the Association's activities was voted down.

Frustrated, the insurgents formed the China League, with R. A. Yerburgh as Chairman and George Jamieson as Secretary, and stumped the country, concentrating their first efforts on the Chambers of Commerce. Manchester was approached with the argument that political indifference to Britain's interest in the Far East was due to sheer ignorance of its potentialities, and of the gravity of the current situation. "The magnitude of the problem, the want of precise information as to the issues involved, and the fear of foreign complications, have combined to produce an acquiescence in the attitude of successive Governments, which has hitherto been practically a policy of waiting on events." The League had been formed to combat this situation and asked for Manchester support.[11] The Board agreed merely to bring it to the attention of its members. The League got off to a slow start and remained quiescent for almost a year. The roster of its organizing committee is instructive: R. A. Yerburgh, Ernest Beckett, John Gretton, E. F. G. Hatch, D. B. Jones, E. R. P. Moon, J. Walton, all members of Parliament organized in the so-called China bloc; R. M. Campbell and C. J. Dudgeon of the Shanghai Committee of the China Association; George Jamieson, former Consul, as Secretary; A. R. Colquhoun, of Burma route fame; and the Reverend C. Poyntz Sanderson, representing the missionary interest.

The first recruiting letter sent out by this committee is worth quoting as an index of the temper of Old China Hand opinion even *before* the Boxer crisis unfolded:

In view of the extreme gravity of events now happening in China and the important question presently up for consideration as to the future of Anglo-Chinese relations, the time is opportune for the formation of an organisation of all who are interested in the Far East, and who desire the maintenance of the commercial and political supremacy which we have hitherto held in these regions.

The importance of China as an open market for our manufactures, and the immense possibilities which that country presents as a legitimate field for British enterprise, are generally recognized by H.M. Government, but owing to the difficult and complex nature of the problem and the variety of interests involved, they have hesitated to embark on a definite line of policy without the support of a strong popular voice. On the other hand, popular information as to the issues at stake is of a most elementary kind. . . .

It is the object of the League to remedy both these defects. In the first place it would seek by means of popular addresses, pamphlets, etc., to build up in the country at large a sound body of public opinion on the Far Eastern question; and, secondly, through a strong parliamentary party it would endeavour to assist and support H.M. Government in the task of formulating and maintaining a clear and consistent line of policy.

This policy is nowise intended to be aggressive. It would aim, in the first place, at the maintenance intact of all existing rights throughout the whole of the territories of the Chinese Empire, and the furtherance of British interests, by all legitimate means. Secondly, it would endeavour to support . . . a progressive Government in China, which by moderate and steady reform would secure the tranquility, prosperity and independence of that Empire. Thirdly, its object would be to see that there shall be no such disturbance of the balance of power in the Far East as would endanger our Imperial position or affect the safety of our Indian Empire.[12]

In essence, this policy did not differ from that of the China Association. As has been noted, Collaborationists and Insurgents were split on strategy, not objectives. The cause of the insurgents fed upon official reaction to the Boxer crisis. Generally regarded as a high-point in Anglo-Chinese relations, the Boxer Rebellion did not affect the fundamental bases of British Far Eastern policy, despite the efforts of mercantile circles. For the latter, the Boxer affair was not in itself a causative factor in their attitude, but rather a heightened occasion for its expression. It served the same purpose as had the Tientsin Affair exactly thirty years before, as rationalization and justification for traditional demands.

Anti-foreign disturbances in Shantung in the winter of 1899–1900, led by the Boxers, an anti-foreign society which appeared to have the secret support of the Dowager-Empress, moved north in June of 1900, threatening the Legations in Peking. Shanghai was alarmed almost to the point of hysteria by the news that the Boxers were advancing on the capital and that insufficient forces were available to resist them. No less than five telegrams were addressed to the General Committee in the ten days following June 12, all of which asked for protection and for various action. Gundry called at the Foreign Office and was assured that the Government had promised the Yangtze Viceroys effective help in putting down outbreaks, a point stressed in the Shanghai communications.[13] The Government was actually moving with speed in ordering military support in the North [14] and support of the Nanking and Hankow Viceroys "assuring them of British protection in maintaining order." [15]

Gundry did not regard this as sufficient and asked for a "more explicit guarantee" in view of the alleged complicity of the palace in the insurrection. It was feared that the "same encouragement" would be given to anti-foreign movements in other provinces. A draft letter was prepared emphasizing the necessity for giving full support to the Viceroys and protecting Shanghai. The intent of the Old China Hands soon became clear. This was an opportunity for exercising those measures which would clearly assert Britain's suzerainty in the Yangtze Valley and Jamieson, of the China League, first broached the suggestion that the Viceroys should be upheld even *against* Peking. "If they were dismissed we should insist on their restoration." [16] It was also agreed that a sizable British force should be dispatched to Shanghai, for the same reason. The inevitable suggestion was forthcoming that the capital be removed to Nanking, but Gundry remarked that that "lay in the future." The first step was to put down the Empress and her advisers and support the Viceroys.

The letter to Lord Salisbury of June 28 embodied these suggestions, stressing the need for dispatch of a force to Shanghai to protect British interests in the Yangtze and an offer of support to the Nanking and Wuchang Viceroys against any action or reprisals by their own government. This view was supported by letters from Shanghai, dated June 14 and June 18.[17] The Foreign Office refused permission to publish the letter, and Gundry agreed on the ground that it might prove embarrassing. "The Government might be willing to do regarding the Yangtze more than it might be willing to state officially at a moment when it was undesirable to raise any question of separate action." [18] But the general reaction of the Foreign Office was cool. Nor would it give "a clear and explicit promise . . . to the Yangtze Viceroys that they not only would be supported in maintaining order but upheld and protected against possible pressure or vengeance from Peking." [19] Yerburgh was, therefore, instructed to ask a question about this point in Commons. Thus far, the Government had on June 19 merely given the assurance that Britain "will, if necessary, cooperate with the Viceroys on the Yangtze in the maintenance of order," a pledge which was renewed a month later.[20]

Yerburgh's interpellation referred specifically to the China Association letter, amended however to spare Peking's sensibilities by asking for "a clear and explicit expression of the intention of Her Majesty's Government to uphold and protect those who have ventured to range themselves on the side of order and loyalty to their obligations." [21] Mr. Broderick refused to budge, maintaining that "assurances they have asked for have been given." In addition, three further suggestions by the China Association met with Foreign Office rebuffs. On urgent representations from Shanghai, the Association had recommended that

Mr. Pelham-Warren, Acting Consul-General at Shanghai, who was known to favor mercantile views on handling the Viceroys, be promoted to the diplomatic rank of chargé d'affaires so that he might treat with the Viceroys on an equal footing. The Foreign Office reply was that this "would create a general revolt in the diplomatic service," leading Gundry to remark that "that raised the question whether the country was created for the Diplomatic Service or the Diplomatic Service for the country." [22]

Similarly, recommendation for the appointment of a high-ranking diplomat to head a special mission to take charge of the Boxer negotiations so that "we should have in China a chief prepared to take charge of them" was denied. The China Association had in mind someone "like Lord Elgin." The names of Lords Cromer, Dufferin, Rosebery, and Pauncefote were mentioned. Finally, the China Association feared that on Sir Claude MacDonald's retirement owing to ill-health, Sir Ernest Satow, Minister at Tokyo, would be appointed to replace him. Gundry expressed the mercantile view that "he did not think Sir Ernest would be generally regarded as a fitting man." [23] The Foreign Office nevertheless appeared to have gone ahead with plans for the appointment.

Gundry was now convinced that the China Association had lost all influence on Anglo-Chinese affairs and was being persuaded that the Insurgents were right. On July 20 he wrote a bitter letter to Keswick, intimating the futility of their efforts:

The experience of the past five years shows that the Government have neglected every suggestion of a political character which the Association has made. We pointed out the danger to Port Arthur more than two years before the crisis occurred, and . . . we were entitled to consider the event a deception. The surrender of Port Arthur to Russia will be recognised in future years as a turning point in the history of the Far East, and as a primary cause, in my opinion, of all the troubles that have since occurred. We have pointed out the dangerous consequences to be expected from the *coup d'état* of 1898. We suggested, last year, various steps which we thought might be usefully taken for the purpose of inaugurating closer relations with the Chinese officials in the Yangtze region. . . . The suggestion was neglected. . . .[24]

Gundry recapitulated his complaints to the General Committee four days later, adding that Hongkong had written for a "mobile force" available for dispatch to any part of China in an emergency, a suggestion communicated to the Foreign Office which had "of course, been neglected." [25] So exercised was he by these events that he tendered his resignation as Secretary. Gundry was the "heart and brain" of the Association, as one member remarked, and his resignation was a serious threat. "The simple truth," Gundry offered in explanation, "was that they had been bombinating in a vacuum," and that as Sir Richard Rennie had remarked, the Government "paid not the slightest attention to their representations." To the objection of one member that Gundry himself had quoted "quite a list of important concessions which the Association had obtained," he countered that these had nothing to do with political questions in which the Association's influence was non-existent. It was a question of policy. Unless the Association was prepared to assert its own dignity he could not continue; he added the veiled hint that his services might be employed elsewhere, meaning the China League. Gundry consented to stay if the Committee would insist on publication of the China Association's letters of June 13, 1899, and June 28, 1900, omitting any references inconsistent with the public interest. No decision was taken, as Keswick's suggestion that action should not take the form of an ultimatum was rejected by Gundry. However, the latter consented to carry on the office business until the next meeting at which the matter would be decided. The *affaire Gundry* was resolved by Keswick's consent to send a strong letter to Lord Salisbury protesting "against the want of sufficient energy on the part of the Government in their Eastern policy," and requesting permission to publish the letters setting forth the program of 1899 and the more recent recommendations.[26]

But the issues remained. Alarming telegrams continued to arrive from Shanghai urging the need for a mobile force "in view of the increasingly unfriendly attitude of the Reactionary party in the Provinces," [27] and continuing agitation for taking "friendly Viceroys" under British protection.[28] The arrival of British troops at Shanghai was hailed as a good sign but the Shanghai branch insisted that "any hesitation about landing them would be fatal to British prestige" as "Chinese regard it as great weakness if we appear afraid [to] carry out declared intent." [29] The China Association continued to press upon the Foreign Office the need for early fulfillment of its recent recommendations: that Pelham Warren be given a "rank befitting the importance of the duties he was called upon to perform"; that the Viceroys be promised "the full moral and material support" of the British Government, including protection against Peking; and that "a special mission with a diplomatist of European rank and reputation as its chief—supported, as Lord Elgin was supported forty years ago, by one or more of the ablest and strongest members of the consular service as adviser—will be appointed to represent the important interests of the British Empire in the Far East." Gundry stressed that he was speaking not alone for the interests of Britain but for the "British Empire." [30]

A logical by-product of this strong stand taken by the China Association was a temporary rapprochement with the China League. The latter offered to put the services of their lecturers and propagandists at the disposal of the Association "in the way of holding meetings and proposing resolutions" on behalf of the Yangtze protectorate and the reforms recommended by the Association. Gundry refused the offer, holding that the "Yangtze question should be handled with extreme discretion." [31] The League's main function, of course, was to be indiscreet. But so closely linked were their views that Mr. Barkill, the League's Secretary and also a member of the China Association, was invited to draw up a memorandum setting forth the issues on which the two agencies might cooperate. Nothing further was heard of this proposal.

Under Gundry's energetic pressure, the China Association renewed its political efforts. A recommendation was submitted to the Foreign Office that the Peking Government be reorganized under British tutelage, with "reforming advisers and a progressive council" consisting of dependable Viceroys.[32] Again the Foreign Office acknowledged but disregarded the suggestion. The Association, anticipating the China League, sought the support of the home Chambers. A circular letter was sent to the Chambers of Commerce in London, Liverpool, Manchester, Blackburn, Halifax, Bradford, Leeds and Glasgow, requesting them to urge upon the Government the special mission project conceived by the Association.[33]

Favorable replies were received from London, Liverpool, Manchester and Halifax, all of whom wrote to the Foreign Office.[34] Manchester's resolution, typical of the rest, called for "earnest representations [to] be made to Her Majesty's Government in favor of the dispatch to China of a special mission, accompanied by a diplomatist of first rank in order that the existing critical condition of affairs may be wisely dealt with." [35] Bradford refused to associate itself with the move, as did Glasgow which, though sympathetic, was sure the Government knew best. Blackburn thought it was too late for such action.[36] The venture was dropped.

More delicate was the issue raised by mercantile opposition to the appointment of Sir Ernest Satow to replace MacDonald at Peking. The Shanghai letter of September 24, 1900, coupled the need for a special mission with strong objection to the Satow appointment.[37] Gundry raised the question unofficially at the Foreign Office and, having received no response, considered a campaign among the Chambers. The leadership of the Association was very wary of raising an issue so personal it was sure to tread on Foreign Office toes. Criticism was also voiced of Gundry's contemplated letter to *The Times* on the matter. To the objection of one member that the Association was commercial and should not go beyond its function and attempt to dictate a political appointment, Gundry replied emphatically: "it is impossible to divorce commerce from politics in China." [38]

But Gundry was outvoted. It was agreed, however, confidentially to sound out the home Chambers and absent members. The response was none too encouraging. The President of the Manchester Chamber refused to become involved and held that "unless there is a very strong case against Sir Ernest Satow I am inclined to think the Board will hesitate to take so unusual a step as to protest against his appointment." He inquired for more facts as to the grounds for objection, but Gundry could not reply that Satow (a) was not a first-class man and (b) was a "student," not a "man of action." There was hardly a "very strong case" against Satow, except that he was not Sir Harry Parkes. The other Chambers also refused to go along.[39]

The essence of the issue, of course, was not mentioned. A strong "man of action" was needed in order to keep alive agitation in this year of decision. If the mercantile program were not now achieved there would perhaps be no other opportunity. The Satow affair was Gundry's means of easing the China Association closer to the Insurgent position. This, too, was evident from the replies received from absent members of the General Committee, of which only one was favorable to Gundry's attitude. Rutherford voiced the mercantile "regret that the British Government have not regarded the situation in China as of sufficient gravity and importance to call for the appointment of a diplomat of the first rank." [40] It was the conviction that they were being left which accounts for the bitterness aroused among Old China Hands at Satow's appointment.

Other replies exhibited the collaborationist taint.

However greatly we may be disappointed at the appointment of Satow [wrote one] I hope we shall not commit ourselves to any adverse criticism on the subject at the present moment. . . . It is probable that Lord Salisbury did not know what else to do in the circumstances . . . while the special mission which we suggested may not be desirable even if practicable at the present moment.[41]

Ewen Cameron of the Hongkong and Shanghai Bank also advised discretion. The appointment was a *fait accompli* and it was senseless to antagonize the Foreign Office. As for Gundry's suggestion, made in private, that the Committee resign in protest if their recommendation were not accepted, Cameron thought it "ridiculous." The Foreign Office should be given the benefit of the doubt. "You can easily conceive of circumstances under which the Government could not carry out our recommendations although recognizing their wisdom, and even anxious to do what we advise." The attitude of this faction was well summed up by Sir

Alfred Dent: "Personally I am not in favour of adopting too strong an attitude against the decisions of the Foreign Office and Government in political matters. If they do not take our advice they no doubt have very good reasons for doing so."

Faced with this kind of opposition, Gundry dropped the entire matter. Nor was progress any happier with regard to the more basic question of British action in the Yangtze Valley. Aside from a limited assurance to the Viceroys and the dispatch of a contingent of troops to the North and to Shanghai, the Government showed no signs of implementing its protectorate. On the contrary, Lord Salisbury jumped at the offer of Japan to take upon herself the major military burden of relieving the Legations,[42] and pursued throughout a policy of close collaboration with the other Powers aimed at reestablishing the *status quo ante*.

There was obviously to be no change in policy, nor did Britain appear to be assuming the leadership. In October the Shanghai Committee warned that action must soon be taken to prevent supplies being sent from the Yangtze to the rebels, but that such action must *not* be international as that would arouse the opposition of the Viceroys. Instead: "If Great Britain alone [took action] good reasons for thinking peaceful arrangements still possible; active British intervention imperative; promise of support no longer sufficient; delay threatens great danger widespread disturbance." [43] Gundry had promptly communicated this telegram to the Foreign Office, pointing out how completely it justified the Association's letter of June 28 that the situation "required not only promise of help in putting down possible disturbance but a clear and explicit expression of intention of Her Majesty's Government to uphold and protect officials who have ranged themselves on the side of order and loyalty to their obligations." The Foreign Office was not moved.

As the year 1901 opened, relations between Old China Hands and the Foreign Office were at their lowest point since 1870. Only the strong hands of the Collaborationists kept the situation from developing into open rebellion. The Shanghai and Hongkong Committees complained that the Far East was being neglected. Hongkong was furious that in the publication of the correspondence regarding a special mission and a successor to MacDonald at Peking, the name of Satow had been suppressed,[44] and proposed to Shanghai to join them in "a protest against the methods of the London Committee." [45] Shanghai dissented from this blanket condemnation and urged upon Hongkong Gundry's plea that they were laboring under difficulties. But neither felt assurance about the basic situation. Shanghai was concerned over the continued occupation of Newchwang by Russian troops (under the Boxer settlement) and what appeared to be the declaration of a protectorate over Manchuria.[46]

There was every reason to fear that Britain was being squeezed out of her preeminent position in China. Manchuria was lost, British prestige was low, no effort had been made to implement the Yangtze sphere, and the sole communication the China Association received from the Foreign Office at this time was the intelligence that the Managing Director of the Hamburg-America line was about to visit Singapore and Japan with a view to consolidating the Far Eastern operations of the company. This naive glee in the prosperity of other nations was the last measure of insult. In all seriousness members suggested the following reply to this communication: "It is not evident where the interest of the China Association came in unless the Government were prepared to follow the example of Germany in increasing subventions for the purpose of extending British shipping."

So dismal did the situation appear that Gundry made another gesture at resigning at the Annual Meeting on April 17, 1901. (He was back the following month.) To the membership he complained that "he was oppressed by a sense of inutility"; he meant not only the Report, which few members bothered to read, but the entire work of the China Association appeared to lead nowhere. While Sir Claude MacDonald was at Peking, some progress might have been made; but the situation was now hopeless.

Meanwhile, because of the China Association's reluctance to mobilize public opinion despite its lack of success with the Foreign Office, the China League again became active. In January, 1901, it renewed its campaign with the proposal to hold a series of public meetings in the principal cities.[47] But it failed to make much headway against public apathy. In Manchester, a meeting was held in the Board Room of the Chamber in the afternoon of March 6 and another in the evening "with lantern slides." Though sympathetic, the Chamber refused to join as a group; later that year it consented to subscribe a guinea a year to the China League, but that was the extent of its interest.[48] Liverpool was even more cautious. The Council of the Chamber, after consulting with Manchester, London and Glasgow and finding they were not disposed to join as a body and "in view of some of its objects being political," recommended that any adherence to the League should be on a strictly individual basis.[49] The China League never gained popularity, nor did it ever rival the larger propaganda agencies in the field of foreign and imperial relations. Rather, it remained the preserve of the insurgent faction among Old China Hands dissatisfied with the leadership of the China Association.

Mercantile circles made one final effort to turn the Boxer affair to account. The Shanghai Committee was the first to suggest the possibility of employing the indemnity as a lever for advancing the mercantile program and its suggestion was eagerly taken up by the home Chambers. On April 4, 1901, Shanghai telegraphed:

Re indemnity there is every reason to believe certain powers propose international guaranteed loan secured [by] simple process of drastic tariff increase. Strongest possible protest should be made, as although increased tariff admissible, such hasty action [in] treatment of tariff destroys only available lever redress present grievances, besides menacing trade expansion. Should bring pressure to bear China provide service indemnity from existing sources native revenue which honestly collected known capable adequate expansion. Present conference eleven Ministers, several [of whom represent] no commercial interests, eminently unsuited settle complex commercial questions which should be reserved for future settlement later by leading commercial Powers.[50]

The Foreign Office replied that this accorded with official views: "No drastic increase of import duties except in return for largely increased trade facilities was exactly the line they had taken up." [51] It was an accord on the surface only. The Foreign Office was granting the China Association position of 1896 that no increase would be tolerated without "largely increased trade facilities." But what Shanghai and the Chambers were demanding was something different: in effect, that the indemnity itself be employed as a lever for the adoption of the mercantile reform program. The China Association, in any event, felt that British interests were being neglected in the Peking negotiations. On the urging of Sir Cecil Smith (still smarting over the fact that he had been overlooked in the Peking appointment) it was recommended to the Foreign Office that negotiations be transferred to London.

Shanghai's proposal was taken up by the Associated Chambers of Commerce which organized a deputation to Lord Landsdowne in support of its resolution adopted at the spring session:

That in the opinion of the Associated Chambers it is essential that Her Majesty's Government should take adequate measures for the safeguarding of the vast commercial and political interests of the British Empire in China, and that in connection with the settlement following the recent hostilities reparation should be sought in increased facilities for trade rather than by a money indemnity.[52]

After some delay the delegation was received by Lord Cranborne, Parliamentary Undersecretary, accompanied by Bertie and F. A. Campbell, head of the China Department at the Foreign Office. W. H. Holland,

M.P., who presented the resolution, noted that its premise was based on the conviction they all held of "the immense potentialities for improvement of the China market; we had only touched the outer fringe." Prosperity of trade for the next generation was "largely in the hands of the Foreign Office." [53] John Walton, M.P., a leader of the China League, noted that they were concerned with policy. In addition to "all possible support" for the Yangtze Viceroys, he urged the following concessions in place of an indemnity as a means of settlement: abolition of *likin* and apportionment of a share of tariff collections to provincial treasuries; British supervision of fiscal reform; the "complete opening" of inland waterways; the same import duty on land frontiers as prevailed at the ports; and extension of railway facilities.

Lord Cranborne, while agreeing with the importance of the problem, stressed what Salisbury and MacDonald had also mentioned: that the furtherance of trade must "in the first instance" depend on free enterprise and the efforts of traders themselves. Theirs was the risk, not the Government's. The duty of government was to secure for traders the full opportunity for exercising their business and he insisted that the Government had in the past few years fulfilled that responsibility. At the same time he emphasized that official policy would resist any tendency toward partition, involved in pursuing an unilateral Yangtze policy, and that Britain must avoid "international swagger." Internal reform in China must be slow; the Government agreed that the indemnity should be limited and no burden imposed on China which might be so severe as to endanger her stability or progress.[54]

The Boxer crisis had offered the last chance for a reversal of the Government policy toward China. Mercantile attempts in 1899 and again in the summer of 1900 to modify that policy had failed. As Gundry well realized, the essence of the Old China Hand program lay in persuading the Government to accept new responsibilities in China, firstly with regard to a vigorous assertion of a British protectorate over the Yangtze through effective occupation and "protection" of the Viceroys, and more broadly by committing itself to the fiscal and administrative reform of China under British tutelage. And although several further efforts were made to mobilize public opinion behind this program, they had neither the drive nor conviction of the crucial period of 1898–1900.

It was the end of an era, as the period from 1902 to 1905 was to demonstrate. Henceforth, the China Association concentrated on attaining gains piecemeal. The larger dream faded and, in its place, attention was turned to solving the remaining commercial questions, particularly *likin,* and protecting British interests against Russian encroachment. (With the end of the Russo-Japanese war these suspicions were diverted to Japan.) Through it all there ran the traditional mercantile cry that Chinese backwardness was the chief enemy and the conviction that by refusing to accept the responsibility of guiding China on the path of reform Britain had lost an Empire.

At least on paper the mercantile community succeeded in solving the *likin* question through the Mackay Treaty of 1902. But, except for the opening of five more treaty ports, that was the extent of the commercial concessions obtained. Revision of the Treaty of Tientsin went little further in 1902 than in 1869. Indeed, it is a striking commentary on that element of *déjà vu* in Anglo-Chinese relations, mentioned above, to note how closely the attitudes and issues of 1902 and 1869 coincided. The Chinese démarche for increased tariff rates as the price of treaty revision had been made in 1896, as was noted above, and the position of the China Association remained what it had been in their famous letter of November, 1896. No increase would be acceptable without a broadening of trade facilities and a solution of the *likin* problem. The Foreign Office, as susceptible of mercantile opinion in such matters as ever, again canvassed the attitude of the Chambers in 1901. In March of that year the Minister at Peking circularized the British communities in China.

The reply of the Shanghai Committee of the China Association, which is representative of mercantile opinion, was addressed to Byron Brenan, Consul-General at Shanghai, at the end of May. The very headings of its letter indicated how closely the issues resembled those of 1869: inland residence, railway construction, inland steam navigation, *likin,* etc. Shanghai itself noted the parallel:

It is indeed noteworthy to remark how little many of these questions have altered during the last forty years, what little progress has been made toward their elucidation, and how closely the representations of British merchants to-day coincide with those made by their predecessors at the time of attempted revision of Treaties in 1869.[55]

Shanghai considered the separate issues. (a) *Inland Residence:* The Minister had suggested extending this right to "some of the more important commercial centres through which railways are expected to run." But Shanghai insisted that the only solution lay in the suggestion made in the Shanghai Memorial of 1867! That is, insisting that Article IX of the Tientsin Treaty gave them the right to travel throughout the interior and Article XII the right to build houses and warehouses at "other places," Shanghai demanded the "comprehensive right" granted by that treaty which "has been rendered inoperative by Chinese obstruction." (b) *Railways:* Calling attention to the China Association letter of July, 1898, Shanghai emphasized again that anxiety was caused by international rivalry in which "railways constructed by Foreign States, under State auspices, with State aid, may . . . in the near future be held to constitute territorial claims." They pressed for the establishment of a Railway Department which might impose uniformity on railway lines, but above everything insisted that without State aid British railway enterprise in China could never compete. (c) *Inland Steam Navigation:* Granting that the right conceded in 1898 to navigate China's inland waters "is probably the most important concession obtained from China since the Treaty of 1858," Shanghai insisted that its purpose had been defeated by the regulations governing this privilege.[56] The hostility of provincial officials, fearing interference with sources of revenue, complications arising through conditions attaching to the carrying of goods and the fact that inland trade as such was not permitted made this right nugatory. (d) *Likin:* This "dead wall of obstruction" had made impossible a workable tariff system. Its total abolition was urged. Shanghai urged that guarantees be established protecting the Transit Pass which would cover a commuted tax, with provincial authorities sharing in the customs revenue. It was the standard solution.

The Mackay Treaty incorporated the last of these suggestions; the other recommendations were dropped. For nearly a year mercantile circles were agitated by discussions over the size of the increase in tariff which would be acceptable and what "guarantees" should be demanded. The China Association objected to the choice of Sir James L. Mackay to conduct the negotiations as he was an "Indian" and "incompetent" and suggested that he be assisted by a Consul as joint commissioner. The Foreign Office wanted no man from the consular service but finally consented to Dudgeon (of the Shanghai Committee) as adviser.[57]

The Mackay negotiations dragged on throughout the winter of 1901–02 and in February the Foreign Office confidentially inquired of the Chambers whether they would approve of the Mackay proposals to increase the tariff (including the commuted *likin* rate) to 15 percent in exchange for abolition of taxation barriers and guarantees for the safeguarding of provincial revenues.[58] The China Association telegraphed to Shanghai and found opinion varied. Keswick thought the advantage of abolition of all internal tax barriers "would fully compensate for the extra duty," but other members thought further concessions should be demanded. And they were skeptical of guarantees. The clash in interests was evident from the murmur of some members that China was trying to hold them up in order to meet its increased public debt, which was the very reason why representatives of the Hongkong and Shanghai Bank approved of it.[59] As the result of this difference an equivocal letter was sent to the Foreign Office, which withheld decision and merely noted that

the abolition of likin and like tax has long been considered ideal but of doubtful practicability, until the opening of Inland Communications by Rail and Water bring local officials within touch of Western methods: and the stipulation that if the engagement was not strictly adhered to, H.M. Government would revert to present Tariffs would possibly not be easy to enforce. . . .[60]

In Manchester there was no such hesitation. The China tariff subcommittee branded the proposal for increased customs dues as "impracticable" and "it is surprising that they should be seriously put forward by His Majesty's Representatives in the interest of British trade." The surtax of 10 percent would be a "heavy blow" to the trade in piece goods and would reduce consumption of Manchester products. It was held that no arrangement for abolition of *likin* barriers would prove effective.[61] No other Chamber adopted the extreme view of Manchester and the Foreign Office sent an extensive reply claiming that an all-inclusive rate of 15 percent would actually reduce the laying down cost of goods which would now be free from "vexatious delay and uncertainty." As for guarantees the system which worked with opium could be extended. Actually, during the indemnity negotiations a majority of Powers had favored doubling the import tariff, the Foreign Office revealed, and it was only British resistance which was securing some concession for the inevitable increase. Manchester was not impressed and continued to lead the agitation against the Mackay proposals.

Under the influence of Keswick the China Association had come around to accepting the Mackay proposal "on the distinct understanding that sufficient guarantees are obtained that every form of inland taxation . . . on merchandise shall be abolished within the limits of China." [62] In Shanghai, however, sentiment was split and a movement arose in the London Committee to insist on further guarantees and a lower surtax than the proposed 10 percent.[63] The China League also organized a deputation to the Foreign Office on April 18 against the Mackay proposal,[64] while in Shanghai the local branch of the China Association voted 24 to 21 against it.[65] At a meeting of the General Committee on April 25 the whole issue was reopened.[66] F. A. Anderson advanced an alternative proposal providing for a surtax of 5 percent which would be earmarked for provincial revenues in exchange for concessions including inland residence, free navigation of inland waterways and a "liberal policy" with regard to railway development.[67] The essence of this proposal, of course, was to force the issue of reform through treaty revision. Under Keswick's influence, however, the Association agreed not to press the issue at that time and tacit agreement was given to the Mackay plan.

Despite the opposition of Manchester and majority sentiment in Shanghai, therefore, this solution was adopted. On July 16 Mackay informed the Foreign Office that the following provisions had been incorporated in the treaty revision: (a) Removal of all *likin* barriers and collections, except for a consumption tax on native goods; (b) a surtax of 7½ percent to be imposed on foreign imports leaving the treaty ports, to be added to the basic tariff rate which remained set at 5 percent ad valorem; (c) supervision of native customs by the Imperial Maritime Customs, including collection of salt, opium and consumption taxes; and (d) five treaty ports opened to foreign trade, including Changsha in Hunan, Wanhsien in Szechuen, Nganking in Anhui, and Waichow and Kongmon in Kwangtung. These provisions were incorporated in the final agreement signed at Shanghai on September 5, 1902.[68] The surtax, however, was not to be levied until the arrangement was accepted by the other foreign Powers.

This, then, was the extent of treaty revision. *Likin* ceased to be a major issue thereafter, but mercantile circles could not but feel that treaty revision had been as empty as in 1869. The major demands—for inland residence, for freer navigation, for an expanded program of railway construction and, above all, for administrative reform, had not been met. Nor was it to be. The Mackay Treaty remained the basis of Anglo-Chinese commercial relations until the abolition of extraterritoriality by treaty in January, 1943.

Until the defeat of Russia in the Russo-Japanese War of 1904–1905, the China Association concentrated its political attention on the menace to British interests of Russian maneuvers in North China. The feeling that a bad bargain had been made in 1899 continued. Britain had failed to secure the Yangtze, while Russian moves indicated that Manchuria and perhaps even Chihli might be lost to British enterprise. During the Boxer affair Russia had occupied stretches of the Peking-Shanhaikwan line and land on the north bank of the Peiho in Tientsin presumably as prelude to a Concession; Manchuria was now treated as a virtual protectorate and the South Manchurian line pushed without regard to previous restrictions as to route and territory.[69] Shanghai's alarm over these developments was communicated to the London Committee where a resolution was hastily drafted by Gundry.

That this Association would view with regret the cession of the Imperial Chinese North Railway to Russia, as injurious to British interests and prestige, and as tending to confirm and extend over North China the influence of a Power which is certain to discriminate against British shipping and commerce in territories under its control; and trusts that the endeavour of the Russian authorities to thwart its development by occupying land alleged to have been acquired by it on the North Bank of the Peiho will be firmly resisted.[70]

A major interest, not mentioned in the resolution, was that of the Hongkong and Shanghai Bank in the line held as security for its loan and which it had taken pains to repair, against Russian obstruction, following the Boxer disturbances.[71] The stand being taken by the China Association, as Keswick pointed out, was in harmony with the views of the Foreign Office which, he revealed, was "quite determined to insist on the full observance of the conditions laid down in the prospectus" of the Newchwang loan.[72] The second point, Keswick noted, was that British trade in North China and Manchuria was based on treaty rights which the Foreign Office would protect. "We should use every endeavour that, whatever Russia might do, there would be no interference with them."

Anderson mentioned the fear of British interests that Russia would charge differential railway rates if she secured control of the Newchwang line. But that was not the major source of anxiety. As Gundry pointed out, the issue of railway rivalries and consequent territorial stakes was not dead. At one time he had favored handing the Newchwang line to Russia for a concession over the Peking-Hankow. Now not only was the latter lost to Britain, but the Belgian Syndicate which represented the Russo-French group had gained control of the American interest in the Canton-Hankow concession.[73]

By inference Gundry was criticizing the British & Chinese Corporation for its slowness in reaching final agreements on the railway concessions it had obtained in 1898. Keswick, in explanation, advanced the traditional complaint of British financial interests: so long as the British Government refused to accept responsibility for guaranteeing British concessions as other Governments had done, "British concessions could not be operative." Without this "State finance" or guarantee, money would not be forthcoming. That explained why the British & Chinese had been unable to compete for the Canton-Hankow concession which American capital had decided to release. Gundry disputed the point, claiming that the Peking-Hankow had been financed without government guarantee. It was to be an issue for the next several years.

The resolution was passed. But, as members recognized, it did no more than register a protest, for the Government would never take strong action against "Russian aggression." Far from moving in, Britain appeared to Old China Hands to be moving out of the situation. Shanghai telegraphed in panic on August 27, 1901, protesting the proposed reduction of the British garrison at Shanghai to a point where it would be no larger than the German, with the senior command possibly in the hands of the latter. What was more, Germany was building barracks for its troops while British soldiers remained under canvass. There was, Gundry pointed out, a matter of prestige involved which the Government overlooked. Reduction of the British regiment to 750 with that of Germany at 1000 men was a serious matter. "Germany clearly meant to be predomin't, and we shouldn't allow it," Michie warned the Committee. "If they put 1,000 men we should put more, and take care that our commanding officer was always senior to theirs." [74] Shanghai refused to drop the matter until assurances were given by the Foreign Office that there was nothing in the rumor. [75]

It was not a detail about which Old China Hands were concerned but the principle of maintaining the British position. Prestige meant protection as well as the assertion of a commitment by the Government. The same issue was involved in the Russian menace to the Maritime Customs in Manchuria where, *The Times* reported on December 4, 1902, Russia was about to take over customs collection. This, said Gundry, was "merely another step towards annexation." [76] The China Association wrote a vigorous note to the Foreign Office about the matter but obtained no satisfaction.

The proposal to appoint Russian officers to collect Chinese import and export duties on Chinese soil . . . is not only a usurpation of sovereign rights, which Russia would not dare to attempt unless she believed China to be weak and friendless, but it aims a blow at the one well managed branch of the Chinese national income. . . . The entire revenue of the Imperial Maritime Customs is pledged for the service of foreign loans, and it is not possible to look complacently on any interference with any portion of it. . . . It may not be premature to indicate a possible menace in Russian action to the integrity of the present Customs Administration. The jealousy with which other Powers regard the provision that the Inspector General shall be a British subject, and the likelihood that an attempt will be made to transmute the post into an International Commission are matters of common notoriety, and any step likely to lead to a change in the present arrangement are regarded by this Association as being fraught with the greatest danger to commercial interests. [77]

It was not to be the last such observation by the China Association. A sense of insecurity, of having lost ground in China, pervaded all its communications to the Foreign Office. The continued Russian occupation of Southern Manchuria, particularly Newchwang where British commercial interests were concentrated, and which was the terminus of the Chinese line built by British capital, continued to exercise the Association until the outbreak of the Russo-Japanese War. It was regarded not only as "injurious to British trade at that port, but also a violation of British treaty rights." [78]

On October 19, 1903, the Association addressed one of its periodic letters on this point to the Foreign Office, noting that "this Association has been awaiting with increasing anxiety the fulfillment by Russia of her obligations as regards Manchuria and especially as regards her forcible intrusion on the Treaty Port of Newchwang." Over and over again, they noted, Russia had renewed assurances given to the British Ambassador in February, 1901, that Manchuria would be restored to its former position as soon as conditions permitted, and that measures of administration and occupation were temporary. Recently—mainly due to "the energetic remonstrances on the part of the Government of the United States" Gundry noted—the evacuation date had been set at October 8, 1903; but so far no move indicating that she was withdrawing had been made. "Every day that such a situation is allowed to continue must end to weaken our relations with China, because it indicates that this country is willing to submit to its rights and privileges being abused without our insisting upon their being duly observed." [79]

The Foreign Office reply denied the seriousness of the situation, noting that the customs revenues at Newchwang were paid into the Russo-Chinese Bank to the credit of the Chinese Government and that the Customs Commissioner, though a Russian, was under the supervision of Hart. It also denied the implicit charge that the United States had exhibited more zeal than London in pressing for evacuation. The date of October 8, 1903, it noted, "can hardly be attributed to remonstrances on the part of the United States, as the date was fixed by the Russo-Chinese Convention signed as long ago as April 8, 1902." [80]

Such a reply hardly proved satisfactory to the China Association. It was still true that "a treaty port in China is in the hands of Russia." In any event, these details were of minor importance. Again they pressed the significant issue: maintenance of British prestige and position in China. "These details, however, are of comparative unimportance when taken into consideration with the loss of prestige which this country must sustain in the face of China by our not requiring without further delay that the status quo ante shall be restored in Newchwang. . . ." [81] Support of the home Chambers was also enlisted, Liverpool exhibiting particular interest.[82]

Particularly irritating was the suspicion that Great Britain was allowing leadership in Far Eastern affairs to slip into other hands. Both the United States and Japan had concluded agreements with China for the appointment of Consuls at Mukden and Antung, moves calculated to reassert Chinese sovereignty in Manchuria. The China Association drew the following gloomy conclusion:

It is seen that, whereas the foremost position in regard to foreign relations with China was won by this country by an expenditure of blood and treasure far in excess of that incurred by any other Power, and that British interests, as illustrated by trade and shipping, are predominant, yet that at the present juncture the endeavour to hold Russia to her Treaty obligations and to maintain the integrity of China, is being, and has been actively prosecuted by Powers whose interests cannot be compared in extent with those of the British Empire.[83]

It was inevitable that with the outbreak of the Russo-Japanese War in February, 1904, mercantile opinion should favor the Island Empire as the champion of British interests against the Russian menace. There is, in China Association documents, no evidence that mercantile circles influenced the conclusion of the Anglo-Japanese Alliance in January of 1902.[84] Nor—and this is even more significant—did the Association regard the Alliance as having altered the nature of Anglo-Chinese relations; no perceptible effect on British policy or on the mercantile program is reflected in its records. It was only with the coming of war that the business interests saw in Japan a means of frustrating Russian designs in Manchuria. What Japan was doing, a speaker at the Annual Meeting of the China Association remarked, was calculated to "give us that security in North China which we hope will lead to the extension of commerce in Manchuria"; another expressed the hope that Japan would establish the open door in that area if, as was to be hoped, she triumphed.[85]

Of course, it was not out of love for Japan that this sentiment prevailed. Indeed, the suspicion soon gained ground that in North China British interests may have traded one menace for another. As early as March, 1904, the China League cautioned the Foreign Office to guard against a settlement adverse to British interests following the Russo-Japanese War.[86] In October the Associated Chambers of Commerce wrote to the Foreign Office in the same vein.[87] Despite mercantile praise for Japanese "moderation and justice" at the Portsmouth settlement,[88] the suspicion grew that in Manchuria Japanese infiltration was replacing Russian occupation as the major threat to British interests. Shanghai telegraphed in January, 1906, that British residents in Newchwang were alarmed lest the reported Japanese demands for control of the telegraph, railway and industrial enterprises in Manchuria be subversive of the open door. Serious misgivings were aroused by the Japanese refusal to permit British vessels to continue the export trade in cocoons at Tatung. The situation, Shanghai noted, "required vigilance." [89] The China Association pressed the matter at the Foreign Office, adding another instance of Japanese "highhanded action" in restricting the sugar trade to its own nationals. Moreover, it was reported that all officers of the Maritime Customs had been removed and their posts filled by Japanese, while the Japanese administration required that plans of buildings in Manchuria by foreigners should be submitted to it for approval.[90]

Despite Foreign Office assurances that the Japanese "firmly intend to carry out the principle of equal commercial liberty for traders of all nations in Corea and Manchuria," [91] the China Association felt the situation was serious. Nor were they pleased at the Foreign Office attitude that the Customs situation at Newchwang was governed by other factors because it had been in Russian hands and never under the actual control of Hart.[92] For this was equivalent to acquiescence in the surrender of British equality in that area.

At a meeting of the General Committee on December 17, 1906, Sir Cecil Smith recalled the fears he had expressed earlier that year "as to the difficulties we were likely to encounter in the future from the Japanese in China," adding prophetically that "he could not overrate the importance of the matter of the future action of the Japanese in and towards China. . . . He was afraid Japan might prove a lion in the path, and that they, for all their protestations, were not likely to move out of the way in our favor." [93] Sir Walter Hillier, formerly of the Legation at Peking, supported Sir Cecil's views. Byron Brenan thought they were exaggerating the evil and that "for the time" Japan would leave the door "widely enough open for us to pass through," to which Sir Walter retorted: "not with a pack upon our back." It was decided to address a strong letter to the Foreign Office emphasizing the report from British residents in Newchwang that Japan was conspiring to divert the trade to Dalny (Talienwan), at the terminus of the railway.

Intermittent protests about Japanese action followed, but the China Association, itself, was not of one mind on the issue involved. One faction, led by Gundry, maintained that so long as Britain insisted on preponderance in the Yangtze, Japanese preference in Manchuria must be recognized. A memorandum from British residents in Newchwang advocating establishment of an International Settlement to counter Japanese monopoly was not forwarded to the Foreign Office because of Gundry's argument that it would weaken traditional British insistence on predominance in the Settlement at Shanghai. What Britain did in Shanghai Japan should be permitted to do in Manchuria.[94]

Mercantile concern with the maintenance of British prestige in the face of the changing situation brought about by the Russo-Japanese war was expressed in yet another matter. Although the China Association had been none too enthusiastic about the acquisition of Weihaiwei, the fear that Japanese occupation of Port Arthur would terminate the lease of Weihaiwei (originally leased so long as Russia held Port Arthur) stirred the General Committee as early as May, 1904. Renewal of the lease and readjustment of its terms to take into account Japanese occupation of Port Arthur was pressed on the Foreign Office. The reasons given were unique: the increasing importance of the North Pacific trade, and Weihaiwei's use as a naval repair and supply base, and as a rest center for naval personnel. Its commercial advantages were not mentioned; but the motive behind the Association's move was clearly set forth: "Too much importance cannot be attached to the principle that when the British flag has once been hoisted on any territory in China, no retirement can possibly take place from that territory without serious loss of prestige, which will affect our relations with the Government and people of the country in almost every direction." [95] A similar warning was repeated some months later when news arrived that Port Arthur had fallen into Japanese hands.

Despite Foreign Office assurances that the importance of the issue was realized, agitation continued throughout 1905. The China League stirred up the home Chambers and Liverpool addressed Lord Landsdowne, urging renewal of the Weihaiwei lease "for the better protection of British commerce in the neighboring seas." [96] Shanghai repeated its concern in November and the China Association again approached the Foreign Office. Sir Cecil Smith revealed to the General Committee that while the Foreign Office and Colonial Office favored retention of Weihaiwei, the Admiralty opposed it as a naval station: it was thought this was due to the personal inconvenience suffered by the Captain of the *Barfleur,* stationed there in mid-winter, who had returned an unfavorable report.[97] Members again urged renewal of the lease if only on the ground that "we might not always be friends with Japan." Assurances were received shortly thereafter and when it became evident that Whitehall had no intention of moving out of Weihaiwei the issue was dropped.

These sporadic outbursts by the China Association, this intermittent concern with the maintenance of British prestige, but reflected mercantile fears that the China dream had finally been dissipated. The grand schemes of 1899 and 1900 which envisaged a British protectorate of the Yangtze and British leadership in the fiscal and administrative reform of China were gradually dropped. Insurgent resentment was bitter, but the China Association, under the leadership of the representatives of the British & Chinese Corporation, soft-pedalled any protest against the Foreign Office policy of international collaboration and limited liability in China. Whitehall would accept no further commitments. This was clearly evident from the progress, or lack of it, in the implementation of the railway concessions obtained in 1898. The British Government would neither guarantee the loans nor would it bring pressure to bear on the Chinese to grant loan conditions which would have secured control of the railways by the British company. Consequently, flotations were delayed, as the Hongkong and Shanghai Bank was convinced that investors would refuse to risk their capital under such conditions. Of the five concessions secured by the British & Chinese Corporation in 1898 not one had been advanced to the point of a final loan agreement in 1903. Meanwhile, the Belgian Syndicate had proceeded with the construction of the Peking-Hankow and had its eye on the Canton-Hankow trunk line. It was further rumored in the spring of 1903 that this Syndicate was actively pressing for the concession of the Honan line from Kaifeng to Chengtu, and the report that the application of a British company for the line from Sinyang to Chengtu had been denied profoundly stirred the Shanghai Committee.[98] This line ran parallel to the Yangtze and Shanghai emphasized the menace to the British sphere.

The China Association earnestly pressed the matter on the attention of the Foreign Office, "deeming it to be of utmost importance to British interests and to the maintenance of the British sphere of influence that any railway running from East to West in the region of the Yangtze Valley should be under British control to the exclusion of all other nationals." [99] The Foreign Office, without committing itself on the "sphere" element in the Association's argument, assured it that British interests were in fact receiving official support:

His Majesty's Government are quite alive to the importance of securing for British enterprise the concession for any railway running from East to West in the region of the Yangtze Valley. This Department is in communication with the British and Chinese Corporation and with the Peking Syndicate on the subject and His Majesty's Chargé d'affaires at Peking has been instructed to support the application of the Representatives of the two companies in China.[100]

Keswick, too, assured the General Committee that the Government was "earnest in support of British enterprise," and that delay had originally been caused by German protest against encroachment on their sphere, but that the matter had been settled jointly by the Peking Syndicate and the British & Chinese Corporation for the construction of a railway from Pukow (opposite Nanking) to Sinyang and thence to

Chengtu. It was all part of an agreement reached with German interests with regard to sharing the Tientsin-Pukow (formerly the Tientsin-Chinkiang) concession.[101]

But the dissidents were not reassured. Delay in signing the final agreements for the Shanghai-Nanking and Canton-Kowloon lines had now lasted more than five years. The Hongkong Committee wrote again on December 12, 1903, complaining of the delay in the Canton-Kowloon line, suggesting an alternate route if, as had been suggested, surveys had encountered engineering difficulties. Pressed for an explanation, Keswick said everything depended on the signature of the Shanghai-Nanking Agreement which was to serve as a model for the other contracts. He attributed delay to the state of affairs in China owing to the Boxer disturbances and the hesitation of the British Government in pressing China to agree to British control of the line as a security measure. Moreover, in the case of the Canton-Kowloon line, a portion ran through British territory and the Corporation was approaching the Government for a special guarantee on that section.[102]

Gundry, only partially exonerating the British & Chinese Corporation and the Foreign Office, noted in his Annual Report to the membership that while railways "in construction under guidance of the continental powers" had made some progress, "railways which are concessions to British interests have lacked progress" owing to political obstacles. It had been "almost impossible" to get conditions framed so as to admit of a prospectus being issued under the British Companies Act for the guidance of investors owing to lack of sufficient security and reluctance of the British Government to advance an official guarantee. Such conditions had, however, finally been secured in the Shanghai-Nanking Agreement, but the outbreak of the Russo-Japanese War had put a stop to the loan issue.[103]

The Shanghai-Nanking Railway Agreement was the sole British concession contract with which Old China Hands were satisfied. It provided for a loan—it should be emphasized again that all British concessions were loan contracts and not outright titles to railway enterprises—by the British & Chinese Corporation of a sum up to £3,250,000, secured by Imperial bonds at 5 percent, and to be taken up by the Corporation at the profitable figure of 90. The loan was secured by a first mortgage on the entire undertaking, including land, rolling stock, and revenue, with the Corporation appointing trustees for the bondholders. The construction and operation of the line was to be in the hands of a Board appointed by Chinese authorities but with two British members representing the Corporation. Bonds to the extent of two and a quarter mil-

lion pounds were issued in London in July, 1904, and the construction
of the line commenced in the fall.[104]

This was regarded as the first real triumph of British finance, but it
was soon forgotten in the series of protests which continued to flow from
Hongkong over delay in the Canton-Kowloon line. Keswick explained
that this could be attributed to difference with the Chinese over questions of management and control and division of profits. The portion
running through British territory would be more costly to build and
ought therefore to receive a larger share of the profits. Moreover, the
British & Chinese Corporation insisted on representation on the Board
of Control until the entire cost of the line had been met.[105]

Criticism from Hongkong because of the "inaction on the part of
British concessionaires" continued throughout 1905, it "being strongly
felt that if Hongkong was to remain the distributing centre for South
China railway communication between the colony and Canton was
essential." [106] The Hongkong Committee telegraphed in alarm that
American interests were endeavoring to obtain a concession for a deep-
water port near Whampoa (Canton) as the terminus for a trunk line to
Hankow. Keswick checked with the Foreign Office, which denied the
rumor,[107] and assured the General Committee that progress on the
Canton-Kowloon line was being made. The Foreign Office, too, in response to the Hongkong letter of April 21, 1905, renewed assurances
of support:

As you are aware, negotiations are at present in progress between the British
and Chinese Corporation and the Chinese Government for the conclusion of
the Final Agreement for the Canton-Kowloon railway and the Minister at Peking has been instructed to make it clear to the Chinese Government that His
Majesty's Government expect the matter to be settled without any undue
delay.[108]

An agreement was finally arrived at on March 7, 1907, approximately
on the same terms as the Shanghai-Nanking Agreement, with the important exception, however, that control of the line was vested not in a
joint Board but in "a Chinese managing director (appointed by the
Viceroy) with whom will be associated a British engineer-in-chief and a
British chief accountant." [109]

The significant note in all these negotiations was that for Old China
Hands the railway question had been transformed from a problem of
international rivalries to one of making headway against Chinese obstruction. It was the ancient complaint: that the Foreign Office was too
reluctant to apply pressure on the Chinese. On October 23, 1905, the

China Association had again found it necessary to address the Foreign Office (against the advice of Keswick and the collaborationists) about delay in construction of the Canton-Kowloon line.

The delay is understood to be due to sheer obstructiveness, His Majesty's Minister having been unable to obtain the signature of the Chinese Government on account of the alleged opposition of the populace which there is reason to believe factitious. Intrigue of the kind is no novelty in China; but it is believed that no notice would have been taken in Peking of the agitation had it been directed against any enterprise favoured by the Imperial Government, and it seems unreasonable that it should be allowed to hinder the fulfillment of a contract already agreed upon and recognised in its preliminary stage.[110]

The implication was obvious. According to the Association, British interests, as usual, were getting a traditional run-around due to lack of zeal on the part of the Foreign Office. All that was needed was firmness, that which mercantile circles had been urging for years. Other Powers seemed to get what they wanted: "The concession made about the same time to Germany to construct a railway in Shantung . . . was promptly carried into effect." [111]

Keswick, too, in his apologia to the General Committee over the delay noted that "Chinese inertia" was to blame. Peking had not yet appointed an official to negotiate with representatives of the Corporation, and when the latter applied for transfer of the negotiations to Canton it had been denied. "He thought that the Foreign Office was beginning to realize that much of the abuse which had been heaped on the British & Chinese Corporation for delay was undeserved, and that even the support of the Colonial and Foreign Offices and the British Minister could not readily overcome the inertia of the Chinese." [112]

No more fitting commentary on mercantile disillusionment at the end of this period can be quoted than the letter which Gundry, then President of the China Association, addressed to Sir Edward Grey, the Foreign Minister, in the mid-summer of 1906, when Chinese recalcitrance appeared to be holding up all progress in the implementation of British concessions:

Experience has shown that the period of compliance in China has rarely exceeded, long, the period of pressure. It is little surprising, therefore, that the lessons of the Chino-Japanese war and of the Boxer campaign should be already obliterated. It is historically consistent, even, that Peking officials should feel their amour propre injured because Japan has declared certain places in Manchuria open to trade; the irony of such pretension, in regard to territory which they neither tried nor were able to defend, being characteristically unperceived.

But it was perhaps not foreseen that the sense of security imparted by the Anglo-Japanese treaty would inspire an attitude of resistance to foreigners and foreign enterprise reminiscent of fifty years ago. Yet that is, obviously, the attitude which has been engendered—an attitude consistent with the traditional bearing of China towards foreigners. . . .

Regarded in this light, the failure of the Imperial Government to implement engagements regarding the construction of railways, the persistent intrigues against the position of the Shanghai Municipality, and the recent encroachment on the administration of the Imperial Maritime Customs appear to the Association to assume graver significance.

Viewed singly, opposition even to the construction by a British company of the Soochow-Hangchow Railway might be pleaded as the expression of a patriotic desire that China should make her own railways herself. And Tang Shao-yi seems to have explained the appointment of himself and Tieh-Liang as Imperial High Commissioners of the Imperial Maritime Customs as a mere titular assertion of national dignity, implying no design either against the status of the service or the appropriation of receipts.

Viewed collectively, however, such incidents present the appearance of a policy of extrusion which may entail serious difficulties if it is not firmly resisted.

China has always desired to keep foreigners out; but the West decided long ago that national isolation was inadmissible. . . .

It is regrettable that the necessity for making these representations, after fifty years of Treaty relations, should still exist. The mere fact places China in an exceptional position. This Association feels constrained to urge again the importance of never yielding rights which have been secured by Treaty or by less formal negotiation. Any tendency in that direction is regarded by the Chinese as a sign of weakness and a base for further encroachments. . . .

The Chinese character is not about to change, and the experience of the past may guide us still.[113]

This broadside, which might properly be labelled "Confessions of an Old China Hand," marks the end of an era and an admission of failure. For, as Gundry complained, the problem had been the same for fifty years, from the mercantile point of view: Chinese backwardness and "obstructiveness" was the enemy and the sole solution lay in foreign pressure and British willingness to assume the responsibility of suzerainty. But all efforts to enlist support for the mercantile maximum program had failed; and Gundry's letter is as much a swan song as an appeal for further support. The Foreign Office policy of limited liability and of restricting its support to the chosen instrument, represented by the British & Chinese Corporation, continued. The fact that the latter was given a free hand was interpreted by Old China Hands not as a triumph for British business interests, but on the contrary as a betrayal of the "national" program which Old China Hands had been advancing since 1869 and more particularly since 1899.[114] This was their interpretation of the agreement in 1908 between the Corporation and German financial interests for a sharing of the Tientsin-Pukow line in a contract which loosened the security requirements written into the Shanghai-Nanking Agreement. This international collaboration, extended in 1909 to embrace the "Four Nations Syndicate" (Great Britain, France, Germany, United States) for sharing the Hukwang loan and expanded three years later into the famous Consortium for financing the reorganization of the Chinese Government,[115] was regarded by the Insurgents as a defeat and betrayal. It was the final abdication by the British Government of its position of leadership in the Far East, according to Old China Hands.

Moreover, it was interpreted as the natural sequence of the defeat of the Insurgents in the struggle waged in the 1900's. For a short period following the formation of the China League in 1900 and the vigorous stand taken by the Association under Gundry's prodding the feud between Collaborationists and Insurgents had simmered down. But, as it became evident that the action of the General Committee was no more than a gesture of appeasement, Shanghai became disturbed. Under the leadership of Charles Dudgeon, for many years head of the Shanghai Branch, and of J. O. P. Bland, publicist and free-lance business man, the cry was raised at the end of 1903 that the London Committee was selling out the broader interests of British merchants and entrepreneurs, by continuing to pursue its tactic of collaboration with the Foreign Office.

The opening gun was fired by the Shanghai Committee in January, 1904, with the passing of a resolution calling on the London leadership "to broaden the basis of the China Association's work," by amalgamation with the more vigorous China League or by engaging "on broader and more independent" lines in relations with the home Chambers and "with such public bodies and individuals as are generally identified with British interests in the Far East." [116] So that there might be no mistake as to intent, Dudgeon wrote privately to Gundry in a letter dated December 24, 1903, that Shanghai members had grown increasingly critical of those in the London Committee who had "axes to grind."

The implication in the Shanghai charge was that the London Committee was content to abandon the commercial interests of the treaty ports in order to protect the more narrow interests of the concessionaires. The General Committee refused to take this move seriously and voted not to join the League or to adopt "an attitude of hostility towards the

Government" as this "would impair the usefulness of the China Association." Nothing, it was persuaded, would be gained by "attempting to drive the Foreign Office to adopt any particular line of action." [117]

Rebuffed, Shanghai threatened mass action, notifying the London Committee that a general meeting was being called at which the leaders of the Shanghai branch intended to submit their resignations. In his defense Keswick reiterated to the General Committee his conviction that "it was a mistake to think that the London Committee had not always done their best to lay before the Foreign Office every subject for reasonable complaint or any matter concerning the welfare and promotion of British interests in the Far East." [118] But, as all were aware, this was not the point at issue. Basically the question was: whom did the China Association represent, the totality of British interests in China, as it pretended, or the vested financial and mercantile interests in the British & Chinese Corporation? Pressing the issue, Bland resigned as Secretary of the Shanghai Committee.[119] Gundry's efforts to have Bland reconsider his resignation failed, but Dudgeon promised to keep the Shanghai branch together until he surveyed the situation personally in London. The General Committee held fast, attributing the tempest to the China League and the parliamentary ambitions of the China bloc in the House of Commons.[120]

This attempt to dismiss the entire matter only added another grievance to the long list drawn up in Shanghai. It was felt that the General Committee was intent on pigeon-holing the affair by its refusal to submit the issue to a general meeting. Byron Brenan, who had been present at the Shanghai meeting which adopted the resolution, told the General Committee that the feeling in Shanghai was high and that if London's answer was unfavorable, the Shanghai branch would sever its connection with the central body.

Both Dudgeon and Bland returned to London and appeared at a special meeting of the General Committee to discuss "the difference arisen between the London and Shanghai Committees." [121] Keswick, as the principal object of attack, released the chair to Sir Alfred Dent after understating the issue as arising from "the impression prevailing that London had not shown that active and intelligent representation of the interests of the Association; also that there had been a lack of independence in our action, and . . . an absence of that force and moving power which are so essential."

Dudgeon, who opened the case for Shanghai, noted that the dissension may have arisen from London's failure to appreciate the "new conditions in Shanghai" and the low estate to which British influence had fallen.

British influence, formerly paramount, was no longer so. Every question that arose became a matter of "political intrigue" and of international jealousy, and in these changed conditions . . . a reconsideration of the hitherto policy of the Association is advisable; we believe that the potentiality of the China Association could be more effectually used by stepping beyond the narrow line to which it has confined itself, lines which limit membership to those with direct connection with China, and which have been interpreted as confining our connection with our Government and our officials to private representation.

Again Dudgeon urged the sense of the resolution, that the Association broaden its scope to form "a strong expression of public opinion to move the Government." Shanghai wished the issue submitted to a general meeting of the membership. Sir Cecil Smith replied that no such meeting had been called because there was no one to speak on the side of Shanghai. All were agreed that there was no point in joining the China League. "I am certain," he concluded, "that so long as government is conducted in the form in which it is in the present time, more is to be got by friendly relations with the Foreign Office than by attacking it in the public press." Dudgeon's attitude, however, was strongly supported by Michie and Sir Edward Ackroyd who represented the manufacturing North.

Dudgeon in his argument had pointed toward conciliation; Bland showed no such scruples. The Shanghai resolution, he opened, was concerned with the "better promotion of British interests, national, political and commercial," while the chief object of the London Committee had been to maintain the "social side" of the Association. This, of course, was nonsense, but Bland proceeded to show what he was aiming at. History had shown the need for the creation of "a definite British policy in China." ("When has there ever been one?" Sir Cecil interjected.) Reviewing events since 1895, Bland maintained that at no time have "we had an intelligent recognition by our government of the importance of the Chinese question." This was so because it had not been under public pressure, for the Foreign Office, he argued, is not the Government.

Even if our relations with the Foreign Office produced entirely satisfactory results, we hold that unless we have an active public opinion which will make the Government move we shall never get any definite recognition of the importance of the Chinese question. The British Government always waits on public opinion and unless someone worries them, they will not act.

With Keswick sitting opposite, Bland then proceeded to charge that the China Association had failed to mobilize public opinion behind a vigorous policy because of the affiliations of its leadership.

Having much to do with the Shanghai resolution [was the conviction that] it was bad for the Association to be actively represented by anyone whose particular or business interests may possibly conflict with the general or wider interests which the China Association was pledged to advance. . . . There were some who had other fish to fry, some were looking for honours and individual advancement. . . . we can hardly expect an independent attitude and fearless criticism of the Foreign Office from anyone who, in another capacity, may be compelled to look to the Foreign Office for assistance and protection.

"It is," he hastened to add, "a matter of principle, not personalities."

The unspoken suspicion which had been buzzing in Old China Hand circles since the formation of the British & Chinese Corporation and its choice by the Foreign Office as the chosen instrument of concession politics was now in the open. The special general meeting of the membership, which the Shanghai insurgents now demanded, was scheduled for July 31, 1905. It did not arouse the interest expected, while the few absent Committee members canvassed by mail stood firmly behind Keswick. Typical comments included the opinion that "the Shanghai malcontents are entirely mistaken in advocating a coercive attitude towards the British Government," and that the remarks regarding the Chairman (Keswick) should be condemned.[122] Another member inquired if the Shanghai representatives had "a mandate to attack the London Committee" and criticized any move toward amalgamation with the China League, "composed of politicians who have personal interests to serve. We can have no alliance with such a body."[123] Sir Thomas Sutherland, M.P., Chairman of the Peninsular & Oriental and one of the founders of the Hongkong and Shanghai Bank, came out firmly against an alliance with "the political." "We are 'Chinamen' and in that capacity removed from all political parties," he noted adding that the Association had done useful work and he was not sure that "any greater progress would have been attained by beating a big drum in the political world."[124]

Fewer than fifty members attended to hear the Shanghai insurgents state their case.[125] Dudgeon added nothing to his earlier remarks to the General Committee except to note that the question had been brewing for some time:

As long ago as 1896, the view began to be expressed in Shanghai that the work of the Association was being conducted on too narrow and confined lines. The close of the Chino-Japanese War had introduced new problems into the Far Eastern question, and political affairs in China had assumed a new and plainly critical aspect, an aspect which seemed to demand the awakening of Great Britain from the complacency with which she was seemingly content to regard her position in China; for it began to be strongly felt that our Government either did not appreciate the situation or that they were too much engaged elsewhere to pay proper attention to it.

The adverse decision in 1900 against merging forces with the China League had not been popular in Shanghai and subsequent attempts to revive the issue had been ignored in London, leading to the present moribund state of the Shanghai branch.

Bland renewed his plea that the China Association intensify its work as a pressure group, for the China question was no longer "of individual but of national interest."

Here in England, as well as in the Far East, those who have realised the gradual undermining of our position, the loss of our opportunities, and the surrender of our natural advantages to our Continental rivals, recognise the fact that our Government, for lack of that pressure of public opinion which is absolutely necessary, fails today, as it has failed in the past, to appreciate the national importance of our interests in the Far East. . . . Government should realise the fact that in China our commercial and political interests are inseparable. . . .

The present policy of the Association—the policy of friendly relations with the Foreign Office and social gatherings—may have been adequate ten years ago, before our rivals had gained the footing which they now hold throughout China; but I submit that it is entirely inadequate today. If we would hold our position we must take a leaf out of the book of our rivals, display some of their energy and obtain some measure of the active Government support which these foreign nations enjoy. . . .

The railway question had been mishandled from the start, Bland claimed, because it had been treated not as a national issue but solely as private undertakings, a view which the Foreign Office was only too glad to adopt. Instead, it must be realized that these are "powerful instruments to advance our commercial interests all over China, and that we should regard them as national, not private enterprises."

The vote was close, but the Insurgents lost (nineteen to eighteen) on Sir Alfred Dent's motion that the Shanghai resolution be not put. From this rebuff the dissidents never recovered. The Shanghai Committee ceased to function for a time, and the London leadership started a search for "anyone of influence in Shanghai who could be relied on to form a new Committee." Sir Cecil Smith suggested that heads of firms in London bring pressure on their representatives in Shanghai with the object of keeping together a branch there.[126] Dudgeon and Bland returned to Shanghai and reported their London reception to an extraordinary meeting on January 5, 1906, where a provisional committee was formed to carry on until the results of the Annual Meeting in London were known. Unless some reorganization of the London leadership occurred the branch agreed to sever relations with the China Association.[127]

Shanghai scored a partial success. Under their pressure Keswick resigned from the London executive,[128] and at the Annual Meeting a constitutional amendment was adopted limiting the terms of President and Chairman to three successive years.[129] Shanghai, somewhat mollified, continued to operate on a provisional basis. But there had been no real retreat in London, for the China Association did not depart from its policy of collaboration. No further attempts were made to mobilize public opinion on a large scale behind that "definite policy" embodying the mercantile maximum program which Shanghai desired. Nor were the plans of 1899 and 1900 which sought to give British predominance in China political substance ever revived. The British & Chinese Corporation continued to serve as the chosen instrument of the Foreign Office in its limited liability policy toward China. The China Association continued to occupy itself with individual issues as they arose, but the dream of a British protectorate was dropped. The defeat of the Insurgents was complete.

X

Retrospect

THE defeat of the Insurgents marked the end of an era. For, although later attempts were made to enlist the support of the Foreign Office on behalf of British interests in China, never again was a concerted effort made by Old China Hands to redirect official policy toward China along the lines advocated by the merchants' memorials of 1869 and the China Association letter of July 13, 1899. Of the grand imperialist scheme which envisaged penetration by British trade and enterprise of the inner reaches of China and saw British official advisers at the side of every Yangtze and South China Viceroy only overtones remained. The half-century conflict between Old China Hands and the Foreign Office over the premises of Anglo-Chinese relations and, consequently, the extent to which British commitments should be pushed, ended without being resolved. But it ended with a definite realization that China would never be another British India; not even an Egypt. With it also there faded the China dream, dear to mercantile hearts, of a fabulous market for trade and enterprise; Pottinger's vision had proved to be a mirage.

What had the conflict been about? Certainly not about the nature of British interests in China; commercial interests, as Balfour repeated, were Britain's "sole interests" there. Nor was the difference over the advisability of protecting trade and enterprise in those regions. Rather the conflict arose when Britain's business-adventurers and policy-makers clashed over the prospects of the China trade and the wisdom of an accelerated penetration and exploitation of its fabulous market. Whitehall rejected the mercantile premise that British interests in the treaty ports, though comparatively small, were capable of almost limitless expansion and therefore warranted the assumption by Government of the commitment to protect and promote those interests to the point, if necessary, of war and the substitution of British for Chinese sovereignty if China collapsed.

Twice the issue had been joined. At the end of the sixties, the merchants saw in treaty revision an opportunity for penetrating Eldorado by British insistence on the right to internal trade and residence, to the navigation of inland waters by foreign steamers, and to railway construction by British enterprise. But, as Alcock emphasized time and again, under a regime of extraterritoriality to make such demands on Peking would imply the British assertion of suzerainty over China. For it would mean the extension of British law into the interior to provide a basis for trade and enterprise and of British police power to protect them. The Board of Trade convinced the Foreign Office that the potentialities of the China market did not warrant the undertaking of such a commitment. The Alcock Convention, consequently, embodied a very limited advance, rejecting the mercantile plea for fundamental reform. Under mercantile pressure it was not ratified, but this did not alter the direction of the official policy of limited commercial reform and "benevolent non-interference" inaugurated after the Treaty of Tientsin. Old China Hands had lost the first round.

Thirty years later the conflict was essentially the same. International rivalry, with its corollary of British exclusion from foreign spheres in the event of China's partition, added an element of urgency to the traditional mercantile program. More than ever it was imperative that China be opened, and in the settlement following the Sino-Japanese War Old China Hands saw the grand occasion for realization of the reforms desired in 1869—steam navigation on inland waterways, penetration of the internal market, and railway construction. The China Association letter of November 2, 1896, however, pointed out that the opening of China would prove meaningless unless the British Government assumed responsibility for fiscal and administrative reform. Thus, although their list of particular commercial concessions was implemented by the Salisbury-MacDonald diplomatic triumphs of 1897 and of 1898, Old China Hands were far from being satisfied. Without a new political basis in China individual commercial concessions could never bear fruit. In the summer of 1899, therefore, the conflict was renewed. Old China Hands advanced a three-point program calling for a British protectorate over the Yangtze Valley through "effective occupation," governmental guarantee of British investment in railway and industrial enterprises, and the fiscal and administrative reform of China, à l'Egypte, under British tutelage. This program Whitehall rejected, convinced that the country would never countenance it. In its place the formula of Balfour, as stated in the House of Commons on April 5, 1898, was adopted: Britain would accept no responsibility for suzerainty, for ruling natives, but it would insist on taking Weihaiwei as "counterpoise" to Kiaochow and Port Arthur. Added to the policy of counterpoise was that of "counter-concession," implemented in the summer of 1898, when five railway concessions were extorted and handed over to the British and Chinese Corporation, representing the vested interest of the Hongkong and Shanghai Bank and Jardine, Matheson & Company.

Only the latter regarded this as even a partial triumph. For the Old China Hands the policy of counterpoise and counter-concession involved the outright repudiation of their own program. It meant—and later events during the Boxer affair proved the point to their satisfaction— that the British Government had refused to depart from its policy of limited liability and limited commitments in China. Far from being a departure from traditional policy, as it is generally interpreted, Britain's acquisition of Weihaiwei and the railway concessions of the Yangtze were seen by the treaty ports as belated and inadequate responses to Continental gambits in the China game. For them it was final evidence that Whitehall continued to accept the premises of 1869: British interests in China, present and potential, were comparatively minor and therefore warranted neither war nor the assumption of sovereignty. The fact that the country was so concerned with the Boer War that it had no time for China affairs but confirmed their conviction that Old China Hands had become the victims of the great underestimation.

The Insurgents among them (as they have been termed in this book) realized fully the nature of the political problem with which they were confronted; it was the same as that with which any pressure group is faced. Unless they could convince public opinion and the Government that their interests were "national interests," their cause was marked for defeat. In Rousseauist terms, their problem was that of translating their particular will into the general will. They must persuade the country that not alone their profits but national interests were at stake; and that national interest demanded the commitment of national force to the attainment of their goal. In the final analysis, any study of pressure group influence on the formation of foreign policy will center on this point. And that is the contemporary significance of this study. No matter how eager the Foreign Office might be to promote and protect vested interests in the treaty ports, the Government's refusal to accept the premise of the mercantile community about the national importance of the China market made inevitable the failure of Old China Hand politics. It explains, too, the British Government's refusal to go beyond a policy of counterpoise and limited commitments. In sum, it solves the historical riddle of why China never became another India.

Notes

INTRODUCTION

1. China Association, Correspondence, Misc. Series, No. 3, Shanghai Branch to Byron Brenan, May 31, 1901.
2. Thus, M. Dabry, French Consul at Hankow, complaining to M. Libois, Procureur-General of the *Missions Etrangères*, of the difficulties encountered in attempting to secure a French concession at Hankow, wrote on July 1, 1863: "Figurez vous cher père que si je n'étais pas arrivé au mois du janvier, il ne serait pas resté un seul pouce de terrain pour le commerce français. . . . Nos braves alliés ont pris la plus grande partie de ce qui était bon à prendre en attendant que la Chine leur accorde une concession—ils sont convaincus que le mond entier leur appartient et partant de ce principe ils agissent en conquérants. . . ."—*Missions Etrangères*, Correspondence, vol. 330, p. 350 (Ms.).
3. C. F. Remer, *The Foreign Trade of China* (Shanghai, 1926), p. 231.
4. C. S. See, *The Foreign Trade of China* (New York, 1919), chart opp. page 282.
5. Remer, op. cit., p. 233.

CHAPTER I

ABBREVIATIONS AND SOURCES

B.T.: Original manuscripts in archives of the British Board of Trade, London. Reference is to volumes as titled and arranged in the Library of the Board of Trade, and to date of document.

B.F.S.P.: *British and Foreign State Papers*.

F.O.: Original manuscripts of Foreign Office documents in archives of the British Public Records Office, London. Reference is to collection series and volume, and date of document. *E.g.*, F.O. 17/287 refers to Foreign Office, series 17 (diplomatic documents pertaining to Anglo-Chinese relations), volume 287.

J.M. & Co.: Original manuscript correspondence in the files of Jardine, Matheson and Co. (Hongkong Office), now in archives of University Library, Cambridge University. Reference is to original Letter Books or boxed series as arranged by Curator.

Manch. C.C.: Original manuscript minutes of proceedings of the Manchester

Chamber of Commerce, Manchester. Reference is to volumes as originally bound.

P.P.: Parliamentary Papers.

NOTES

1. A. J. Sargent, *Anglo-Chinese Commerce and Diplomacy* (Oxford, 1907), pp. 132–33.

2. J.M. & Co., Box G.B., 1846–50, Robberds & Co. to Jardine, Matheson & Co., March 31, 1846.

3. Though neither a branch nor a partner in its relation to Jardine, Matheson & Co., the London firm of Matheson & Co. acted as the commercial and financial *alter ego* of the Far Eastern house. Matheson & Co. served as the financial clearing house and commercial agency for Jardine's.

4. J.M. & Co., Box G.B., 1846–50, Geo. Armstrong (Liverpool) to Jardine, Matheson & Co., May 23, 1846.

5. Ibid., reported by Jardine's Manchester agent, August 22, 1848.

6. J.M. & Co., Box G.B., 1846–50, Jardine, Matheson & Co. to Matheson & Co., London, and R. R. Calvert, Manchester, June 22, 1850.

7. P.P., Report from the Select Committee of the Commons on Commercial Relations with China, with Minutes of Evidence. 1847, V.

8. Loc. cit.

9. Ibid., #2706 in Minutes of Evidence.

10. #2707 in Minutes of Evidence.

11. Manch. C.C., *Proceedings*, 1849–1858, May 22, 1849.

12. Ibid.

13. Ibid., July 19, 1849.

14. Loc. cit.

15. Manch. C.C., *Proceedings*, 1849–1858, Feb. 11, 1850.

16. Ibid.

17. Ibid., June 13, 1850.

18. Ibid., January 19, 1854.

19. Ibid., January 26, 1854.

20. J.M. & Co., London Box, 1847–51, Thomas Ross to Matheson & Co., March 2, 1850.

21. J.M. & Co., Letter Book, 1851, Hongkong, Jardine, Matheson & Co., to R. R. Calvert, Feb. 26, 1851.

22. F.O. 17/287, Elgin to Foreign Office, March 31, 1858. A Foreign Office minute on the envelope reads: "I think your Lordship would be interested by the inclosure. It appears it was not sent home by Sir G. Bonham."

23. F.O. 17/287, March 31, 1858.

24. Evident throughout his papers. See, *e.g.*, T. Walrond, *Letters and Journals of James, Eighth Earl of Elgin* (London, 1872), pp. 305, 325, and *passim*.

25. Ibid., p. 305.

26. F.O. 17/287, included in Elgin's dispatch, dated March 31, 1858.

27. F.O. 17/287 contains the original of this famous address. Also in Walrond, op. cit., p. 240.

28. See, *e.g.*, memorial of East India & China Association of Liverpool, cited in Sargent, op. cit., p. 101.

29. P.P., Correspondence relative to the Earl of Elgin's Special Missions to China and Japan, 1857–1859. 1859 Sess. 2, XXXIII, No. 49.

30. Ibid., No. 50. Memorial of British Chamber of Commerce, Shanghai.

31. F.O. 228/318, Memorandum by Lord Elgin, Feb. 8, 1862.

32. Text in B.F.S.P., 1857–1858, vol. 48, p. 47f.

33. Cf. note 30.

34. J.M. & Co., Letter Book, 1858–59, August 9, 1858.

35. J.M. & Co., Letter Book, Hongkong, 1860–61, Jardine, Matheson & Co., to Matheson & Co., Dec. 31, 1860.

36. J.M. & Co., London Box, 1859, John Thacker to Jardine, Matheson & Co., Sept. 15, 1859.

37. Quoted in Sargent, op. cit., p. 145.

38. See, *e.g.*, Jardine, Matheson & Co. to Matheson & Co., May 1, 1861, Letter Book, 1861–62; R. Barbour to Jardine, Matheson & Co., Sept. 28, 1862, Box G.B., 1862–63; R. R. Calvert to Jardine, Matheson & Co., Dec. 27, 1862, Ibid.

39. J.M. & Co., Letter Book, Hongkong-Europe, 1862. Jardine, Matheson & Co. to Sam Mendel (Manchester), July 26, 1862.

40. J.M. & Co., Letter Book, 1861–62, to Matheson & Co., May 1, 1861.

41. Ibid.

42. Sargent, op. cit., p. 148.

43. B.T., Gen. Dept., Letters Written 1856, 1004/56, Nos. 547, 548, 673, and 791. The correspondence on the subject is voluminous.

44. Ibid., No. 673.

45. B.T., Gen. Dept., Letters Written July–Dec. 1857, No. 776, December 3, 1857.

46. J.M. & Co., Letter Book, March 1861–Jan. 1862.

47. Ibid., Jardine, Matheson & Co. to Matheson & Co., June 28, 1861.

48. Loc. cit.

49. F.O. 228/298, Glasgow Chamber of Commerce to Lord Russell, November 14, 1861.

50. J.M. & Co., Box. G.B. 1862–63, W. Paton to Jardine, Matheson & Co., January 25, 1862.

51. F.O. 228/298, Hongkong Chamber of Commerce to Glasgow Chamber.

52. J.M. & Co., Letter Book, Honkong-Europe 1862, to Matheson & Co., February 16, 1862.

53. B.T., Gen. Dept., Letters Written Jan.–June 1862, February 15, 1862.

54. J.M. & Co., Box G.B. 1862–63, W. Paton to Jardine, Matheson & Co., January 25, 1862.

55. Manch. C.C., *Proceedings* 1858–1867, January 8, 1862.

56. Ibid., January 27, 1862.

57. F.O. 228/318, February 8, 1862.

58. B.T., Gen. Dept., Letters Written Jan.–June 1862, B.T. to F.O., February 15, 1862.

59. November 29, 1862.

60. December 11, 1862.

61. F.O. 17/390, Bruce to Foreign Office, Jan. 20, 1863.

62. Excerpts enclosed by Bruce, ibid.

63. P. 20.

64. Full text in B.T., Gen. Dept., 114/1863, Shanghae Chamber of Commerce to Lord Russell, September 4, 1862.

65. Ibid., Bruce to Russell, September 17, 1862.

66. Ibid., #130, Bruce to Russell, September 22, 1862.

67. Ibid.

68. F.O. 17/358.

69. B.T., Gen. Dept., 114/1863, minute initialed "L.M. 10 Feb '63."

70. B.T., op. cit., draft letter to Foreign Office, February 17, 1863.

71. Ibid.

72. F.O. 228/337. Hammond to Shanghai Chamber of Commerce, February 19, 1863.

73. The legend of a sudden shift in policy as a result of the Burlinghame mission and the Clarendon Declaration became part of mercantile folklore and will be explored in the next chapter. F. W. Williams, *Anson Burlinghame and the First Chinese Mission to the Foreign Powers* (New York, 1912) perpetuates this thesis and it has been repeated from authority to authority. Cf. R. McCordock, *British Far Eastern Policy* (New York, 1931), p. 66: "The Burlinghame Mission and the accession of the Liberal Government in 1868 produced a change in Great Britain's Chinese policy."

74. F.O. 228/297, Russell to Consul W. H. Fittock, January 11, 1861.

75. F.O. 228/319, Bruce reprimanded Consul W. R. Gingell at Hankow for siding with British subjects who attended, uninvited, a celebration at the local prefect's pavilion, where they were insulted and beaten. July 2, 1862.

76. F.O. 228/319, Bruce to Consul Forrest, July 2, 1862.

77. Ibid., October 7, 1862.

78. F.O. 17/390. G. P. Browne to Moresby, November 25, 1863.

79. See, *e.g.,* Russell's severe censure of Consul Gardner's independent use of force to redress local grievances. F.O. 228/379, January 26, 1865.

80. F.O. 228/425. Stanley to Alcock, January 8, 1867.

CHAPTER II

ABBREVIATIONS AND SOURCES

A.C.C.: Associated Chambers of Commerce of Great Britain, Annual Reports, London.

B.T.: Board of Trade, London. Manuscript records.

F.O.: Foreign Office documents in archives of the Public Records Office, London.

J.M. & C.: Jardine, Matheson & Co. archives, Cambridge.

M.E.: *Missions Etrangères* archives, Rue du Bac, Paris.

P.P.: Parliamentary Papers.

NOTES

1. J.M. & Co., Letter Box, Europe, 1865–66, to Matheson & Co., August 28, 1865.

2. Loc. cit.

3. F.O. 17/503, Memorandum on Shanghai Trade, 1867.

4. J.M. & Co., Letter Book 1865–66, May 12, 1866.

5. Ibid.

6. J.M. & Co., Letter Book 1866–67, Jan. 1, 1867.

7. F.O. 17/503.

8. F.O. 17/558.

9. Enclosed in F.O. 17/562.

10. F.O. 17/507.

11. F.O. 17/504. Canton Trade Report enclosed in Alcock to Hammond, June 28, 1868.

12. F.O. 17/532, September 22, 1869; F.O. 17/534, Reports of Consuls at Amoy, Foochow and Hankow. See also correspondence in P.P., China No. 3, 1870, Reports on Consular Establishments in China, 1869.

13. F.O. 17/534.

14. F.O. 17/533, enclosed in Alcock's dispatch of October 11, 1869.

15. F.O. 17/571.

16. Ibid., British merchants at Chefoo to Alcock, May 18, 1867.

17. Ibid., Address by British merchants at Chinkiang, May 6, 1867.

18. F.O. 17/571, Alcock's reply to Kiukiang merchants, May 6, 1867.

19. F.O. 17/571, Stanley to Alcock, August 17, 1867.

20. F.O. 17/571.

21. B.T., Commercial Dept., Letters Written 1867, No. 425, Aug. 28, 1867.

22. F.O. 17/571.

23. B.T., Commercial Dept., Letters Written 1868, Jan. 8, 1868.

24. For texts of memorials and F.O. comment see F.O. 17/571; also in P.P., Memorials addressed by Chambers of Commerce in China to the British Minister at Peking on Revision of Treaty of Tientsin, 1867–68, vol. 73.

25. F.O. 17/571.

26. Louis Mallet at the Board of Trade scribbled a furious minute of approval at this point in his reading of Winchester's dispatch.

27. The Hongkong Memorial was sent to the Colonial Office rather than to the Minister at Peking. Robertson, the British Consul at Canton, forwarded a copy to Hammond at the Foreign Office with his own views added as marginal commentary. F.O. 17/571, October 30, 1867.

28. F.O. 17/571, Alcock to Foreign Office, Nov. 27, 1867.

29. F.O. 17/571, Jardine, Matheson & Co. to Governor of Hongkong, Nov. 28, 1867.

30. Alcock to Stanley, Nov. 15, 1867, ibid.

31. F.O. 17/572, December 23, 1867.

32. See excerpt in F.O. 17/572.

33. F.O. 17/572. Shanghai Chamber of Commerce to Chambers of Commerce in Great Britain, Jan. 24, 1868.

34. P.P., China No. 5 (1871), vol. 70, Belfast Chamber of Commerce, Mar. 6, 1868, p. 100. See also memorials of other Chambers, ibid., Nos. 6–17, 30, 45, and 47.

35. A.C.C., *Annual Report*, 1868, London.

36. Liverpool Chamber of Commerce, *Semi-Annual Report*, August 1868. Resolution adopted was passed at May meeting. For text of letter to Hammond see P.P.. China No. 5 (1871), No. 47.

37. F.O. 17/572, Alcock to Stanley, Jan. 1, 1868. Confidential.

38. Ibid.

39. U.S., *Foreign Affairs*, 1868, II, Burlinghame to Seward, Dec. 14, 1867, p. 494. The standard, though somewhat idealistic, account of the Burlinghame Mission remains F. W. Williams, *Anson Burlinghame and the First Chinese Mission to Foreign Powers* (New York, 1912).

40. F.O. 17/496, January 6, 1868.

41. London *Daily News*, Feb. 28, 1868. Quoted in Williams, op. cit., pp. 92–93.

42. F.O. 228/446, Stanley to Alcock, Jan. 27, 1868. See also Stanley to Lyons (Paris), Feb. 8, 1868.

43. F.O. 17/572, Alcock to Stanley, May 5, 1868.

44. Cited by Alcock, ibid.

45. F.O. 17/572.

46. Ibid.

47. F.O. 17/497, Alcock to Winchester, May 19, 1868.

48. Ibid.

49. F.O. 17/498, enclosed in Alcock to Stanley, June 20, 1868 (Separate & Confidential).

50. Ibid.

51. F.O. 17/498, loc. cit.

52. Quoted in Williams, op. cit., p. 136.

53. *The Westminster Review,* New Ser., vol. 37, 1870, p. 181.

54. *North China Herald,* "A Retrospect of Political and Commercial Affairs in China, 1868 to 1872" (Shanghai, 1873), p. 8.

55. Published in Shanghai, 1872, p. 891.

56. Ibid., p. 287.

57. Williams, op. cit., pp. 141–42.

58. U.S., *Treaties and Conventions concluded between the United States of America and Other Powers* (Washington, 1889), p. 181.

59. F.O. 17/499, Alcock to Stanley, Sept. 26, 1868 (Separate & Confidential).

60. Ibid.

61. See, *e.g.,* Prince Kung to Alcock, Dec. 5, 1868, F.O. 17/574.

62. H. Cordier, *Histoire des Rélations de la Chine avec les Puissances Occidentales* (Paris, 1901), vol. I, p. 295.

63. "The policy which Mr. Burlinghame was assured H.M. Government wished to observe towards China . . . is no other than the policy which has been carefully observed since the ratification of the Treaty of Tientsin in 1860. It was uniformly adhered to by my predecessor Sir. F. Bruce, by Mr. Wade as Chargé d'affaires before my arrival and by myself since that date." Alcock to Foreign Office, March 29, 1868, F.O. 17/520.

64. And which accounts for Cordier's observation: "Jamais pour les agents européens à Peking, la situation ne fut plus pénible que pendant les mois qui suivirent l'arrivée de Burlinghame à Londres. . . . Alcock, mélancolique, constatait qu'il avait préparé sa propre ruine et qu'une révision favorable du traité de 1858 devenait une chimère en présence de l'attitude des hauts dignitaires chinois." Cordier, op. cit., pp. 295–96.

65. F.O. 17/503, October 3, 1868.

66. "I find a most wholesome alarm prevalent amongst all classes as regards the advent and intentions of H.M. Ships." Medhurst to Alcock, Nov. 6, 1868, F.O. 17/503.

67. F.O. 17/500, Oct. 12, 1868, minute by Hammond (italics mine).

68. Cf. supra n. 63.

69. F.O. 17/504. Published in P.P., China No. 1 (1869). Text also quoted in Williams, op. cit., pp. 173–76.

70. Ibid., text as quoted from F.O. 17/504.

71. On Jan. 1, 1869. F.O. 17/516, Clarendon to Alcock, Jan. 12, 1869.

72. Enclosed ibid.

73. F.O. 17/516; also in Clarendon to Alcock, Jan. 13, 1869, F.O. 228/466.

74. F.O. 17/521, Alcock to Burlinghame, April 2, 1869.

75. F.O. 228/467, Clarendon to Burlinghame, June 21, 1869. See also Hammond to Brown (Secretary to the Burlinghame Mission), May 31, 1869: "I hoped that

Mr. Burlinghame would make the Chinese Government clearly understand that, although the British Government did not choose that British consuls and British naval officers should act independently of the authority of their government, as they had done of late in several cases, yet that they held the Chinese Government itself responsible for the exact fulfillment of its treaty engagements, and for the protection of British subjects, and for the exercise of efficient control over their local authorities; and that if the Chinese Government did not do its duty in these respects, the questions which would arise would not be such as would admit of being adjusted by local action between the Consuls and those authorities; but would have to be settled between the Chinese Government and the British Government, which would be a much more serious affair."

76. F.O. 17/504, Gladstone's minute on Clarendon draft, Dec. 28, 1868.

77. P.P., China No. 3 (1869), Correspondence respecting Missionary Disturbances at Chefoo and Taiwan; China No. 7 (1869), Correspondence respecting Attack on Boats of H.M.S. *Cockchafer* by Villagers near Swatow; China No. 9 (1869), Papers respecting Proceedings of H.M.S. *Janus* at Sharp Peak Island.

78. F.O. 17/516, Jan. 28, 1869.

79. F.O. 228/466, Clarendon to Alcock, Jan. 28, 1869.

80. F.O. 17/520, March 15, 1869. Clarendon's reaction, minuted on the dispatch, would have puzzled the taipans: "Sir R. Alcock cannot disguise his antipathy to our moderate policy. The application of force is clearly his means of overcoming every difficulty in China."

81. Ibid., cited supra n. 63.

82. *The Westminster Review*, New Ser., vol. 37, 1870, p. 182.

83. A. R. Colquhoun, *China in Transformation* (London, 1899), p. 221.

84. Williams, op. cit., pp. 177, 179.

85. Surveyed in *London & China Telegraph*, March 22, 1869.

86. Dispatch dated March 15, 1869. *London & China Telegraph*, June 7, 1869.

87. Ibid., May 1, 1869.

88. Quoted in *London & China Telegraph*, July 29, 1869.

89. M.E., vol. 316b, f. 549, M. Osouf to Directeurs du Séminaire, May 19, 1869.

90. F.O. 17/516, Clarendon to Alcock, April 19, 1869.

91. Quoted in *London & China Telegraph*, Jan. 4, 1869.

92. Hansard's *Parliamentary Debates*, 3 ser., vol. 194, p. 939, Mar. 9, 1869. Peers approved of Earl Grey's statement that "we have abused our superior force" and urged restriction of consular protection to treaty ports.

93. Hansard's *Parliamentary Debates*, 3 ser., vol. 195, p. 1855, April 29, 1869.

94. Hansard's *Parliamentary Debates*, 3 ser., vol. 197, p. 1796f.

95. "If England demanded that her citizens should have power to reside under exceptional circumstances in China, with ex-territorial rights, all other nations having treaty rights would demand the same thing, and they would have inextricable confusion, tending to the disorganization of the Empire." Ibid., p. 1799.

96. *The Standard*, July 15, 1869.

97. Text reprinted in *London & China Telegraph*, Nov. 1, 1869.

98. Text reprinted in *London & China Telegraph*, Oct. 4, 1869.

99. Ibid., Oct. 18, 1869.

100. Quoted in Williams, op. cit., p. 199.

101. On Nov. 23, 1868. Revealed in *London & China Telegraph*, Sept. 7, 1869.

102. Williams, op. cit., p. 202.

103. Browne's Memorandum to the United States Department of State, reprinted as Appendix III, Williams, op. cit., pp. 298–314.

104. See, *e.g.*, *Overland China Mail*, Aug. 5, 1869; *London & China Telegraph*, Sept. 7, 1869.

105. H. B. Morse, *The International Relations of the Chinese Empire* (London-New York, 1918), vol. II, App. C.

106. Sept. 27, 1869.

107. Quoted in *London & China Telegraph*, Sept. 27, 1869.

108. "The 'Times' on British Policy in China," *London & China Telegraph*, Mar. 7, 1870.

109. *China Mail*, Mar. 1, 1870, reprinted in *London & China Telegraph*, April 11, 1870.

110. Hansard's *Parliamentary Debates*, 3 ser., vol. 200, p. 842, Mar. 29, 1870.

CHAPTER III

ABBREVIATIONS AND SOURCES

A.C.C.: Associated Chambers of Commerce of Great Britain, Annual Reports, London.

B.T.: Board of Trade, London. Manuscript records.

F.O.: Foreign Office documents in archives of Public Records Office, London.

Manch. C.C.: Manchester Chamber of Commerce. Manuscript records.

P.P.: Parliamentary Papers.

NOTES

1. F.O. 17/574, Alcock to Hart, July 4, 1868.

2. F. O. 17/574, Hart to Alcock, May 29, 1868, enclosed in Alcock's dispatch of Dec. 7, 1868.

3. F.O. 17/574, Alcock to Stanley, Dec. 6, 1868.

4. Ibid.

5. F.O. 17/574, Alcock to Stanley, Dec. 23, 1868.

6. Ibid. It is instructive to note that Alcock is writing to Lord Stanley when he speaks of the "policy of absolute non-intervention" as the accepted one.

7. P.P., China No. 5 (1871), No. 89, Shanghai Chamber of Commerce to Medhurst, Feb. 1, 1869. Minutes of meeting, ibid., p. 294.

8. Ibid., No. 90, p. 296; No. 91, p. 299; No. 92, p. 302; and passim.

9. B.T., Commercial Dept., Letters Written 1869, Dec. No. 211/1869, May 19, 1869. Also in P.P., China No. 5 (1871), No. 107, pp. 345–55.

10. Ibid., p. 355 in published version.

11. F.O. 228/467, Clarendon to Alcock, May 21, 1869.

12. F.O. 228/467, Clarendon to Alcock, June 4, 1869, confidential.

13. F.O. 228/466 and F.O. 228/467 contain diplomatic correspondence on treaty revision. The United States supported the British decision, Fish to Thornton, June 12, 1869, F.O. 228/467. Bismarck went along. France led the opposition, recommending postponement of revision until the Emperor's majority, de la Valette to Lyons, June 28, 1869, P.P., China No. 5 (1871), No. 129, p. 378. Belgium, though consent-

ing, read the Foreign Office a lesson on the treatment of China, suggesting an international consortium which would assume the white man's burden, Vanderstichelen's communication, F.O. 228/467.

14. P.P., China No. 5 (1871), Inc. 1 in No. 152, p. 414 f. Convention signed on October 23, 1869. Also published as P.P., China No. 1 (1870) "Despatch from Sir Rutherford Alcock respecting a Supplementary Convention to the Treaty of Tien-Tsin, signed by him on October 23, 1869."

15. Ibid., China No. 5 (1871) p. 421; China No. 1 (1870), p. 13, Alcock to M. Rehfus (doyen), Oct. 20, 1869.

16. *London & China Telegraph*, Jan. 17, 1870.

17. Memorial from the Shanghae Chamber of Commerce, Dec. 31, 1869, China No. 4 (1870), No. 2, p. 7; also printed as supplement to *North China Herald*, Jan. 11, 1870.

18. F.O. 17/580, Jan. 21, 1870. Also in P.P., China No. 6 (1870) No. 3, p. 8, where a careless copyist at the Foreign Office transmuted the Chairman's name from Keswick to Kesurir.

19. F.O. 17/580 contains the fullest account. The Memorial of Jan. 13, 1870, is published in China No. 4 (1870), No. 1, p. 1, 1870, vol. 69.

20. A.C.C., 10th *Annual Report,* Report of Special Meeting of the Executive Council, Nov. 16, 1869.

21. All in China No. 4 (1870), Nos. 3, 4, 5, 6.

22. Manch. C.C., *Proceedings*, 1867–72, Jan. 12, 1870.

23. Ibid., Jan. 26, 1870.

24. Ibid., Feb. 17, 1870. Also in China No. 4 (1870), No. 7, p. 25.

25. *London & China Telegraph*, Feb. 7, 1870.

26. Liverpool Chamber of Commerce, *Semi-Annual Report*, Sept. 13, 1870.

27. Quoted in *London & China Telegraph*, Jan. 17, 1870.

28. Quoted ibid., Jan. 17, 1870.

29. Ibid., Feb. 7, 1870.

30. F.O. 17/580, Feb. 11, 1870.

31. B.T., Commercial Dept., Letters Written 1870, No. 106, Feb. 25, 1870.

32. F.O. 17/580 contains a full account of the interview. Also reported in *The Times,* March 1, 1870.

33. *London & China Telegraph*, Mar. 7, 1870.

34. *The Times,* Mar. 1, 1870.

35. Mar. 2, 1870.

36. Mar. 1, 1870.

37. Mar. 2, 1870.

38. F.O. 17/580, Hammond to Shaw Lefevre (private), Mar. 3, 1870.

39. Ibid.

40. F.O. 17/580, Shaw Lefevre to Hammond (private), Mar. 7, 1870.

41. F.O. 17/580, Hugh Matheson, Chairman of the Committee of London Merchants, Mar. 14, 1870. Also in P.P., China No. 6, (1870), No. 2, p. 5.

42. F.O. 17/580, Halifax Chamber of Commerce to Lord Clarendon, Mar. 22, 1870. Also in P.P., China No. 6 (1870), No. 6, p. 24.

43. P.P., China No. 6 (1870), No. 7, p. 24, Mar. 23, 1870.

44. F.O. 17/580, Granville to Clarendon, Mar. 18, 1870.

45. P.P., China No. 6 (1870), D. Sassoon & Co. to Lord Clarendon, Mar. 22, 1870, p. 21.

46. Mar. 26, 1870, p. 397.

47. F.O. 17/580.

48. F.O. 17/580, Memorandum by Alcock, May 3, 1870; printed for Foreign Office use, June 8, 1870. Published as P.P., China No. 10 (1870), "Letter to Chambers of Commerce, &c., respecting the China Treaty Revision Convention," 1870, vol. 69.

49. F.O. 17/580, Alcock to Hammond (private) May 4, 1870.

50. F.O. 17/580, Memorandum from M. de la Valette, May 11, 1870.

51. B.T., Commercial Dept., Letters Written 1870, No. 250, June 2, 1870. Also in F.O. 17/581, dated June 1, 1870.

52. F.O. 17/581. Respective minutes dated June 2, 1870.

53. Ibid., Clarendon minute, June 3.

54. F.O. 17/580, Hammond draft dated June 6, 1870, with minutes by Clarendon and Otway.

55. P.P., China No. 10 (1870), June 9, 1870. Copies were sent to the London Committee, the East India and China Association of Liverpool, the Associated Chambers of Commerce, the Sassoons, the Manchester, Halifax, Glasgow, Leith, Dundee, Edinburgh and Macclesfield Chambers of Commerce. See F.O. 17/581.

56. F.O. 17/581, June 21, 1870.

57. Manch. C.C., *Proceedings* 1868–72, June 20, 1870.

58. F.O. 17/581, June 20, 1870.

59. *London & China Telegraph,* June 27, 1870.

60. F.O. 17/581, Hammond to Wade (private), June 30, 1870.

61. F.O. 17/581, Hammond to Granville, July 1, 1870.

62. Exact date not given. F.O. 17/581, Granville minute on *pro-memoria* from M. de la Valette, July 7, 1870.

63. F.O. 17/581, July 25, 1870. P.P., China No. 11 (1870), No. 7; also in China No. 5 (1871), No. 153, p. 428.

64. F.O. 17/581, July 29, 1870.

65. See views expressed in *London & China Telegraph,* July 18, 1870.

66. *The Standard,* July 7, 1870, letter signed "A.B."

67. F.O. 228/487, Clarendon to Wade, April 7, 1870.

68. Account in P.P., China No. 1 (1871), "Papers relating to the Massacre of Europeans at Tien-Tsin on the 21st June, 1870." Narrative in H. Cordier, *Histoire des Rélations de la Chine avec les Puissances Occidentales* (Paris, 1901), vol. I, pp. 348–90.

69. Cordier, op. cit., p. 362.

69a. China No. 1 (1871), Granville to M. de la Valette, Aug. 25, 1870, No. 10, p. 8.

70. August 29, 1870. French missionaries, on the other hand, were more concerned with the reassertion of prestige. Writing to his superiors in Paris, M. Lemmonier, Procureur at Shanghai, warns: "Si la France ne frémit pas d'indignation et ne s'élève pas en masse pour forcer le gouvernement français à demander une éclatante réparation, c'est qu'elle est morte. Et si la France cette fois n'inflige pas un châtiment exemplaire et se contente d'une punition dérisoire . . . s'en est fait de son influence dans ces pays ci, elle sera descendue dans son tombeau, avec le Consulat et le drapeau français, le 21 Juin 1870." *Missions Etrangères,* v. 330, f. 956, July 14, 1870. Missionaries and merchants were agreed, however, on the imperative need for putting the fear of God into the mandarins.

71. Aug. 2, 1870. Excerpt in F.O. 17/606.

72. *North China Herald,* July 14, 1870.

73. F.O. 17/606, July 16, 1870.

74. P.P., China No. 1 (1871), Granville to M. de la Valette, Aug. 25, 1870.

75. F.O. 228/488. Published in P.P., China No. 1 (1871), Granville to Wade, Sept. 15, 1870, p. 50.

76. F.O. 228/488, Sept. 15, 1870. Account in P.P., China No. 1 (1871), Matheson to Granville, Sept. 15, 1870, p. 51.

77. Ibid.

78. F.O. 228/488, Otway to Matheson, Sept. 16, 1870. Also in China No. 1 (1871), p. 52.

79. *London & China Telegraph,* Oct. 12, 1870.

80. Liverpool Chamber of Commerce, *Semi-Annual Report,* February, 1871.

81. F.O. 17/609.

82. P.P., China No. 1 (1871), Inc. 2 in No. 83, p. 136; No. 143, p. 206.

83. F.O. 228/488.

84. Oct. 12, 1870.

85. F.O. 228/488, Sept. 26, 1870. Drafted by Hammond, approved by Gladstone and Granville.

86. F.O. 228/488, Oct. 6, 1870.

87. F.O. 17/581, Sept. 28, 1870. Minuted by Gladstone.

88. F.O. 17/609.

89. F.O. 17/559, Wade to Hammond, Oct. 14/15, 1870.

90. F.O. 17/546, Hammond draft dated Dec. 29, 1870.

91. F.O. 228/488, Hammond to A. Michie, Chairman of Shanghai Chamber of Commerce, Dec. 28, 1870. Also in P.P., China No. 1 (1871), No. 157, p. 220.

92. *The Times,* Nov. 2, 1870.

93. Nov. 7, 1870.

94. Cordier, op. cit., I, p. 378.

95. *Pall Mall Gazette,* Dec. 30, 1870 and Jan. 9, 1871.

96. G. Thin, *The Tientsin Massacre.* The Causes of the Late Disturbances and How to Secure Permanent Peace. (Edinburgh, 1870).

97. *The Edinburgh Review,* January 1871, pp. 176–206.

98. See, *e.g.,* H. Paul, *A History of Modern England* (London, 1904), vol. II, Ch. V, pp. 66–81.

99. Hansard's *Parliamentary Debates,* 3rd ser., vol. 204, p. 6. February 9, 1871.

100. *London & China Telegraph,* Feb. 13, 1871.

101. Hansard's *Parliamentary Debates,* 3rd ser., vol. 205, Mar. 24, 1871, pp. 545–64.

102. *London & China Telegraph,* May 1, 1871.

103. Hansard's *Parliamentary Debates,* 3rd ser., vol. 205, May 1, 1871, p. 1911, question by Earl of Carnarvon in the Lords; p. 1934, question by Mr. Magniac in the Commons. Mr. Magniac exhibited an almost unparliamentary bitterness in this exchange.

104. *London & China Telegraph,* May 15, 1871.

105. Oct. 2, 1871.

106. July 24, 1871.

107. See, *e.g.,* reports published in *London & China Telegraph,* Aug. 1, 1871, warning that China was preparing for war and was bent on abrogating treaty rights.

108. F.O. 17/625, Hammond to Wade (private), Jan. 24, 1872.

CHAPTER IV

ABBREVIATIONS AND SOURCES

A.C.C.: Associated Chambers of Commerce of Great Britain, Annual Reports,
    London.
B.T.: Board of Trade, London. Manuscript records.
F.O.: Foreign Office documents, archives of Public Records Office, London.
J.M. & Co.: Jardine, Matheson & Co. archives, Cambridge.
Manch. C.C.: Manchester Chamber of Commerce, Manchester. Manuscript rec-
    ords.
M.E.: *Missions Etrangères*, Paris.
P.P.: Parliamentary Papers.

NOTES

1. February 5, 1872.
2. See, *e.g.*, China No. 1 (1873, 66), Report by Mr. Malet, H.M. Secretary of
Legation upon the Fluctuation of Foreign Trade between the Years 1864 and 1871.
3. M.E., Lemmonier to M. Tesson, Oct. 16, 1872, v. 330, f. 1177.
4. *North China Herald*, Jan. 16, 1873.
5. J.M. & Co., G.B. Box 1872, Sam Mendel to J.M. & Co., Jan. 25, 1872.
6. J.M. & Co., Letter Book Europe: Jan. 1872–April 1873, to Matheson & Co.,
Sept. 20, 1872.
7. J. H. Clapham, *An Economic History of Modern Britain*, vol. II, (Cambridge,
1932), p. 385.
8. A. J. Sargent, *Anglo-Chinese Commerce and Diplomacy* (Oxford, 1907), pp.
199, 251.
9. Ibid., p. 201.
10. H. Schumacher, "Die Organisation des Fremdhandels in China," *Weltwirtschaftliche Studien* (Leipzig, 1911), pp. 430–62. But Schumacher fails to note that
"Kommissionsgeschaeft" and native competition had begun to undermine the position of the merchant princes long before 1870.
11. F.O. 17/662.
12. F.O. 17/665, July 1, 1873.
13. F.O. 17/682. It is indeed rare to find a Consular statement so closely reflecting
mercantile views: "Let but the trade be freed from its tributary bondage to Peking
and let local governments be permitted to draw their full share of benefit therefrom
and there can be little doubt that foreign goods will find many new outlets."
14. F.O. 17/633, Robertson to Hammond (private), Nov. 11, 1873.
15. F.O. 17/654, May 16, 1873.
16. Ibid.
17. F.O. 17/625, Hammond to Wade (private), Jan. 24, 1872.
18. F.O. 17/650.
19. Ibid.
20. F.O. 17/717, Wade to Granville, Sept. 11, 1871.
21. F.O. 17/626, Idem to Idem, Jan. 31, 1872.
22. F.O. 17/717, Wade to Granville (Confid.), April 22, 1872.

23. F.O. 228/510, July 11, 1872.

24. F.O. 17/717, Malet to Wade (Confid.), Sept. 6, 1872.

25. F.O. 17/717, Idem to Idem, Oct. 24, 1872.

26. F.O. 17/717, Johnson to Wade, Oct. 8, 1872.

27. F.O. 228/520, Granville to Comte d'Harcourt, Oct. 3, 1873.

28. Ibid., Granville's minute.

29. F.O. 17/632, Oct. 27, 1872.

30. F.O. 17/674, June 22, 1874.

31. A.C.C., *12th Annual Report*, 1872, Jan. 22, 1872; also in F.O. 228/510, Granville to Wade, Jan. 31, 1872.

32. F.O. 228/510, July 11, 1872.

33. F.O. 17/631, Sept. 5, 1872.

34. F.O. 228/529, Mar. 17, 1874.

35. *North China Herald,* April 3, 1873, listing on p. 304.

36. *London & China Telegraph,* July 14, 1873.

37. Manch. C.C., *Proceedings* 1872–1879, July 9, 1873.

38. F.O. 17/655, Wade to Hammond (private), Aug. 22, 1873.

39. F.O. 17/655, Wade to Sutherland, Sept. 3, 1873.

40. J.M. & Co. documents add nothing significant to the account in P. H. Kent, *Railway Enterprise in China* (London, 1908), Chap. II.

41. *London & China Telegraph,* Feb. 24, 1873.

42. *The Times,* Feb. 27, 1873.

43. *The Times,* Mar. 7, 1873.

44. F.O. 17/654, May 13, 1873.

45. May 1, 1874.

46. *London & China Telegraph,* June 28, 1875.

47. Sargent, op. cit., p. 225.

48. *London & China Telegraph,* July 12, Aug. 9, Sept. 6, Sept. 20, 1875.

49. F.O. 17/470. This volume and the subsequent one, F.O. 17/471, contain the voluminous Sprye correspondence.

50. F.O. 17/470, April 14, 1858.

51. F.O. 17/470.

52. Ibid., June 7, 1858.

53. Sept. 2, 1858.

54. Nov. 17, 1858.

55. F.O. 17/470, Oct. 29, 1859.

56. Ibid., Nov. 22, 1859.

57. F.O. 17/470 and F.O. 17/471.

58. See, *e.g.,* Hammond's minute on Sprye's letter of Mar. 5, 1860, F.O. 17/471: "These are the indefatigable gentlemen who for two or three years have been advocating a communication with China through Burmah to be set on foot through their instrumentality employed on public account and at public expence."

59. *The Times,* Mar. 9, 1870. Though how *The Times* had the news is puzzling, for Sprye assured the Foreign Office that, while making headway with press and Chambers in the North and Midlands, he had refrained from sending his pamphlet to the London papers so as not to excite the jealousy of the French!

60. Manch. C.C., *Proceedings* 1858–60, July 12, 1860.

61. F.O. 17/471, Aug. 7, 1860.

62. Ibid., Sept. 17, 1860.

63. Ibid., Sept. 22, 1860.

64. *The Times*, July 19, 1861; *London & China Telegraph*, July 29, 1861.

65. F.O. 17/471, Dec. 2, 1862.

66. P.P., Rangoon and West of China, Memorial of the Association of the Chambers of Commerce, 17 Feb. 1873 (1873, 61), p. 8. Also, P.P., Letter from Capt. Richard Sprye to the Secretary of State for India, 15th Jan. 1866, etc., (1866, 52).

67. Enclosed in F.O. 17/471.

68. F.O. 17/471, Stanley minute of July 25, 1866.

69. P.P., Rangoon and Western China, No. 233, (1867, 50), p. 10, Sept. 29, 1866.

70. P.P., Rangoon and West of China, Memorial of the Association of the Chambers of Commerce, Feb. 17, 1873 (1873, 61), p. 12.

71. F.O. 17, 498, June 30, 1868.

72. F.O. 17/490, July 30, 1868.

73. H. Cordier, *Rélations de la Chine avec les Puissances Occidentales* (Paris, 1901), I, p. 551.

74. P.P., Memorial of the Huddersfield Chamber of Commerce, April, 1869.

75. Liverpool Chamber of Commerce, *Semi-Annual Report*, August, 1869.

76. Jan. 25, 1870.

77. A.C.C., *11th Annual Report*, 1871, pp. 121–26, Meeting held at Bradford, Nov. 24, 1870.

78. A.C.C., *12th Annual Report*, 1872, Meeting held at Plymouth, Sept. 26–27, 1871.

79. *London & China Telegraph*, Aug. 26, 1872.

80. A.C.C., *13th Annual Report*, 1873, pp. 41–43.

81. P.P., Rangoon and West of China, Memorial of the Association of Chambers of Commerce of the United Kingdom, Feb. 17, 1873 (1873, 61).

82. A.C.C., *14th Annual Report*, 1874, Report of Proceedings at Provincial Meeting, Cardiff, Sept. 23–25, 1873, p. 47.

83. A.C.C., *15th Annual Report*, 1875, Meeting held on Sept. 22, 1874.

84. See correspondence in F.O. 228/520.

85. F.O. 228/527, correspondence dated May 20, 1873, July 24, 1873, and Aug. 23, 1873.

86. F.O. 228/527, Chief Commissioner to Government of India, July 17, 1873.

87. F.O. 228/531, Salisbury to Derby, April 17, 1874.

88. Ibid., enclosure in Tenterden to Wade, June 20, 1874.

89. F.O. 17/674, July 15, 1874.

90. F.O. 17/675.

91. H. Cordier, op. cit., I, p. 563. For an account of immediate developments leading up to the Margary murder see P.P., Papers connected with the Development of Trade between British Burmah and Western China and with the Mission to Yunnan of 1874–5. (1876, 56).

92. P.P., China No. 1 (1876), enc. 3, in No. 14, Wade to Prince Kung, April 28, 1875.

93. *London & China Telegraph*, June 14, 1875, reprints the letter which appeared in the *North China Daily News*.

94. Hansard's *Parliamentary Reports*, 3rd ser., vol. 223, p. 1448, April 22, 1875.

95. *London & China Telegraph*, April 22, 1875.

96. *The Times*, March 5, 1875.

97. March 16, 1875.

98. July 5, 1875.

99. P.P., China No. 1 (1876) and China No. 4 (1876).

100. *Pall Mall Gazette*, quoted in *London & China Telegraph*, July 5, 1875.

101. Hansard's *Parliamentary Debates*, 3rd ser., vol. 227, p. 3, Feb. 8, 1876.

102. *London & China Telegraph*, Aug. 23, 1875.

103. F.O. 228/563, Derby to Wade, Jan. 1, 1876.

104. P.P., China No. 3 (1877), p. 64f. (1877, 88).

105. F.O. 17/775; see also Cordier, op. cit., II, Chap. 4.

106. F.O. 17/775, Fraser to Derby, June 26, 1877.

107. F.O. 17/776, Sept. 17, 1877.

108. F.O. 17/776, Sept. 25, 1877; Oct. 4, 1877; Oct. 26, 1877, with minute by Tenterden.

109. F.O. 17/775, Memorial from D. Sassoon & Co.

110. F.O. 17/776, Society for the Suppression of the Opium Trade, Oct. 4, 1877.

111. F.O. 17/776, Oct. 15, 1877, gives the following firms as represented: Matheson & Co.; Dent, Palmer & Co.; T. A. Gibbs & Co.; Adamson & Co.; B. Smith & Co.; A. Ranken & Co.; L. Reiss Bros. & Co.; Zimmern & Co.; Henderson & Co.; R. Brand & Co.; Dent Brothers; Shaw, Brand & Co.; and Dufour Brothers.

112. F.O. 17/776, Nov. 12, 1877.

113. F.O. 17/776, Bradford Chamber of Commerce to Lord Derby, Nov. 23, 1877.

114. Ibid., Halifax Chamber of Commerce, Nov. 29, 1877.

115. Ibid., Liverpool Chamber of Commerce, Dec. 20, 1877.

116. Manch. C.C., *Proceedings* 1872–79, minutes of meetings on Sept. 26, Nov. 28, and Nov. 30, 1877.

117. Liverpool Chamber of Commerce, *Semi-Annual Report*, February, 1879.

118. Manch. C.C., *Proceedings* 1872–79, Sept. 25, 1878 and Oct. 30, 1878.

119. Oct. 31, 1878.

120. See Manch. C.C., *Proceedings* 1872–79, meetings of Feb. 12, Feb. 26, and March 10, 1879.

121. Liverpool Chamber of Commerce, *Semi-Annual Report*, August, 1881, Special Meeting of April 13, 1881.

CHAPTER V

ABBREVIATIONS AND SOURCES

A.C.C.: Associated Chambers of Commerce, *Annual Reports*, London.
B.F.S.P.: *British and Foreign State Papers*.
B.T.: Board of Trade, London, manuscript records.
F.O.: Foreign Office archives, Public Records Office, London.
L.C.C.: London Chamber of Commerce, *Journal*.
Manch. C.C.: Manchester Chamber of Commerce, manuscript records.

NOTES

1. See, *e.g.*, Hansard's *Parliamentary Debates*, 3rd ser., vol. 246, May 9, 1879.

2. Hansard's *Parliamentary Debates*, 3rd ser., vol. 277, April 3, 1883, p. 1351.

3. F.O. 17/838 and F.O. 17/839 containing Consular Reports for January–December 1880.

4. F.O. 17/838, Consul Bullock's Report for 1879.

5. It was the major single issue throughout the period. Typical cases are noted in F.O. 17/926, Grosvenor to Foreign Office, Nov. 9, 1883 and F.O. 17/924, Aug. 30, 1883.

6. Thus, in 1873, the *London & China Telegraph* noted that treaty port residents regretted the absence of the German Minister from Peking during discussions on the audience question. Even allowing for editorial exuberance, the following is remarkable: "The prestige which Great Britain had gained by means of a firm and decided line of conduct has been in great measure frittered away to please a class of politicians who are willing to sacrifice the true interests of their countrymen in the East for the sake of cutting down the public expenditure. . . . Our place should be taken by the ambitious and unflinching countrymen of Prince Bismarck." (May 12, 1873)

7. *North China Herald*, Oct. 18, 1881.

8. *North China Herald*, Jan. 8, 1880.

9. E. V. G. Kiernan, *British Diplomacy in China, 1880–1885* (Cambridge, 1939), p. 252. By 1897 the figures were: 374 British firms and 4,929 residents.

10. *London & China Telegraph,* Feb. 25, 1878.

11. Hansard's *Parliamentary Debates,* 3rd ser., vol. 277, p. 1351.

12. Thus the Foreign Office refused a letter of introduction to the Peking Government requested by an arms merchant, on the ground that they "cannot recommend any particular Firm to a Foreign Government for supplying it, and the letter which you request would imply such a recommendation." F.O. 228/563, to Mark Firth, Mar. 24, 1876.

13. An expression employed by Mr. Leveson of the Bank during an interview in London, April 28, 1939.

14. J.M. & Co., Europe Letter Book: 1874–75, to Matheson & Co., Dec. 3, 1874 and Dec. 9, 1874.

15. Quoted in *London & China Telegraph,* Mar. 8, 1875.

16. F.O. 17/921, Jan. 27, 1883.

17. *North China Herald,* June 29, 1880, listing on p. 575.

18. Kiernan, op. cit., p. 260.

19. *North China Herald,* April 8, 1885, p. 424.

20. Kent, op. cit., p. 2.

21. F.O. 228/549, Fergusson to Lord Derby, Feb. 18, 1875.

22. In addition to the account in Kent, op. cit., Chap. II, there is some correspondence on the Woosung affair in F.O. 228/564 which confirms the vigor of Chinese opposition to the venture.

23. Kent, op. cit., Chap. III, the line being actually carried to Lutai in 1886.

24. F.O. 17/779, Fraser to Foreign Office, Jan. 31, 1878, when the idea was first projected by Li.

25. Kent, op. cit., p. 30.

26. Kiernan, op. cit., p. 270.

27. *North China Herald,* June 29, 1880, quotation on p. 575.

28. F.O. 228/500, Hammond to Hyde Clark, April 26, 1871. The occasion was an interview between Granville and the Council of Foreign Bondholders on Mar. 29, 1871, regarding claims on Venezuela.

29. F.O. 17/825, Memo to Byron Brenan, Oct. 9, 1877.

30. F.O. 17/825, Oct. 8, 1877.

31. F.O. 17/825, Fraser to Derby, Oct. 15, 1877.

32. Memorial of (Chinese) Board of Revenue on foreign loans, 1881, enc. in F.O. 17/862.

33. F.O. 17/949, Parkes to Granville, Mar. 31, 1884.

34. F.O. 17/949, minute on above, initialled "J. P. 29/5/84."

35. Ibid., initialled "HWC 31st."

36. Ibid., minute dated June 7, '84.

37. *The Times*, Aug. 16, 1884.

38. *The Times*, Aug. 14, 1884. "The fact is, the merchant comes to China to make money and retire as soon as possible. It was only the other day I heard the whole question disposed of by a successful business man.—'My dear Sir, I am not working for posterity.'" Colquhoun's series of articles, it is instructive to note, was an attempt to explain the stagnation of trade with China as the result of lack of vigor in Britain's policy toward China.

39. A. R. Colquhoun, *English Policy in the Far East* (A tract), (London, 1885), p. 21.

40. Kiernan, op. cit., pp. 181–83.

41. F.O. 228/582, Wade to Tenterden, June 4, 1877. By far the best account of the crisis, particularly from the diplomatic angle, is in Kiernan, op. cit., Chaps. III and IV.

42. Cf. Kiernan, op. cit., Chap. III; Cordier, op. cit., vol. II, Chaps. IX–XII.

43. Kiernan, op. cit., p. 42.

44. Russia's diplomatic efforts to convince Britain that the emancipation or strengthening of China would prove disastrous to Western Powers were not of recent vintage. See, *e.g.*, F.O. 228/563, Loftus to Derby, Dec. 21, 1875, enclosing two articles from the semi-official *Novoi Vremia* advising England to doubt China's fidelity in the settlement of the Margary affair and arguing that a strong China would be a dangerous neighbor for Europe.

45. F.O. 17/829, Jan. 28, 1880, quoted in Kiernan, op. cit., p. 44.

46. *North China Herald*, June 8, 1880.

47. Kiernan, op. cit., p. 52.

48. *North China Herald*, June 22, 1880.

49. *North China Herald*, Sept. 11, 1880.

50. Memorials by British Chambers of Commerce in F.O. 17/912, cited in Kiernan, op. cit., p. 71.

51. A. R. Colquhoun, *The Truth About Tonking* (London, 1884).

52. F.O. 17/627, Wade to F.O., March 25, 1872.

53. F.O. 228/531, Lyons to Derby, Mar. 8, 1874; and, June 23, 1874.

54. F.O. 17/673, April 2, 1874.

55. F.O. 228/549, April 9, 1874.

56. Ibid., Carnarvon to Derby, July 7, 1874.

57. F.O. 17/683, Robertson to Hammond (private) Feb. 3, 1874.

58. Quoted in Robertson to Hammond (private), Oct. 14, 1873, F.O. 17/663.

59. Cordier, op. cit., vol. II, pp. 308–309.

60. "Had the French been content to swallow Annam quietly and remain south of Hanoi, China might have kept equally quiet: once Tonking was put in question, Peking was compelled to make a stand." Kiernan, op. cit., p. 88.

61. Manch. C.C., *Proceedings* 1879–1885, Sept. 24, 1881.

62. Kiernan, op. cit., p. 90.

63. Cordier, op. cit., p. 361.

64. Cordier suggests that this may have been due to the hostility of a "clique locale" of French residents in Shanghai, whose plans for strengthening Gallic control of the municipal council in the French concession M. Bourée had thwarted. Ibid., pp. 364–65.

65. Kiernan, op. cit., p. 93.

66. F.O. 17/923, Grosvenor to Currie, May 4, 1883, cited by Kiernan, op. cit., p. 186.

67. Ibid., pp. 96–97.

68. F.O. 17/925, Oct. 29, 1883.

69. *North China Herald*, July 11, 1884.

70. F.O. 17/954, Parkes' telegram dated Jan. 19, 1884.

71. F.O. 17/968, Jan. 3, 1884.

72. F.O. 17/954, Minute by Pauncefote on Parkes' telegram.

73. *North China Herald*, July 11, 1884.

74. Manch. C.C., *Proceedings* 1879–1885, Nov. 26, 1884.

75. Kiernan, op. cit., pp. 172–73.

76. See, *e.g., North China Herald*, July 18, 1884.

77. *North China Herald*, July 25, 1885.

78. On Aug. 15, 1884, cited by Kiernan, op. cit., p. 141.

79. *North China Herald*, Aug. 22, 1884; see also *North China Herald*, Sept. 20, 1884.

80. Quoted in *North China Herald*, Aug. 22, 1884, pp. 206–207: "Much of the present depressed condition of commerce is due to the weakness which the French have displayed."

81. As evidence see resolution passed at a meeting of Shanghai residents, reported in *North China Herald*, Sept. 20, 1884.

82. *North China Herald*, Oct. 15, 1884.

83. Ibid., Oct. 22, 1884.

84. Home press survey in *North China Herald*, Oct. 29, 1884. On reaction to blockade see *North China Herald*, Feb. 11, 1885.

85. F.O. 97/621, Granville Papers, Mar. 31, 1885.

86. Ibid., O'Conor to Sanderson, April 9, 1885.

87. Kiernan, op. cit., p. 178.

88. See, *e.g.,* letter signed "A Scotchman" in *North China Herald*, Dec. 3, 1884.

89. April 8, 1885.

90. May 29, 1885.

91. Text of treaty in Cordier, op. cit., II, p. 531ff.

92. B.T., Letters Written 1885, Aug. 5, 1885.

93. Cordier, op. cit., p. 556f. April 25, 1886.

94. Manch. C.C., *Proceedings* 1885–1890, Sept. 28, 1886 and Oct. 27, 1886.

95. B.F.S.P., 1885–86, vol. 77, pp. 80–81.

96. A.C.C., *17th Annual Report*, 1877, pp. 122–24.

97. A.C.C., *18th Annual Report*, 1878, p. x.

98. A journey described in A. R. Colquhoun, "Exploration in Southern and South-Western China," *Royal Geographical Society: Supplementary Papers*, vol. II (London, 1889).

99. L.C.C., *Journal*, Nov. 15, 1882.

100. L.C.C., *Journal*, Dec. 1, 1882.

101. Manch. C.C., *Proceedings* 1879–1885, Nov. 29, 1882; Dec. 27, 1882; Jan. 24, 1883.

102. L.C.C., *Journal*, Feb. 5, 1883; June 5, 1883.

103. Manch. C.C., *Proceedings* 1879–1885, Nov. 28, 1883.

104. A. R. Colquhoun, *Report on the Railway Construction of Burmah and China* (London, 1884).

105. L.C.C., *Journal*, May 5, 1885.

106. Manch. C.C., *Proceedings* 1879–1885, April 29, 1885.

107. Ibid., July 29, 1885.

108. Ibid., Sept. 30, 1885.

109. L.C.C., *Journal*, Oct. 5, 1885.

110. Liverpool Chamber of Commerce, *Semi-Annual Report*, Feb. 1886.

111. Professor Langer implies that interest grew "in the later 1880's," but actually, although it did not subside entirely, it failed to reach the proportions of the sixties, the period from 1873–1875, or that just described. W. L. Langer, *Diplomacy of Imperialism, 1890–1902*, vol. I (New York, 1935), p. 392.

112. L.C.C., *Journal*, Nov. 5, 1887.

113. Ibid., July 5, 1888.

114. Ibid., April 5, 1886.

CHAPTER VI

ABBREVIATIONS AND SOURCES

B.D.O.W.: *British Documents on the Origin of the War*, London, 1927, vol. I.

B.F.S.P.: *British and Foreign State Papers*, London.

C.A.: China Association, London.

> *Annual Reports*, 1889—.
>
> Correspondence, File 1895–1899. Ms.
>
> Minute Books, A, 1889–1895. Manuscript minutes of meetings of the Executive Committee, General Committee and special committees of the China Association; including various documents and correspondence placed before the General Committee.

D.G.P.: *Die Grosse Politik der Europaeischen Kabinette, 1871–1914*, Berlin, 1924, vol. IX.

Manch. C.C.: Manchester Chamber of Commerce, manuscript records.

NOTES

1. London Chamber of Commerce *Journal*, Nov. 5, 1888.

2. Archibald J. Wolfe, *Commercial Organizations in the United Kingdom*, Department of Commerce, Special Agent Series No. 102 (Washington, 1915), p. 9.

3. Cf. B. H. Brown, *The Tariff Reform Movement in Great Britain, 1881–1895* (New York, 1943).

4. C.A., Minute Book A. 1889, April 11, 1889.

5. But a suggestion that Manila be added was rejected on the ground that "it would be beyond the powers of the Committee to intervene in any matter affecting the interests of British subjects in Manila, in the same way they were prepared to do in the case of China, Hongkong and Japan." C.A., Annual Report 1889–90, p. 2.

6. C.A., Minute Book A, 1890, Gen. Cmt., April 15, 1890.

7. See correspondence in F.O. 17/1010 and F.O. 17/1011.

8. C.A., Annual Report, 1890–91, p. 5.

9. Sir Thomas H. Sanderson (1841–1923), then Assistant Undersecretary at the Foreign Office; Permanent Undersecretary from 1894 to 1906.

10. C.A., Annual Report, 1890–91, Appendix.

11. A. J. Sargent, *Anglo-Chinese Commerce and Diplomacy* (Oxford, 1907), p. 251.

12. C.A., Minute Book A, 1891, Gen. Cmt., April 22, 1891.

13. Manch. C.C., *Proceedings* 1889–1894, July 15, 1891.

14. C.A., Minute Book A, 1891, Gen. Cmt., April 22, 1891.

15. H. Cordier, *Rélations de la Chine avec les Puissances Occidentales* (Paris, 1901), vol. III, pp. 55–66.

16. C.A., Minute Book A, 1891, Gen. Cmt., Dec. 2, 1891.

17. Ibid.

18. "It has been suggested that executions of the poorer class of Chinese for implication in these riots offer no satisfactory guarantee against the revival of troubles that are believed to be inspired by their superiors who commonly escape punishment. . . . But the punishment even of these really responsible persons would hardly furnish such an effective guarantee as might be hoped from opportunities of more extended intercourse with the people, for it is in the acquisition by the Chinese of a better knowledge of foreigners that the best safeguards for the future are to be found. And although it might be going out of our way to argue these points as questions of abstract policy, we might perhaps found on them a claim for freer communications and, specifically, for opening a port in Hunan to foreign trade. The opening of the West River was understood to have been actually under negociation a while ago, but seems to have dropped out of sight again. On the same ground, a revival of the claim for access to Chungking by steamer might be urged. . . . There is the question, too, of the right of foreigners to set up manufactures at the open ports. . . . There is nothing new in all this. . . . But points have never been authoritatively put forward in a comprehensive form; and I am desired by the Committee to suggest whether your Chamber would think it worthwhile to formulate . . . a statement. . . ." C.A., Annual Report, 1891–92, App. E, China Association to Shanghai Chamber of Commerce, Dec. 4, 1891.

19. C.A., Minute Book A, 1892, Gen. Cmt., Jan. 20, 1892.

20. Ibid., Gen. Cmt., May 25, 1892.

21. C.A., Minute Book A, 1893, Exec. Cmt., Jan. 24, 1893.

22. "The occasion was therefore deemed opportune to ask Lord Rosebery's attention to the whole question of commercial intercourse with the Southern Viceroyalty." C.A., Annual Report, 1892–1893.

23. Ibid., Gundry to Lord Rosebery, Oct. 14, 1892.

24. Liverpool Chamber of Commerce, *Annual Report,* 1893. The Manchester Chamber adopted without reservation the treaty port interpretation of Article 28 of the Tientsin Treaty that the commutation tax freed goods from all further taxation of any kind. Manch. C.C., *Proceedings* 1889–94, Minutes of the India, China and Colonial Committee, Oct. 26, 1892.

25. C.A., Annual Report, 1892–93.

26. C.A., Annual Report, 1893–94, App. D., Memorial of the Hongkong Chamber of Commerce to Lord Rosebery, July 31, 1893.

27. B.F.S.P., 1885–86, vol. 77, pp. 80–81.

28. B.F.S.P., 1894–95, vol. 87, p. 1311f. "Convention between Great Britain and China, giving effect to Article III of the Convention of the 24th July, 1886, relative to Burmah and Thibet." This involved the retrocession of frontier territory with the "sole proviso that His Majesty the Emperor of China shall not, without previously coming to an agreement with her Britannic Majesty, cede either Munglem or Kiang Hung . . . to any other nation," a clause later employed by Britain to protest the cession of this territory to France.

28a. B.F.S.P., 1892–93, vol. 85, p. 1235f.

29. Cf. Sargent, op. cit., p. 231.

30. C.A., Annual Report, 1893–94, App. D, China Association to Foreign Office, Nov. 30, 1893.

31. Liverpool Chamber of Commerce, *Annual Report,* 1894.

32. Manch. C.C., *Proceedings* 1889–1894, Minutes of the India, China and Colonial Committee, Oct. 26, 1893.

33. C.A., Minute Book A, 1893, Feb. 21, 1893.

34. C.A., Minute Book A, 1894, Gen. Cmt., April 10, 1894.

35. Ibid., Gen. Cmt., May 7, 1894.

36. Ibid., Gen. Cmt., Aug. 9, 1894.

37. Manch. C.C., *Proceedings* 1889–1894, Minutes of the India, China and Colonial Committee, Aug. 27, 1894.

38. C.A., Minute Book A, 1894, Aug. 9, 1894.

39. See *U.S. Foreign Relations,* 1894, App. I, Denby to Gresham, July 6, 1894, No. 21, p. 30.

40. Cf. R. S. McCordock, *British Far Eastern Policy* 1894–1900, (New York, 1931), pp. 89–96. But, until Foreign Office documents for the period are available, there is no decisive evidence of the extent of official "indignation."

41. *The Times,* Aug. 9, 1894.

41a. *U.S. Foreign Relations,* 1894, App. I, Denby to Gresham, July 28, 1894, No. 32, p. 41.

42. *The Times,* Aug. 9, 1894.

43. See R. S. Gundry, "Corea, China and Japan," *Fortnightly Review,* Nov. 1894, vol. 56 (new ser.), p. 618.

44. See *U.S. Foreign Relations,* 1894, App. I, Denby to Gresham, Sept. 15, 1894, No. 48, p. 58.

45. Ibid., Goschen to Gresham, Oct. 6, 1894, No. 56, p. 70; Idem to idem, Oct. 14, 1894, No. 59, p. 70.

46. McCordock, op. cit., p. 111.

47. C.A., Minute Book A, Gen. Cmt., Meetings in November and December.

48. C.A., Annual Report, 1894–95, App. E.

49. Ibid.

50. Ibid., China Association to Shanghai and Hongkong Committees, Dec. 20, 1894.

51. C.A., Minute Book A, 1895, Annual Meeting, Feb. 26, 1895.

52. March 5, 1895.

53. Jan. 23, 1895, p. 2.

54. Jan. 28, 1895.

55. Cf. Philip Joseph, *Foreign Diplomacy in China,* 1894–1900 (London, 1928), pp. 78–83.

56. Ibid., p. 79.

57. *The Times,* Mar. 9, 1895. This statement "may be taken absolutely as giving Japan's view at the present juncture," according to *The Times.*

58. Supra, pp. 169–170.

59. C.A., Minute Book A, 1895, Gen. Cmt., Mar. 26, 1895.

60. Ibid.

61. Reported ibid.

62. Ibid.

63. Embodied in China Association to Foreign Office, Mar. 28, 1895, C.A., Annual Report, 1895–96, App. B. The text was toned down in the final draft to express the Association's confidence in Foreign Office judgment.

64. C.A., Minute Book A, 1895, April 2, 1895.

65. C.A., Annual Report, 1895–96, pp. B, Shanghai Committee to China Association, Mar. 23, 1895.

66. McCordock, op. cit., p. 118.

67. Cf. Joseph, op. cit., p. 86.

68. Quoted in Joseph, op. cit., pp. 89–90.

69. *London & China Telegraph*, Mar. 18, 1895.

70. *London & China Telegraph*, Mar. 23, 1895.

71. C.A., Annual Report, 1895–96, App. B, Shanghai Committee to China Association, April 10, 1895.

72. Supra, pp. 165–166.

73. C.A., Annual Report, 1895–96, App. B, Hongkong Chamber of Commerce to China Association, May 29, 1895.

74. C.A., Minute Book A, 1895, Gen. Cmt., June 5, 1895.

75. Cf. *The Times*' (Mar. 30, 1895) comment on the armistice concluded between Japan and China.

76. B.F.S.P., 1894–95, vol. 87, pp. 799–804. "Treaty between China and Japan— Signed at Shimonoseki, April 17, 1895. Ratifications exchanged at Chefoo, May 8, 1895."

77. Cf. Joseph, op. cit., p. 106.

78. D.G.P., No. 2236, Hatzfeldt to Auswaertige Amt, April 6, 1895. At this time, Lord Kimberley stated that the British Cabinet had not yet reached a decision.

79. Ibid., No. 2239, Idem to idem, April 8, 1895.

80. *The Times*, April 8, 1895. "We have no title to meddle in these negotiations unless British interests are injured or imperilled," was the way *The Times* put it, counselling China that "the terms are not in excess of what the defeated Power ought to have been prepared for." It even welcomed Japanese annexation of Formosa as a step toward the development of its resources.

81. Joseph, op. cit., p. 124f. It is of interest to note that Lord Kimberley rejected a final appeal to join the Dreibund on the ground that British public opinion had expressed itself "in the most determined fashion" against intervention. D.G.P., No. 2248, Hatzfeldt to Auswaertige Amt, April 22, 1895.

82. C.A., Annual Report, 1895–96, Secretary's Report.

83. C.A., Annual Report, 1895–96, App. C, Butterfield & Swire to O'Conor, May 16, 1895.

84. Ibid., China Association to Foreign Office, Aug. 16, 1895.

85. Ibid., O'Conor to Shanghai Committee, June 12, 1895.

86. Ibid., Secretary's Report.

87. C.A., Minute Book A, 1895, Gen. Cmt., June 5, 1895.

88. C.A., Annual Report, 1895–96, China Association to Foreign Office, July 1, 1895.

89. Ibid., Shanghai Committee to China Association, July 25, 1895.

90. Ibid., Shanghai Committee to O'Conor, July 19, 1895.

91. *Daily Graphic* (London) May 2, 1895.

92. C.A., Correspondence File 1895–1899, Hornby to Gundry (private), June 13, 1895.

93. See *London & China Telegraph*, May 13 and May 20, 1895.

94. See C.A., Minute Book A, 1895, Gen. Cmt., June 5, 1895.

95. C.A., Annual Report, 1895–96, Secretary's Report.

96. Joseph, op. cit., p. 134.

97. D.G.P., No. 2276, Marschall to Gutschmid, June 7, 1895.

98. B.D.O.W., vol. I, Memorandum by J. A. Tilley, Jan. 14, 1905, p. 1.

99. J. V. A., MacMurray, *Treaties and Agreements with and Concerning China 1894–1919*, vol. I, Contract for Chinese 4% Gold Loan of 1895, p. 35; Protocol

of Exchange of Declarations concerning the Chinese 4% Gold Loan of 1895, pp. 40–41.

100. B.F.S.P., 1894–95, vol. 87, p. 523; also in MacMurray, op. cit., p. 26.

101. See Joseph, op. cit., p. 147. For clause prohibiting cession of this territory without British consent, see supra, note 28.

102. B.F.S.P., 1894–95, vol. 87, p. 525f. Both treaties were dated June 20, 1895.

103. C.A., Annual Report, 1895–96, C. P. Chater to Sir William Robinson (Governor of Hongkong), Nov. 13, 1894.

104. *London & China Telegraph,* July 1, 1895; Aug. 10, 1895.

105. C.A., Annual Report, 1895–96, Hongkong Committee to China Association, Sept. 20, 1895.

106. Ibid., Secretary's Report; and Chater to Governor of Hongkong, Sept. 16, 1895.

107. Sept. 23, 1895.

108. *The Times,* Oct. 25, 1895.

109. *The Times,* Oct. 28, 1895.

110. In his Guildhall Speech, Nov. 9, 1895. See infra, p. 185–186.

111. *Le Temps* (Paris), Oct. 30, 1895, quoted in *The Times,* Oct. 31, 1895.

112. C.A., Minute Book A, 1895, Nov. 4, 1895.

113. C.A., Minute Book A, 1895, Gen. Cmt., Nov. 6, 1895.

114. Ibid.

115. Ibid.

116. C.A., Minute Book A, 1895, Gen. Cmt., Nov. 7, 1895.

117. Ibid. The quotation, of course, is from the report in the Minute Book and not necessarily a verbatim account of Keswick's words.

118. See McCordock, op. cit., p. 213.

119. *The Times,* Nov. 11, 1895, gives the text of the Guildhall Speech.

120. Ibid., p. 10.

121. *London & China Telegraph,* Nov. 18, 1895.

122. C.A., Minute Book A, 1895, Nov. 16, 1895. The account of the interview with Lord Salisbury is given under that date.

CHAPTER VII

ABBREVIATIONS AND SOURCES

A.C.C.: Associated Chambers of Commerce of Great Britain, *Annual Reports,* London.

B.D.O.W.: *British Documents on the Origin of the War,* London, 1927, vol. I.

B.F.S.P.: *British and Foreign State Papers,* London.

C.A.: China Association, London.
  Annual Reports, 1896—.
  Correspondence, File 1895–1899. Ms.
  Minute Books A and B, 1896–1898. Manuscript minutes of China Association meetings, including correspondence and documents submitted to General Committee.

D.G.P.: *Die Grosse Politik der Europaeischen Kabinette, 1871–1914,* Berlin, 1924. Vol. XIV (1).

Manch. C.C.: Manchester Chamber of Commerce, manuscript records.

P.P.: Parliamentary Papers.

NOTES

1. P. Joseph, *Foreign Diplomacy in China* (London, 1928), p. 149. See A. Gerard, *Ma Mission en Chine* (Paris, 1918), pp. 131–33. It was, on the face of it, a strictly commercial contract between the Company's engineer and the Yamen.

2. W. L. Langer, *The Diplomacy of Imperialism* (New York, 1935), vol. I, pp. 399–404, gives the best account. See also Joseph, op. cit., pp. 161–67.

3. It was revealed to the London *Daily Telegraph* by Li's son in 1910, and made officially public at the Washington Conference in 1921; but its basic terms were published as the "Cassini Convention" in December, 1896, and believed accurate in Old China Hand circles despite repeated Russian denial.

4. *The Times,* Feb. 4, 1896.

5. C.A., Minute Book A, 1896, Annual Gen. Meeting, Feb. 19, 1896.

6. Valentine Chirol, *The Far Eastern Question,* (London, 1896), p. 180. Chirol acted as *Times* correspondent and his book is one of the best journalistic statements of Old China Hand attitude, especially in its emphasis on Chinese backwardness as the major target for attack.

7. C.A., Annual Report, 1896–97, Shanghai Committee to General Committee, July 10, 1896.

8. Manch. C.C., *Monthly Record,* Jan. 31, 1895, p. 29.

9. A. J. Sargent, *Anglo-Chinese Commerce and Diplomacy* (Oxford, 1907), pp. 249–267.

10. Ibid., p. 251.

11. *London & China Telegraph,* May 12, 1896.

12. Ibid., May 13, 1896.

13. Ibid., Sept. 4, 1895.

14. Grover Clark, *Economic Rivalries in China* (New Haven, 1932), pp. 78–79.

15. *London & China Telegraph,* July 7 and July 14, 1896.

16. B.F.S.P., 1895–96, vol. 88, p. 473f.

17. B.D.O.W., vol. I, No. 1, Memorandum by J. A. C. Tilley.

18. Joseph, op. cit., p. 152. See Gérard, op. cit., pp. 126–129.

19. B.D.O.W., vol. I, p. 1.

20. J. V. A. MacMurray, *Treaties and Agreements with and Concerning China* 1894–1919, vol. I, p. 57, Art. III.

21. C.A., Minute Book A, 1896, Annual Gen. Meeting, Feb. 19, 1896.

22. Ibid.

23. C.A., Minute Book A, 1896, Gen. Cmt., April 28, 1896.

24. C.A., Annual Report, 1896–97, China Association to Hongkong and Shanghai Committees, May 15, 1896.

25. Ibid., Secretary's report, "Proposal to Increase Customs Dues."

26. Ibid., Hongkong Committee to China Association, May 20, 1896.

27. Ibid., China Association to Lord Salisbury, June 26, 1896; Foreign Office to China Association, July 2, 1896.

28. See C.A., Minute Book A, 1896, Gen. Cmt., July 21, 1896.

29. Ibid.

30. C.A., Annual Report, 1896–97, China Association to Hongkong and Shanghai Committees, July 23, 1896.

31. Ibid., Hongkong Committee to China Association, July 10, 1896.

32. Supra p. 195.

33. C.A., Annual Report, 1896–97, Shanghai Committee to China Association, July 31, 1896.

34. Supra p. 174.

35. Text in C.A., Annual Report, 1896–97, Shanghai Committee to Gen. Cmt., July 10, 1896.

36. Ibid., China Association to Shanghai Committee, September 25, 1896.

37. C.A., Minute Book A, 1896, Gen. Cmt., Sept. 15, 1896.

38. Ibid., Gen. Cmt., Aug. 20, 1896.

39. C.A., Annual Report, 1896–97, Memorandum, Aug. 31, 1896.

40. Ibid., Secretary's report, "Proposal to Increase Customs Dues."

41. Manch. C.C., *Proceedings* 1894–99, Minutes of India, China, and Colonial Committee, Sept. 8, 1896; Board Meeting, Sept. 30, 1896.

42. A.C.C., *Annual Report*, 1897, Cir. No. 367, Dec. 8, 1896.

43. C.A., Minute Book A, 1896, Gen. Cmt., Sept. 15, 1896.

44. Ibid., Gen. Cmt., Oct. 22, 1896.

45. C.A., Annual Report, 1896–97, China Association to Lord Salisbury, Nov. 2, 1896.

46. Ibid., Secretary's Report, "Proposal to Increase Customs Dues."

47. C.A., Annual Report, 1897–98, MacDonald to Salisbury, Feb. 16, 1897.

48. Ibid., China Association to Foreign Office, April 29, 1897.

49. See C.A., Correspondence File 1895–1899, Gundry to Bertie (private), May 1, 1897.

50. C.A., Minute Book B, 1897, Gen. Cmt., Sept. 9, 1897.

51. C.A., Annual Report, 1897–98, Memorandum on "Lekin on Foreign Imports," Nov. 30, 1897. "It is hardly an exaggeration to say that Lekin has been the bete noire of foreign merchants in China for the last forty years."

52. R. S. McCordock, *British Far Eastern Policy* 1894–1900 (New York, 1931), p. 155. Joseph, op. cit., p. 181.

53. Liverpool Chamber of Commerce, *Annual Report,* 1894.

54. Manch. C.C., *Proceedings* 1894–1902, Sept. 25, 1895.

55. Liverpool Chamber of Commerce, *Annual Report,* 1896, India Office to Liverpool Chamber of Commerce, Oct. 19, 1895.

56. Manch. C.C., *Proceedings* 1894–1902, Nov. 13, 1895.

57. B.F.S.P., 1895–96, vol. 88, p. 13.

58. A.C.C., *Annual Report,* 1897, Annual Meeting, Mar. 24–26, 1896.

59. *London & China Telegraph,* June 15, 1896.

60. B.F.S.P., 1896–97, vol. 89, p. 25f. MacMurray, op. cit., vol. I, p. 94.

61. See Chapter VI, note 28.

62. C.A., Annual Report, 1897–98, Secretary's report.

63. Dec. 12, 1896.

64. Joseph, op. cit., pp. 179–180.

65. *Parliamentary Debates,* 4 ser., vol. 37, Feb. 14, 1896, p. 346.

66. Ibid., Feb. 25, 1896, p. 1079.

67. Ibid., Feb. 27, 1896, p. 1254; vol. 38, Mar. 19, 1896, p. 1342.

68. Ibid., vol. 50, July 9, 1897, p. 1469.

69. C.A., Minute Book B, 1897, Gen. Cmt., July 28, 1897.

70. Ibid.

71. Ibid.

72. C.A., Minute Book B, 1897, Gen. Cmt., Sept. 8, 1897.

73. Bare reference to these negotiations is made in B.D.O.W., vol. I, No. 1, Memorandum by J. A. C. Tilley.

74. P.P., China No. 1 (1898), No. 13, MacDonald to Salisbury, Oct. 17, 1897. China No. 1 (1898) is in 1898–CV.

75. Ibid., No. 14, MacDonald to Salisbury, Oct. 19, 1897.

76. D.G.P., xiv (1), No. 3645, Marschall to Hollmann, Mar. 11, 1895. See Joseph, op. cit., pp. 191–99.

77. D.G.P., xiv (1), No. 3650, Rotenhan's Memorandum, Sept. 9, 1895.

78. D.G.P., xiv (1), No. 3664, Heyking to Hohenlohe, Aug. 22, 1896.

79. That it would probably be a missionary incident was also foreseen. D.G.P., xiv (1), No. 3669, Nov. 28, 1896.

80. Joseph, op. cit., p. 198.

81. C.A., Minute Book B, 1897, Gen. Cmt., June 15, 1897.

82. Ibid.

83. C.A., Minute Book B, 1897, Gen. Cmt., Nov. 30, 1897.

84. Joseph, op. cit., p. 199. Relevant documents in D.G.P., xiv (1), Chap. 90, Sec. B.

85. Joseph, op. cit., pp. 200–203.

86. D.G.P., xiv (1), No. 3708, Hatzfeldt, Nov. 17, 1897.

87. China No. 1 (1898), No. 5, MacDonald to Salisbury, Nov. 22, 1897.

88. Ibid., No. 6, Salisbury to MacDonald, Nov. 23, 1897.

89. Ibid., No. 20, MacDonald to Salisbury, Dec. 14, 1897.

90. Ibid., No. 21, Salisbury to MacDonald, Dec. 15, 1897.

91. Joseph, op. cit., pp. 215–16.

92. China No. 1 (1898), No. 15, Goschen to Salisbury, Dec. 1, 1897, enclosing précis of Novosti article.

93. C.A., Minute Book B, 1897, Gen. Cmt., Nov. 30, 1897.

94. Reported in C.A., Minute Book B, 1897, Dec. 29, 1897.

95. Quoted ibid.

96. Quoted ibid.

97. Quoted ibid.

98. China No. 1 (1898), No. 26, MacDonald to Salisbury, Dec. 22, 1897.

99. Ibid.

100. Ibid., No. 30, Salisbury to MacDonald, Dec. 28, 1897.

101. Ibid., No. 32, MacDonald to Salisbury, Dec. 30, 1897.

102. C.A., Minute Book B, 1897, Gen. Cmt., Dec. 29, 1897.

103. Ibid.

104. China No. 1 (1898), No. 33, China Association to Foreign Office, Dec. 31, 1897. The letter is signed by W. Keswick as Chairman.

105. Account in C.A., Minute Book B, 1898, Jan. 4, 1898. Exact date of interview is not given: it occurred sometime between Dec. 29, 1897 and Jan. 4, 1898.

106. Ibid., Gen. Cmt., meeting, Jan. 4, 1898.

107. C.A., Minute Book B, 1898, Gen. Cmt., Feb. 23, 1898.

108. China No. 1 (1898), No. 43, Salisbury to MacDonald, Jan. 5, 1898.

109. Supra, p. 210.

110. *The Times*, Jan. 11, 1898.

111. Quoted in Joseph, op. cit., p. 238.

112. B.D.O.W., vol. I, No. 9, Salisbury to O'Conor, Jan. 25, 1898.

113. Ibid., No. 13, O'Conor to Salisbury, Feb. 7, 1898.

114. Ibid., No. 15, Salisbury to MacDonald, Feb. 11, 1898.

115. Ibid., No. 1, Memorandum to J. A. C. Tilley, p. 2.

116. China No. 1 (1898), No. 78, MacDonald to Salisbury, Feb. 4, 1898.

117. Ibid., No. 80, Salisbury to MacDonald, Feb. 5, 1898.

118. Ibid., No. 62, MacDonald to Salisbury, Jan. 21, 1898.

119. B.D.O.W., vol. I, No. 1, Memorandum to J. A. C. Tilley.

120. P.P., China No. 1 (1899), No. 20, MacDonald to Salisbury, Feb. 20, 1898. China No. 1 (1899) is in 1899–CIX.

121. Ibid., Inc. 3 in No. 20, Yamen to MacDonald, Feb. 11, 1898.

122. Ibid., Inc. 5 in No. 20, Yamen to MacDonald, Feb. 13, 1898.

123. Ibid., Inc. 1 in No. 20, MacDonald to Yamen, Feb. 9, 1898.

124. China No. 1 (1898), No. 88, MacDonald to Salisbury, Feb. 19, 1898.

125. China No. 1 (1899), No. 59, Idem to idem, Mar. 18, 1898.

126. MacMurray, op. cit., vol. I, p. 108f, Art. VI.

127. C.A., Minute Book B, 1898, Gen. Cmt., Feb. 23, 1898.

128. Ibid.

129. Ibid., Annual Meeting, Mar. 23, 1898.

130. *Parliamentary Debates*, 4 ser., vol. 34, Mar. 1, 1898, p. 309.

131. "Wherever the Russian Power obtains control, all British commerce is practically excluded." Ibid., p. 300.

132. Ibid., p. 332.

133. Ibid., p. 339.

134. Ibid., p. 321.

CHAPTER VIII

ABBREVIATIONS AND SOURCES

A.C.C.: Associated Chamber of Commerce of Great Britain, *Annual Reports,* London.

B.D.O.W.: *British Documents on the Origin of the War,* London, 1927, vol. I.

C.A.: China Association, London.
> Annual Reports, 1898—.
> Correspondence, File 1895–1899. Ms.
> Minute Book B, 1898–1899. Ms.

D.G.P.: *Die Grosse Politik der Europaeischen Kabinette, 1871–1914,* Berlin, 1924. Vol. xiv (1).

Liv. C.C.: Liverpool Chamber of Commerce, *Annual Reports.*

Manch. C.C.: Manchester Chamber of Commerce, Proceedings and *Monthly Record,* Manchester.

P.P.: Parliamentary Papers.
> China No. 1 (1898). 1898–CV
> China No. 1 (1899). 1899–CIX
> China No. 2 (1899). 1899–CIX

NOTES

1. P.P., China No. 1 (1898), No. 101, O'Conor to Salisbury, Mar. 9, 1898.

2. Ibid., No. 103, Salisbury to O'Conor, Mar. 10, 1898.

3. Ibid., No. 108, O'Conor to Salisbury, Mar. 8, 1898.

4. B.D.O.W., vol. I, No. 23, O'Conor to Salisbury, Mar. 13, 1898.

5. China No. 1 (1898), No. 125, O'Conor to Salisbury, Mar. 23, 1898.

6. J. V. A. MacMurray, *Treaties and Agreements with and concerning China* 1894–1919, vol. I, p. 127f. Arts. III, V.

7. P.P., China No. 1 (1899), No. 22, Monson to Salisbury, April 13, 1898. See also P. H. Kent, *Railway Enterprise in China* (London, 1908), pp. 160–161.

8. R. S. McCordock, *British Far Eastern Policy* 1894–1900, (New York, 1931), pp. 218–19.

9. Dated Mar. 9, 1898. C.A., Minute Book B, 1898, Gen. Cmt., Mar. 23, 1898.

10. Dated Mar. 17, 1898. Ibid.

11. Ibid.

12. C.A., Minute Book B, 1898, Annual Meeting, Mar. 23, 1898.

13. *Parliamentary Debates,* 4 ser., vol. 54, Mar. 1, 1898, pp. 339, 331.

14. Ibid., p. 332.

15. See B.D.O.W., vol. I, No. 9, Salisbury to O'Conor, Jan. 25, 1898.

16. *Parliamentary Debates,* vol. 55, Mar. 24, 1898, p. 782.

17. Ibid., p. 785.

18. B.D.O.W., vol. I, No. 23, O'Conor to Salisbury, Mar. 13, 1898.

19. Ibid., No. 24, Memorandum by Mr. Bertie, Mar. 14, 1898.

20. Ibid., No. 32, Balfour to MacDonald, Mar. 19, 1898.

21. China No. 1 (1898), No. 129, Salisbury to MacDonald, Mar. 25, 1898.

22. P. Joseph, *Foreign Diplomacy in China* (London, 1928), p. 302.

23. *Parliamentary Debates,* vol. 56, April 5, 1898, pp. 226–27.

24. China No. 1 (1899), No. 40, MacDonald to Salisbury, April 25, 1898.

25. Ibid., No. 69, MacDonald to Salisbury, May 5, 1898.

26. C.A., Minute Book B, 1898, Gen. Cmt., April 6, 1898.

27. Dated Mar. 29, 1898, Ibid.

28. Ibid.

29. A.C.C., *38th Annual Report,* 1898, p. 89f. Meeting held on Mar. 15–17, 1898.

30. Ibid., p. 89.

31. Manch. C.C., *Proceedings* 1894–1902, Minutes of meetings on April 13 and April 27, 1898.

32. Manch. C.C., *Monthly Record,* April 30, 1898, Manchester Chamber of Commerce to Foreign Office, April 27, 1898.

33. C.A., Minute Book B, 1898, Gen. Cmt., April 6, 1898.

34. Original telegraphic demands in China No. 1 (1899), No. 21, Balfour to MacDonald, April 13, 1898.

35. C.A., Minute Book B, 1898, April 14, 1898.

36. *The Times,* April 28, 1898. Also in China No. 1 (1899), No. 25, China Association to Lord Salisbury, April 14, 1898. Although the letter and its contents are referred to in the Minute Book, no copy of the original text was discovered in the China Association records.

37. Joseph, op. cit., p. 330.

38. China No. 1 (1899), No. 5, Hongkong & Shanghai Bank to Foreign Office, April 4, 1898.

39. D.G.P., vol. xiv (1), No. 3771, von Buelow to Hatzfeldt, April 30, 1898.

40. Ibid., p. 173.

41. D.G.P., vol. xiv (1), No. 3773, Hatzfeldt to Auswaertige Amt, May 3, 1898.

42. C.A., Minute Book B, 1898, April 6, 1898.

43. D.G.P., vol. xiv (1), No. 3776, Hatzfeldt to Auswaertige Amt, May 5, 1898.

44. D.G.P., vol. xiv (1), No. 3776, Hatzfeldt to Hohenlohe, May 12, 1898, editorial footnote.

45. Ibid., the expression is that of the German Ambassador.

46. Kent, op. cit., p. 131.

47. C.A., Minute Book B, 1898, Gen. Cmt., May 26, 1898.

48. China No. 1 (1899), No. 96, Salisbury to Lascelles, May 13, 1898.

49. Ibid., No. 173, Salisbury to MacDonald, June 8, 1898.

50. C.A., Minute Book B, 1898, Gen. Cmt., May 26, 1898.

51. Kent, op. cit., p. 161.

52. China No. 1 (1899), No. 173, Salisbury to MacDonald, June 8, 1898.

53. Ibid., No. 135, Salisbury to MacDonald, May 24, 1898.

54. Ibid., No. 139, MacDonald to Salisbury, May 26, 1898.

55. C.A., Minute Book B, 1898, May 26, 1898.

56. China No. 1 (1899), No. 175, Salisbury to MacDonald, June 9, 1898.

57. Kent, op. cit., App. B, No. 1 & No. 2, pp. 224–34.

58. Ibid., p. 99.

59. Ibid., p. 101.

60. China No. 2 (1899), No. 9, MacDonald to Salisbury, Aug. 6, 1898.

61. Ibid., No. 7, Salisbury to MacDonald, July 24, 1898.

62. Ibid., No. 12, MacDonald to Salisbury, Aug. 10, 1898.

63. C.A., Annual Report, 1898–99, Shanghai Committee to General Committee, June 24, 1898.

64. Loc. cit.

65. A.C.C., *39th Annual Report*, 1899, Report of the Executive Council, Mar. 14, 1899.

66. Ibid.

67. C.A., Minute Book B, 1898, Gen. Cmt., June 21, 1898.

68. Contract for construction of this line was signed by the Russo-Chinese Bank on May 21, 1898. Kent, op. cit., p. 170.

69. C.A., Minute Book B, 1898, Gen. Cmt., July 7, 1898.

70. Ibid.

71. Ibid.

72. C.A., Annual Report, 1898–1899, China Association to Foreign Office, July 8, 1898. Also in China No. 1 (1899), No. 214, p. 141.

73. Supra, pp. 200–201.

74. *Parliamentary Debates*, 4 ser., vol. 65, Aug. 10, 1898, pp. 826–27.

75. Ibid., speech by Sir William Harcourt, pp. 806–16.

76. China No. 1 (1899), No. 286, Balfour to MacDonald, Aug. 17, 1898. Concessions listed in No. 278, Aug. 13, 1898.

77. Ibid., No. 383, MacDonald to Salisbury, Sept. 21, 1898.

78. Ibid., No. 306, Balfour to MacDonald, Aug. 30, 1898.

79. Ibid., No. 307, Balfour to Lascelles, Aug. 30, 1898.

80. Ibid., Inc. 2 in No. 312, Hongkong & Shanghai Banking Corporation to Shanghai Agent, Sept. 3, 1898.

81. Ibid., Inc. 1 in No. 312, Minutes of Meetings held at New Court, St. Swithin's Lane, London, on September 1 and 2, 1898.

82. China No. 2 (1899), No. 13, Balfour to Scott, Aug. 12, 1898.

83. Ibid., No. 18, Balfour to Scott, Aug. 19, 1898, and No. 19, Scott to Balfour, Aug. 21, 1898.

84. Ibid., No. 25, Scott to Balfour, Sept. 2, 1898.

85. Ibid., No. 48, Scott to Salisbury, Sept. 22, 1898.

86. Kent, op. cit., p. 206, App. A, No. 2, Oct. 10, 1898, Definitive Agreement between the British & Chinese Corporation and Director-General Hu respecting the Peking-Newchwang Loan.

87. China No. 2 (1899), No. 57, Hongkong & Shanghai Banking Corporation to Foreign Office, Nov. 23, 1898, and No. 66, Foreign Office to Hongkong & Shanghai Banking Corporation, Dec. 29, 1898.

88. Kent, op. cit., App. A, No. 5, p. 220.

89. C.A., Minute Book B, 1898, Annual Meeting, Nov. 1, 1898.

90. Manch. C.C., *Monthly Record*, Oct. 31, 1898, Report of Quarterly Meeting, Oct. 26, 1898.

91. Liv. C.C., *49th Annual Report*, 1899, Meeting of Nov. 10, 1898.

92. Ibid., Appendix, "Address by R. A. Yerburgh, M.P."

93. Ibid., pp. 20–21.

94. Manch. C.C., *Monthly Record*, Jan. 31, 1899, Manchester Chamber of Commerce to Liverpool Chamber of Commerce, Jan. 26, 1899. "It is apparent to the Board that to claim 'preferential rights' in any part of China for British Enterprise would be inconsistent with the equality advocated in the Chamber's letter to Lord Salisbury of April, 1898."

95. Manch. C.C., *Monthly Record*, Feb. 28, 1899, p. 48. See also Manch. C.C., *Proceedings*, Minutes of India, China and Colonial Committee, 1894–1899, Jan. 18, 1899.

96. C.A., Corespondence File 1895–1899, Dudgeon to Gundry, Jan. 2, 1899.

97. Ibid., Shanghai Branch Memorandum, Jan. 23, 1899.

98. Manch. C.C., *Proceedings*, Minutes of India, China and Colonial Committee, 1894–1899, April 19, 1899.

99. C.A., Minute Book B, 1899, Gen. Cmt., April 5, 1899.

100. A.C.C., *40th Annual Report*, 1900, Mar. 14, 1899, p. 82.

101. Joseph, op. cit., p. 390.

102. C.A., Minute Book B, 1899, Gen. Cmt., April 5, 1899.

103. C.A., Correspondence File 1895–1899, Whitehead to Henderson, May 4, 1899.

104. Ibid., Shanghai Committee to London Committee, May 17, 1899.

105. Ibid., Shanghai Committee to London Committee, May 9, 1899.

106. Ibid., Gundry to Campbell, May 18, 1899.

107. C.A., Minute Book B, 1899, Gen. Cmt., May 30, 1899.

108. Ibid.

109. Ibid.

110. C.A., Correspondence File 1895–1899, No. 9a, June 6, 1899.

111. C.A., Minute Book B, 1899, Gen. Cmt., June 20, 1899.

112. Ibid.

113. Supra, pp. 237–238.

114. C.A., Correspondence File 1895–1899, No. 9a, June 6, 1899.

115. C.A., Minute Book B, 1899, Gen. Cmt., July 10, 1899.

116. Ibid.

117. C.A., Correspondence File 1895–1899, Shanghai Committee to Hongkong Committee, June 17, 1899.

118. Ibid., Gundry to Bertie, July 5, 1899.

119. Conversation reported in C.A., Minute Book B, 1899, Gen. Cmt., July 10, 1899.

120. Ibid., Gen. Cmt., Oct. 18, 1899.

121. *North China Herald*, July 31, 1899, p. 216.

122. C.A., Correspondence File 1895–1899, Dudgeon to Gundry, Sept. 7, 1899.

123. Ibid., Gundry to Campbell, Oct. 20, 1899.

124. C.A., Minute Book B, 1899, Sept. 28, 1899.

125. Mr. Broderick in House of Commons, *Parliamentary Debates*, 4 ser., vol. 72,

p. 803. Quoted in W. L. Langer, *The Diplomacy of Imperialism* (New York, 1935), vol. II, p. 684. Professor Langer's account also emphasizes the fact, substantiated by mercantile sources, that the official policy of limited liability regarding sphere politics was crystallized in the summer of 1899 and merely confirmed by Britain's reaction to the Hay Note.

126. Ibid., p. 686. Professor Langer notes that the Hay Note was based on a memorandum by Mr. Rockhill of the State Department presumed to have been inspired by A. E. Hippisley, an Englishman with the Chinese Maritime Customs.

127. Quoted in full in Joseph, op. cit., pp. 400–402.

128. C.A., Minute Book B, 1900, Gen. Cmt., June 28, 1900.

CHAPTER IX

ABBREVIATIONS AND SOURCES

A.C.C.: Associated Chamber of Commerce of Great Britain, *Annual Reports,* London.

B.F.S.P.: *British and Foreign State Papers,* London.

C.A.: China Association, London.
 Annual Reports, 1899—.
 Correspondence, Ms., variously filed
  File 1895–1899, 1895–1900
  Misc. Folder 1900
  File F.O. 1900
  File F.O. 1902/3
  File F.O. 1904
  File F.O. 1905
  File Outward F.O. 1906/8
  Misc. Series, Documents, etc.
  Minute Books B and C, 1899–1907

Liv. C.C.: Liverpool Chamber of Commerce, *Annual Reports.*

Manch. C.C.: Manchester Chamber of Commerce, Proceedings and Minutes of India, China and Colonial Committee, 1894–1907, and *Monthly Record.*

NOTES

1. C.A., Minute Book B, 1899, Gen. Cmt., Dec. 11, 1899.

2. Ibid.

3. Foreign imports to China averaged 200 million taels in 1896–1898, with an increase to 264 million taels in 1899. Sterling value of the tael at the time averaged 3 shillings.

4. C.A., Minute Book B, 1899, Gen. Cmt., Dec. 11, 1899.

5. C.A., Minute Book B, 1900, Gen. Cmt., Mar. 13, 1900.

6. Ibid.

7. Supra, pp. 242–245.

8. Liv. C.C., *Annual Report*, 1901, p. 36. Fourth Congress of Chambers of Commerce of the Empire, June 29, 1900.

9. C.A., Minute Book B, 1900, Gen. Cmt., June 7, 1900.

10. Ibid.

11. Manch. C.C., *Monthly Record,* July 31, 1900. Jamieson to Manch. C.C., July 2, 1900.

12. Manch. C.C., *Proceedings* 1894–1902, China League to Manchester Chamber of Commerce, July 2, 1900.

13. C.A., Minute Book B, 1900, Gen. Cmt., June 28, 1900.

14. China No. 3 (1900), No. 92, Foreign Office to War Office, June 8, 1900.

15. Ibid., No. 135, Salisbury to Acting Consul-General Warren, June 15, 1900.

16. C.A., Minute Book B, 1900, Gen. Cmt., June 28, 1900.

17. C.A., Minute Book B, 1900, Gen. Cmt., July 24, 1900.

18. C.A., Minute Book B, 1900, Gen. Cmt., June 28, 1900.

19. C.A., Minute Book B, 1900, Gen. Cmt., July 24, 1900.

20. *Parliamentary Debates,* 4 ser., vol. 84, June 19, 1900, p. 442; vol. 86, July 19, 1900, p. 456.

21. Ibid., vol. 86, July 23, 1900, pp. 850–51.

22. C.A., Minute Book B, 1900, Gen. Cmt., July 24, 1900. See also Mr. Broderick's reply to Yerburgh's question on the same matter, *Parliamentary Debates,* 4 ser., vol. 86, July 20, 1900, p. 641.

23. C.A., Minute Book B, 1900, Gen. Cmt., June 28, 1900.

24. C.A., Correspondence, Misc. Folder 1900, July 20, 1900.

25. C.A., Minute Book B, 1900, Gen. Cmt., July 24, 1900.

26. C.A., Minute Book B, 1900, Gen. Cmt., Aug. 14, 1900.

27. Dated July 28, 1900. C.A., Minute Book B, 1900, Aug. 2, 1900.

28. C.A., Minute Book B, 1900, Gen. Cmt., Aug. 14, 1900.

29. Ibid., dated Aug. 14, 1900.

30. C.A., Correspondence, Misc. Folder 1900, China Association to Foreign Office, Aug. 27, 1900.

31. C.A., Minute Book B, 1900, Gen. Cmt., Sept. 12, 1900.

32. Ibid.

33. Dated Oct. 2, 1900. C.A., Minute Book B, 1900, Gen. Cmt., Nov. 29, 1900.

34. C.A., Correspondence, File 1895–1899 (sic!), No. 13, Chambers of Commerce and Special Communications, 1900. Letters variously dated, Oct. 15–Nov. 10, 1900.

35. Manch. C.C., *Proceedings* 1894–1902, Board Meeting, Oct. 17, 1900. Also in Manch. C.C., *Monthly Record,* Oct. 31, 1900.

36. C.A., Correspondence, File 1895–1899, No. 14e, Blackburn C.C. to Gundry, Oct. 19, 1900; No. 14g, Glasgow C.C. to Gundry, Nov. 15, 1900; No. 14h, Bradford C.C. to Gundry, Oct. 26, 1900.

37. C.A., Minute Book B, 1900, Gen. Cmt., Nov. 29, 1900.

38. C.A., Minute Book B, 1900, Gen. Cmt., Sept. 27, 1900.

39. C.A., Correspondence, File 1895–1900, President Manchester C.C. to Gundry, Oct. 8, 1900; also letter of Oct. 10, 1900.

40. Ibid., Rutherford to Gundry, Sept. 27, 1900.

41. Ibid., Member (signature illegible) to Gundry, Sept. 27, 1900.

42. R. S. McCordock, *British Far Eastern Policy* 1894–1900 (New York, 1931), p. 336.

43. Dated Oct. 15, 1900. C.A., Minute Book B, 1900, Gen. Cmt., Nov. 29, 1900.

44. C.A., Minute Book B, 1901, Gen. Cmt., Jan. 9, 1901.

45. C.A., Minute Book B, 1901, Gen. Cmt., April 15, 1901.

46. C.A., Minute Book B, 1901, Gen. Cmt., Jan. 9, 1901.

47. Manch. C.C., *Proceedings* 1894–1902, Jan. 23, 1901. Yerburgh to Manch. C.C., Jan. 4, 1901.

48. Ibid., Mar. 6, 1901 and Oct. 16, 1901.
49. Liv. C.C., *Annual Report*, 1901, p. 166.
50. C.A., Minute Book B, 1901, Gen. Cmt., April 15, 1901.
51. Ibid.
52. Manch. C.C., *Proceedings* 1894–1902, May 8, 1901.
53. Manch. C.C., *Monthly Record*, June 29, 1901.
54. Ibid. See also A.C.C., *Annual Report*, 1902, Report of the Executive Council, Mar. 4, 1902, pp. 5–8.
55. C.A., Correspondence, Misc. Series, Shanghai Committee to Byron Brenan, May 31, 1901.
56. C.A., Annual Report, 1899–1900, pp. 66–90.
57. C.A., Minute Book C, 1901, Gen. Cmt., Sept. 9, 1901.
58. C.A., Correspondence, File F.O. 1902/3, Foreign Office to China Association, Feb. 13, 1902. Manch. C.C., Minutes of the India, China and Colonial Committee, 1900–1905, Feb. 21, 1902.
59. C.A., Minute Book C, 1902, Feb. 24, 1902.
60. C.A., Correspondence, File F.O. 1902/3, China Association to Foreign Office, Feb. 27, 1902.
61. Manch. C.C., Minutes of the India, China and Colonial Committee, 1900–1905, Feb. 21, 1902; and Mar. 10, 1902.
62. C.A., Correspondence, File F.O. 1902/3, China Association to Foreign Office, Mar. 25, 1902.
63. C.A., Minute Book C, 1902, Gen. Cmt., April 15, 1902.
64. Manch. C.C., Minutes of India, China and Colonial Committee, 1900–1905, April 23, 1902.
65. C.A., Correspondence, File F.O. 1902/3. Telegram from Shanghai Branch of China Association to Foreign Office, April 28, 1902.
66. C.A., Minute Book C, 1902, Gen. Cmt., April 25, 1902.
67. C.A., Correspondence, File F.O. 1902/3, Memorandum by F. A. Anderson, April 19, 1902.
68. B.F.S.P., vol. 95, 1901–02, p. 39f. The essence is contained in Article VIII, pp. 40–47.
69. P. H. Kent, *Railway Enterprise in China* (London, 1908), Chaps. VII and VIII.
70. C.A., Minute Book B, 1901, Gen. Cmt., May 14, 1901.
71. Kent, op. cit., pp. 62, 66.
72. C.A., Minute Book B, 1901, Gen. Cmt., May 14, 1901.
73. Kent, op. cit., pp. 109–121 tells the story of this attempt to gain control of the Canton-Hankow; it proved to be only temporary.
74. C.A., Minute Book C, 1901, Sept. 9, 1901.
75. C.A., Minute Book C, 1902, Gen. Cmt., Jan. 21, 1902.
76. C.A., Minute Book C, 1902, Gen. Cmt., Dec. 19, 1902.
77. C.A., Correspondence, File F.O. 1902/3, China Association to Foreign Office, Dec. 17, 1902.
78. C.A., Minute Book C, 1903, Gen. Cmt., Oct. 13, 1903, remarks by Sir Cecil Smith.
79. C.A., Correspondence, File F.O. 1902/3, China Association to Landsdowne, Oct. 19, 1903.
80. C.A., Correspondence, File F.O. 1902/3, Foreign Office to China Association, Nov. 3, 1903.

81. Ibid., China Association to Foreign Office, Nov. 13, 1903.

82. Liv. C.C., *Annual Report,* 1904, Liverpool C.C. to Foreign Office, Oct. 27, 1903; Memorial to Foreign Office, Jan. 29, 1904.

83. C.A., Correspondence, File F.O. 1904, China Association to Foreign Office, Jan. 28, 1904.

84. B.F.S.P., vol. 95, 1901–02, pp. 83–84.

85. C.A., Minute Book C, 1904, Annual Meeting, Mar. 15, 1904.

86. Liv. C.C., *Annual Report,* 1905, p. 107.

87. A.C.C., *Annual Report,* 1905, Report of Executive Council, Feb. 28, 1905, and A.C.C. to Foreign Office, Oct. 19, 1904.

88. A.C.C., *Annual Report,* 1906, Report of Autumnal Meeting, Sept. 5, 1905.

89. C.A., Minute Book C, 1906, Gen. Cmt., Jan. 3, 1906.

90. Ibid. Exchange of correspondence in C.A., Correspondence, File Outward F.O. 1906/8.

91. C.A., Correspondence, File Outward F.O. 1906/8, Mar. 27, 1906.

92. Ibid., Foreign Office to China Association, May 15, 1906.

93. C.A., Minute Book D, 1906–07, Gen. Cmt., Dec. 17, 1906.

94. Ibid., Gen. Cmt., Jan. 8, 1907.

95. C.A., Correspondence, File F.O. 1904, China Association to Foreign Office, May 20, 1904.

96. Liv. C.C., *Annual Report,* 1906, Liv. C.C. to Landsdowne, Oct. 18, 1905.

97. C.A., Minute Book C, 1905, Gen. Cmt., Nov. 15, 1905.

98. C.A., Correspondence, File F.O. 1902/3, telegram, Shanghai Committee, May 23, 1903 in China Association to Foreign Office, May 25, 1903.

99. Ibid. Endorsed by General Committee in C.A., Minute Book C, 1903, June 2, 1903.

100. C.A., Correspondence, File F.O. 1902/3, Foreign Office to China Association, May 30, 1903.

101. C.A., Minute Book C, 1903, Gen. Cmt., June 2, 1903.

102. C.A., Minute Book C, 1904, Gen. Cmt., Jan. 22, 1904.

103. Ibid., Annual Meeting, Mar. 15, 1904.

104. Kent, op. cit., App. D, pp. 244–258.

105. C.A., Minute Book C, 1904, Gen. Cmt., Dec. 6, 1904.

106. Kent, op. cit., p. 173.

107. C.A., Minute Book C, 1905, Gen. Cmt., April 11, 1905.

108. C.A., Correspondence, File F.O. 1905, Foreign Office to China Association, May 27, 1905.

109. Kent, op. cit., p. 175.

110. C.A., Correspondence, File F.O. 1905, China Association to Foreign Office, Oct. 23, 1905.

111. Ibid.

112. C.A., Minute Book C, 1905, Gen. Cmt., Nov. 15, 1905.

113. Ibid., Gundry to Sir Edward Grey, July 16, 1906.

114. See J. O. P. Bland, "The Finance of China," *National Review,* April, 1912.

115. See W. Straight, "China's Loan Negotiations," in G. H. Blakeslee (ed.), *Recent Developments in China* (New York, 1913), pp. 119–61.

116. Resolution dated Jan. 12, 1904 in C.A., Minute Book C, Gen. Cmt., Jan. 22, 1904.

117. C.A., Minute Book C, 1904, Gen. Cmt., Mar. 22, 1904.

118. Ibid., Gen. Cmt., June 22, 1904.

119. Ibid., Gen. Cmt., Sept. 5, 1904.

120. Ibid., Gen. Cmt., Dec. 6, 1904.

121. C.A., Minute Book C, 1905, Minutes of Gen. Cmt. Meeting July 12, 1905, specially printed for information of members.

122. Ibid., W. S. Young to General Committee, July 26, 1905.

123. Ibid., Reid to General Committee, July 27, 1905.

124. Quoted in C.A., Minute Book C, 1905, Minutes of Special General Meeting, July 31, 1905 (printed form).

125. Ibid.

126. C.A., Minute Book C, 1905, Gen. Cmt., Sept. 14, 1905.

127. C.A., Minute Book C, 1906, Minutes of extraordinary meeting, Shanghai Committee, Jan. 5, 1906.

128. C.A., Minute Book C, 1906, Gen. Cmt., Mar. 21, 1906.

129. Ibid., Annual Meeting, April 10, 1906.

Bibliography

I. DOCUMENTARY SOURCES: MANUSCRIPT

Board of Trade (B.T.): Correspondence and memoranda of the Commercial and General Departments, British Board of Trade, for the period from 1856 to 1885. Reference is to volumes as bound, titled and stored in archives of the Board of Trade Library, London.

China Association (C.A.):

(a) Minute Books A, B, and C cover the period from 1889 to 1906. Contain original minutes of Annual Meetings and of meetings of the General Committee and Executive Committee of the China Association, London, as well as various documents and memoranda presented to the General Committee. In the files of the China Association, The Strand, London.

(b) Correspondence. Files of original correspondence of the China Association, principally with the Foreign Office, covering the period from 1895 to 1908. Filed in the offices of the China Association, London, as follows:

File 1895–1899
File 1895–1900
Miscellaneous Folder, 1900
File F.O. 1900
File F.O. 1902/3
File F.O. 1904
File F.O. 1905
File Outward F.O. 1906/8
Miscellaneous Series & Documents

Foreign Office (F.O.): Foreign Office correspondence and other documents relating to Anglo-Chinese relations covering the period from 1856 to 1885, filed under series F.O. 17/—and F.O. 228/—, in Public Records Office, London.

Jardine, Matheson & Co. (J.M. & Co.): Original correspondence of Jardine, Matheson & Co. removed from the main office at Hongkong; boxed and stored at University Library, Cambridge University, Cambridge. Covers mainly the period from 1840 to 1880.

Manchester Chamber of Commerce (Manch. C.C.): Records and proceedings of the Manchester Chamber of Commerce, including minutes of the Board and the India, China and Colonial Committee, bound and stored at the Manchester Public Library, Manchester. Covers the entire period here under review.

Missions Etrangères (M.E.): Correspondence filed at Rue du Bac, Paris.

II. DOCUMENTARY SOURCES: PUBLISHED

Associated Chambers of Commerce, London, *Annual Reports,* 1860—.

British and Foreign State Papers, London.

British Documents on the Origin of the War, vol. I, London, 1927.

Die Grosse Politik der Europaeischen Kabinette, 1871–1914, vols. IX and XIV (1), Berlin, 1924.

China Association, *Annual Reports,* 1889—, London.

China, Imperial Maritime Customs, *Decennial Reports,* 1882–91, 1892–1901, Shanghai.

Liverpool Chamber of Commerce, *Semi-Annual Reports,* 1868–1890.

———, *Annual Reports,* 1890—.

London Chamber of Commerce, *Journal,* 1881—.

Manchester Chamber of Commerce, *Monthly Record,* 1890—.

MacMurray, J. V. A., *Treaties and Agreements with and Concerning China,* 1894–1919, 2 vols., New York, 1921.

Parliamentary Debates

(British) *Parliamentary Papers:*

Report from the Select Committee on Commercial Relations with China, 1847.

Correspondence relative to the Earl of Elgin's Special Missions to China and Japan, 1857–59, 1859.

Correspondence respecting Affairs in China, 1861.

Correspondence respecting the opening of the Yangtze to Foreign Trade, 1861.

Memorials of Chambers of Commerce in China on the subject of the Revision of the Treaty of Tientsin, 1867–68.

China No. 3 (1869), China No. 7 (1869), China No. 9 (1869).

China No. 3 (1870), China No. 4 (1870), China No. 6 (1870), China No. 10 (1870).

China No. 1 (1871), China No. 5 (1871).

China No. 1 (1873).

Rangoon and West China, Memorial of the Association of Chambers of Commerce to Mr. Gladstone, 1873.

China No. 1 (1876), China No. 4 (1876).

China No. 3 (1877).

China No. 1 (1898).

China No. 1 (1899), China No. 2 (1899).

China No. 1 (1900), China No. 2 (1900), China No. 3 (1900).

United States, *Foreign Relations,* 1868, II; 1894, Appendix I.

III. CONTEMPORARY NEWSPAPERS AND PERIODICALS

(Files for 1860–1906, except where otherwise indicated)
London & China Telegraph (London)
North China Herald, The (Shanghai)
Pall Mall Gazette (London)
Standard, The (London)
Times, The (London)
Contemporary Review, November 1894, May 1895, February–December, 1898, April 1910, and May 1912.
Edinburgh Review, July 1895, January 1896, and July 1898.
Fortnightly Review, October 1894, April 1895, September 1896, April–May 1898, May 1911.
National Review, April 1912.
Quarterly Review, April 1898, January 1900, October 1900, July 1901.
Westminster Review, January 1870.

IV. SELECTED WORKS

Bank of China, *Chinese Government Foreign Loan Obligations,* Shanghai, 1935.
Bau, M. J., *The Foreign Relations of China,* New York, 1921.
———, *Foreign Navigation in Chinese Waters,* Shanghai, 1931.
Beresford, Lord Charles, *The Break-Up of China,* London and New York, 1899.
Bland, J. O. P., *Recent Events and Present Policies in China,* London, 1912.
Blakeslee, G. H., (ed.), *Recent Developments in China,* New York, 1913.
Bredon, Juliet, *Sir Robert Hart,* London, 1909.
Brenier, Henri, Chambre de Commerce de Lyon, *Rapport Général de la Mission Lyonnaise d'Exploration Commerciale en Chine,* Lyon, 1897.
Buss, C. A., *War and Diplomacy in Eastern Asia,* New York, 1941.
Chirol, V., *The Far Eastern Question,* London, 1896.
Clements, P., *The Boxer Rebellion,* New York, 1915.
Clark, Grover, *Economic Rivalries in China,* New Haven, 1932.
Clapham, J. H., *An Economic History of Modern Britain,* vol. II, Cambridge, 1932.
Colquhoun, A. R., *Across Chryse,* London, 1883.
———, *China in Transformation,* London, 1898; new edition, 1912.
———, *English Policy in the Far East,* London, 1895. Pamphlet.
———, *The Problem in China and British Policy,* London, 1900. Pamphlet.
———, "Exploration in Southern and South-Western China," *Royal Geographical Society, Supplementary Papers,* vol. II, London, 1889.
——— and Hallett, H., *Report on the Railway Connexion of Burmah and China,* London, 1888.

Cordier, Henri, *Histoire des Rélations de la Chine avec les Puissances Occidentales*, 1860–1902, 3 vols., Paris, 1902.

Croly, Herbert, *Willard Straight*, New York, 1925.

Curzon, G. W., *Problems of the Far East*, London, 1896.

Davies, H. R., *Yunnan, The Link between India and the Yangtze*, London, 1909.

Dennett, Tyler, *Americans in Eastern Asia*, New York, 1922.

Dennys, N. B., *China and Her Apologist*, Hongkong, 1876. Pamphlet.

Dickinson, G. L., *Letters from John Chinaman*, 1902.

Dilke, C. W., *Greater Britain* (8th ed.), London, 1885.

Dugdale, B. E. C., *Arthur James Balfour*, vol. I, New York, 1937.

Eames, J. B., *The English in China*, London, 1909.

Eitel, E., *Europe in China*, London, 1895.

Eldridge, F. R., *Trading with Asia*, New York, 1921.

Field, F. V., *American Participation in the China Consortium*, New York, 1931.

Flournoy, F. R., *British Policy towards Morocco in the Age of Palmerston*, London, 1935.

Friedman, I. S., *British Relations with China: 1931–1939*, New York, 1940.

G., R., *Overland Communication with Western China*, 1872.

Gérard, A., *Ma Mission en Chine*, Paris, 1918.

Griswold, A. W., *The Far Eastern Policy of the United States*, New York, 1938.

Gundry, R. S., *China and Her Neighbours*, London, 1893.

———, *China, Present and Past*, London, 1895.

Gwynn, S., and Tuckwell, G., *Life of Sir Charles Dilke*, London, 1917.

Hall, R. O., *China and Great Britain*, London, 1927.

Hart, Sir Robert, *These from the Land of Sinim*, London, 1901.

Hauser, E., *Shanghai: City for Sale*, New York, 1940.

Holcombe, A. N., *The Chinese Revolution*, Cambridge, 1930.

Hornbeck, Stanley, *Contemporary Far Eastern Politics*, New York, 1916.

Hornby, Sir Edmund, *Autobiography*, London, 1928.

Hosie, A., *Three Years in Western China*, 1897.

Hsu, M. C., *Railway Problems in China*, New York, 1915.

Hubbard, G. E., *Eastern Industrialization and Its Effect on the West*, London, 1935.

———, *British Far Eastern Policy*, London, 1939. Pamphlet.

Jernigan, T. R., *China in Law and Commerce*, New York and London, 1905.

Johnstone, W. C., *The Shanghai Problem*, Stanford, 1936.

Joseph, Philip, *Foreign Diplomacy in China: 1894–1900*, London, 1928.

Kent, P. H., *Railway Enterprise in China*, London, 1908.

Kiernan, E. V. G., *British Diplomacy in China: 1880–1885*, Cambridge, 1939.

Lane-Poole, S., *Life of Sir Harry Parkes*, 2 vols., London, 1894.

Latourette, K. S., *The Development of China*, Boston, 1924.

Lattimore, Owen, *Solution in Asia*, New York, 1945.

Little, A., *Gleanings from Fifty Years in China*, London, 1910.

MacNair, H. F., *China in Revolution*, Chicago, 1931.

McCordock, R. S., *British Far Eastern Policy 1894–1900*, New York, 1931.

Michie, A., *The Englishman in China*, 2 vols., Edinburgh, 1900.

Morse, H. B., *The International Relations of the Chinese Empire*, 3 vols., London, 1910–1918.

———, *The Trade and Administration of China*, London, 1921.

Norman, H., *Peoples and Politics of the Far East*, New York, 1923.

Overlach, T. W., *Foreign Financial Control in China*, New York, 1919.

Peffer, N., *China: The Collapse of a Civilization*, New York, 1930.

Pinon, R., and de Marcillac, J., *La Chine qui s'ouvre*, Paris, 1900.

Remer, C. F., *The Foreign Trade of China*, Shanghai, 1926.

———, *Foreign Investments in China*, New York, 1933.

Sargent, A. J., *Anglo-Chinese Commerce and Diplomacy*, Oxford, 1907.

See, C. S., *The Foreign Trade of China*, New York, 1919.

Schumacher, H., "Die Organisation des Fremdhandels in China," *Weltwirtschaftliche Studien*, Leipzig, 1911.

Shanghai Chamber of Commerce, *Report of Delegates on Trade of the Upper Yangtze*, 1869. Pamphlet.

Soothill, W. E., *China and England*, London, 1928.

Stimson, H. L., *The Far Eastern Crisis*, New York, 1936.

Tilley, J., and Gaselee, S., *The Foreign Office*, London, 1933.

Walrond, T., *Letters and Journals of James, Eighth Earl of Elgin*, London, 1872.

Whitehead, T. H., *Letter to a Friend in England*, Hongkong, 1897. Pamphlet.

———, *The Expansion of Trade with China*, London, 1901. Pamphlet.

Whyte, Sir F., *China and the Foreign Powers*, London, 1927.

Williams, F. W., *Anson Burlinghame and the First Chinese Mission to the Foreign Powers*, New York, 1912.

Willoughby, W. W., *Foreign Rights and Interests in China*, 2 vols., Baltimore, 1927.

Wolfe, Archibald, "Commercial Organizations in the United Kingdom," Department of Commerce, Special Agent Series, No. 102, Washington, 1915.

Index